P9-BIX-169

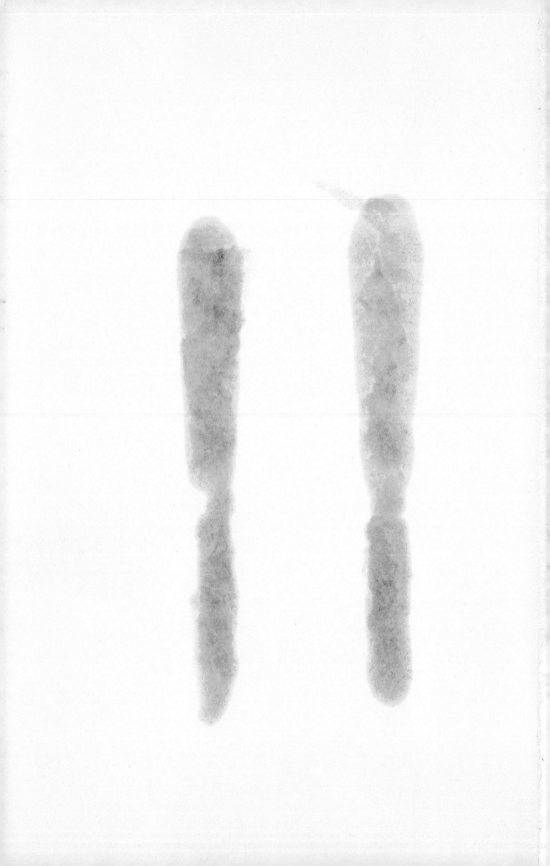

THE GREAT FRONTIER

BOOKS BY
WALTER PRESCOTT WEBB

The Great Plains
The Texas Rangers
Divided We Stand
More Water for Texas
The Great Frontier

The Great Frontier

WALTER PRESCOTT WEBB

Introduction by
ARNOLD J. TOYNBEE

UNIVERSITY OF TEXAS PRESS, AUSTIN

International Standard Book Number 0–292–73253–8 (cloth)
0–292–72706–2 (paper)
Library of Congress Catalog Card Number 64–10321   8/10/76
Copyright 1951 and 1952 by Walter Prescott Webb
Copyright © 1964 by Terrell D. Webb
All rights reserved
Printed in the United States of America
Fourth printing of University of Texas Press edition, 1975

TO JANE
AND THE STUDENTS IN
THE FRONTIER SEMINAR
1938–1952

INTRODUCTION

WALTER PRESCOTT WEBB was a scholar whose mind went on growing all through his life. Though he was not young when he died, we can be sure that his intellectual growth would have continued if a fatal accident had not tragically cut his life short. If he had lived longer, then probably *The Great Frontier* would not have been his last major work. Fate, however, has decided that this book should be the culminating achievement of his intellectual career, and it worthily fills that role. His own university is making a fitting memorial to him in republishing *The Great Frontier* and in deciding, from now onwards, to keep this arresting book permanently in print.

Being, as he was, a thinker whose mind never stopped producing new thoughts, Walter Prescott Webb became an historian of a kind that is not very common in our time. He managed to combine mastery of a special area of history with a vision of the total history of the world. Like most historians in his generation, he started as a specialist. He set out to study something that lay at his door and that was personally familiar to him: the American people's conquest of the Great Plains of the North American continent. He had the imaginative power to see, and to convey, the drama of this story. The pioneers who stepped out of the forests of eastern North America into those vast bare expanses were, he perceived, cutting themselves loose from a physical setting which had been their ancestors' environment since time immemorial. When North-West Europeans had crossed the Atlantic and had struck new roots in the New World, they found themselves still in the forest setting with which they and their forefathers had been wrestling in the Old World. For them, these ubiquitous forests had been ambivalent. The forest had been at once man's friend and his enemy: his enemy while he was doing the back-breaking work of hewing down the trees to clear the ground for cultivation; but his friend, in retrospect, as soon as he left the standing

vii

trees behind. Western Man then discovered how dependent he had been on lumber for manufacturing the apparatus of civilization. When he launched out on to the Great Plains, he had to find substitutes for lumber; and it was through Yankee ingenuity and inventiveness that the pioneers' physical conquest of the Great Plains became a practical possibility.

In *The Great Plains,* Webb told a thrilling story, but the imaginativeness and the comprehensiveness of his treatment were indications that he was not going to stop there; and he did not. He now saw that the frontier which the American people had carried into the Great Plains, and across them, out of the eastern forests of northern Europe and of North America, had been a phase of a global movement westward. In the United States, the descendants of West European colonists had occupied effectively vast habitable spaces which previously had been virtually empty or else had been occupied ineffectively and utilised inefficiently by their former inhabitants. But this had been happening not only in the United States; it had been happening also in Canada, in southern South America, in Australia, in New Zealand. Moreover, this effective occupation of more or less empty spaces had not been the only form that the West European peoples' expansion had taken. While they had been supplanting the world's surviving food-gathering, hunting, and pastoral nomadic peoples, they had also been subjugating the civilized, but technologically backward, agricultural peoples of Mexico and Peru and Asia and Africa. In one or the other of these two ways the West European peoples and their overseas daughter-nations had been expanding literally all over the planet in the course of the four hundred years that came to a climax in the nineteenth century.

Webb's vision now extended from the Great Plains of the United States and Canada to the world as a whole; and his intimate knowledge of the history of Western Man's expansion in the United States gave him a clue to what was in store for Western Man everywhere else as well. In the eighteen-nineties the westward-moving North American frontier had come to a halt, except here and there, as, for instance, in Oklahoma and in the northwestern fringe of the prairie provinces of Canada. In general, the limit had now been reached in the long process of bringing North America under the plough. There was even a slight recession in the area of cultivated land. At about the same time other Western peoples were reaching the limit of their domination over non-Western peoples. These were learning, from their Western conquerors themselves, the political arts of resistance and of national self-assertion. These anti-Western resistance movements were overt in the Asian and African subject countries; and they were only thinly veiled in Mexico, Guatemala, Bolivia, and other countries in the subtropical or tropical zone of the Americas—countries in which the Pre-Columbian element in the population was preponderant over the new blood that had been infused since the sixteenth century from Europe and from Africa. It was evident that the West's expansion of every kind and in every continent was coming to an end: and, then, what next? This is the fateful question that *The Great Frontier* raises. It is fateful because by the time this book was being written the expansion of the West had been going on for the best part of five hundred years; and throughout this half-millennium it had been the dominant movement in world history. Any historian who, seeing the world as a unity, might be trying to write a global history of the human race during this five-hundred-years-long period must take this theme, and only this, as his leading note. When this theme petered out, what was to follow?

The ending of the West's five-hundred-years-long world-wide expansion wrote a formidable question mark on the dark curtain that always veils the future. This curtain is, of course, always receding as time goes on; and, already, we can discern some glimmer of an answer to the question which *The Great Frontier* poses. In fact, the subject for a third book in the Webb series is now taking shape. And who can doubt that Walter Prescott Webb himself would have been the writer of it if he had been spared to live his life out to its natural term? The loss of his potential third major work is a sad loss for history. This third book will have to be written by somebody some day, but no one else will be able to write it with so sure a hand or with so true an eye for the historical perspective.

At least two important features of the current new chapter of world history are already apparent, and these two features, at any rate, are surprising, or at least unexpected. One thing that we now know is that the non-Western nationalists who have reacted—and, in the end, victoriously—against Western domination, political or economic or both, are not reacting also against the Western way of life. So far from that, they are using the freedom of choice that they have won since their political liberation in order to induct their respective coun-

tries, as quickly and as effectively as they can, into membership in a
new society. This new society is going to be a world society united by
a common allegiance to a modern world civilization; but this modern
world civilization will be based, to begin with, on the Western way of
life. This is bound to be so if such a thing as a world civilization is to
be got under way at all, because it is the West, alone, that has provided a possible foundation and initial framework for world unity by
expanding on a truly world-wide scale and drawing all the rest of the
human race together in the meshes of a Western net. All the same, the
Western orientation of the leaders of the non-Western liberation
movements is remarkable. Their objective in struggling so persistently
to throw off the domination of the Western peoples turns out to have
been to go Western, themselves, in a radical way.

A second unexpected feature of the chapter of history through
which we are now living is that the Western peoples are not going to
be ruined by the halting of their geographical expansion and the
liquidation of their political and economic ascendancy. Ruin might
have seemed to be staring them in the face, since for five hundred
years their expansion at other peoples' expense was apparently the
basis of their prosperity. Yet the United States was never before so
prosperous as she has been since the closing of her frontier, which
happened about seventy years ago; and the West European countries have never been so prosperous as they have been since they gave
up, or lost, their former colonial empires during and after World
War II.

This continuing and increasing prosperity of the deposed or abdi-
cating Western peoples is not really the paradox that it might seem to
be at first sight. The truth is that the factor that is making them still
prosperous today, since their geographical expansion and their ascendancy over other peoples have come to an end, is the same factor
that, in the preceding chapter of history, enabled the West to spread
itself so triumphantly over the whole face of the earth. Ever since the
fifteenth century, at latest, the Western peoples' winning card has
been their technological precocity. Since the seventeenth century
they have also been consciously and deliberately improving their
technology by applying science to it. And this characteristically Western cooperation between science and technology has never before
brought in such huge economic and social returns as it is bringing to
us in the West in our generation. Today the West is investing its scientific and technological ability, experience, and skill in the home

market, and this redirection of its energies inwards is bringing the West a golden harvest.

So cannot the West now forget the rest of the world and look forward to living happily ever after? No human beings, outside fairy stories, ever can, or do, live happily ever after; and if we Westerners were callous enough to be willing to forget the rest of the world our fellow human beings would not let us do it. They have power to compel us to give them our attention, because they are in an overwhelming majority, and they have a motive for importuning us, because they are hungry. They are certainly going to be much more numerous, and are possibly going to be a good deal more hungry, by the end of this century. The two things seemingly must go together. The population explosion opens up a vista of famine for most of the human race, while the Western minority is going to produce larger and larger surpluses of food which it will not be able either to consume at home or to sell abroad at an economic price. Thus our Western business interests conspire with prudence and human feelings to make us recognize that, whether we like it or not, we are our non-Western brothers' keepers.

The task before us in the West in our day is to reopen the West's economic frontier at a new moral level. We have now to be disinterested enough to help the developing, but not yet adequately developed, countries to learn how to help themselves by mastering modern science and technology up to a standard approaching our own. And, meanwhile, our Western taxpayers may have to pay our Western farmers to produce still bigger unsaleable food surpluses to be given away in order to tide over the population crisis. The cause of the present population explosion is a magnificent reduction in the premature death rate, thanks to the application of preventive medicine and the introduction of public health services, but this without any immediate corresponding reduction in the traditional birth rate. We may hope that the movement of population will come back into equilibrium in the non-Western countries, as it has in the West already. But this is going to take time; and this is the time—a critical time for the whole world—in which the Western minority's help is going to be most needed by the majority of mankind.

Here, surely, are subjects for a third major work in the Webb series. If only Walter Prescott Webb were still with us to develop these new themes in his own masterly way.

ARNOLD J. TOYNBEE

FOREWORD

THE PURPOSE OF THIS BOOK is to present an historical hypothesis set forth in the first chapter and elaborated in the succeeding ones for the consideration of scholars in divers fields of learning. It is important that the reader understand two terms which appear throughout and are given a special meaning. The Great Frontier is one and the Metropolis is the other. The first term is applied to all the new lands discovered at the opening of the sixteenth century; the second refers to the community of western Europe without regard to political divisions. The Great Frontier and the Metropolis, when used in reference to the whole frontier and the whole of Europe, are capitalized, but the unmodified frontier as adjective or noun is not.

The story is intended to outline some of the relationships between the Great Frontier and the Metropolis during modern times, and to show how the individual fared in the interaction between these two forces. Ideally the reader should not be able to determine the nationality of the author, but as things are it will not be difficult for anyone to see that the book is of American origin, and that most of the illustrations on the frontier side are drawn from the American experience. A similar story, with different emphasis and a different set of illustrations equally valid, could have come, and can come, from any country, frontier or metropolitan, with frontier experience. America happens to be important in frontier development and study, and the author happens to be an American.

The validity of the study depends on the validity of the boom hypothesis of modern history which is also set forth in the first chapter. There is so much evidence that the opening up of the resources of the Great Frontier precipitated a boom of long duration on the Metropolis such as to make the boom hypothesis less risky than it may at first seem. Even if figures were lacking, reason would tell us that the sudden acquisition of a new hemisphere could not be without economic significance to those who found it.

Because of the point of view from which the study has been approached, that of viewing the interaction between the Great Frontier and the Metropolis, many familiar features in history appear in a different perspective, take on another meaning. The mere act of looking at the whole frontier on the one hand and the whole metropolitan region on the other reveals relationships which are not apparent in examining fragments. In some respects the whole is simpler than the separate parts—simpler because function and meaning become apparent and aid understanding. The reader should have no trouble in discovering variations, some slight and some more pronounced, from some accepted views about both property and freedom and their possession.

Though the interaction of the Great Frontier and the Metropolis is the general theme, the two factors are not treated equally. The accent is on the frontier side. It is put there partly to redress a balance, but primarily because there is where the author set out to put it. The frontier is the subject, and the Metropolis gets into the account solely because of its connection and only to the extent that it was connected. In the history of Western civilization the two are inseparable, as this book attempts to illustrate.

The scope of the work and the magnitude of the two principal factors mentioned above made it impossible to develop in one volume the many leads that are suggested but are not followed out. The excursion has been down the main street, but there have been many observations about views up the side alleys, some of which have been explored tentatively for a short distance. This procedure may lead some to conclude that the work lacks a satisfying completeness, that it falls short of the possibilities. That is exactly the effect desired. The author would have been much gratified to complete the story rather than begin it, but since he could not complete it, the next best thing was to suggest to others the possibilities without exhausting them. He who explores the Great Frontier intellectually is subject to the same errors as those who explored it physically. Those who wish to avoid such risks should never invade any frontier, but should remain close at home with easy access to such pillars of certitude as the policeman and the encyclopedia. Many explorers made mistakes in the American wilderness, but nevertheless came back with or sent back valuable information.

Chapters X to XII are directed to those who are not satisfied with what has been done here, who feel that there are further possibilities. The three chapters are done under the general head of "What the Frontier Touched," and are intended to call attention to the relation of the frontier to the various fields of knowledge. The last section in Chapter XII is addressed to the historians, and contains some account of historical procedure and something about method. Ordinarily this material might have been given here, but it seemed more appropriate to put it near the end of the book. It is hoped that this introductory study will open up a broad front of investigation, in the humanities and in the sciences, which will eventually determine the validity of the thesis and reveal just how important the opening and closing of the Great Frontier has been and will be in the history and destiny of mankind.

The obligations incurred during the long period of study prior to writing this book extend over the United States and to Europe. They are acknowledged here and in greater detail at the end of the volume.

WALTER PRESCOTT WEBB

Austin, Texas
April 1, 1952

CONTENTS

THE GREAT FRONTIER

CHAPTER ONE

THE FRONTIER FACTOR IN MODERN HISTORY

THE FRONTIER as a determining factor in modern Western civilization has never been fully examined by historians or other scholars. Therefore it is important, in undertaking such an examination, to make clear the basis on which the inquiry proceeds, and it is equally important for the reader to keep in mind the point of view presented and the simple postulates upon which the superstructure is erected. It may well be that many readers, especially those in the United States, will feel that they know all about the frontier and its influence on American life. But this study is not primarily concerned with American life except as a detail, and an illustration, of a much larger and far more important story than one country, however important, could afford. The historical analysis here attempted could have been made, with important variations, had the United States never existed, but for obvious reasons the United States furnishes an excellent example of what a frontier means to a society, and what a frontier society is. In addition to that, the writer finds it easier to draw on American history than on that of other frontier countries. Despite this American slant, what follows is not about the American frontier; but as the title of the chapter and of the book indicate, it is concerned with the frontier factor in modern Western civilization since about 1500.

The first section, intended primarily for those not familiar with American history, shows how the frontier concept developed a meaning in the United States which has not been intensively studied abroad. The second section defines the Great Frontier as the term will be used throughout this study and sets it off against the Metropolis which is also defined and

1

used throughout with an unusual but appropriate meaning. The third section. "The Boom Hypothesis of Modern History," presents the underlying postulate of the entire work. If the reader will examine the frontier concept, visualize the Great Frontier and the Metropolis as they are defined, and accept tentatively the boom hypothesis of modern history, he will be in position to understand the analysis here attempted.

1. The American Frontier Concept

The word frontier appears in similar form in nearly all the western European languages; and, as used in Europe, it means the boundary between two nations and is represented on maps by a thin line. It implies that the nations must not cross that line except by permission or at national peril; it is "the sharp edge of sovereignty," the door or bastion of a neighbor, friendly or hostile as the case may be. There protocol and diplomacy become important and a "frontier incident" may well become an international affair. In the United States the word frontier has an entirely different meaning, and carries a different set of implications and connotations. It becomes a concept with such wide ramifications and so many shades of meaning that it cannot be wrapped up in a neat definition like a word whose growth has ceased and whose meaning has become frozen. It is something that lives, moves geographically, and eventually dies.

In America the word is hardly used at all to indicate the nation's limits. No American would refer to the line separating the United States from Canada or that from Mexico as the frontier, and to apply it to them in this sense would lead to misunderstanding.[1] The American thinks of the frontier as lying *within*, and not at the edge of a country. It is not a line to stop at, but an *area* inviting entrance. Instead of having one dimension, length, as in Europe, the American frontier has two

[1] The line separating the United States from Canada is generally referred to as the boundary; that separating the country from Mexico is likely to be called the border. The distinction is a nice one, and probably comes from the historic fact that there has been more friction between the United States and Mexico than between it and Canada. There has also been more lawlessness on both sides along the southern line, and the word border suggests that.

dimensions, length and breadth. In Europe the frontier is stationary and presumably permanent; in America it *was* transient and temporal.[2]

The concept of a moving frontier is applicable where a civilized people are advancing into a wilderness, an unsettled area, or one sparsely populated by primitive people. It was the sort of land into which the Boers moved in South Africa, the English in Australia, and the Americans and Canadians in their progress westward across North America. The frontier movement is an invasion of a land assumed to be vacant as distinguished from an invasion of an occupied or civilized country, an advance against nature rather than against men. On a frontier the invaders often have immediate and exclusive possession whereas in a nonfrontier the invaders have to contend with the original inhabitants whom they always find troublesome and frequently too much for them. Inherent in the American concept of a moving frontier is the idea of a body of free land which can be had for the taking.

This expanded concept of the frontier grew out of the American experience as the sole proprietor of an unsettled contiguous territory. Always, for three centuries, to the west of the settlements there stretched an empty country inviting settlement, luring the venturesome toward the sunset. Of this territory the United States came piece by piece into undisputed possession. No foreign power contended for it; it therefore did not present a problem in sovereignty, and movement into it was civilian, not military.[3] The territory was adjacent to the settled area, and the journey there did not involve a sea voyage, a long trek, or any considerable outlay of capital. The settlers who went there were not colonists, and the land to which they went was in no sense a colony. The settlers were citizens moving into territory owned by the nation. The only thing that distinguished these citizens and this territory from

[2] See Fulmer Mood, "Notes on the History of the Word *Frontier*," *Agricultural History*, XXII (April, 1948), pp. 78–83. The evolution of the American meaning of the word is here traced from 1623 to recent times.

[3] I am ignoring the scattered Indian population who did present some resistance but were not a major problem except for the few people who were in contact with them on the farthest fringes of settlement. In the present area of the United States the Indian population was probably not more than 500,000, one Indian to about six square miles.

the older region was the fact that the processes current were a step or two behind the processes of the older region, say in Virginia or Massachusetts.[4] It was understood on all sides that the status of the individual as a citizen was unchanged, and that within a short time the new territory would become automatically a state in the Union whose status would not differ from that of the oldest member. The absence of the military, the proximity of the new land to the old, the ease of migration, and the absence of any attempt on the part of government to regulate or control the process made the whole American situation the last word in simplicity, so simple that it amounted to chaos. In these respects the movement of the American people into the frontier after independence was unlike the movement of people from European nations into their overseas colonial possessions.

American historians assume that the frontier process began with the English settlement at Jamestown, Virginia, in 1607. Since the process depended on the act of taking possession of new land, it would go on as long as there was new land to be taken. The year 1890 is usually accepted as marking the date when there was no more frontier available, when the new land was no longer new. Though there is some quibbling about the date, 1890 does approximate the end of the frontier process in the United States, an experience of almost three centuries.[5]

It is the magnitude and the unbroken continuity of the experience that makes the frontier of major importance in American development. It made no difference what other tasks the

[4] The American method of expansion was simple and, for the people, highly impersonal. When new territory was acquired, it was understood that within a short time it would be cut up into states which would be admited to the union. The process was as follows:

1. Acquisition of an area by purchase, conquest, or treaty.
2. Government of the area as unorganized territory.
3. Territorial organization of prospective state or states.
4. Admission of organized territory into Union.

From the time of acquisition until admission, the territory, organized or unorganized, was governed by the United States Congress. After admission, state and local government was in the hands of the resident people. Any citizen of the United States could migrate to and become a legal resident of a territory without permit or formality of any sort. The land was never a colony nor the resident a colonist.

[5] The year 1890 is generally given as the date marking the close of the frontier. Actually the closing was gradual, covering the period from 1880 to 1910.

Americans had on their hands at a given time, there was the additional, ever-present task of moving into and settling new country. They did it while they fought for independence, before and after; they did it while they hammered out the principles of a democratic government and that government was eventually shaped to the needs of frontier men; and they did not cease doing it in the period of civil strife. They rarely reached the limits of the vacancy they owned before they acquired another vacancy, the Louisiana territory by purchase, the Florida country by negotiation, Texas by treaty, and the southwestern quarter of the United States by conquest.[6] In every case the frontiersmen had infiltrated the country before the nation acquired it. Like locusts they swarmed, always to the west, and only the Pacific Ocean stopped them.

It would be strange indeed if such an experience as this should have had no effect on the people and the nation. Could people have as their main task for three centuries working with raw land without getting its dirt under their nails and deep under their skins? The effects were present everywhere, in democratic government, in boisterous politics, in exploitive agriculture, in mobility of population, in disregard for conventions, in rude manners, and in unbridled optimism. Though these effects were present everywhere, they were not understood anywhere by the people who felt and reflected them. The frontier lacked its philosopher, the thinker who could view the whole scene and the whole dramatic experience and tell what was its meaning. This philosopher arrived three years after the experience ended and told the American people that from the beginning the American frontier had been the dominant force, the determining influence in their history.

It was in 1893 that a young and unknown historian appeared before the American Historical Association and read a paper entitled "The Significance of the Frontier in American History." That paper made him a scholar with honor in his own

[6] The territorial expansion of the United States occurred in the following order: Louisiana territory, 1803; Florida, 1819; Texas, 1845; the Oregon country, 1846; the Southwestern territory, including all or part of seven present states, 1848. These acquisitions were all made in advance of the migratory horde that was moving west with the result that vacant land was available throughout the nineteenth century.

country, for, brief though his essay is, it is recognized as the most influential single piece of historical writing ever done in the United States. It altered the whole course of American historical scholarship. The young man was Frederick Jackson Turner of the University of Wisconsin. Following Turner's lead, there arose in the United States a whole school of frontier historians who have worked out in many directions the rich mine that Turner opened up. It is not necesary here to elaborate Turner's famous thesis except to reiterate that it expounded the overwhelming importance of the frontier as the dominant force in creating a democracy and making the individual free from Old World restrictions.[7]

What should be emphasized is that Turner confined his attention to *American* history. The frontier that he talked about was the new *American* land lying west of the *American* settlements. His disciples and followers have not greatly extended the scope of his investigation. Most of them have treated the frontier as if it were something exclusively American, as if the United States were the only nation that had felt the powerful influence of access to vacant land. As for historians in other countries,[8] in the New World or the Old World, they have with few exceptions ignored the frontier completely, have never become more than vaguely conscious of its existence. As stated above, the European scholars, excepting W. K. Hancock of Oxford (formerly of Australia), Eric A. Walker of Cambridge (formerly of South Africa), and Fred Alexander of Aus-

[7] The essay appears in various places but is most accessible in Frederick Jackson Turner, *The Frontier in American History* (New York: Henry Holt and Co., Inc., 1920), pp. 1–38. For the pros and cons of the Turner thesis see George Rogers Taylor (ed.), *The Turner Thesis Concerning the Role of the Frontier in American History* (Boston: D. C. Heath and Co., 1949). A much quoted passage from the opening paragraph reads: "Up to our own day American history has been in a large degree the history of the colonization of the Great West. *The existence of an area of free land, its continuous recession, and the advance of American settlement westward, explain American development.*" (Italics supplied.)

Though Turner's interpretation has been challenged, it has continued to grow, and its influence has spread to literature, political science, philosophy, and even to psychiatry. It is today imbedded in the fabric of American thought, and is slowly invading other frontier societies.

[8] Canada is an exception. Its proximity to the United States has made it impossible for Canadian historians to escape the frontier hypothesis.

tralia,[9] have not even noticed the frontier concept, have not broadened the meaning of the term beyond its application to a boundary line.

I have often thought that each nation has something peculiar to itself that could be borrowed with advantage by its neighbors. If I could export one thing American to European scholars, something which, I believe, would help them to a better understanding of their troubled world, our troubled world, it would be an understanding of the frontier — not the American frontier, but their own — and its significance in their history and in their present lives. It is the American frontier concept that needs to be lifted out of its present national setting and applied on a much larger scale to all of Western civilization in modern times. This application will be of interest to European scholars only insofar as it helps them to a better understanding of their own history. The basic assumption for the discussion of the frontier as a factor in western European civilization is that Europe, too, had a frontier.

Europe had a frontier within the American concept more than a century before the United States was settled. Europe's frontier was much greater than that of the United States, included the present United States, and was the greatest frontier of world record. The frontier was almost if not quite as important in determining the life and institutions of modern Europe as it was in shaping the course of American history. Without its frontier modern Europe would be so different from what it is that it could hardly be considered modern at all. The close of Europe's frontier may mark the end of an epoch in Western civilization, and as a result of that close, many of the institutions designed to function in a society dominated by frontier forces should find themselves in strain and crisis.

The relation between Europe and its frontier must be surveyed from the date the relationship was established, say about the year 1500, down to the present year (1950), in the perspec-

[9] Eric A. Walker, *The Frontier Tradition in South Africa* (London: Oxford University Press, 1930); W. K. Hancock, *Survey of British Commonwealth Affairs* (London: Oxford University Press, 1940), chap. I; Fred Alexander, *Moving Frontiers* (Melbourne: University Press, 1947).

tive of 450 years. But before examining this relationship it is necessary to define the terms mentioned earlier so that we may not be lost in the complexities of the long period of history. The nature of the subject makes it necessary for us to ignore the artificial subdivisions of the two reciprocal regions whose relationships are to be examined. To divide Europe as the politicians have done is to invite confusion, and to divide the frontier as the Europeans did is to confound the confusion. Our task is to discover and impose a unity on each one which is not superficially apparent, the unity of western Europe and the unity of its opposite, the frontier. Once we conceive of western Europe as a unified, densely populated small region with a common culture and civilization — which it has always had basically — and once we see the frontier also as a unit, as a vast and vacant land without culture, we are in position to view the interaction between the two as a simple but gigantic operation extending over more than four centuries, an operation which may well appear as the drama of modern civilization.[10]

2. *The Metropolis and the Frontier*

It has seemed necessary to find a suitable name for western Europe, one which will emphasize its essential unity, and at the same time set it off in sharp contrast to that opposite land, the frontier. The name chosen is the Metropolis, a good name, implying what Europe really was, a cultural center holding within it everything pertaining to Western civilization. Prior

[10] Adam Smith was able to view Europe, the Metropolis, as a unit, and to see that the frontier (colonies) exerted an influence on the whole. He wrote:

"The general advantages which Europe, *considered as a great country*, has derived from the discovery and colonization of America, consist, first, in the increase of its enjoyments; and secondly, in the augmentation of its industry. [Italics supplied.]

"The surplus produce of America, imported into Europe, furnishes the inhabitants of this great continent with a variety of commodities which they could not otherwise have possessed. . . .

"The discovery and colonization of America . . . have contributed to augment the industry, first, of all the countries which trade to it directly . . . and, secondly, of all those which, without trading to it directly, send, through the medium of other countries, goods to it of their own produce." — Adam Smith, *An Inquiry into the Nature and Causes of the Wealth of Nations*, Edwin Cannan, ed. (London: Methuen and Co., 1904), vol. II, chap. VII, pt. III, p. 92.

He goes on to elaborate the indivisible influence of the new country on Europe.

to 1500 the Metropolis comprised all the known world save Asia, which was vaguely known and has no part in this exposition.[11] Its area was about 3,750,000 square miles and its population is estimated at 100,000,000 people.

There is no need to elaborate here the conditions under which these people lived in 1500. It should be remembered, however, that by modern standards the society was a static one with well-defined classes. The population pressed hard on the means of subsistence.[12] There was not much food, and practically no means of escape for those people living in a closed world. The idea of progress had not been born. Heaven alone, which could be reached only through the portals of death, offered hope to the masses of the Metropolis.

Then came the miracle that was to change everything, the emancipator bearing rich gifts of land and more land, of gold and silver, and of new foods for every empty belly and new clothing stuffs for every half-naked back. Europe, the Metropolis, knocked on the door of the Great Frontier, and when the door was opened it was seen to be golden, for within there was undreamed of treasure, enough to make the whole Metropolis rich. The long quest of a half-starved people had at last been rewarded with a prospect beyond human comprehension.

Columbus, a Genoese navigator in the service of Spain, has been accepted as the symbol, as the key that unlocked the golden door to a new world, but we know that he was only

[11] Asia is ruled out because it was actually civilized and densely populated. This study is confined to the empty lands of North and South America, Australia, and that portion of the Dark Continent comprised in the Union of South Africa.

[12] The situation in France may be taken as typical for the period under consideration. By 1328 the population is given at 22,000,000, and it fluctuated around that figure for four centuries, standing at 26,000,000 in 1789. It fluctuated from 86.9 persons per square mile at its lowest to 125 per square mile at its highest. Abbott Payson Usher writes:

"A population of about one hundred persons to the square mile would represent the normal possibilities of adequate maintenance in view of the agricultural technique of the period. . . . Until the Industrial Revolution this figure of one hundred persons to the square mile represents about the normal density for Europe." — Abbott Payson Usher, *An Introduction to the Industrial History of England* (Boston: Houghton Mifflin Co., 1920), pp. 88 ff.

Usher's density figure for Europe is far in excess of that of the Metropolis as used in this study. The Metropolis includes a much greater area than Usher's Europe.

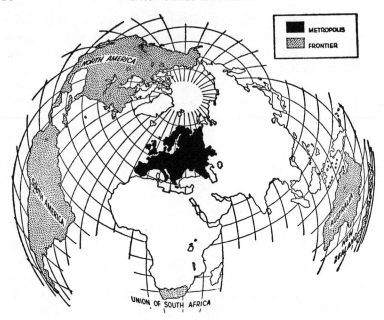

From Harper's Magazine
THE GREAT FRONTIER

one of a group of curious investigators, Portuguese, Spanish, English, Dutch, and Scandinavian, men of the Metropolis and not of one country. Within the brief period, as history is told, Columbus and his prying associates pulled back the curtains of ignorance and revealed to the Metropolis three new continents, a large part of a fourth, and thousands of islands in oceans hitherto hardly known. They brought all of these — continents, oceans, and islands — and deposited them as a free gift at the feet of the impoverished Metropolis. What they brought was the Great Frontier, a new ingredient in history.[13]

It was stated above that the Great Frontier was a unit, and

[13] The long-range effect of the discoveries was well stated in a review of Germán Arciniegas, *Caribbean: Sea of the New World* (New York: A. A. Knopf, 1946). The review, quoted below, appeared in the Book Review section of the *New York Times*, Aug. 11, 1946, p. 25:

"With the discovery of this sea and its lands, the whole tight medieval world became unsettled. Appear now lands and people that the Bible knew naught of, an altogether new dimension, a 'change from plane to solid geometry' — the Golden Age hitherto put into the past, is now placed overseas."

it will be considered as such in examining the interplay between it and the Metropolis. The fact that the frontier was scattered geographically should not obscure its common characteristics and the unity of the force it exerted. Nor should the fact that fragments of it claimed by fragments of the Metropolis hide the unity of either. The ensuing story of the Great Frontier and the Metropolis rises high above the fragments of both. What went on between them has been referred to as the drama of modern history. Let us so consider the drama by imagining the stage of the Western World set for the long historical interplay, with the Metropolis and the frontier in the leading roles. From the right side comes the Metropolis clad in the culture of an old civilization, rich in ideas and institutions, equipped with experience in government and skilled in all the known arts, accompanied by a host of attendants; but with all this, the Metropolis is poor in worldly goods, a little threadbare of garment and extremely short of food, a condition shared generously with the supporting cast. From the opposite side apears a rude figure, lacking in all the refinements, ignorant of government and law, shy on arts and letters, and almost devoid of attendants. The contrast is heightened because the frontier comes laden with what the Metropolis lacks, and craves more than anything else to have, and that is a burden of wealth, or of the stuff that wealth is made of, in such quantity and variety as the Metropolis never hoped to see. There was every reason why the two actors should become interested in each other, and enter into a mutual exchange of benefits, one gaining wealth and the other culture, eventually blending their fortunes only to find in the end both have become quite different from what they were when the curtain rose on the first act.

The presentation of the frontier as a dramatic character is of course a bit of historical license used by way of emphasizing it as a unified force. It was highly impersonal, without volition, and for our purpose inanimate. It was a vast property which had suddenly been bestowed on the Metropolis, and to the Metropolis as the new owner we must look to see what was done with it. It may be assumed that the Metropolis would ask some pertinent questions about the land that had been given it. (1) How big is it? (2) Who lives in it? (3) What is its inherent worth, what is it good for, and what can *I* get out of it?

The answer to the first question would be that the frontier, or that part of it we shall deal with, had an area five or six times the size of Europe. As to the second question — Who lives in it? — the answer would be, practically nobody. Outside of a few primitive inhabitants, whose rights need not and will not be respected, it is all vacant country. The way there cannot long be disputed by the present inhabitants. And to the third question — What is the land good for? What can *I* get out of it? — the answer comes clear and strong: You can get everything of a material nature you want, more than you ever dreamed of having, from gold and silver to furs and foods, and in any quantity you want, provided only that you are willing to venture and work. And something you have never had within your historical memory will come to you as a by-product, and that is an extraordinary degree of freedom.

The Metropolitans, having received such encouraging answers to their questions, decided to accept the gift, and they began the process of taking it. Instantly the divisions in Europe were projected into divisions of the frontier. Instead of making the new lands available to all the people, each little European Power seized a section of the frontier bigger than itself and tried to fight all the others off. Each nation wanted it all. The result was a series of wars lasting from 1689 to 1763, wars of elimination, from which three European Powers — England, France, and Spain — emerged with apparent success, as chief owners of the frontier world. Their success was more apparent than real, for within less than fifty years England had lost her chief prize while Spain and France had lost practically everything.

Though the Metropolis had by 1820 lost *title* to most of the new lands, it had not lost something more precious than title, namely, the benefits that the frontier exerted on the older country. For example, England probably derived more advantage from the United States after that country established its independence than it had derived prior to separation. The political separation of North and South America relieved the Metropolis of responsibility and onerous obligations, but it did not cut off the abundance or the profits. Europe continued to share in the wealth and the opportunity that the opening of the golden door had made available. The overriding influence of the frontier on the Metropolis, on Western civilization, is of such importance as to require special emphasis.

3. The Boom Hypothesis of Modern History

In order to appreciate this influence, it is necessary to examine the inherent quality of the new historical ingredient. What was the essential character of the frontier? *It was inherently a vast body of wealth without proprietors.* It was an empty land five to six times the size of western Europe, a land whose resources had not been exploited. When this great area was made available to the crowded and impoverished people of the Metropolis, they swarmed out like bees to suck up the nectar of wealth, much of which they brought home to the mother hive. *This sudden, continuing, and ever-increasing flood of wealth precipitated on the Metropolis a business boom such as the world had never known before and probably never can know again.* The Metropolis seethed with excitement. What with all the coming and going, the wharves were piled high with new strange goods, the tables were set with exotic foods of delightful flavors, and new-minted coins of gold and silver rattled in the coffers of the marketplace. This boom began when Columbus returned from his first voyage, rose slowly, and continued at an ever-accelerating pace until the frontier which fed it was no more. *Assuming that the frontier closed in 1890 or 1900, it may be said that the boom lasted about four hundred years.*

A hypothesis such as this cannot be presented like dogma to critical thinkers. They must have the supporting facts before they can accept such a radical doctrine as the boom theory of modern history. Before presenting the supporting facts, a corollary of the boom hypothesis should be examined. Assuming that there was a boom, and that it lasted four hundred years or more, it follows that a set of institutions, economic, political, and social, would in that time evolve to meet the needs of a world in boom. It is generally accepted that a set of institutions has developed since 1500, and we speak of them as modern to distinguish them from medieval institutions. Therefore, these boom-born institutions, economic systems, political systems, social systems — in short, the present superstructure of Western civilization — are today founded on boom conditions.

The boom hypothesis has implications that are far-reaching and important. It means that the modern age was an abnormal age, and not a progressive orderly development which mankind was destined to make anyway. It means that the institutions developed in this exceptional period are exceptional institutions, something out of the ordinary, and something quite different from what might be expected in the course of human affairs. They and their attendant ideas about human beings, government, and economics are very highly specialized to meet boom conditions, and may be expected to undergo much change when those conditions have passed away and history returns to normal. It is too early to guess what the changes will be, for the boom is not yet quite over everywhere, but the end of it is near enough to promote tendencies which give some hint of tomorrow. So much for the hypothesis; let us now return to proof of the boom on which it rests.

If all the problems connected with this study could be proved as conclusively as the existence of the boom in modern times, the task would be less difficult and the conclusions more satisfying. It is a matter of common knowledge that since 1500 Western man's condition has improved, not in a moderate way but extraordinarily. Any table of national wealth for any Western nation would show a constant upward curve until comparatively recent times, and of course the total for all nations would show the same trend. In certain periods and for the most forward nations, the advance would be spectacular. Paralleling the upward curve of material well-being there has been comparable progress in science, arts and letters, and a general admission of more and more people to the possession of property and to the benefits of learning once reserved for the few. Our failure, or refusal, to think of this extraordinary era as an abnormal period of boom, our natural preference to think of it as merely another logical step in the orderly progress of an endowed people, detracts nothing from the reality of the boom, the most naked reality of the modern age.

The causes which created it are another matter. The idea advanced here is that the frontier furnished directly the major factor of material wealth upon which the boom was founded, and indirectly contributed much to the subsidiary accompaniments in the realm of culture.[14] Our task then is to supply evidence that powerful factors favorable to a boom did exist after the discoveries and because of them, and that those factors which were most potent derived their strength from the frontier. The factors involved, though gigantic in magnitude, are simple in nature and in their relation to one another. There are three of them to deal with, and when they are brought together in proper proportion, a boom is of high probability. Given the social and economic situation of Europe in 1500, it was almost certainly inevitable. The factors are population, land, and capital. Before examining each of these separately, it should be said that all three were present prior to the discovery, but the proportions, the ratios were wrong for a boom. It was the change of ratios which set off the spark for the elec-

---

[14] It should be said that the academic argument as to the source of culture and institutions can probably never be settled to the satisfaction of those who must argue. One theory is that all ideas and institutions come from the brain and thought processes of man. The argument must be accepted. The opponents contend that environment presses man in certain directions, and compels him to do what he does. This argument cannot be denied. If man could exist entirely apart from environment, he could receive full credit for all that he does, which would be nothing. If environment existed without man (and it can exist) there would be no human institutions at all, no ideas, no culture. In either extreme we come out with the same result, which is nothing. But historically we never deal with the extremes; we always deal with man in an environment, and we believe that the two are reciprocal factors which complement and adjust themselves to each other. To the historian, at least to me, any argument as to which is the more important smacks of medieval scholasticism. I shall doubtless be charged with attributing too much to the environment, but the reason is not difficult to see. The environment I am dealing with is the *new* ingredient, the special factor whose influence is being followed on special assignment. The historian should have the choice of working the side of the street he sets out to work. The other side has been well canvassed.

tric upsurge of modern prosperity. The Metropolis furnished the population and the labor, but the frontier upset the ratios by supplying a *surplus* of land and a *surplus* of capital. It was the union of these factors, two of them radically modified by the frontier, and the opportunity for them to interact on one another, that made the transformation of Western civilization possible.

The population of the Metropolis in the year 1500 was, according to the best estimates, about 100,000,000 people. These people were crowded into an area of some 3,750,000 square miles. This means that there was an average density of 26.7 persons per square mile, an average of about 24 acres, good or bad, for each individual. The population was fairly stable, varying little between 1300 and 1650. The scarcity of land in relation to population was reflected in inheritance laws, in late marriage, and in enforced celibacy on those who lacked inheritance and dowery.[15] Primogeniture grew out of it. It is not an exaggeration to say that the land was saturated with people, with a labor supply.

It is inconceivable that this many people, confined to this small area, could by any stretch of their genius or by any invention they might make produce the wealth and create the boom which they enjoyed during the four following centuries. Even with all the advances they have made, Europeans of the same number could not from their own resources maintain the standards which they have enjoyed, and which but for their own foolish wars they might still enjoy. The essential truth was stated by William Graham Sumner when he said, "It is

15 For a discussion of the limitation on marriage and the custom of inheritance, see George Caspar Homans, *English Villagers of the Thirteenth Century* (Cambridge, Mass.: Harvard University Press, 1941). Homans says (p. 159):

"The working rule, no land, no marriage, had two aspects. First, men and women who were not to inherit a family tenement did not marry unless they could secure land for themselves. Second, in many places, the man who was to inherit the tenement did not marry until its last holder was ready to turn it over to him. In this manner the sentiments and customs of men secured a stable adaption of society to its economic conditions. Despite the logic of Malthus, they limited the number of persons who pressed on the land for subsistence."

this ratio of population to land which determines what are the possibilities of human development or the limits of what men can attain in civilization and comfort." [16]

It was the opening of the frontier which upset the whole European situation by altering the balance that had been struck between the amount of land and the number of people. The effects would have been readily apparent if by some magic the land, clothed with all its resources, could have risen out of the sea adjacent to what is present in Europe, but the distant position of the land, the fact that it lay over the seas, does not in final analysis matter. What does matter is that it was *additional* land, something extra, a great surplus.[17] To the 100,000 people of the Metropolis was suddenly made available nearly 20,000,-000 square miles of fabulously rich land practically devoid of population, an area more than five times as great as all Europe. Adding this area to that of Europe, the population density was reduced to less than five persons per square mile, and each individual could have an average of 148 acres instead of 24. One of the important aspects of modern times has been the flow of population from the Metropolis into the frontiers with the result that the population increased and the man-land ratio began to climb from its low of less than 5 to 1, slowly at first but more rapidly as time went on, until in the decade from

[16] William Graham Sumner, "Earth-Hunger or the Philosophy of Land Grabbing," in Albert G. Keller (ed.), *Earth-Hunger and other Essays* (New Haven: Yale University Press, 1913), p. 31.

[17] On November 21, 1882, Robert Griffin, Esq., President of the Statistical Society, London, read as his inaugural address a paper entitled "The Utility of Common Statistics," which appeared in *The Journal of the Statistical Society* for December, 1882, pp. 517–46. In this paper the author anticipated Turner by ten years and predicted that the disappearance of free land which would come by 1900 would alter the history of both Europe and the United States. "The history of Europe we may well say would have been entirely different from what it has been during the last century but for the new countries. It is difficult indeed to over-estimate the extent to which the existence of a new field for population . . . has dominated the recent economic history of Europe. We are so accustomed to a set of economic circumstances in which population . . . finds practically unlimited means of expansion, that we can hardly understand economists like Malthus who were oppressed by the only too evident limits which nature, at the time he wrote, had apparently set. "It seems impossible, however, not to see that a period in which the pressure of limits to growth and expansion may again be felt is not far off. . . . We are in measurable distance of very great changes." — Pp. 536–37.

1920 to 1930 it passed the point it registered in Europe prior to 1500. The surplus of land is no more, and noting this led Dean Inge in 1938 to remark that "the house is full." By 1940 the big house was much fuller than the little house was in 1500.[18]

Capital, the third factor in the boom, will be considered in two forms, as gold and silver and as Things, meaning goods and commodities. Our task is to show that here, as in land, the surplus came largely from the frontier. At the starting point in 1500 the Metropolis was short of both these forms of wealth. There is no way of knowing the exact amount of gold and silver in the Metropolis, but we do know that the production was small, and the scanty supply of precious metals had a way of drifting off to the Orient never to return. It is estimated by Michel Chevalier that all Europe had a little less than $200,-000,000.[19] Certainly there was not enough to serve the needs of exchange much of which was carried on by barter or to give rise to erudite theories of a money economy. By 1500 the Spaniards had cracked the treasure houses of the New World and set a stream of gold and silver flowing into the Metropolis that continued without abatement for 150 years and that still continues. The results were instantaneous. This flood of

---

[18] Man-land ratio in the Metropolis was 26.7 people per square mile. In the Metropolis plus the frontier after 1500, the man-land ratio was as follows:

1650	4.8
1750	6.5
1800	9.0
1850	13.9
1900	23.5
1930	29.5
1940	34.8

A comparison of the figures after 1500 and for 1930 is significant. It is interesting to observe that at the last date the Western World was gripped in depression — a coincidence no doubt, but perhaps of some significance. The above ratios are based on a study by Betty Brooke Eakle, "The Frontier and Population: A Study of the Influence of the New World on Population Growth," unpublished Master's thesis, University of Texas, 1948, p. 70.

[19] Michel Chevalier, *Remarks on the Production of the Precious Metals and on the Depreciation of Gold* (London: Smith Elder & Co., 1853), p. 21. Chevalier's estimate of the total supply of gold and silver in 1492 was slightly less than $200,000,000:

Gold	$ 56,843,000
Silver	139,756,050
Total	$ 196,599,050

treasure, the amount of which will be noticed shortly, changed all the relations that had existed between man and money, between gold and a bushel of wheat or a *fanega* of barley. It set the whole Metropolis in a frenzy of daring and adventure which gave character to the age. But, even so, the gold and silver were of less importance than the form of wealth that was to follow.

Fortunately, the data on the amount of gold and silver produced in the world since 1493 is available. Compared with the pre-Columbian period, the amount is so great that it has been commented on by historians and economists of all Western nations. What is important for the present study is the place of origin, the geographical source of the surplus. The total production of gold in ounces up to 1940 is 1,374,941,037. The total of silver for the same period is 17,253,108,920 ounces. The modern value up to 1934 may be arrived at in dollars by multiplying the number of ounces of gold by $20.67, and the number of ounces of silver by $1.38 per ounce until 1701, after which market values are used. After the devaluation of the dollar in 1934, the value in dollars is obtained by multiplying the number of ounces of gold by $35.00 If we accept the old basis, the amount of gold produced since 1493 would be worth $28,415,448,098; but if we accept the new basis adopted in 1934, the same amount at $35.00 per ounce would have a value of $48,122,936,295. Actual value used here is $31,927,983,709. This is arrived at by taking gold produced prior to 1934 at $20.67 per ounce and that produced since 1934 at $35.00 per ounce. The production of silver would, at $0.8958 per ounce, have a value of $15,454,326,543. The total value of both gold and silver would be $47,382,310,252, an increase on the esti· mated value for 1500 of 24,101 per cent. Assuming that the Western World today has $31.98 billion of gold, each of the 800,000 inhabitants could have on an average of $39.975. Each individual could have about twenty times the amount of money in gold dollars that he had in 1500. If the silver is added, each of the 800,000,000 inhabitants would have approximately $60 or thirty times the amount per individual in 1500.

The spectacular nature of the first influx of wealth in the

form of precious metals should not obscure the fact that it was but the initial wave of wealth or capital washing back from the Great Frontier onto the Metropolis. Wave followed wave in endless succession in the form of material things, and each deposit left the Metropolis richer than before. Unfortunately the amount of material goods cannot be measured because men were not so careful of their records here as they were in respect to gold and silver. It is known that prior to 1500 the people of the Metropolis had little to wear and hardly enough to eat, and that after 1500 their condition gradually and constantly improved until quite recent times. South America sent them coffee and Africa cocoa and the West Indies sent them sugar to sweeten it. Strange and flavorsome fruits came from the tropics. From primeval forests came ship timbers, pitch and tar with which to build the fleets for merchants and warriors. North America sent furs for the rich and cotton for the poor so that all could have more than one garment. It sent the potato which, adapted to the Metropolis, became second to bread as the staff of life. It gave corn, or Indian maize, and rich lands on which to grow it, and in time hides and beef from the plains and pampas of the New World. Everywhere in Europe from the royal palaces to the humble cottages men smoked American tobacco and in the soothing smoke they dreamed of far countries, wealth, and adventure. Scientists brought home strange plants and herbs and made plant experiment stations in scores of European gardens. In South America they found the bark of a tree from which quinine was derived to cure the plague of malaria and another plant which was sent to the East Indies to establish the rubber industry and add to the fortunes of Holland and Britain. No, it is not possible to measure the amount of goods flowing from the frontier into the Metropolis, but it can be said that the frontier hung like a horn of plenty over the Metropolis and emptied out on it an avalanche of wealth beyond human comprehension, almost beyond the dreams of the most avaricious. Men have not seen this great interplay because they have insisted on cutting the Metropolis up into fragments which they called nations and states, insisted on cutting the frontier up into fragments called colonies and empires. What they have not seen is that the influence of the frontier on the Metropolis was indivisible, having little relation to who claimed what. The Spanish gold prospered England and Holland and France, and English sugar sweetened coffee and tea all over the continent.[20]

We have now examined each of the three factors involved in the boom of the modern Western world. We have shown that the Metropolis furnished the population, and that the population did not increase rapidly until near the opening of the nineteenth century. The frontier furnished the *excess* of the other two factors, land and capital, and it was this excess, this additional amount of real and potential wealth, which incited the acts of appropriation that created a boom condition. It is the ratio between the quantity of land and capital of all kinds and the number of people which furnishes indisputable proof that conditions were highly favorable to an era of exceptional prosperity and economic progress. This excess of wealth over population does not mean that a boom was inevitable, but it does mean that if the society had the acquisitive instinct and the necessary skills and techniques, it would find in the new abundance unusual opportunities to satisfy its acquisitive desires and to develop its techniques through experienced practice. It happened that in Europe at that period, the acquisitive instinct was highly developed, the techniques for a beginning were present, and so the boom got promptly under way.

If we assume that the boom came about because wealth suddenly became available, increasing in quantity out of all proportion to increase in population, then we may assume that the boom will continue as long as the quantity of wealth to be had is abundant and out of proportion to the number of peo-

---

20 For an account of the effects of the New World on one European country, the reader should consult James E. Gillespie's excellent study, *The Influence of Oversea Expansion on England to 1700* (New York: Columbia University Press, 1920). Gillespie takes into account the influence of the Orient as well as that of the frontier as defined in this study.

Cornelius Walford has found that from the year 1000 to 1600 there was an average of thirteen famines per year. By contrast, he records three in the seventeenth century, four in the eighteenth century, and two in the nineteenth century, prior to 1879. — Cornelius Walford, *The Famines of the World: Past and Present* (London: 1879).

There is no famine recorded for England between 1880 and 1900.

ple. To tell the story of the relationship between wealth and population over a period of more than four centuries would be a complicated task. We can, however, show graphically what the relationship has been between population and land and between population and capital in the form of gold and silver, all of which factors can be measured with reasonable accuracy. What we cannot measure is the quantity of goods (Things) *produced* at a given time because the records on annual production of goods are not available. Even though we cannot measure the annual production of that form of wealth classed as Things or commodities, we can make some reasonable guesses as to the relative volume of this production by examining the economic theory that dominated economic thought in a given age.

Let us then set up four categories, each of which will be represented quantitatively by the height of the column. The categories are:

1. Population (measurable)

2. Land (measurable)

3. Gold and Silver (measurable)

4. Things, Goods or Commodities (not measurable)

The quantity of each of the above categories may be indicated by a column, and the heights of the respective columns at any date will reveal a certain relationship or ratio. It should be noted that categories 2, 3, and 4 represent wealth in some form, and the main relationship we are after is that between category 1 and the other three, i.e., between population and the total quantity of wealth. It should be observed that the land area remains the same throughout. The other three categories show a constant increase, and it is the difference in the *rate* of increase that is important. The base for beginning the calculation is 1500, and the amount of population, land, gold and silver, and Things on hand in 1500 is the unit of measurement. The height of a column is a multiple of this base, rather than the absolute amount. The land column rises quickly to about

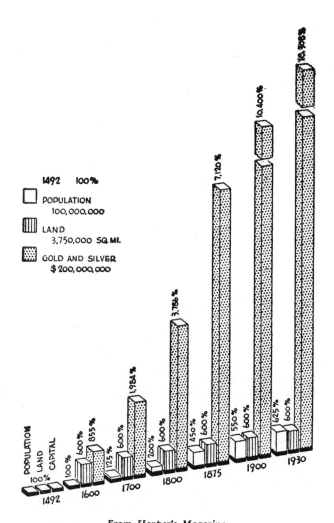

From Harper's Magazine

THE RELATION OF POPULATION TO LAND AND WEALTH

The chart illustrates the manner in which the Great Frontier changed
the ratio between the number of people on the one hand and the
amount of land and of the precious metals on the other at different
periods throughout the modern age. A study of these ratios will

indicate clearly that a boom was in progress as measured by the excess of land and the excess of precious metals in proportion to population. It will be noted that by 1930 the population column had risen above the land column, indicating that the excess of land has passed away. In the text reference is made to a fourth column, representing Things or commodities, the real wealth. Since the height of this column cannot be determined, it is not included in the chart, but may be imagined in relation to the others. It is suggested that its height was a strong factor in determining the prevailing economic theory of a given time. It is probable that prior to 1700 the Things column was lower than the precious-metals column, explaining the price revolution and making valid the mercantile theory. In the eighteenth century it rose above the precious-metals column, introducing an age of abundance, and making tenable for a long period the theory of laissez faire. The theory of laissez faire was in its turn rendered untenable by the recent rise of the population column above the land column. See Chapter I, Section 3.

six times the original base, and remains fixed throughout the period. The population column represents the total population of European origin in the Western World at given dates. The gold and silver column is accumulative, no deduction being made for loss or destruction of these metals. There was, of course, some loss, but when we take into consideration the total amount of gold on hand at any given time, and compare it with the accumulated production up to that time, it appears that the actual loss was inconsiderable. The unrecorded gold probably more than compensates for the loss and destruction. At any rate, the loss, whatever it was, would not change to any extent the relationship of gold and silver to people. We saw that in 1500 each individual would have only $2, but the gold supply of $24,000,000,000 now buried in Kentucky would give each of the 800,000,000 people in the Western World $30 each, not to mention gold reserves in other nations and that absorbed by industry.

With this explanation we are ready to examine the relationship between the population and the three categories of wealth. They are each represented in 1500 by small rectangles, the Things rectangle being in special design to show that we have no knowledge as to the amount of production. We only assume the amount in 1500 to represent 100 per cent. Therefore our graph would appear in this form:

Population (100 million)	Land (3,750,000 sq. mi.)	Gold and Silver $200,000,000	Things (?)
100%	100%	100%	100%

The four symbols, which merely represent 100 per cent of what was on hand, imply that a balance had been struck prior to the opening of the New World. In the preceding figure, the disturbance of this balance is apparent as we record the situation at intervals throughout modern history. By 1600 the population had not changed appreciably. The land area had increased to more than 600 per cent, and the gold and silver had increased to 855 per cent.[21] Since we have no knowledge of the production of Things, we cannot be certain as to the height the fourth column should be. It is safe to assume that it would stand below the land column, and, as indicated by the price revolution, far below the precious metals column. The popularity, and the practicality, of the mercantile theory until well into the eighteenth century, may be explained by the fact that Things had not yet begun to flow from the frontiers in sufficient quantity to free the people from an intense desire to have the luxuries from the Orient, luxuries which could be obtained only in return for gold and silver.[22]

The situation in 1700 shows no significant change. The population column is beginning to creep upward, the land column remains the same, but the gold and silver column rises to 1,984 per cent of what it was in 1500. The Things column is mounting, but probably is still only a little ahead

[21] The percentage figures for land and precious metals are arrived at by adding the new land and the new treasure to what was on hand. Population is, of course, not subject to this treatment.

[22] It will surprise some economists, and many historians, to find the much abused mercantile theory treated as a sound and practical one for the age it served. The subject will be discussed again in Chapter Three.

of land. By 1800 the population column has a little more than doubled, the precious metals have shot up to 3,786 per cent, and the Things column was almost certainly much higher, and had been since about 1720. This tremendous increase in Things made the old money supply inadequate, even with all its increases, led to the wide adoption of credit to supplement hard money, and prepared the way for the abandonment of the mercantile theory and the adoption of the economic theory of laissez faire.[23] It is only when Things are abundant that the principle of laissez faire can be applied with practicality. By 1875 there was no change in the relation of population to land and capital, except that the excess of land had been reduced and the excess of gold and silver had continued to increase. By this time the industrial revolution had speeded up the production of Things enormously so that the Things column must have been very high indeed. This was the Victorian age when the white man's burden was a real joy.

By 1900 something of great significance was in the offing, and that was the fact that population had risen almost to the height of the land column, 550 as against 600. The gold and silver column stood at 10,400 per cent, and without doubt the Things column was much higher. By 1930 the significant thing had happened. The population column stood *above* the land column, at 625. This meant many things: That the excess of land furnished by the frontier no longer existed in relation to population; that the bars to immigration from the Metropolis to the frontier countries would go up everywhere; and that the excluded nations who had formerly had an outlet for their surplus populations would demand living room, and failing to find it, would radically alter their forms of government and undertake to gain by force the privileges to which they had long been accustomed. It meant that so far as the Western World was concerned it was back to the man-land ratio which obtained in Europe prior to the opening of the frontiers. It meant more than that, because population was increasing at breakneck speed with the result that by 1940 there

---

[23] See Chapter VII, "Three Unwise Bubbles," for a further discussion.

were about 34.8 people per square mile instead of 26.7 as in 1500. It meant that in terms of 1500 the big house was fuller than the small house had been four centuries earlier. It may be an accident that the world depression came in 1929, just before the 1930 census revealed the return of the land-man ratio to approximately what it was just before the frontier precipitated the boom.

It is quite clear that if the existence of an excess of land in proportion to population was a factor in producing the boom, then after 1930 that factor ceased to operate in that direction. Where else could the boom come from? Superficially, it might seem to come from the excess of gold and silver which in 1930 had risen to the astronomical figure of 18,308 per cent of what it was in 1500. A knowledge of elementary economics, or plain common sense, tells us that this is not true, that gold and silver are practically useless except for what they will procure. Things are of utmost importance, such things as food, clothing, and shelter, and therefore we must come at last to our column of Things. The boom, if it continues, can exist and continue only if the column of Things remains high above population so that there will be enough for everybody.

The abundance of Things, and our great facility in making them available, obscures a fundamental truth which we need to see very clearly if we are to have any hope of meeting the main problem confronting Western civilization today. That basic truth is that the Things which are so abundant, even the gold and silver itself, rest upon the land and are derived from it. The land has only so much to offer, and when it is crowded, it has less to offer each one than when it exists in excess. Regardless of any techniques which may be developed to extract more from the land, there is a limit beyond which we cannot go; and if our techniques speed up the process of utilization and destruction, as they are now doing, they hasten the day when the substance on which they feed and on which a swollen population temporarily subsists will approach scarcity or exhaustion. Then the scholars will look back on the age when the Golden Door opened, and men marched out to the Great Frontier to create the greatest boom that the world has known; they will make myths and legends about it, and in poetry and literature express their poignant ·yearning for New Frontiers. They will see the frontier as the great factor in the age called modern, see it clearly as the lost factor which they would so love to find.

CHAPTER TWO

THE EMERGENCE OF THE INDIVIDUAL

THE PURPOSE of this chapter is to show that the frontier furnished conditions exceptionally favorable to the emergence of the individual, who has played such an important role in modern history. In the first section the idea is developed that the frontier acted as an abrasive on the metropolitan institutions, wearing them down until man stepped forth with old human restraints stripped off, old institutions of aid or hindrance dissolved, leaving him relatively free of man-made masters. The new master he faced was nature, but since nature is passive, man was the only active agent present, and was free to do what he would. It was in the exercise of this freedom that the particular kind of individualism associated with frontier society developed.

The second section illustrates the principle suggested in the first by showing how Jim Brown, knowing how to act in a frontier, took the lead over his more distinguished companions who represented the best products of the Metropolis. It was the new master, nature, that moved him to the top position and that led his companions to recognize without dispute the promotion.

Having discarded the trappings of the old master, nature again decided what the emancipated individual should go in for. It settled this issue by offering a high premium to him who worked. It was work that paid off more than anything else, and turned men toward what was material, practical, and useful in a narrow sense. The third section explains why the frontiersman enthroned work as a god and worshiped it.

The fourth and final section is concerned with the new faith in work as it appears historically. What is the individual who worships work to do when he can no longer enter the temples of his chosen deity? He remembers that when the frontier furnished the substance, the god of work drove him with relentless fury to his task, and he made folklore of his hardships; but now that the substance had dried up, he is left to beat on a closed door.

1. Masters — Old and New

The suggestion has been advanced that democracy is a frontier institution so far as the modern world is concerned. Though the frontier exerted powerful influence in originating or developing such institutions as mercantilism and its concomitant commercial revolution, capitalism, and the Industrial Revolution, it did not actually create these or for that matter nourish them in its own bosom. In response to the needs and opportunities provided by the frontier, Europe created or fostered these institutions and practices and retained their centers in the homeland. It was quite different with democracy. The center of it was established on the frontier, and it has as yet not been transferred to Europe in its frontier form. Europe mothered mercantilism, commercialism, capitalism, and industrialism, but the frontiers mothered democracy. We must seek out its beginnings, its habits and early tendencies in the forest glades of the New World, and to be more specific, along the eastern coast line of America where Englishmen had come to make their homes.

Here we need to take warning of confusion resulting from the assumption that political democracy is synonymous with democracy itself. Politics is an opportunist, coming forward to lay its eggs after the nest has been fully constructed. The frontier had built a nest, and built it well, before politics and statecraft came to lay a new government which was called democratic. The fledgling found the nest just right and the whole social and economic and mental environment suited to its growth.

When a handful of Europeans entered the American forests at the opening of the seventeenth century they found their relationship with both man and nature changed in the most extreme manner. All their previous lives in Europe had been dominated by contact with their fellow man. They were controlled by man's institutions, guided by his laws, influenced by his opinions, regulated by his taboos, frightened by his religion, and often intimidated by his government. Men and women everywhere — in England, in Holland, in France — were surrounded by man-made things. Nature — the land, water, air, and vegetation — was recessive. Wherever man turned, some guardian was telling him what to do, what to believe, what to think. All around he was walled in by authority which saw to it that he moved in a prescribed groove. Everywhere he looked he saw that the great struggle was that of man against man. Nature, passive and recessive, had been pushed into the background by civilization.

When these first men, many of them smarting under the man-made restraints of economics and religion, came to America they indeed and in truth entered a new world. It is with difficulty that I find language to express its newness to the children of civilization. In driving across the vast expanses of America I have often tried to visualize it as it was in this beginning, not the beginning of America, but the beginning of the European's experience with it. Even at the distance of four hundred years, more or less, I find myself caught up with the combined emotions of wonder, amazement, and awe. Here were new forests, new soil, and new streams; here was new silence and immensity, too silent and extensive to be broken by a single individual or by any number then available. How small man feels in such presence. But with this consciousness of insignificance goes that of elation which comes when man feels himself blended with nature where his vision is unobstructed and his acts unimpeded by other men. What men had done to him all his life now fell away in a single instant: nowhere was there policeman, priest, or overlord to push him around. All the barricades that men had placed around him came down, and he stepped forth freer of man than he or any of his fellows had been for a very long time. Then and there he took a long step toward democracy, not political democracy but psychological, social, and economic liberty without which political democracy cannot long endure.

Though the European walls had fallen away, new ones rose around him, for he stood in the presence of a new master. That master was nature, the forests and plains, the streams and deserts, the wind and the weather. It is doubtful if man should be asked to change from one master to another with such contrasting temperaments. Civilization shouts, gives orders, writes rules, puts man in institutions, and intimidates him with a thousand irritating directives. In return it offers him protection, soul salvation, and a living if he can find it. Nature looks down on him and broods in silence. It never shouts, writes rules or builds prisons, and it makes no suggestion about destiny or the future. Its noises of running streams and wind in the trees are its own, not directed at but soothing to him because he heard them before he heard the noises of civilization. Nature makes no promises, writes no insurance, and cares not for the soul. It is passive, receiving whatever is given to it, never striking back for vengeance or justice. *Thus frontier man became the only active agent on the scene, and his acts were unrestrained by other men.* In Europe the theme of life was man against man, man against civilization; but on the frontier the theme was man against nature.

In order to understand the long-time influence of the frontier, it is necessary to emphasize that the experience described above was not a momentary one, nor was it that of only a few. It was not as if the Virginians and the Pilgrim Fathers had this experience once, solved the problems connected with it, and then laid it away on the shelf of remembered things. The experience of man with the frontier was renewed over and over again by every man, every family, who took another step into the wilderness. It was this repetition of the experience for three hundred years as the frontier of America moved slowly and on a broad front from the Atlantic to the Pacific which put the indelible frontier stamp on United States psychology, ideas, and institutions. Any so-called conquest of a frontier is unlike a conquest in a battle, a campaign or a war. In such cases you have two opponents, both active and aggressive, each bent on triumphing over the other. The result is that the fight is of short duration, a matter of hours or days or at most of a few years. The outcome settles the issue, not only where the battle occurred but also over a much larger area as well. The case is different in a frontier conquest where all the fighting is done by one side. Since the opposing force is passive, it can never be defeated; it can only be destroyed. Moreover, the destruction or conquest settles the issue only in the spot where it occurred; it settles nothing in the adjoining spot. Therefore, for a country with an extensive frontier, such as the United States, Australia, or Brazil had, the forces emanating therefrom made a stream pouring back into the currents of civilization, giving them color and direction.

Scholars, being civilized persons, have long busied themselves inquiring what civilization did for the new lands which they have been wont to speak of in the possessive as colonies, empires, and dependencies, and not as the impersonal, passive yet powerful frontier that I have described. Our task is to reverse the approach and inquire as to what the frontiers did to civilization in general and more specifically to the individual man who came there as its representative.

Man brought with him to the frontier of North America his whole European culture complex. That consisted of his institutions of economics, religion, and government; it consisted of his ideas, mechanical techniques, tools, clothes, and his habit of dependence on those forces of civilization which pushed in on him from all sides to hold him fast in his groove of class and circumstance. I propose to show how nature, i.e., the frontier, went to work on this complicated culture complex, and despite all resistance, changed its pattern into something else. It was not so much that this new master, nature, imposed the change. The change to new ways and attitudes came because nature would not yield to the old ones, and man had to devise something to which it would finally yield. It was only the things that work, and in the last analysis, those that man acting with a minimum of social support can make work, that endured in frontier society.

If we seek out a single word to describe the principle on which the frontier operated on man-made institutions, we find no better one than disintegration. This disintegrative effect can be illustrated with many examples in American history, and likewise in the history of other frontier commonwealths.

The examples I shall use will be drawn from the American experience. I think the case may be better put this way: European institutions and practices wore themselves out against the abrasive frontier grindstone. It was the fact that they wore out — everybody knew they had worn out, and were not thrown out — that distinguishes a frontier revolution from a revolution in a highly organized society. In civilization institutions may cease to be useful or to function as intended, but they still have defenders, advocates with vested interests, and all that; the result is that they often have to be discarded by force. The frontier, being passive and impersonal, is not concerned with what institutions or tools are used against it; it has no vested interest in them, no advocates for them, but by the time the frontier gets through with either a tool or an institution that will not work, everybody is glad to lay it aside for one that will. Therefore it comes about that when man enters the frontier with equipment derived from civilization, the distintegration begins at once and goes on rapidly. It is this process that we may now examine. We shall see the individual survive his institutions, and remain the indestructible element which even the roughest emery of the frontier could not erode away.

The first step, and really the most important of all steps, I have tried to make clear by the figure of the crumbling of man-made walls, which fell from around the frontier man when he found himself alone in the presence of nature. It was his aloneness and the passivity and impersonality of the force against which he moved that explains much that we in the United States have called American. Fundamentally his aloneness meant that man was at last really on his own. He could do in this new environment anything he wanted to do and as much of it as he wanted to do without human opposition. For example, if he wanted to cut down trees, kill game, or navigate streams, he could cut, kill, and navigate without seeking a permit or running afoul of a policeman. The hazard that the tree might fall on him, the game tear him to pieces, or the stream drown him was his own lookout; he was neither prohibited nor rescued from his own acts. Nature viewed anything he did with a cold and impersonal, though sometimes a kindly eye. He found his own rewards and his own punishments, a double responsibility which in the first instance developed his boldness, initiative, and aggressiveness, and in the second fostered wariness, caution, and circumspection — acknowledged frontier traits. The fact that this man found his own rewards and punishments, and complete self-responsibility for his fortunes, did things to his psychology. It was natural that he who survives in such a situation would come to think very well of himself. It is true that many did not survive, "could not stand the frontier," and so they dropped out of the problem, leaving the stage to those who had learned their lines.

It was the men that survived, learned to play the game, who formulated the standards of conduct and value which were eventually accepted as the ideals of the society. They wrote the rules for the neophytes in the mores of frontier people. They accepted the practices and attitudes which necessity had compelled them to adopt, formulated them into a creed, and insisted that their creed was about the only one that was worth having. The creed was notoriously intolerant and narrow, as anyone knows who has a passing acquaintance with the frontier; but it was highly practical in the conditions for which it was designed. All over the United States, and probably in other countries, the creed remains after the conditions that created it have in large measure passed away.

The main point of this section needs to be emphasized because it seems to have been obscured by a rather abstract discussion of man on the frontier. The *man* got in the foreground for the very reason that he alone weathered the frontier storm, losing all his baggage, as it were, with which he started out from the Metropolis. It is the lost baggage which deserves our attention, baggage consisting of Old World or Metropolitan ideas about rank, status, and relative position; baggage consisting of institutions of control and direction for all. Throughout this book much attention will be devoted to institutions, how they were broken and reformed, but the details cannot be given here. With the subject of status and rank we can do something because here we are dealing with ideas which may for a time survive institutions, as they must precede them in origin. When the man enters the frontier, the walls of institutions are for the time being down as a physical fact, but memory of old relationships, of rank and status, remains as a psychological fact. They must be removed by experience on the frontier and not by mere presence there. How experience changes rank and status is illustrated in the following section, an imaginative example of an actual process.

2. *Jim Brown Knows the Way*

The case is that of five men who set out on an expedition into the frontier as it existed in some broad region in the area of the United States from 1607 to, let us say, 1850. Let us assume that the five men are going into the Mississippi Valley in about the year 1800, that all are of good natural intelligence. Four of them are exceptional in that they have risen to high position in their respective occupations. They represent civilization at its best. The fifth man — and the one on which we must keep an eye — has not so distinguished himself. He might be the man we have been talking about in this chapter. Let us give each man his name and respective rank.

1. General William Folwell was born somewhere in Europe. He took military training and at an early age entered the king's service as an officer. He fought in all the wars that came his way, rose from one position to another until he became a general. He had in the end thousands of men under his command; and until circumstances made it necessary for him to come to America, he enjoyed great power. He had many decorations, medals and certificates of merit. Imperious by nature, he liked to wear the smart military uniform, give orders, and wear his medals as a mark of honors civilization had conferred on him. We shall let him wear his uniform and medals on this expedition. We naturally assume that he is in charge of it.

2. Mr. Charles J. Claybrook represents business, the business world. He is the head of large commercial enterprises, a director of banks, a man who owns and controls much money. He has long been accustomed to the power, the obsequious

service and the prestige that the possession of money conveys. He knows all its rules, habits, and attitudes, and how to bring it forth from secret places. We will of course permit him to take as much of his money as he desires on this expedition, assuming that he is on the lookout for a "good proposition." He represents the best that civilization has produced in his line. He is still young, able-bodied but a little plump from being waited on too much with too much. His clothes are of the finest material, especially tailored for roughing it.

3. Professor Ernest J. Fairchilds represents learning and erudition. He speaks many languages (European, of course) and is spoken of with great respect at Oxford, Cambridge, Heidelberg, and perhaps at Harvard. His scientific discoveries and investigations have pushed out the boundaries of knowledge in that great movement which corresponded with the expansion of the frontiers. He has studied so hard that he has ruined his digestion, and has to be very careful of what he eats. His interest in the expedition is purely that of the scholar. We will permit him to carry such books and apparatus as he may wish. General Folwell and Mr. Claybrook, being practical persons, are not too enthusiastic about him and note with concern his dyspeptic pallor. They do respect him because he represents the best that civilization has done in the field of scholarship.

4. The Reverend Henderson Fowler is one of the best representatives of religion that European civilization has produced. A jolly sort, you know, brought up in the correct tradition with a thorough knowledge of and a reasonable belief in the Ten Commandments and with enough Latin and Greek to enable him to get by anywhere. His muscular frame and sound constitution have not been undermined by too much hard study. He represents a finger of some European creed extended to feel the religious pulse of the frontier. His performance there would surprise no one more than himself, but of that he is as yet fortunately ignorant. He anticipates that the report he will write is bound to bring favor from his superiors because he has a good style.

5. James Daniel Brown is the fifth member of the party, and for him civilization has done very little. He never had an

honor, wore an epaulette, or went much farther than b-a baker in Webster's Blue-Backed Speller. Having a good mind and being a curious person, he has continued to read and knows enough arithmetic to figure up what is due him. He did manage to learn a little about surveying by carrying the chain one year in the western territory. His given names — James and Daniel — indicate that his family read the Old and New Testaments, if not immediately, far back, and that they had respect for the apostle and the prophet. He would be startled himself on hearing these names because he is known everywhere in his community as Jim Brown, just plain Jim Brown. The neighbors call him Jim, and though they respect him for his good sense, they have never thought of giving him a title.

The attitude of the other four members toward Jim Brown varies as they vary in disposition and psychology. General Folwell addressed him once as "boy," but for some reason he discontinued that army term without knowing just why. Mr. Claybrook gave him businesslike instructions about what he wanted done with his luggage, and called him Brown. The scholar and minister were through long habit more reserved.

Perhaps Jim Brown's attitude toward the four men is also worthy of notice. There seemed to be no occasion for him to call any of them by title. Titles tended to stick in his throat and he avoided them by talking little, and addressing each in such a manner that there could be no doubt as to identity. Jim did whatever was necessary to get the party off, and he seemed rather expert at doing things, but no one could long maintain the feeling that he was in any sense a servant. Jim least of all. So far as he felt, there were five men going into the forest and he was one of them. They all looked pretty much alike to Jim. Of course, Jim never analyzed his feelings and attitudes. The real fact is that he did not know the differences among his companions. The military medals of the general, the money background of Mr. Claybrook, the scholarship of Professor Fairchilds had little significance for Jim, and much talk about them seemed positively silly. Jim could do inimitable satires of persons who differed from him, and among those of his own kind he would mimic them, and his mimicry would nearly always end up with the quite serious query:

"What good is all that stuff *here?*" Don't you see that Jim was a little narrow; he felt that whatever did not exist in his world, the frontier, did not exist *for him* anywhere, and moreover he doubted its right to exist. That was the basis of his intolerance. The important point for us is that here was a party of five men going into the forest, and that he was one of them. Their distinctions in their respective fields meant little to him. He would in the end measure them by his own standards and each would determine his own stature each day in the field. For him and all his fellows nothing had disintegrated faster than civilization's stamp of human inequalities. And so the five men set off into the forest for a two-year experiment with the frontier.

In this purely fanciful example I trust it will not be necessary to give the destination of the party or their geographic itinerary. We are interested in the disintegrative process of the frontier as it worked itself out on the members of this party, stripping them of the habiliments of civilization, reshuffling them as to rank, and bringing them back as different from their original character as they were from their original appearance. We present three scenes placed at suitable intervals.

Scene I. Time, the first day. The men have taken the trail, entering a dark and magnificent forest which is as yet untouched by civilized hands. The way leads west. The forest is full of wild game. Each man carries a gun and a knife, and whatever else he may have desired. It was Jim who insisted that the minister should carry a gun, even though the minister insisted he could never shoot it. For our purpose we are compelled to let the whole party walk, but the story would be the same if they were mounted, but more complicated; we would have to dismount them somewhere, and we might as well do it now. The general leads out, and why not? It has long been his business to lead expeditions. He has a map of the country and a compass which tells him that he is headed west. He looks rather swank in his new uniform, and the sun, falling through the trees, flashes its rays on his medals. Next comes Charles J. Claybrook, who has never ranked third in any society. He thinks of the money in his belt, and wonders if he has brought enough. He never felt better in his life. Professor Fairchilds is third, and not too happy about the prospect. He makes sure that his notebooks are in place, and wonders if he can find the right kind of food for his stomach. Henderson Fowler and Jim Brown bring up the rear. The minister is thinking of the report he will write, and finds something of a thrill in having possession of a fine rifle which at the last moment Jim thrust into his hands. All four men carry baggage, Jim Brown less than any. In no way does he seem to stand out in this forest, but rather to be a part of it.

It is not long before they come to a place over which they cannot follow the compass. There are suggestions as to what alternative to take. It is not until a decision is reached that Jim Brown suggests probable difficulties on the route proposed and mentions another. He can give no very clear reason for his opinion, but says something about the "lay of the land" which means little to his well-trained companions. Jim is overruled and the party sets off, only to meet an obstacle they cannot surmount. They turn back and try Jim's route, which they find feasible. We will pass over the events of the day, with its more and more frequent rests. Jim Brown doesn't seem to need so much rest, and goes off prowling around the bivouacs to examine things that interest him, trails, tracks, streams, and trees. Jim sees many things which the others cannot see at all. He is an experienced translator of the silent language of nature, though he knows no word save his own language and a little Indian, both sign and spoken.

Camp is struck very early this day and for most necessary reasons numbering exactly four. Everybody except Jim Brown is exhausted, and the general has a blister on his heel. Under these circumstances it falls to Jim Brown to make the fire and prepare the meal. He knew early that there would be an early camp, and had shot a turkey which he saw on a glade where the others saw nothing. This night you would have thought Jim was a servant because he did nearly everything, with some help from Henderson Fowler, whose recuperative powers seemed to be considerable. Each man had brought some food, but Jim said they had better go heavy on turkey and save as much of their store as possible. Appetites were excellent, and

Mr. Claybrook mentioned that he had never tasted better fowl at the King's Inn. Professor Fairchilds forgot his stomach and took a second helping. The general rubbed his feet, put a little tallow on his blistered heel, and all went to bed, feet to the fire. The stars and the forest looked down on four sleeping men. Jim Brown was listening to the sweet noises of the night and thinking of what he was in for. We may omit a description of stiff joints and sore muscles on the next morning. The ground in this forest made a hard bed for civilized men. It may be mentioned that when they got into their clothes, they lacked the fresh and natty appearance they presented the morning before. Jim Brown's appearance had changed less than any. The forest had gone to work on their clothes, and this brings us to the second scene.

Scene II. Time, six weeks later. Place, one hundred miles in the forest. A camp stands under some great trees by a bubbling spring. A fire is going and over it meat is cooking on a spit. A rifle may be seen leaning against a tree, and the man's eyes fall on it often as he works. He is a strange-looking creature. He wears tattered shoes through which his toes may be seen. You can tell that the soles are gone because of the respect he has for live coals that may have fallen from the fire. He puts his feet down very carefully; they may be tender, but more likely they are sore. All of his trousers are gone up to his knees, and his shirt is equally tattered. His skin is brown as a coffee berry, for the Reverend Henderson Fowler tans easily. There is strength in his muscles and the buoyancy of health in his movements. He has learned much in six weeks.

Another figure, equally ragged and unkempt, comes up from the spring bringing water in a wild gourd which has been hollowed out for that very purpose. He is none other than financier Charles J. Claybrook himself, who has learned to be quite handy around the camps. He is slimmer, harder, and there is a new light in his eye. His muscles do not cry out now against use. He still has his money belt with a lot of money in it around his waist, but you would never guess it. He wears little else, and what he does wear will obviously not be with him long. The two begin to talk.

"They ought to be coming in soon," says Claybrook, setting

the gourd down and, with two sticks for tongs, dumping some hot rocks into it to heat the water.

"Yes, any time now. I want this venison done because they will be hungry. Do you think they will get any more deer?"

"Sure, *he* will find the deer if anybody can. He never fails. I don't see how he does it."

"Do you think he can do it?"

"You mean the clothes? Well, if he can't we are in a hell of a shape in these rags. We'll all be naked as Indians in ten more days, and barefooted, too. See that — " and the financier extended his foot and wiggled all his toes.

"He says we ought to stay in this camp at least ten days, until we can get a new outfit. I hope the weather stays clear because you can't work hides in wet weather."

Just then two men appear coming through the forest. They are the professor and the general, each carrying the end of a stout stick from which hangs a deer suspended by thongs around its feet. They are talking and laughing as they come. The general's uniform is all gone except some fragments, and there is not a sign of a medal. The scholar is in no better shape as to clothes, but the physical change in him is quite noticeable. All the pallor has left him, his shoulders have become almost erect, his complexion quite ruddy, and it is often mentioned by the others that he seems to have the stomach of an ostrich. They place the deer on the ground and go to work with hunting knives removing the hide. Their conversation is beyond earshot.

Now another figure emerges from the forest, carrying three rifles, his own and those of the other two men. Jim Brown's clothes are in bad condition, but are perceptibly better than the garments of his companions. He walks with the swinging easy gait of an Indian.

Jim Brown approaches the two men who are skinning the deer and watches for a moment. "Here," he says, "let me show you," and he takes the knife and bends over the animal. "Be careful to see that you separate the hide clean from the meat so that we'll have no trouble in tanning." He then goes to the fire where the venison is roasting. "How are the ashes coming?" he asks.

"Oh, fine," says the preacher. "See, we have quite a pile. I have saved them all, and have burnt only oak wood as you said."

"Well, we can start tanning tomorrow. I think we have enough brains and ashes to do the job."

And so the task of frontier clothes-making gets under way. Brains and ashes are applied to deerskins in such a way as to leave them soft and pliable. Needles are improvised from bone and thongs are used as thread. We will now leave the men to their labor.

On the last day they make their departure early. We see them from a distance, moving single file across an opening in the forest. At that distance you can hardly tell one from the other because they are all dressed alike, in skins. The first step in disintegration has been completed; the frontier has destroyed the clothes of civilization. Yes, there is another change, which we had not at first noticed. Jim Brown is in the lead, followed by Henderson Fowler. General Folwell, who is having some trouble with his moccasins, brings up the rear. Men are taking their places on the frontier in an order different from that prescribed and supported by civilization.

Scene III. Time, a month later. Place, hostile Indian territory, farther west. For days now the party has been in hostile country where the Indians are on the warpath. Ours is not a war party, but it has no choice. It must either fight or perish. Henderson Fowler had changed his mind about shooting a gun. It was necessary for him to learn in order that he might do his part in providing food. His good eyesight and steady nervous system have made him a crack shot. When he thinks about it, he still resolves that he will never use the gun against a human being, even an Indian.

As we come upon them, the party is being attacked. Indians seem to be all around them. The general is lying behind a log, a sort of frontier foxhole. His gun is near to his shoulder as he watches a clump of trees for movement. The professor's slim form is protected by a giant beechnut tree, and his buckskin suit blends well with the bark. The banker is of course well protected, watching a long opening, hoping that he will get a shot. He has forgotten all about the money in his belt. That leaves Henderson Fowler and Jim Brown, who are near together. At this moment things begin to happen very fast in their sector. Two Indians jump right out of the forest in their faces. Jim Brown brings the leader down, and that leaves him with an empty gun. The other Indian keeps coming, is almost up on him as Jim reaches for the only other weapon available, his knife. He wishes for Fowler's gun, but just then the preacher's gun cracks and down goes the Sixth Commandment. The preacher remembers later that on this memorable occasion he felt a strange sense of exaltation, one he had never known before. He was a little ashamed when he thought of what he had done, when he viewed it through his civilized eyes; but he did not think of things that way very often now. After this episode he is one of the best Indian fighters in the outfit. In the new theology of the forest, the Sixth Commandment does not apply to Indians.

We need not follow the party farther except to say that all got back safely. The frontier had done more to them than wear out their clothes. It had worked them over inside. We saw how it happened to Henderson Fowler. The professor had lost his indigestion, the banker and the general had lost their habit of giving orders and depending on others; all had gained physical strength and a large measure of self-reliance. They had approached Jim Brown's standards, and would have by popular election chosen him as the leader simply because he knew how to lead in that land. Each of the four had seen room for expanding his own field of action, whether military, financial, scholarly, or religious, but none had been able to do much about it. That part is another story. As Mr. Claybrook removed his buckskin suit and got into civilized clothes, he unbuckled his money belt, remarking that this had been the most economical trip he had ever made. All the money he had started with was in the belt. There was not a medal or button in the whole outfit. Whatever went into the forest, there returned — just five men.

If the reader can grant the existence of Jim Brown as an example of what the frontier produced, then I ask him to imagine thousands just like him. From long before the American Revolution down to the end of the nineteenth century the United States was full of his type and more and more of them were growing up all the time on the western fringe. Even those in the interior were old Jim Browns who had lived the life and thought the thoughts a generation earlier. They still maintained their old attitude, and in many places their descendants maintain it today.

It should be easy to see how natural political democracy came to this type. These men had already adopted everything pertaining to democracy save political practice. They were living democracy in the truest sense of the word, and had been ever since John Smith in Virginia, a plain and egotistical common man, told a perishing colony that all who would eat must work and made it stick by a generous application of cold water. It was the Jim Brown type who fought at King's Mountain, who elected Andrew Jackson President, and then wrecked the White House by climbing over the furniture after the whiskey to celebrate the victory. The American army was a Jim Brown army where — up to and through the Civil War — many company officers were elected by the men and in some instances the regimental officers as well. In a Jim Brown army there wasn't a man who did not feel fully competent to elect a general. The European creed of "I know my place" was replaced by the frontier creed, "I am as good as any man." And the frontier man almost believed it.

Thus far I have dealt with an imagined case, but one which I believe represents a fundamental truth. It remains to cite examples from history of institutions and practices which wore themselves out or underwent radical alteration on the American frontier. Some of the examples are important, can be substantiated abundantly from the records, and several are treated at length in Chapter VIII. Another group may be considered trivial, but they are indicative.

Titles of nobility furnish a fine example of a European custom which nowhere survived the rigors of the frontier. Titles not only disappeared from the English colonies of North America, but they also vanished almost as quickly in the Latin-American countries. They have not been of indigenous growth in South Africa, Australia, New Zealand, or Canada. It may be argued that they naturally disappeared when the revolution from 1776 to 1815 shook off the monarchs of Europe who spawned them and gave them their being. It remains for those who make this argument to explain why the new nations made little attempt or none to establish a nobility on a new basis. It is also necessary for those who hold this view to explain why titles of nobility are, aside from a few royal officials, almost as scarce in the self-governing dominions as they are in the American republics.

Primogeniture and entail, which formed the basis of the laws of inheritance, gave place to the principle of equal division of intestate property in the thirteen colonies, in the United States and in other frontier countries. The English law pertaining to the uses of water was modified in the eastern United States, radically altered in the middle-western and Pacific coast states, and completely abrogated in the eight states lying in the heart of the arid region. (See Chapter VIII.) Indenture was widely practiced in Europe, and was used extensively in colonizing the original thirteen colonies. The system operated with reasonable success, but was not able to survive amidst the abundance of the New World. Escape from abject poverty was too easy to permit the rise of a class subject to indenture.

Three trivial changes in custom may be noted, namely, informality of dress, the use of the fork in the right hand instead of the left, and driving on the right-hand side of the road. The records on how these changes came about are scant. Still, when one understands the conditions under which a frontier society lived, it is not difficult to arrive at some very good reasons for the change.

Living conditions on the frontier were too hard to permit people to go in much for formal dress. It simply was not practical to dress for dinner, or for any other occasions. Church vestments were discarded, evening suits were practically nonexistent, and even servants disliked any dress indicating their status, for they had no expectation of being servants tomorrow. Soon the dislike for formality entered into the mores of the people, and any pretense at formality met with such social disapprobation that none but the doughiest could go through with it.

The American habit of using the fork in the right hand is quite in contrast with the European custom of never permitting it to leave the left. I have never seen any attempt to explain why the American decided that he could use both implements with one hand, and therefore what I shall have to say about the subject is conjecture based on rather intimate acquaintance with frontier conditions. In the first place the colonies were settled before the fork came into common use, and it is possible that fork etiquette was not fully developed when the foundations of American society were laid.[1] But even if it had been developed, the Americans might easily have forgotten it in their hard struggle with nature. On the frontier food was simple, utensils such as china and silverware scant, and appetites large. Food was served family style, and a second helping often depended on the speed with which the first one was dispatched. Experience soon taught that ordinarily the right hand was more efficient than the left, and so the custom of using the fork in the right hand arose and was accepted.

The last example is also one for conjecture. Today the English drive on the left-hand side of the road and the Americans on the right. No one knows when the change occurred, but a possible explanation came to me one day in Oxford when I saw a cart coming up High Street drawn by one horse. The man in charge was walking next to the curb, managing the horse with a rein held in his *right* hand. In that land of short distances and small horsepower that form of hauling must have been dominant prior to the coming of the automobile. For the man to have ridden the horse or in the cart would have added too much to the burden of one horse, and so the man walked. Naturally, he would want to handle the reins with his right hand and therefore he would prefer to travel on the left-hand side of the road.

In America the distances were great, the roads bad, and horses numerous. It was unthinkable and uneconomical to send one man on a long journey with one horse, or even with two. Four or six or eight were customary. They were hitched

[1] The scarcity of cutlery in frontier homes is illustrated by a story told by my father. In making preparation for company a mother inquired of her daughter if she had put the knives on the table. "Yes, Ma," the girl replied, "I've got old case- and cob-handle, little butch and big butch, and Dad's durned old pocket knife."

to a great wagon, and the driver, who had no thought of walking, mounted the heavy seat, politely called a spring seat, which
put him high above his team. He managed the brake with one
foot, braced himself with the other, held from two to four pairs
of lines in one hand, and the stock of a twenty-foot blacksnake
whip in the other. The average driver, being right handed,
would want his right foot on the brake and his right hand free
to handle the whip. The driver, thus mounted, preferred the
right-hand side of the road.

Had he traveled on the left side, he would have had to
swing his whip *in* the road, and that might have brought on
unpleasant conversation with passing drivers, a breed noted for
direct speech. If the American drove oxen, as he often did, the
need for the free use of the whip was more imperative, for oxen
were controlled exclusively with the whip.

3. The Religion of Work

It was observed at the end of Section 1 that despite all effort
to deal with institutions, it was impossible to keep man out of the
foreground. It is in the nature of society on the frontier that
the individual takes precedence over institutions, is the indestructible residue left after the institutions have been stripped
away and the ideas forced to change. He is important because
he about all that is left of a former complex structure which
in civilization had crusted him over. This is a fact so important that it must be constantly borne in mind by those who
would understand the influence of the frontier on institutions.
It is a point of view which enables us to see why at the core
of our most important modern institutions, regardless of how
big or complex they may be, we always find the individual, an
individual, there imbedded, again crusted over, but still important historically. It is the business of the historian to begin
with this simple element and trace the process of re-encrusta-
tion as it has gone on to the present.

The man himself determined by his choice and action the
nature of the first institutional crust formed around him. That
layer resulted from his decision as to what he would go in for
chiefly in his new situation. And what he went in for chiefly,

while depending on his physical surroundings, would result eventually in the formation of his most important institution, the one which would have the dominant influence on the society whose foundations he was laying down. The frontier man should not receive too much credit for the decision he made because he really had little choice in the matter, but he does deserve some credit. It was his situation and circumstance that forced him to be very practical, and he should receive credit for being practical.

If the man on the frontier lost the values that obtained in civilization, what values did he substitute in their stead? What counted most, not in London or Paris, but in the heart of the forest? It is important to remember that everything was up to him and he could expect society to do nothing for him. If any rewards were to be had, he must *take* them; there was no one to *give* them to him. This all means that he was free to act as he desired, having regard only for circumstance and condition. Therefore we need not be surprised that frontier man set up favored words to describe himself, and all these words emphasize his ego, his importance to himself, if not to others. Some of these favored words are freedom, independence, individualism, self-reliance, courage, initiative, aggressiveness, and finally industry. All these words thrust out, or imply a willingness, almost eagerness to do so. There is not a suggestion of defense, retreat, or compromise in the lot, and not one of them hints at a desire for guaranteed security.

All these thrusting, driving words became the slogans which expressed the folk ideals because they pointed to attributes that when exercised paid extraordinary dividends. The absence of timid words in American or democratic frontier folklore arises from the fact that by and large there was no great need for defense there. The main force against which man moved was nature, a passive force which never attacked, and this being true, there was no need for defense and no danger in attack. For aggressiveness there was nearly always a premium.

All the high words the frontier man used to describe himself and to express his egoistic ideal, meant *work* of one sort or another. Courage, initiative, aggressiveness, and industry can be best expressed in action, movement; that is, in work. Independence, freedom, self-reliance, and individualism mean that each man expects to act for himself. It is *I* who possess these attributes; every man on the frontier is an *I* because society has been atomized down to its elemental particles each of which is an *I*.

It has been said that the genius of America is expressed in the word work. Americans are good at getting things done. In any task calling for organization, power, and mass production they equal the best and excel most. They excel in the art of dealing with tangible things such as bridges, tunnels, skyscrapers, farm machinery, and automobiles by the millions. Their civilization has been called material because they have excelled in the production of things. They have not founded a religion or excelled in poetry or prose or equaled Europe in music, painting, sculpture, or architecture. Only one philosophy has come out of their thinking, and that is, as we might now guess, the philosophy of what is practical, what works. Pragmatism is accepted in America but it is scarcely recognized in the Old World as philosophy at all. Americans or any other frontier people are not much given to introspection and contemplation. *Work was what the frontier man first went in for.*

It may be argued that this devotion to work was imported from Europe, and did not develop in America at all. Though the argument cannot be settled, there is a good deal of historical evidence to show that work became something special in the New World. The present-day European attitude does not indicate that the worship of work is highly developed there. The Englishman does not regard it as an end in itself. He does a reasonable amount of it, but is not averse to interruptions which the American until recently would not tolerate. Socially the Englishman does not consider his industry an asset, and he rarely mentions it in company, and when he does he lets you feel that it is something he practices with his left hand, a sort of aside to living. Nor do the Latin people set too much store by work, having if possible other less strenuous interests. The European people who can afford leisure sit in cafés by the hour to talk, listen to music, and let life flow by as they relax under the gentle tonic of purposeless leisure. They are puzzled, and perhaps amused by the American who seems full of purpose, even when there is nothing to do. They note that he eats hurriedly and cannot understand why the bill is not brought with his coffee; and that if the conversation turns to art, music, the theater, philosophy, or literature, the American is likely to be ill at ease — he wants to get away and *do* something. If the European is a little ashamed of his work, the American is very proud of his because it is what he knows best.[2]

The American's devotion to work has expressed itself in a mania for efficiency. The Europeans exhibit no such mania. England and America show a quaint and characteristic contrast in all public service and in their universities. All sorts of service in England is slow by American standards, from telephone connections to cleaning and pressing. Service while you wait finds no favor there.[3] In the matter of education the contrast is most marked. American universities run full blast for thirty-six weeks with an extra session of from six to twelve weeks in the summer. The English universities, Oxford and Cambridge, operate for twenty-four weeks, broken by three vacations, two of six weeks and one of sixteen weeks. The Englishman assumes that education is acquired through the purposeful use of leisure; the American comes at it by busyness. Modern American universities devote most of their energies to training people to work, for jobs as accountants, reporters, and what not; English universities train their young men, it is said with considerable truth, to think. The work is up to them after they are educated. It would seem that if the Americans inherited their attitude toward work from their English forefathers, they have been caught in a case of arrested development because the English have evolved out of that attitude.

[2] What is said above applies to the middle class, people who might have leisure if they wanted it. The American does not like toil if he can avoid it, and the European immigrants, especially those from the continent, are better at it than he. I would say that the American is devoted to getting work done, rather than doing it himself. What he exhibits is the spirit of work, an absorbing interest in the business.

[3] In 1942 I was in England and broke my glasses. The optician, to my consternation, told me it would require two weeks to get a new lens. Fortunately, the break could be mended with glue. Not less than two or three days were required to sole a pair of shoes or press a suit. Three days were required to get a book out of the British Museum.

If the American attitude toward work developed in America, did it arise in the frontier period or later? There is an abundance of evidence to show that it developed very early, and over considerable resistance. John Smith was an early exponent of work, making it a condition in Virginia for all those who wanted to eat. Good eating on the frontier seemed always directly connected with work, dependent on it, but it was not until the latter part of the eighteenth century that work found its philosopher.

Benjamin Franklin was not only a philosopher, but he was also the apostle of the frontier faith in work. He glorified it, dignified it, made it seem the most respectable of man's occupations. In his eyes work that was useful conferred rank and status above birth, which he professed to dislike. While representing the new nation in Paris, he was disturbed by the false expectations of people who were contemplating removal to America. Bluntly, he informed them that "America is the land of labor." Nothing else counted. He assumed to speak for the Americans, to say how they looked on titles, leisure, officeholders, and geniuses; such things might have a place in Europe, but they had none in America. Americans honor the husbandman and mechanic "because their employments are useful." The Americans have a saying that "God Almighty is himself a mechanic, the greatest in the universe, and he is respected more for the variety, ingenuity, and utility of his handiwork than for the antiquity of his family." It is doubtful that many Americans of that day would have had the impiety to think of the Maker of the universe as a top mechanic, but Franklin wanted to make it clear that in America there was no room for genius, no market for birth, no tolerance of anything that was not "useful." He went further, and told the Europeans something which seems not to be true now, namely, that the American would feel more indebted to a genealogist

> who could prove for him that his ancestors and relations for ten generations back had been plowmen, smiths, carpenters, turners, weavers, tanners, or even shoemakers, and consequently that they were useful members of society, than if he could only prove that they were gentlemen, doing nothing of value, but living idly on the labor of others.

Franklin's most cruel draft from the well of American feeling is his Negro folk biography of the hog:

> Boccarora (meaning the white man) make de black man workee, make de horse workee, make de ox workee, make eberyting workee; only de hog. He, de hog, no workee; he eat, he drink, he walk about, he go to sleep when he please, he live like a gempleman.[4]

Here Franklin, perhaps with some license, was expressing the typical Jim Brown attitude towards the accepted ideas and institutions of an older civilization, a culture which could not flourish on the frontier. But Franklin was by no means through with the subject of work. He preached its merits interminably to the Americans through the popular medium of *Poor Richard's Almanack*. This was a sly approach by way of the weather, a subject of universal interest, to a broader audience than Franklin could have reached through any other channel. The people would not read his philosophy or his learned theories on science, society, and government, but they all kept the Almanac hanging just to the right of the mantel, and consulted it constantly in planting potatoes and corn, in castrating hogs and calves and colts, and in foretelling the seasons. It probably outranked the Bible in popularity and ran it a close second in respect. The Bible and the Almanac were twin guides, the one directing the way to heaven, the other on earth, and of the earthly guide Franklin had a practical American monopoly. Having secured his audience, having a guarantee that they would have to come back to him annually — for the Almanac, unlike the Bible, got out of date — Franklin proceeded to teach the people his abiding faith in work, and in so doing he exerted an influence in that respect which outlasted him for generations.

Franklin was too shrewd to take to himself credit for all his salty wisdom, and so he created a mythical character, Poor Richard, and attributed it all to him. People might dislike Franklin for personal reasons, but they could have no prejudice against Richard, who like most of them, was poor, and if he did not work, he certainly spoke in favor of it, and in language

4 "Information to Those Who Would Remove to America," written in 1782.

they could understand. In a sense Franklin, though rather sly, was actually very honest in disclaiming credit for maxims which were really not his. What he did was to gather by observation and reading the folk-wisdom of the people, the clues they gave for succesful living, and from the collection he distilled the maxims and phrased them cleverly. As a teacher, he knew the value of reiteration, and so he repeated the maxims in each almanac, driving the nail deeper each year and season. It is clear that the American people, toiling in their shops and on their farms, were themselves Poor Richard, and Franklin was enough of a philosopher to know that people will readily accept their own philosophy. Franklin was consciously teaching the people their unconscious philosophy, just as William James did later.

Though literate people still have some knowledge of Poor Richard's maxims, a few of them may be set down here as a reminder. They are now imbedded in the American language, but they are no longer regarded as practical. Up until about 1900 they appeared often in schoolbooks, but are no longer found there. They exist now as a part of a frontier memory, and therefore may be of interest to those who wonder how the American people came to set such store by work.

God helps them that help themselves.

Sloth like rust consumes faster than labor wears.

The used key is always bright.

But doest thou love life, then do not squander time, for that's the stuff life is made of.

He that riseth late must trot all day, and shall scarce overtake his business at night.

Early to bed and early to rise makes a man healthy, wealthy, and wise.

He that hath a trade hath an estate.

Industry pays debts, while despair increaseth them.

God gives all things to industry.

The cat in gloves catches no mice.

Employ thy time well if thou meanest to gain leisure; and since thou art not sure of a minute, throw not away an hour.

Many without labor would live by their wits only but they break for want of stock.

There are today elderly men who can remember a pioneer father's attitude toward work, and the pains he took to inculcate a respect for it in his sons. This devotion to work is exemplified in the custom of early rising. It is said that one father would on Monday morning at four o'clock shout to his sleeping sons: "Get up, boys! Today's Monday, tomorrow's Tuesday, next day's Wednesday — the week's gone and nothing done!" Men everywhere were going to work early and staying late. Others were driven by example or counted worthless. Idleness, even in the name of art, literature, music, or scholarship was not understood, and he who practiced it enjoyed no prestige. The naturalist Audubon was not able in 1824 to find a single patron who would subscribe to his magnificent work on birds in Philadelphia, and had to go to Europe for publication and support.[5] The devotion to work, which began as a necessity, became a creed and the principal article of economic faith. It brought many rewards, but it ruthlessly crushed out many fine qualities which human beings derive from leisure. The rewards were largely material rather than artistic and spiritual, and so in time it came to be said that America developed a materialistic culture with the dollar mark as its symbol. Other interests than work slowly developed as the culture matured, but they have had to make their way against the vested interests and traditions of useful work.

If man on the frontier worked at first because of necessity, he continued to work for the very good reason that there was immediate tangible reward for his effort. Work put a roof on the house, corn in the crib, potatoes in the hill, apples and cider in the cellar, and it extended the limits of the farm. These things he could have without purchase; he obtained them by his own labor. In his situation he got no such tangible or satisfactory results from other forms of activity. If he painted a picture, there were few to look at it, fewer to appreciate it, and none to buy it; if he wrote poetry or prose his neighbors

[5] In 1829 Audubon returned from Europe where he had obtained a publisher and a number of subscriptions for his book on American birds. He hoped to get more in America, but was unsuccessful. He could not obtain a single subscription, either in New York or Philadelphia. He had obtained one subscription on the voyage from Europe, later got one from the Library of Congress, three in Baltimore, and four in Philadelphia. — Constance Rourke, *Audubon* (New York: Harcourt, Brace and Co., 1936), pp. 234 ff.

had no conception of their merit; he might know all the Greek and Latin, science, or economics, but unless these things could "help out with the work" they brought no rewards. The finer vibrations made by the delicate instruments of civilization were recorded but faintly on the tympanum of the frontier. It heard the crack of the hunter's rifle, the sharp notes of the woodsman's axe, the whine of the saw, and the clangor of a thousand anvils where blacksmiths shaped the instruments for the great American symphony of work.

Another reason why men worked was that they never lacked something to work on. Nowhere in all the world had they found themselves in the presence of such an abundance of materials. Before them lay soil, forests, minerals, and water which were theirs for the taking. Here was a situation in which work paid off. With only a little of it a man in America could possess land comparable in amount to that of an aristocratic overlord in Europe. Never was there greater incentive to develop and satisfy if possible the acquisitive instinct. Here in one place necessity, motive, material, and reward all combined to drive men along the road of useful work. In a world of increasing leisure, we cannot condemn them too severely for following it.

4. Folklore Replaces Faith

The sociologists might tell us that a society is inclined to preserve its folk ideals in the legends it creates, in the mythical folk characters. Aside from Uncle Remus, who was the creation of one man, the original American folk characters, those who have sprung from the soil, are notable for one thing, and that is work. We have borrowed Cinderella, Little Red Riding Hood, Dick Whittington, and Mother Goose from England; Santa Claus from Germany; the Ugly Duckling from Denmark, and others from Holland. Aside from Santa Claus, not one of them was much involved in work, and his was but seasonal. In many of the borrowed legends somebody of noble blood was lurking around to be recognized as a princess or to become one.

America, on the contrary, and insofar as it has developed

folk characters, has turned out such a set of workers as the world as probably not seen before. There is a mythical character for many occupations. The most famous is Paul Bunyan and his Blue Ox, Babe, who performs wonders in the lumber camps of the Northwest; Mike Fink manages keelboats and Kemp Morgan, the mighty oil well driller, runs the fields of the Southwest; the immortal Casey Jones comes to his tragic end as a railroad man devoted to putting the trains through; in the Southeast John Henry is a steamboat roustabout and a great cotton picker; and in the steel rolling mills there is Joe Magarac, who performs prodigious feats; while Old Stormalong commands the wildest windjammers and rides out the roughest weather of the seas. Among them there are no fairy godmothers, gossamer wings, vacant principalities, or available princesses — not even a mayoralty. It is not their purpose to get out of work, to escape to a status of luxury and idleness, but to do more work than anybody else can do, to set the world an example. They are, these legendary and ingenious workers, a folk manifest of Franklin's dictum when he said, "In short, America is the land of labor."

With all this emphasis on work it would be a mistake for anyone to assume that all men on the frontier were devoted to thrift and industry. Foreign observers, and others from metropolitan districts, often commented on the shiftlessness of frontier people. In the freedom they enjoyed and in the absence of social compulsions, men could loaf if they pleased, and loaf many of them did. But the loafers did not win the prizes in the frontier sweepstakes of work. They did not set the standards; they were not the men that the neighbors named their children for. They were often pleasant to have around, but they did not become important. They, like Blackie Scantling of *Hound-dog Man*, were more popular with children than with men, and with men than with women, especially mothers.[6]

It was easy for men to loaf or do a minimum of work on the frontier where a living could be had from the forests and

---

[6] Fred Gipson, *Hound-dog Man* (New York: Harper and Bros., 1949). Blackie Scantling was a typical frontier loafer, carried over into the period of about 1900, a frontier survival.

streams, where food could be had as a by-product of the pleasant diversion of hunting and fishing, and, as Crèvecoeur remarked, "once hunters, farewell to the plow." Franklin left the impression that in America men must work to live, but he was careful not to say that they could live by working very little. The first pioneers were not always the estimable characters represented by Jim Brown. When civilization caught up with those who first penetrated the forest, it often found them strangely impractical. Only a few of the pioneer families were farsighted enough to realize that the condition in which they lived would not continue, and to profit by that knowledge. It was only natural that when the seedpods of human desires were released from pressure they exploded and the desires were borne by frontier breezes in all directions, toward idleness, lawlessness, and viciousness as well as toward industry, self-discipline, and integrity. The common denominator in all these was individualism which expresses itself in bad works as well as in good. Perhaps this is what Walt Whitman meant when he said that American democracy would need strong compellers.

The observations of the Frenchman, Jean de Crèvecoeur, on American life confirm Franklin's and supplement them. He attempts to view American life through the eyes of a recently arrived Englishman:

> He is arrived on a new continent; a modern society offers itself to his contemplation, different from what he had hitherto seen. It is not composed, as in Europe, of great lords who possess everything, and of a herd of people who have nothing. . . . The rich and the poor are not so far removed from each other as they are in Europe. Some few towns excepted, we are still tillers of the earth. . . . We are a people of cultivators, scattered over an immense territory. . . . We are all animated with the spirit of an industry which is unfettered and unrestrained, because each person works for himself. . . . A pleasing uniformity of decent competence appears throughout our habitations.

He notes the absence of titles and believes the Englishman will find difficulty in reconciling himself to the American dictionary "which is but short in words of dignity, and names of honor." By some means the poor of Europe got together in "this great American asylum," and, remembering their past, have no desire to keep alive old national sentiments. They remembered that in Europe they had not a foot of land, but rather the frowns of the rich, the severity of the laws, the jails, and the punishments. But now a metamorphosis has taken place. "Everything has tended to regenerate them; new laws, a new mode of living, a new social system; here they are become men." He compares them to withered plants transferred from poor to fertile soil where they take on their natural growth.

"What then is the American, this new man?" he asks.

. . . *He* is an American, who, leaving behind him all his ancient prejudices and manners, receives new ones from the new mode of life he has embraced, the new government he obeys, and the new rank he holds. . . . The American is a new man, who acts upon new principles; he must therefore entertain new ideas and form new opinions. From involuntary idleness, servile dependence, penury, and useless labour, he has passed to toils of a different nature, rewarded by ample subsistence. — This is an American.

It is Crèvecoeur who supplements Franklin by telling us how shiftless and worthless a frontiersman may be, and was. He describes the farthermost settlements, the first fringe, in the following manner:

He who would wish to see America in its proper light, and have a true idea of its feeble beginnings and barbarous rudiments, must visit our extended line of frontiers where the last settlers dwell, and where he may see the first labours of settlement, the mode of clearing the earth, in all their different appearances; where men are wholly left dependent on their own tempers, and on the spur of uncertain industry, which often fails when not sanctified by the efficacy of a few moral rules. There, remote from the power of example and check of shame, many families exhibit the most hideous parts of our society.[7]

7 J. Hector St. John de Crèvecoeur, *Letters from an American Farmer* (London: J. M. Dent & Sons, Ltd.; New York: E. P. Dutton & Co., 1912), pp. 39–47 *passim*.

The whole thesis of the change which occurred when civilization was transferred from the Metropolis to the frontier is contained in the above quotations. Crèvecoeur records the changes, but he does not attribute them to the influence of the frontier, but to what amounts to the same thing, the ownership of land and private wealth which he admits to be impossible in the

He says, and with some truth, that these are the cast-offs who will be followed in ten or twelve years by the more substantial ones. It did not seem to occur to this acute observer that in this wild society men may have been washing from the institutional linen the dirt and filth of civilization so that those who came after could have the fresh clean garments of liberty and freedom. The fact that this sort could go to the frontier, relieved the old society, and in a sense purified it, was important. While the frontier absorbed and consumed the outcasts, the loafers, and the criminals, it adopted the industrious and ambitious workers who followed, and made them its legatees. Though the frontier received the good and the bad, the shiftless and the industrious with calm impartiality, it furnished conditions which enabled the ones who worked to shape the character of the society.

By way of clearing up a misconception a few words should be said on the subject of frontier hardships. Pioneers and their descendants tend to dwell on the sufferings incident to frontier living, and the older ones like to tell the younger ones how much easier things are now — for young people. Sometimes they glory in their early tasks as illustrated by a bit of South African veld verse:

> Behold, my son, the wheel scarr'd road!
> Be shamed, and be afraid,
> For we, the first, were greater men
> Than those for whom we made.
> We wrought in death and hunger,
> We fought the veld — we few!
> Behold this effort of our hands,
> This road we built for you.[8]

Metropolis. In a loyal aside he attributes the benefits to "our government," which is derived, he says, from "the original genius and strong desire of the people ratified and confirmed by the crown." He was a loyalist writing in 1782 before the independence of the Americans had been recognized, and he may have thrown in this statement to prevent difficulties with publisher and officials. The crown had little to do with the condition he describes; if so, why did not the same conditions prevail in England?

8 Kingsley Fairbridge, *The Story of Kingsley Fairbridge* (London: Oxford University Press, 1941), p. 8. The above appears at the head of the chapter entitled "A New World," and the only identity as to authorship is *Veld Verse*. Since it and other verse so designated bears the unmistakable mark of authorship, it may have been done by Fairbridge or borrowed by him from African writers. The book itself is an excellent story of the rise of a frontier society.

From South Africa also comes the story of *Vrouw Grobelaar* by Percival Gibbon, a story in which the Vrouw records a tale of unremitting toil that almost breaks the heart, the making of brick by her young husband, Kornel.[9] Hamlin Garland, and many others, including O. E. Rølvaag, have expressed the same thing for America. The following from Garland appears among his *Prairie Songs*:

> A tale of toil that's never done, I tell;
>   Of life where love's a fleeting wing
> Across the toiler's murky hell
> Of endless, cheerless journeying.[10]

Whether veld verse or prairie song the plaint is that of work, too much of it for human beings to bear. That is the point, too much work, too long hours, too little leisure. The hardships of the frontier were those of too much employment instead of too little.

How did these hardships of frontier life differ from those of the present time? The difference and the contrast arise from man's relation to employment. On the frontier men suffered because the tasks were beyond their strength, and in their gigantic effort they came to physical exhaustion and death because the journeys were too long and the loads too heavy. It was he who survived the ordeal of work that had a sense of achievement, of fitness and of worth; as the years went by he elaborated his experience, dramatized his importance, and made himself something of a hero to those who came after in softer times. His elation outlasted his fatigue and it may have increased with passing time; literary men caught up the spirit and magnified his worth still more, making a hero of the man who had more work than he could do.

The distress of modern life, of civilization, seems to arise from an opposite source. There is no longer so much occasion, perhaps opportunity would be a better word, for men to break under their burden of physical labor. Labor unions and professional associations are busy making rules and setting stand-

9 Percival Gibbon, *Vrouw Grobelaar* (New York: McClure, Phillips & Co., 1906), pp. 258 ff.
10 Hamlin Garland, "Altruism," *Prairie Songs* (Cambridge and Chicago: Stone & Kimball, 1893), p. 78.

ards to keep out a surplus of workers. Most of the anxiety of our times comes from the fact that there does not seem to be enough for men to do; the fatigue they suffer is that of involuntary idleness, of muscles unused and minds unoccupied. The chief strain is mental, arising from worry and frustration. The frontier men, and women, died as a result of the race while modern men die because they are not permitted to run.

The theme of this chapter has been the effect exerted on a highly developed metropolitan society migrating with its full equipment of ideas and institutions into a primitive frontier. The first effect to be noted was the disintegration of the complicated institutions in the new environment, a disintegration that went on until it left man a mere human nubbin standing in the presence of nature. As he cast about, through trial and error as impelled by necessity, he began to build himself a new home, going in mainly for what paid him. He found in his circumstance that work paid, physical work on material things, and so he turned to it, making of work an ideal. It was a commodity for which there was an insatiable demand at such a profit as to cause him to neglect other worthwhile values, and often made him blind to their existence. Equipped with this ideal, he developed the necessary techniques and moved against the frontier with an accelerated pace until he came to its end. There he found himself in possession of enormous wealth, a technique of marvelous efficiency, and a creed of industry which left his desire for work unabated. He had chiseled a magnificent monument to his ideal, but now, for reasons he does not quite understand, he seems to have run into difficulties.

His difficulties arise from the fact that he had escaped the old institutions and had formed the habit of acting as a free atom in a decrystallized society. In the meantime a recrystallization was going on, and a new set of institutions was growing up around him, and with these he is having some difficulty. In the following chapter an attempt will be made to trace this recrystallization as represented by some well-known modern institutions.

CHAPTER THREE

THE RECRYSTALLIZATION OF SOCIETY

IN THE PRECEDING CHAPTER the hypothesis was advanced that the institutions of the late Middle Ages disintegrated when brought in contact with the frontiers of the New World, and that this process of disintegration left the individual temporarily institutionless in the presence of the new master nature. Since nature is neutral and passive, the institutionless man was the sole active agent on the scene, and was therefore free to do whatever his judgment dictated — with the understanding that he was to bear the whole consequence of his acts. The circumstance was such as to make him an extrovert of the first order, and to develop in him those attributes which have come to be associated with individualism as traditionally understood.

While it may be true that man likes his freedom and chafes at the restraints institutions impose on him, it is impossible for him to remain without them. If conditions destroy one set of institutions, he immediately begins to devise another. If a society should be completely dissolved, leaving all human beings in suspension, each an independent particle in an inchoate mass, a recrystallization would set up, and in a short time institutions would appear to bring order out of chaos. These institutions would again fix the flying human particles in their place and set up relations of dependence such as is revealed throughout history. It is this process of recrystallization of institutions in the atomized society of the frontier that forms the subject of this chapter.[1]

1 The writer is aware of the fact that society was not completely atomized any more than it is ever completely stratified or crystallized. Fortunately, perhaps, history trends never go to the logical extreme. What we are dealing with are prevailing tendencies.

Inasmuch as the individual has been represented as the active agent, acting in the presence of a passive master, it follows logically that he would in large measure determine the kind of institutions resulting from the recrystallization. He would be the chief catalyst, but not the only one. He would have the utmost freedom in proposing, in experimenting, in trying to find what would work, but all his efforts which nature refused to accept would be foredoomed to failure. It was this refusal of nature to accept the old institutions with which he came equipped that gave him the opportunity now before him. In time, by trial and error, he would hit on something that would yield to his efforts, something that nature would permit and perhaps reward. Having found this key, he would open the door to success, and would proceed to develop and adopt the institutions which would promote and guarantee its continuance. Thus would society be recrystallized around what paid off.

We have seen that what paid off in the frontier was economic effort. And this is not strange when we remember that the frontier was an unexampled body of wealth practically without ownership. Thus, in final analysis, it was nature which decided the direction that men did go in their initial efforts on the frontier. It determined that their contributions should for a long period be economic rather than artistic, literary, or spiritual. For this reason the society that resulted has been called, with very good reason, materialistic. The important point for us, however, is the reorganization of society and its recrystallization in a set of institutions made in the interest of the individual man at work.

The process of recrystallization is a most complex one, but it is very essential that it be seen clearly. Therefore let us visualize a single society fully equipped with its institutions marching into a wilderness. There disintegration sets up which strips from that society many of its tested ideas and practices, strips them off until little remains but the individual standing alone in the presence of novel conditions. Immediately reintegration begins, and society re-forms by creating a new set of institutions which will function *in* the wilderness. I hasten to add that not all institutions were discarded, but many were and many others were modified.

Such a revolution as I have envisaged does not come about easily or quickly. Within the frontier it comes peaceably because the chief antagonist of man there is nature, and whatever the obstacle nature may present to man, it never wages war against him. The chief difficulty that has to be overcome in effecting this revolution is the loyalty and devotion of men to their traditions, a reluctance to lay aside the things they previously accepted. It therefore takes a deal of scene-shifting to make the stage ready for the new production. The first section of this chapter undertakes to describe the revolutionary changes that occurred in *theory, motive, method,* and *instrument* before the new *institutions* would be fully formed around the man at work. Since we are dealing with the man at work, the adjective economic may be understood as modifying each noun underlined above. There may be some who will object to the emphasis on the economic aspect of the subject. This emphasis is defensible; more than that, it is inevitable, since work is what man went in for first and first succeeded at. The economic institution that resulted was the modern business corporation which set the pattern that has been followed by nearly all other segments of our society. The other segments are treated in the second division of the chapter under the heading, "A Cross Section of the Corporate Age." In that section we see how the principle of corporateness, first adopted in business, has been extended so that in the end the whole society is tending to become corporate.

1. Theory, Motive, Method, and Instrument of the Man at Work

It is clear that a society composed of free and disconnected individuals bent on developing along economic lines will find it necessary to harmonize all subsidiary elements with the main purpose. The people's philosophy, their theories, their motives, and their methods and tools must all be brought into line and made to contribute to getting on with the main job. When these changes have been made, an institution will emerge in which all the elements are incorporated, and this institution will until the purpose is changed tend to become universal and dominant in the society. It will rule in its chosen field because it is successful, and its success there will lead to its adoption by imitation in other fields. Thus will a single institutional tendency pervade society.

i. The Theory — Laissez Faire

An economic theory may be defined as a formal statement of principles followed by practical men with successful economic results. If the principles acted on lead with reasonable uniformity to success, and if they are discovered and correctly formulated, then and then only is the theory sound. Since a good theory must coincide with sound practice, there can be no such thing as a procedure that is good in theory but bad in practice. Therefore the prevailing theory in a given age can be understood best when it is examined in relation to the practices that were being followed successfully in that age. And since the practices which yield desirable economic results are in large measure dependent on the conditions and circumstances, human and physical, surrounding those engaged in them, we find it impossible to separate the prevailing theory from the prevailing conditions and circumstances. For example, a society having a scarcity of materials, say land, and an abundance of people would be compelled to adopt practices for which a corresponding theory would be formulated, a theory that would be "good" in that situation; but the same practice and the same theory would be "bad," or less good, in a society where materials were abundant and population sparse. Thus it would seem that both practice and theory grow out of the prevailing conditions of society at a given period of time.

It has already been pointed out that in the Metropolis the first condition prevailed, that of scarce materials and abundant population. On the frontier the reverse was true, for there we had, as long as the frontier lasted, an abundance of materials and a sparse people. It would seem to follow that we would expect to find one theory, that of scarcity, dominant in the Metropolis, and quite another, that of abundance, prevailing in the frontier. This would have inevitably been true had the Metropolis and the frontier, once it was seeded, been sealed off from each other. Historically, the situation was mixed because the abundance of the frontier was constantly being emptied into the Metropolis to increase its abundance, and the population in the Metropolis was being drained off to increase the numbers in the frontier. It is not strange therefore that the practice which was followed universally on the frontier was formulated into theory by a man of the Metropolis who had the leisure and the training to view the whole scene. The theory of laissez faire is a theory of abundance, of enough to go around, and cannot endure in any other circumstance. Therefore it was a good theory as long as the frontier or some other source which supplied an excess of materials lasted.

The mercantile theory and practice which dominated the Metropolis until it was pushed aside by laissez faire was a bridge on which economic man crossed over from the age of real scarcity to the age of great abundance. It was put into practice at a time when specie was scarcer than commodities, though both were scarce enough. Its assumption that money and not Things constituted the real wealth of a society is understandable when we recall that the precious metals were an absolute requisite in tapping the luxury markets of the Orient and in keeping these luxuries flowing westward. Europe had little in the way of commodities that the Orient wanted, and the frontier had nothing in the way of luxuries to offer the Orient. Therefore the precious metals were an absolute essential in bringing to Europe what was most craved. In this sense, and in that age, it need not surprise us that for a long period gold and silver were looked upon as the essence of wealth. The theory prevailed at a time when raw materials were flowing into Europe from the West and luxuries from the East, but before the art of manufacture had developed sufficiently to provide a real abundance. It is certain that in the sixteenth century gold and silver were still scarce commodities, and it was in this century that the mercantile theory was applied — a theory of money scarcity. It is quite probable that during the century, owing to the influx of American treasure, money increased faster than commodities, as indicated by the price revolution. It is probable that some time in the seventeenth century commodities increased faster than specie, and eventually they came to be recognized as the paramount factor of a nation's wealth. By the early eighteenth century, commodities had become so abundant that specie was once again relatively scarce, and in order to bring the medium of exchange into balance with the Things available for exchange, an extensive system of credit had to be superimposed on specie, giving rise to the great banking systems of Amsterdam, London, and Paris. It is important to note that this credit superstructure rested on commodities, the collateral, rather than on the hard money. Thus it came about that the new money, credit, sprang from society's collateral of Things. This change was a most fortunate one because it provided a flexible currency, one that could expand and contract with the expansion and contraction of the quantity of Things, which Adam Smith recognized as the real wealth. It is significant that the mercantile theory was not seriously attacked until credit had attained the importance, though not the prestige, of cash. The rise of credit and a knowledge of how to manage it would in itself have in time destroyed the hard-money philosophy of the mercantilists. Certainly when the scholar thought the matter through and found that the real source and support of the new money, credit, was land, cattle, and cargoes, his confidence that the precious metals were the *source* of wealth must have been severely shaken. It was not difficult to take the next step and conclude that gold and silver were mere symbols too, not very different from the paper of credit. They were convenient symbols used in the traffic of things. Though the mercantile theory may have been sound when it was first originated and practiced, it could not survive the flood of abundance which men wanted, and which drove them to create a substitute money whose quantity would vary as commodities and without much regard for the precious metals. Credit destroyed the scarcity of money on which the philosophy and theory of the mercantilists rested.

On the frontier, as represented by the American colonies, mercantilism was never acceptable either in practice or in theory. It would not take hold in a society of men who were practicing the utmost freedom in their pursuit of such wealth as was available to them. While they might be shy of money, they were rich in goods and were too busy appropriating them to be much concerned with theories of any sort. If by chance a theory was called to their attention which ran counter to their interests, they ignored it and evaded any law made to force it upon them. No better example can be found of this than the colonial resistance of the navigation acts which England undertook to enforce, laws made in conformity to the mercantile theory. It was too late. Under the previous century of salutary neglect the people had adopted a practice in harmony with the conditions around them, a procedure that could not be harmonized with mercantilism. In the midst of the abundance of the frontier each man was acting for himself in appropriating wealth in utter disregard for any theory as to the direction that money ought to flow. Instinctively, each man knew if he collected enough goods, some money — enough to get along on — would eventually come his way. Whereas in the Metropolis laissez faire had to make its way over the active opposition of a contrary opponent, in the forests of the Atlantic seaboard there was no opponent at all. The frontiersmen there were following the principles of laissez faire for at least a century before Adam Smith formulated the theory. In the midst of abundance they were ready to swallow the theory based on abundance, hook, line, and sinker. Thus the frontier man at work found a philosophy of work which satisfied him completely because it rationalized and justified what he had been doing and what he was determined to keep on doing anyway. For the time being it was for him a good philosophy and a good theory.

Though we are concerned here with the crystallization of an economic culture complex around the man at work, we may digress to call attention to a parallel development in politics. Man not only wanted to work for himself and as he pleased, but he equally desired to govern himself in the same manner. Only by governing himself could he be sure that he would remain free to pursue his dominating purpose. Actually he had been, in the absence of old institutions, practicing self-government without the formal consent of the governor. He fought the American Revolution to persuade the governor, England, to sanction what had long been practiced, to bring the theory into conformity with the reality. The parallel is more striking because two documents formulating new theories acceptable to frontier men appeared simultaneously. One came from the Metropolis proclaiming economic freedom and the other came from the frontier proclaiming political freedom. In 1776, Adam Smith published *The Wealth of Nations* and Thomas Jefferson wrote the Declaration of Independence. Granting that the individual now had an acceptable economic theory and a highly tolerant government, we are in position to inquire as to his motive and his relation to the circumstances surrounding him.

ii. The Motive — Profit

It is unnecessary to dwell on the motive, the driving force, that actuated the society of individuals on the frontier. When we concede that the individual went in for work, the only thing that would lead nature to yield him much results, and that work did pay off better than any other form of activity, we see him arrive at profit as a reward. Of course the desire for profit was in no sense confined to the frontier; it is well-nigh universal in any society. What distinguished the frontier man from him of the Metropolis was the universality of the devotion to it. It acted like a powerful magnet that polarized every particle of society in greater or less degree. "America is the land of work," said Franklin. Religion, birth, the arts were either discarded or bent in the direction of work, made to contribute to it. Even frontier games such as log rolling, house raising, quilting bees, and corn huskings served to get a lot of work done in the spirit of fun. Not everybody practiced it, but nobody dared disapprove of it in principle, and those who did work dominated the society, shaped the mores, and set the standards.[2]

2 John A. Kouwenhoven, *Made in America: The Arts in Modern Civilization* (New York: Doubleday & Co., Inc., 1948). This book deals with the development of an indigenous art in America as distinguished from traditional European art. I think that his argument boils down to this, that America's contribution to art has come from the task of doing a great deal of work. The indigenous art of America — the vernacular — is functional. It has grown out of making engines, building houses, and constructing bridges.

The end desired by him who works is profit, and any considerable aggregation of profit. becomes capital in the modern sense.[3] Therefore it is not strange that in a society with such devotion to work, capital accumulated rapidly, provided — and the provision is all-important — there was substance on which to work. Here is where the abundance of the frontier made its contribution by providing such a supply of material as men had never known in history. It was this abundance that made the profit motive tenable, and that carried the whole society along the road to capitalism. Without substance the religion of work would have been a superstition and none but stupid men would have believed in it.

iii. The Method — Competition

Competition has been treated by some as if it were a prescription handed down to man as a method, a ritual, which he must follow in carrying out his devotion to the god of work. Some assume that it is a good method, others that it is the best method, and a decreasing number contend that it is the only method. I propose to show that in a frontier society of individuals such as I have described it was a natural method, an inescapable one. I also hope to demonstrate that competition was one thing in an open frontier and quite something else in a closed or frontierless society. If it has objectionable features, they are less apparent in the first than in the last, for reasons that will be stated.

Competition was a natural method of work among men of the frontier because of two relationships that existed there: the relationship among men free of all human restraints, political or economic; and the relationship of these men as a body to the vast quantity of unappropriated wealth which lay before them.

The relationship among men of the frontier has been described in Chapter Two, and illustrated with the story of Jim Brown. There was a simple equality and a lack of institutions, both facts tending to make every man independent. The so-

[3] For a different view see Gordon R. Taylor, *Are Workers Human?* (Boston: Houghton Mifflin Co., 1952).

ciety was but a collection of these men, an aggregation without much form. Since each man acted for himself, there was a
natural rivalry of individual effort, a special kind of competition. Each man tried to do more work than his neighbor at
log-rollings, house-raisings, wrestling matches, and shooting
bees. Each kept an eye on his neighbor and tried to outdo him
in growing corn and fattening pigs. He kept an eye on his
neighbor in accumulating wealth, and did his best to outstrip
him, and if he got the better of him in a horse trade he took
satisfaction in his cleverness. Despite small differences between them — for, as Franklin observed, it was a land of happy
mediocrity, and as Crèvecoeur said, a land of decent compe-
tency — they were still relatively equal.

It was the second relationship, that of the group of men to
the abundance of the frontier, which gave their competition
its peculiar character, which made competition in that period
so blameless. For a man to gather wealth in that situation it
was not necessary, not even desirable, for him to take it away
from another man. It was hardly worth while because the
other man had no great quantity, nothing comparable to what
could be had from nature without incurring opposition. Why
should he "outfox" his neighbor for a quarter-section or a
stand of timber when he could have them from the free frontier? The competition consisted more in appropriating from
the common storehouse than in profiting at one another's expense. Actually men co-operated in this appropriation, helped
each other out in surveying, fencing, and testifying.[4] This co-
operation in helping one another in the common task of appropriation from a public storehouse goes far to explain frontier neighborliness of which we hear so much. This sort of
competition — if it can be called that — was friendly and lacking in the savage cruelty which came to characterize it when

[4] O. E. Rølvaag, *Giants in the Earth* (New York: Harper and Bros., 1927).
In this powerful novel of frontier life in South Dakota, it is not enough for
Per Hansa, the chief character, to make sure of his own free quarter-section.
He shows his neighbors how to secure theirs and leads them in pulling up the
surveyor's stakes and destroying landmarks. Here is an example of frontier
neighborliness in taking land from the sovereign. Had it been a private deal
in which the men were trading with one another, the attitude would have
been quite different.

all frontier wealth had been appropriated, and the only way
one could acquire a disproportionate amount was to take it
away from the others. The first form of competition all men
approved; the second form, which in time displaced it, has
often been criticized. Free competition is par excellence the
method of abundance, and probably cannot be tolerated without disastrous results in an economy of extreme scarcity.

iv. The Instrument — The Machine or Tool

The set of instruments or tools which men use are accepted
by the cultural anthropologist as an index to the stage of
culture they are in. The tools likewise indicate the side of
culture the society is emphasizing. The artifacts in the kitchen
middens of North America tell us that the ancient inhabitants
were in the Stone Age, and that their main emphasis was on
hunting and war. Once this emphasis is discovered, a great
many otherwise meaningless things take on significance. An
observer, coming on a deserted habitation deep in the wilderness, could by examining the contents of the place determine
the primary interests and occupation of the former dweller.
Bits of painter's canvas and splotches of dried pigment and an
improvised easel would indicate one thing; gun shells, steel
traps and dried hides on a bent stick would indicate another;
while axes, saws, barns with corn and hay, and plow tools
would speak plainly of the former occupant.

It has been suggested that what the frontiersman went in
for primarily was work directed against nature for the purpose of economic gain. There were not many easels on the
frontier, but there were many axes, hoes, saws, augers, adzes,
and plows, simple tools universally used by an army of men
advancing on a wilderness. Emerson Hough once remarked
that four instruments were used in the conquest of America:
the axe, the rifle, the boat, and the horse.[5] All were prized
for their practical value, their usefulness, and all in one way
or another sped or lightened the work. The axe, the rifle, and
the boat received so much attention that they became works
of art — lovely to look at and a pleasure to handle. Their

[5] Emerson Hough, *The Way to the West* (Indianapolis: The Bobbs-Merrill
Co., 1903).

grace and beauty combined with their utility to express the genius of the frontier man at work. All four instruments were adapted for use by one man, and three of them were incapable of management by more than one. These simple tools and instruments are a highly significant factor in a society noted for individualism.

Though these simple and individual tools sped the work, they could not do enough to satisfy the men whose motive was gain. They limited the speed with which the wealth available, the abundance of the frontier, could be appropriated. It was the great abundance of raw material which put a high premium on improving the tools, which in turn created an outlet for human ingenuity and improvisation, for invention and practical application of the principles formulated by the thinkers. This outlet for ingenuity and invention is of more importance in understanding the development of the Industrial Revolution than we may have suspected. In the presence of abundant materials, no expense involved in inventing and proving a machine was too great provided it would speed the work. This was the practical side, the place where the inventor left off and the practical man who had work to do took over. It was he who could stand the expense, gamble a short loss against a long profit. This practical man gave impetus to invention and an outlet for mechanical ingenuity by paying the bill — any amount to get on with the task.

It is worth noting here that the Industrial Revolution in its initial stage was effected by the application of the principles of physics almost exclusively, and that physics is, or was at that time, concerned with but two things, matter and energy, physical substance and power. Since substance existed in such abundance on the frontier, and since men there were so devoted to appropriating it through work, where in all the world did physics have a better opportunity or a more favorable human climate to apply the principles it was discovering on such a gigantic scale? It may be objected, and correctly so, that the principles of physics were not discovered on the frontier or for that matter with the purpose of applying them there. This is admitted. It is only contended that regardless of their place of origin the principles were applied in a practical manner on a large scale either in countries which had tapped the abundance of the frontier such as England or in frontier countries such as the United States. It is also significant that the United States, which possessed the greatest quantity of substance, rapidly became the leading exponent of the Industrial Revolution. It became a tremendous physics laboratory where energy was applied to useful work on a scale unknown anywhere else.

Just as the strength of the average man determined the size of the simple tools such as the axe, and the strength of the horse limited the size of the plow, so mechanical tools were limited by the power available to drive them. When a greater source of energy was discovered, it was then possible to increase the size of the tool or the number, and to complicate it into a machine. This enlarged and complicated tool, operated or driven by nonhuman and nonhorse energy, has changed the whole character of the society, by bringing men into different relationship with one another, into different relationship with their tools, and into different relationship with the materials. This is an old story and need not be retold except to say that groups of men, and not the single individual, soon became the *unit* in the production of wealth. The process of institutionalization was now well under way.

It is the idea that the Industrial Revolution attained the importance it did because of the abundance of material furnished by the frontier that is likely to stir up incredulity among many who have thought otherwise. It is certain that the Industrial Revolution could not have existed, or if it existed in theory, could have had no practical results in a vacuum, without substance to work on. In the presence of scarcity it could have had only meager results, and there is little reason to believe that any but simple tools would have ever been needed or justifiable economically. It was in the presence of abundance, whether of forests or minerals or western wheatfields, that the great complicated tools are practical or can be afforded. If we could imagine a society in which materials become less and less, we would see a gradual discarding of the machines until men would eventually be working with the simple tools they had when the Great Frontier was opened to them. In such a society there would be little impetus to further invention and little premium on mechanical ingenuity. The study of physics would become a mere intellectual exercise and technology would go through a process of devolution towards the simple instruments with which it began. Manufacturing machinery, apart from a body of material to be fabricated, cannot exist. So it would seem that the complicated tool of modern industry is a method of doing work which in the last analysis depends on an abundance of material, and we have already shown that that abundance has for the most part been derived from the frontier.

v. The Institution — The Corporation

We have followed the man at work as he set the stage for the change-over from the age of scarcity to the age of abundance. In order that he might work unhindered and to the best effect, he wanted nothing that would not contribute to his main purpose in the condition in which he found himself at the time. The things he adopted, or invented, were those suited to a free and unrestricted individual acting in the presence of an abundance. Therefore he set the stage with the theory of laissez faire, adopted the motive of individual profit, the method of competition, and devised a set of tools commensurate with the power at his command — all these against a backdrop of abundance. It is one of the misfortunes of the historian that the factors he works with are constantly changing while he is solving his problem. If the situation in America could have been frozen as it was in the quarter-century 1800–1825 so that the abundance would have been permanent and the power limited to what men and horses and oxen could furnish, then the motive of profit and the method of competition might have operated indefinitely without too much injustice to any segment of the society.

In order to make clear the changes that did occur, let us move from the early period to the second quarter of the twentieth century. By that time the theory of laissez faire had been abandoned and controls more stringent than those imposed by the mercantile theory had been restored. Any doubt of this may be removed by attempting to transfer money out of any European country. The prevailing belief, though not yet formulated into a theory, is that the country with the most American dollars is the best off. Without understanding the whole situation, this belief may seem as absurd to a later age as the mercantile theory seems to us. The method of competition has also undergone a radical change in character. Restricted by monopoly on one hand and by government regulation on the other, competition lacks the freedom and the number of participants it once had. As a game among individuals it has about played out. The laborers have united on one side, and instead of competing among themselves, they agree to co-operate as to the amount of work they shall do and the amount of remuneration they shall receive. The owners of the tools, a new class that rose in power as the tools grew into machines, combine on the other side and oppose their collective strength against that of the collective laborers. Such competition as is left is between or among groups and not among individuals. Without doubt the basic change affecting the other changes was in the tools with which men worked. Once these were complicated and increased beyond the strength and control and ownership of the individual, they altered the status of the individual and of the entire society. They foreshadowed the recrystallization of society and made imperative the creation of an institution that would encompass all the factors devised in the early period to promote work. One of these factors we have not mentioned because it has remained unchanged. Profit is still the motive of work even though the amount of it does not bear the old relation to the individual.

The institution which in time crystallized around the individual man at work, and that incorporated within itself his early theory of laissez faire, his motive of gain, his method of competition, and his efficient tools, is the modern business corporation. It is important for us to see the corporation as the institutionalization of the ideals and practices of individual men at work in a condition of great abundance. Even though the conditions, both human and physical, have changed very much with the passage of time, and the ideals and attitudes of many individuals have changed correspondingly, the corporation stubbornly maintains the old position. Its purpose is work, its favorite theory is laissez faire, its professed method is competition, and its tools are, as always, the best commensurate with the power available to drive them. It seems hardly necessary to cite advertisements in current magazines to substantiate the above statement. There the corporations boast of their ability to do a great deal of work, ask that government not interfere, claim that their prices and methods are competitive, and praise the efficiency of their machines. They act today very much as the single individual acted a century ago, even to the assumption that the materials available are still unlimited.

What seems quite plain is that the corporation has become what the individual once was and is supposed to be in modern society, acting in the place of the individual and in the same manner as he acted when he was the chief unit of production. To the extent that the corporation has succeeded — and its success has been spectacular — the individual has ceased to be important in the old way, ceased to be anything more than a dependent member of a group. Striking evidence that the corporation did want to move in to the position occupied by the individual is found in the fact that Roscoe Conkling induced the Supreme Court of the United States to hold that the corporation was a person in the legal sense, a legal person enjoying the privileges and immunities accorded by a democratic government to real persons. The far-reaching importance of this decision cannot be overemphasized. It threw a legal and constitutional barricade around the corporation which made its destruction or control by the people, by the component states, or by the nation itself extremely difficult. It prepared the way for corporateness to advance beyond its first field of endeavor and take over one segment of society after another until it became the dominant and all-pervading institution of modern times. If corporateness was good for business, it might also be good for labor, education, the churches, public works, and a miscellaneous and powerful group known as the associations.

2. A Cross Section of the Corporate Age

In Section 1 of this chapter an attempt was made to show the process by which the frontier society first became atomized, breaking down into a mass of individuals, for the reason that the old institutions had disappeared. Their disappearance or failure gave the society an opportunity to constitute itself anew, and to form other institutions which seemed to be in keeping with the ideals and purposes of the members. The result was a recrystallization of institutions designed to accomplish the main purpose. For the main purpose there would emerge the master pattern, the master institution which would be overpowering in its influence on all the others. The master institution was corporate in form, and it expressed itself first in work. In order to do this, it had to have a philosophy or theory, a method, and the necessary equipment. These we have noticed. In this section we turn our attention to an examination of a cross section of a society which is going completely corporate according to the master plan. We shall take a look at the present corporate nature of such things as business, labor, public roads, the churches, education, and of a class hitherto not much noticed which may be called associations.

i. The Business Corporation

He who would understand the modern age must understand corporateness just as he who would understand the Middle Ages must know a great deal about feudalism. Perhaps in another age, when men have moved into another cycle of civilization, scholars will grub in the ruins of this one for its records and fragments. If their research and reconstruction are adequate, they will be bound to conclude that the dominant institution of the moderns was the corporation, an abstraction representing a set of relationships which are established when a society crystallizes a group of separate and amorphous particles into a prevailing form. The first task of the scholar, once he suspects that he has hit upon a key to the mystery, would be to make a collection of corporations to see if they represent all segments of the society he is studying, if corporateness has universality. If he finds that it does have, he warms to his task, understanding that corporations will vary in form, perfection, and function. Now he can classify them under the different categories, and proceed to determine which among all his specimens is the most highly developed and the most perfect. This one he may then analyze.

The specimen he selects turns out, fortunately, to be the business corporation, and for a very long time he gives it the closest attention. He takes it apart in order to see how it was put together, and for what purpose. At the center of the dissected corporation he finds the figure, much shrunken now, of a man in the attitude and with the tools of work. This small figure is the clue he has been looking for, and from it he can make many reasonable deductions. Did it all begin with the man at work? The central position of the figure, its attitude and the tools around it, would seem to indicate work. Was there ever a man named Cyrus McCormick, Andrew Carnegie, John Deere, or Henry Ford who started out to do a lot of work and wound up buried in a corporation? The scanty records of the moderns reveal that such was the case. The small and simple tools tell much, their size that man could use them, their shape that he did use them. For what reason did the man work? The answer in another age with different ideals might not be easy to come at. The American Indian would have said that the man worked because he was a fool, but the scholar must find the reason that would be given by the man himself could he answer the question. He would have said that he worked for gain, to pile up wealth, something called profit, and the scholar must be permitted to arrive at this correct answer. If the man worked, exerted his energy with the tools, against what object did he apply the tools and energy? The nature of the tools would indicate real substance, something that would yield to the axe, the hoe, the spanner, and the plow. Yield what? That which the man was intent on having, wealth. Next the scholar would ask: How many men worked in this manner? To answer this he had to examine the core of many specimens of the particular category, and at the core of each he found the man in a similar attitude with similar though not identical tools. Therefore he could conclude that all men in that category worked in similar manner and for an identical purpose. Having arrived at this point, he could deduce that each man worked separately and independently of all the others, as an individual and not in a unified group.

Now the scholar could visualize many men, each acting separately, applying their energy and tools to substance which they chiseled out and piled up in separate piles, claiming it as their own. Since each took great pride in the size of his pile, he must have striven hard to make it bigger than his neighbor's. This meant friendly and general competition, a game which each man tried to win. Why was the game universal? How could it be? It could be universal because of the abundance of the substance and the absence of institutions restraining men from playing at it. When will it cease to be universal? It will cease to be universal when one of two things happens: when the abundance no longer exists in unlimited quantity or when the man is deprived of his tools. Finally, the scholar comes to the end of his logic, and though the answer to the last question is the easiest, it gives him pause for the civilization whose foundations he has discovered. It means the end of the civilization of the *one* man at work.

When will the game of work as originally carried on cease by becoming impossible?

To answer this question, the scholar turns his attention away from the man to the substance on which he works. What is its nature, its source, and its origin? It is the raw stuff of which wealth is made; its source is the earth, not all of it but only that part which has not yet been appropriated — the frontier. The extent of it once seemed limitless because the Great Frontier section of the earth had but recently been made available, furnishing a place where an unlimited number of men could make a beginning. A beginning? Yes, this single man at work must be just that. Certainly not a corporation, the thing now under analysis. The corporation represents a later stage, perhaps the end stage, and what went on between the beginning and the end stage is the history of the evolution of a simple organism into a most complex one which caught up the men on one side, deprived them of their tools, and brought them together in a compact and closely related mass. It caught up the tools on the other side, connected them, and complicated them into an intricate machine driven now by a new source of power which no man and no group of men could of themselves supply. The process of work had been institutionalized and in the process the old relationship of individuals to one another, and their relation to their tools and to the substance on which they worked was greatly altered and in ways that many could not and cannot understand. The corporation moved into the position occupied by the individual, taking over most of the work, most of the tools, and most of the substance. Its success piled up wealth exceeding all bounds.

These things the scholar learns by pouring over the scanty records left by the moderns. He may easily come to the conclusion that they worshiped a god called business and erected great temples in his honor. Some of the temples were filled with wheels, pulleys, saws, levers, and augers, all driven frantically by an inhuman power. They were called factories. Another class of temples, known as skyscrapers, were filled with papers and filing cases, most of which have disappeared. These strange people seemed to be hurrying about the world, always in search of that which was called profit and bringing it into a place where symbols only were kept. The symbols of profit were known as money, and some of it was of metal, but later other symbols were substituted for the metal, symbols of symbols, as it were. The moderns prized the symbols highly and judged their status by the height of the stack of symbolic symbols, which sometimes reached to the ceiling. As for the metal, they did a most curious thing — they buried it in the ground.

The scholar finally decides that he has found the main axis on which this quaint civilization of the moderns turned, the institution which encompasses within itself their principal ideal and their genius. The business corporation was the lead ox of the corporate herd, the pattern setter, the trail blazer, a sort of herald whose mission it was to convince society that corporateness was a good thing, worth embracing by other segments than business. The scholar now turns his attention to the coming of corporateness into other phases of modern life.

ii. Labor

A survey of the history of labor indicates that it has followed the path of business in becoming corporate. The history began in early America with each man working for himself, with the small tools suited to his strength, working competitively, and retaining control or ownership of what he produced. When the tools grew into giant machines which he alone could neither own nor manage, his status changed from that of an independent worker to that of an employee. He was no longer in a position to compete on personal terms as he once could do, and the only way he could protect himself was to combine with others in like situation in an organization sufficiently powerful to protect the component members. The pattern of the business corporation was before him, and it was natural that its success would encourage him to imitation.

The idea of organizing labor was an old one, going back to the guilds of the Metropolis in the medieval period. Repeated attempts at organization were made in America in the early period, but they were notable for their sporadic character and lack of success as long as the abundance of the frontier was available. There was still an outlet, even in the presence of the growing business corporations, in the free and unoccupied land. It may be a coincidence that the first permanent national labor organization, the American Federation of Labor, was chartered in 1881, contemporaneously with the closing of the American frontier. The pattern set by the business corporation was followed here in that the organization was initiated by one man, a Jewish cigar maker, Samuel Gompers. The first important move toward corporateness was tentative, a federation of more or less independent units. This loose organization was a gesture to the past, to what men had been, marking the transition to the final crystallization of laborers into a tighter, more comprehensive and less tolerant institution. It was not until 1935 that this crystallization took place when John L. Lewis formed the Committee of Industrial Organization, a corporation as powerful in its way as the business corporation is in its chosen field. The primary purpose of the labor corporation was to procure for its component members as much of the wealth produced as is possible. The final stage in labor corporateness will come when the American Federation of Labor and the Congress of Industrial Organizations consolidate their forces and unite on a common program, seeking a monopoly of labor in order to compete against the monopoly of tools and of power by their business opponents.[6] It is significant that neither

[6] This consolidation is predicted by Edwin A. Lahey in an article in *Collier's Weekly*, September 1, 1951, entitled "The AFL Will Absorb the CIO When . . ." The author contends that with the passing of the present generation of leaders, William L. Green of the A.F.L., and Philip Murray of the C.I.O., consolidation is likely to come.

group has demanded a restoration of the tools, but only what they consider a reasonable share of what is produced with them. It is worthy of observation also that within the labor corporation men no longer compete among themselves but rather co-operate. The old spur to competition is not there because the things they make are not theirs. They co-operate because they have been separated from their tools, from the abundance on which they work, and from the ownership of what they produce.

iii. Education

Education furnishes an example of the process of integration and centralization less pronounced than that found in business or labor. Still education tends toward corporateness, the common crystallization of society according to a dominant pattern. Since its motive is not profit, and since it is conducted on a public social basis, education's corporate structure is not so perfect, not so sharply defined as the first forms we have examined. Because its products are intangible, incapable of being measured by any standard unit, it cannot be driven too hard into the corporate mold. It is only when we approach the evolution of public education historically that its tendency to conform to the corporate pattern can be clearly seen.

The frontier school was a most elemental thing. At first a few neighbors came together, provided a schoolhouse, hired a teacher if one were available, and fired him if he did not please them — and he usually didn't for more than a year. "The little red schoolhouse" was one of the sweetest American sentiments, too sweet and too sentimental to endure. In the little red schoolhouse the people *elected* trustees, usually three men, who had charge of the community school, a democratic institution created and maintained by the community. This school stood alone in the forest and was not related to any other school. We need not follow its evolution from this frontier beginning to the modern integrated system, but the use of the word system is indicative of what has happened. The process of building a system was that of enlarging the unit, to the district, to the country, to the state, and finally perhaps to the nation. Today the entire school system, every public schoolhouse in a state, is tied together in one organization. Local trustees are still elected by the citizens, and they still choose the teachers, but they do not do it with the freedom they once exercised. The schools are supervised, directed, and controlled more and more by higher authority, represented by agents of the state and to a less extent of the national government. In 1950 in the state of Texas the choice of the head of the state school system was taken away from the people and lodged in an elective board; and at the same time the title of the head was changed from superintendent to commissioner.[7] All these changes have been made in the name of improvement and progress, and improvement there has been. What we have now is in no sense as democratic, as individualistic, or as independent as what we started with. The integration and systemization have gone on at the expense of the old freedom, as the schools become more corporate.

iv. Public Roads and Highways

Still in the realm of publicly controlled institutions we find another example of systemization in something everyone is familiar with, public roads and highways. Until comparatively recent times the road pattern was determined largely by land surveys and boundaries. The public road had many sharp turns and curves as it made its way by and around quarter- and half-sections. Each landowner determined in some measure how it should respect his place. It was a pretty individualistic road, and was maintained in a most democratic manner, generally under the supervision of the elected county commissioners. Each year able-bodied male citizens in certain age limits were "warned out" to work the road. On designated days the neighbors assembled and worked desultorily with weeding hoes, mattocks, and spades to make the road passable. Then came the automobile and the integration started. The counties tried their hand at road-building with unsatisfactory results. Finally the state took over the job of public road-building and ad-

---

7 In 1950, the elective state superintendent of public instruction was replaced by a Commissioner of Education who is appointed by a State Board composed of twenty-one members elected by popular vote from the twenty-one Senatorial districts.

ministration with some participation by the federal government. The results are known to any motorist. The roads are admirable in design, direct in layout, excellent in construction — but they are not democratic roads. The citizen has next to nothing to do with their routes, construction, or maintenance. All he does now, except to pay taxes, is to vote for a governor who appoints a commission which selects a chief engineer, who is virtually a dictator in his own domain.

v. The Churches

The churches are in general following the pattern of integration, unification, and centralization, becoming rapidly corporate in polity and in the form of worship. This statement may startlé some and displease others, but it should not be rejected before the facts as revealed by the history of church evolution are examined. I hasten to say that it is not my business here to deal with the religious faith of any creed or person, but only with the vehicle which men have constructed through which their faith can more conveniently express itself. These vehicles and the influences they exert on society fall within the purview of the historian.

The churches introduced into the Great Frontier fall into two categories, Catholic and Protestant. The Catholic Church dominated the Spanish frontier, where it exerted tremendous influence on the surviving native populations. It came in corporate form and with a structure so rigid that the frontier was never able to break it. That the frontier did alter its practices, the manner in which the religion was applied to a primitive people, there is not the slightest doubt. It is the genius of this corporation — the Catholic Church — that it will yield under pressure on almost any detail, adapt itself to any circumstance, but it will not yield at the hard inner core of fundamental principle; and it cannot yield there without destroying the foundation on which it rests. It is the viscous exterior, yielding readily to outer force, modifying its form and coloring to suit any human environment, that absorbs the shocks and protects the rigid inner framework that cannot yield without disastrous results to the whole structure. Outwardly the Catholic Church may change, and does; but inwardly it is immovable, a perfect corporation with a complete monopoly on the tools and the commodity it dispenses — a desirable position for any corporate group.

It has been remarked that the frontier hypothesis developed in this study does not seem to apply to Latin America as well as it does to those countries taken over by northern European groups. The process of institutional disintegration which went on in the north until the individual remained in clear relief, free to rebuild his institutions from the beginning, did not take place to any such extent in the southern continent and Mexico. It seems that the rigid character of the Catholic structure was too much for the disintegrative forces which were so successful with the more mundane institutions. The soft and yielding outer surface of the church absorbed the natives without enlightening them too much, while the inner core remained steadfast to the corporate principles as interpreted by the central authority. It is clear that if democracy, defined as government by the will of the people, came to such a society, it would have to come in spite of the prevailing church and not because of it. If the church became the dominant corporation in the Latin South, as the business corporation was in the Anglo-Saxon North, then it would set the pattern for the lesser organizations to follow and eventually bring the whole society into a subordinate harmony with its policies and methods. Insofar as the church was able to do this, it would turn people away from the mad search for wealth, from emphasis on a materialistic culture, and in politics make true democracy more of a form than a reality. The natural companion of an absolute and dominant church is an absolute and agreeable state. It is not strange, therefore, that in the Latin-American or Catholic frontiers the temporal governments have alternated between efforts at democracy and efforts at dictatorship. Though the frontier forces driving men toward freedom and self-government were strong enough to break the political bonds of the Metropolis, discard titles of nobility, and destroy primogeniture, they were never able to break the hold of that powerful human organization, the Catholic Church. Could they have done this, and made the people really free, then the people could, like their northern neighbors, have be-

gun individually on clean ground and built an indigenous society on a substantial basis. As it is, the dominant institution
is an imported one, directed from without, one which the frontier with all of its abrasiveness could not wear out nor much
alter. This rigidity and stability of the Catholic Church has
done more to frustrate the atomizing influence of the frontier than any other single factor operating in the New World.

The frontier had much better luck with the Protestant
churches which were introduced into North America and
other lands occupied by northern Europeans. Though the
Catholic Church does not yield, it can be broken, and it was
broken just at the right moment, when the frontier world was
coming into view, broken in the interest of the common man.
The democratization of religion took a long step forward
when Martin Luther declared that every man was his own
priest, that salvation was a matter between the individual and
God, and that no intermediary was essential to sign visas and
open sacramental gates for him who would travel the straight
and narrow way. In a word, Martin Luther's basic logic destroyed in the minds of those who followed him the sacro-
sanct character of the priesthood and all claims that the church
made as the exclusive earthly agent of the Divinity. According
to Luther's logic priests were ordinary men, and as such might
as well marry and raise families as other men did; the church
itself, said Luther, was a man-made institution which had
through clever design made credulous people believe that it
alone could lead them to eternal salvation. Had this somber
son of an iron founder lived in this age, he hight have pointed
out the church's similarity to a host of other corporations with
a president, a board of directors, a host of obedient employees,
and a multitude of customers: a spiritual cartel with universal
aspirations. But, according to Luther, each man had a direct
wire to God, and need not go through an exchange or submit
to much censorship. The Bible was made a free book which
every literate man could read for himself, not an oracle whose
words could be understood only by the anointed. Luther believed so much that men ought to read the Bible that while
in prison — that study from which so much of literary value
has emerged — he translated it into the language of the common people. By his logic Luther fragmented the institution

of the church until nothing was left but the individual standing naked in the presence of his God. He did to the old religious institution by logic and his fervor what the frontier did to many other ancient institutions by its impassivity. In both instances man was left free to act on his own initiative, without support or institutional go-betweens. It was the splintered faith of the Protestants that went to North America; but it was the corporate faith that stood fast in Latin America.

Institutional distintegration was implicit in Luther's basic idea, and once the principle was established it was inevitable that a further process of fragmentation would go on among Protestant groups. There was no power to prevent division over details of creed, theology, interpretation, or polity. The result was a multiplication of denominations which had got well under way by the time the migration to America had begun. It would be a mistake to assume that, even though they had been set up on a logic of freedom, these bodies were societies of tolerance. Quite the contrary, and Luther himself was forced by circumstance to depart from the principles of his own logic. Each group had to fight for its existence, and all the Protestants together had to resist the constant efforts of the still powerful Catholic corporation to crush what it considered the upstarts and outlaws of religion who were infringing its spiritual patents. There was a general tightening up of controls, sharper definition of creeds, and a greater insistence on conformity within each group. It is very significant that for 150 years during which the foundations of frontier societies were being laid down in the Americas the prevailing condition in the Metropolis was that of religious wars and unprecedented intolerance.[8]

During the last half-century of this period (1600–1650) groups from nearly all the warring denominations adjourned to the English colonies of the Atlantic seaboard, often because they were persecuted in Europe. Puritans, Calvinists, Huguenots, Quakers, Lutherans, and Catholics all came. The Catholics were few and soon yielded to the Protestant majority. Historians have made much of this flight of persecuted peo-

---

[8] The religious wars began about 1520 and are said to have ended with the Thirty Years' War and the Peace of Augsburg in 1648. The intolerance lasted much longer.

ple to "a land of freedom," but they have not told us very
clearly why the mere act of moving not only made them free
but also led them to do what they had at first little intention
of doing, grant freedom to others and soon to all. Having
found a place where they could practice intolerance, how did
it come about that they lost it? Did their dawning tolerance
come from within themselves, or was it imposed upon them
by conditions in which they found themselves? The answer
is that it came from both sources. The logic on which the Protestants acted, on which their creeds were founded, carried them
in the direction of freedom from all institutional restraints.
Every man his own priest; salvation by personal faith alone;
no intermediary between man and God; every man equal before God. All this came from within, a belief in an institutionless religion, a non-corporate faith. From the outside, from
the frontier circumstances in which they found themselves,
came the rich soil in which the seeds of their simple faith
could take hold and grow into practices which corresponded
with their logic and their desires.

It has been represented in this study that the frontier broke
old institutions, stripped them away until little was left but
the individual. Protestantism was one institution whose authority the frontier did not have to break, for that authority
came *broken* and in denominational fragments. There was
complete harmony between the man who stood naked in the
presence of nature and the man who stood naked in the presence of God. In the forests of the frontier the same man stood
naked in the presence of both. He saved himself in the presence of nature by work and not by faith in institutions; he
saved his soul by faith in God and not by work or through any
institution. God, as the Protestants understood Him, was not
a competitor with nature for man's allegiance; they might well
be partners. At any rate, there was no conflict in rendering
to each what each required, aggressiveness toward nature and
humility toward God.

After the American Revolution the principles of complete
toleration and religious freedom, which had long been practiced, were in time incorporated into the political constitu-

tions, state and federal. Our problem now is to trace the process of evolution which took place among Protestant churches within two centuries, and to note the relation of two stages of denominational evolution to the open and closed frontier. The first stage was one of continuous division and multiplication of denominations. There were breaks, schisms, and revolts based on the principle that each man was master of his own fate. There was a lowering of educational standards for the ministry, a departure from formalism and ritual, and an increasing emphasis on the initiative of the individual in attaining salvation. As the frontier moved westward, the denominations continued to multiply. Studies have shown that most of the divisions either took place in the western regions, or if they occurred in the East, the revolters often fled to the West or found their greatest following there. Scores of examples could be given, but the Mormons who fled to Utah in 1846–47 furnish a striking one. It is also true that as the denominations moved west, they became more "radical," that is, they departed further and further from formalism and elaborate ritual. For example, the Anglican Church was quite strong in the older states, especially along the tidewater region of the South, but the Anglican Church with its formal service, prescribed ritual and dignified ceremonial was left behind by the onrush of the pioneers in the frontier. These wanted something more personal and more emotional than the staid dignity of the Anglican Church provided. The Baptist Church, with its pure congregational control, its extreme democracy of polity, its utter lack of formalism, and the Methodist, only a little less democratic and only a little more formal, offered what the frontier people wanted.[9] During the frontier period both adopted the revival meeting method of propagating the faith and their ministers, often wholly uneducated men, exhorted, threatened, and frightened their flocks along the road to God. The people shouted, prayed, and sang in a way that neither Catholics nor Anglicans could understand. There may

[9] For a discussion of the abandonment of Anglican formalism by the Methodists in America, see Mrs. Mauree P. Trahan, "American Methodism and the Frontier, 1760–1880," unpublished Master's thesis, University of Texas, Austin, 1951, pp. 45–47.

have been unity in devotion to God, but there was chaos in the method of finding Him with the result that what Arthur G. Wiederaenders calls *divisiveness* went on and on.[10]

It was not until near the close of the frontier that the multiplication of denominations and sects slowed down. By 1910 the process had gone in reverse, and a decided trend toward unification had begun. This started with mergers among sects of the same denomination whose differences were such as could be easily reconciled. The Northern and Southern Metho· dists effected the biggest single merger when they united in 1939. Union among the Presbyterian sects has progressed to the point that churches throughout the country are studying a tract outlining the provisions for reorganization into one single body. The Northern and Southern Baptists have not yet composed their differences, but with their purely congregational polity there is really no Baptist Church in the corporate sense. There are only Baptists who come together for convenience in congregations and these in associations. There is no unity and no authority higher than the member, only a fellowship of equals. The Lutheran Church followed closely the pattern outlined for the larger denominations.

Thus far we have considered the tendency toward consolidation and unification *within* a given denomination. The facts are so plain, the movement so far developed as to be clearly seen by anyone. This union within groups appears to be a middle stage moving towards union *among* groups, the consolidation of all Protestant denominations into one great church; or, what is more remote, the union of Protestants and Catholics into a universal church. The move to unite all the Protestants is well under way, and there exists a considerable body of literature on the subject. In short, church polity is tending strongly toward unification and centralization just as business and government are, and that tendency has developed rapidly since the closing of the frontier. Like business and government the churches are becoming corporate.

It may be worthwhile to speculate on the results of this

10 Arthur G. Wiederaenders, "The American Frontier as a Factor in Protestant Denominationalism in the United States," unpublished Doctor's dissertation, University of Texas, Austin, 1942.

tendency. If the Protestant churches unify and adopt a centralized government they will because of their nature achieve this end with difficulty. If they insert an institution between man and God and grant it any considerable authority, they will do so at the expense of the fundamental principles on which Protestantism was established, namely, the right of the individual to attain salvation in *his own way*. It is doubtful if the church unity we hear about can be achieved without the imperatives and compulsions that seem necessary in all large corporate organizations. How can Protestants achieve unity without denying the individual the right to differ, or without ignoring the differences to such an extent as to make the unity a farce?

Let us go a step further and assume that Protestant unity has been achieved, and that there is one Protestant Church. The next step would be a union of the Protestants and Catholics, a move that would put an end to denominationalism and bring agreement among Christians. Those who advocate such a program would do well to consider its practical implications and the terms on which it would probably have to be effected. If we can take the historical attitude of the Catholic Church as an indication of its future attitude, we can readily see that such a merger would have to come on Catholic and not on Protestant terms. The fundamental tenet of the Catholic Church is that it is a divine institution, created by God and not to be tampered with by man. It has never yielded this position, this inner core which has given it the strength to stand up under the shocks of the ages. The assumption of the Protestant churches, and presumably of the assumed united Protestant Church, is that churches are human institutions made by man for his convenience in fellowship and worship. If two institutions merge, one immovable because of a divine assumption, the other movable because of its human assumption, there can be little doubt as to which will name the terms of the merger. When complete church unity comes it will have to come on conditions laid down by the Catholic Church.

The idea developed here is that the Protestant denominations are evolving toward corporateness, and it is with them that we are most concerned. The same cannot be said of the

Catholic Church because it is and has long been one of the world's most perfect corporations. Therefore insofar as the Protestant churches are moving in the corporate direction, they are moving closer and closer, however slowly they move, toward both the structure and the ceremonial of the mother church. Every merger, every union is a step in that direction.

The slow return of the modern churches to corporateness is reflected in many ways as the mass of free religious individuals are caught up in the institutional crystallization that is going on. The drive toward unity is a structural change which is advancing. The practices in the larger churches are changing faster than the structure. Formalism is appearing, vestments are being put on, candles are burning again, and symbolism is playing a greater and greater part. The personal sermon, once so important, has become a sermonette, an inconspicuous detail in an elaborate ritual of song, music, prayer, offertory, flickering candles, vestmented processional, a combination of sensory appeals brought together in such a manner as to strike the emotions rather than the intellect. Gone are many of the personal manifestations by the individual sinner who sought by prayer and personal anguish to make contact with God and then by testimony and work to maintain the relation. That is all gone from the modern churches, though not from the fringe sects which flourish in the margins of cities and in the rural byways.

The church edifices are changing architecturally to conform to the new practices, becoming cathedral-like, calculated to inspire awe and reverence, silent participation in a formal ritual.

The conclusion is that the Protestant churches are becoming corporate despite the higly individualistic character of their philosophy or theology as expounded by Luther and other leaders. When these churches were transplanted to America, the individualistic character of the faith was reinforced by a similar philosophy about wealth and politics. Economic theory, political philosophy, and religious theology joined in placing high emphasis on the freedom and independence of the human being, and the result was a balanced culture notable for its respect for free men. The simplicity of the institutions was in keeping with men's conditions and economic aspirations. The society outwardly was noisy and disorderly, as it must be when every man insists on doing everything in his own way, but inwardly it was harmonious and strong because all human wants tended generally in the same direction.

As I have shown, the churches did not retain their simplicity. The disintegrative tendency lasted until the close of the frontier, after which reintegration began and continues to the present. Crystallization within the denominations is going on at a rapid rate, and is reflected in both the service and the houses of worship. Religious practice among Protestants, as it has long been among Catholics, is becoming a matter of institutional procedure, of observing the forms and ceremonies prescribed by the corporation. But for many reasons corporateness will grow tardily among Protestants despite the efforts of some of their leaders to unite them and hasten its coming. Since the church deals with the intangibles, it is under no compulsion to be efficient, to make short cuts or save work. It cannot measure its accomplishments in arbitrary units as the business corporations or the governmental bureau can. A deeper and far more significant hindrance to the full acceptance of corporateness by Protestants is the fundamental idea that made them Protestants, namely, that every man is free to find God in his own way. If they give this idea up in practice, in church polity, they will eventually give it up in theory and in teaching. Then they will no longer be Protestants.

Finally, it must be said that in the sort of society in which we now find ourselves, the future seems to be with the corporate church, with what the Catholic Church has long been, with what the leading Protestant churches are now becoming. Since all the other institutions which began around the individual have wound up in corporate structures, why should religious institutions which began in the same way expect to escape? Insofar as they do escape, they will be out of harmony with the society in which they exist. The Protestant may say so let it be, but again let us examine some implications of letting it be. Insofar as corporateness embraces society, it reduces the individual to a greater and greater dependence. This dependence on corporations, whether it be on General Motors, the C.I.O., or the R.F.C., has the effect of softening up the spirit of man's independence and unbounded faith in himself. He turns to security in the way of pensions, old age assistance, and permanent tenure. He wants these things to come to him with as little exercise of initiative on his part as possible; he wants them to come because he has performed certain rituals, gone through certain legal ceremonies.

It would seem quite reasonable that once the individual is conditioned in this manner, to dependence, he would not look unkindly on a church institution that would provide salvation and spiritual satisfaction on the same terms. Why should he be required to exercise the initiative in making peace with God, why should he carry so much responsibility and experience so much uncertainty, when he can have an institution act for him and receive from the institution complete assurance that the mission has been accomplished? Between a guaranteed living and a guaranteed salvation there is a harmony which appeals to men who are ready to accept either.

In view of what has been said above, it would not be difficult to chart the progress of the two great church groups from the pioneer period to the present time. The country was settled primarily by Protestants, and with few exceptions, they dominated every state and community. Though the Catholic Church made little headway in colonial and early American history, it is making giant strides now. Its membership outnumbers that of any single Protestant denomination, and represents about one third of all church membership.[11] The most perfect corporation is today the leading church in a corporate society.

vi. Associations — Peak and Professional

A word should be said about another class of integrated groups which are less obvious than corporate business or corporate labor, or even the corporate church. I refer to associa-

[11] In 1947 the total church membership in the United States was 73,673,182. The Catholics numbered 24,402,124. — *Statistical Abstract of the United States, 1949*, p. 30.

tions, apparently — but often not actually — loose organizations which appear to be in an embryonic state of development, a sort of corporate foetus. Practically every profession has its national association, an organization which fixes standards, writes a code of ethics, and exerts pressure on any legislation affecting its members. The American Medical Association and the American Bar Association are perhaps the most familiar examples because nearly everyone has had some experience with doctors and lawyers. Others less well known are the American Bankers Association, the American Association of Engineers, and one in each field of academic study. The list could be extended indefinitely. It is a well-known fact that some of these — all of them that are able — exert tremendous pressure on legislators when something comes up affecting their privileges. They may predicate their action on high ground, but actually each seeks to protect its own interest and becomes most active and vociferous when the question involves a choice between the public and the associational welfare.

Two such associations deserve special mention and seem to stand in a class by themselves. These are the National Association of Manufacturers and the United States Chamber of Commerce. The first is in essence an association of business corporations, and probably represents more money and capital than any other group. The United States Chamber of Commerce has a broader base than the N.A.M., representing the thousands of chambers of commerce throughout the nation. Both without doubt represent the interests of business rather than labor, but that is beside the point.

Since the days of Theodore Roosevelt and Lincoln Steffens it has been the custom in the United States to rail in print and on the platform against single business monopoly, to cry out against trusts and holding companies, with the result that a vast body of literature has come into existence on each of these subjects. It remained for Robert A. Brady in his *Business as a System of Power* to point out what he aptly calls the *lacunae* in this literature. In the broad gap between the human individual and the corporate individual stand the numerous associations which have crept into society almost unawares.

The scholars, Brady says, have almost completely neglected this whole field, so pregnant with economic, social, and political significance.

> In American literature there is only one outstanding study of the phenomenon in general, and that, *Employer's Associations in the United States*, by Clarence E. Bonnett, was published in New York in 1922. Even this excellent survey related only to the labor angle of a few highly specialized (at that time) employer associations.[12]

The neglect of the associations and the "institutes," in contrast to the attention paid to the more obvious forms of combination, is set forth by Brady in the following paragraph:

> Thus, while "concentration of economic power" has become sufficiently important to merit the entire attention of one of our most noteworthy governmental investigations, and has become the subject matter of a vast and swiftly proliferating technical literature on forms of "monopoly" and "trust problems," the trade association, the intercorporate "institute," and the chamber of commerce have been almost entirely neglected by the learned fraternities.[13] With but minor exceptions . . . they have largely escaped the dragnet of official inquiry.[14]

Brady's purpose is to point out to the scholars and official inquirers the importance of what they are overlooking, already a powerful force in the national life, well worth study and perhaps official investigation. Once we perceive the importance of these associations, three facts about them strike us with great force: (1) their recent origin, (2) their rapid growth, and (3) their simultaneous appearance in all the industrialized societies. These commercial and industrial organizations, forming a system and a business network, have grown up almost entirely since 1900; they have attained three fourths of their growth since World War I. For example, in

[12] Robert A. Brady, *Business as a System of Power* (New York: Columbia University Press, 1943), p. 9, footnote. Brady makes a comparative study of the tendency to unification and centralization of authority in business in six countries, the United States, England, France, Germany, Italy, and Japan.

[13] Some intercorporate institutes are: The American Steel Institute, the American Meat Institute.

[14] Brady, *Business as a System of Power*, p. 9.

the United States there were not more than forty chambers of commerce in 1870, but in 1930 they were estimated at three thousand, with a membership of a million or more. When the United States government undertook to put into effect the National Recovery Act (the late N.R.A.), it found the key factor to be 3500 state and national trade associations and 10,000 local trade associations and chambers of commerce. In 1931, there were more than 19,000 associational organizations listed, and of these 2634 were interstate, national, and international, 3050 were state and territorial, and 13,625 were local organizations.[15]

The associational movement in the United States is duplicated with variations in England, Germany, France, Italy, and Japan. The German Economic Committee made public a list of 2272 associations affiliated with the Central Committee of German Employers' Association as of 1930. In the other countries accurate data are not available but Brady says "the same trends are observable," and in all cases the "associational machinery is of comparatively recent vintage." Here, it seems, is a reserve force, half hidden from view, which has come quietly up to reinforce the corporations as they go about their conquest of the world. Though they already play an important role in economic and political affairs, they rarely have their name on the program.

Brady's term, "associational machinery," is a real contribution to our thinking, implying as it does a complicated integration of apparently separate entities. It is this integration in which we are interested, particularly in its bearing on the role of corporations in a democratic society. Does this new machinery contribute to democratic life or does it lean to another form? If it tends away from democracy, what form of government does it favor? Brady cites two examples of what happens *through* this associational machinery when the state goes corporate. He says:

> The changes brought about by the Nazis in Germany meant streamlining, not abolition, of this elaborate machinery. A like generalization holds for Italy, where under four strictly

[15] *Ibid.*, p. 10.

business associations out of a total of nine Fascist Confederations there are to be found 91 associational groupings.[16]

The culmination of the integrative process is the "peak" association. The peak association is born when a large number of associations with similar or parallel objectives confederate (consolidate is too strong a term) for common action. When a peak association is formed, it tends to take over the public policy and the task of directing over-all strategy and tactics toward the common objectives of the component members. For example, it will undertake to direct and co-ordinate the policy of manufacturers toward such matters as organized labor and governmental action, presenting to both a united front. Such a peak association would not be concerned with competition among its separate members, however much it might deplore it. Its internal policy must be one that will meet with almost universal approval of its members, and all manufacturers do generally agree in their attitude toward organized labor and governmental regulation.

The peak association has a more exclusive function in dealing with external relations, such as public opinion and legislation. It sends ambassadors to the state and national capitals to promote its interests and protect its privileges. The various "institutes" fill the most expensive magazines with "good will" advertising and are constantly engaged in "educating" the public. No expense is spared to prove that the whole program is designed in the public interest. It seems that activity of this sort is stimulated on occasions when pertinent legislation is pending or when labor and capital are in contest.

The significance of trade associations is indicated by the fact that they have appeared in all the major industrialized nations and have flourished in an economic climate of laissez faire. Like the corporations they are controlled, or directed, by a few people at the center. They have had their greatest growth during the last half-century. They did not disappear in Germany, Italy, and Japan when those countries turned to totalitarianism; with a little streamlining they furnished the machinery for the successful operation of both the Nazi and

16 *Ibid.*, pp. 10–11.

Fascist states. Their future role in the countries that remain democratic is a current question. Finally, they illustrate the extent to which the recrystallization of society has gone.

The above discussion of the corporate development in business should not obscure the fact that the main subject of this chapter is the reintegration of society. Business has furnished the outstanding example of the process, but we need to remember that the example has been and is being copied in practically all walks of life, in all occupations, in all professions, even in the churches that were not already highly integrated. The business corporation — presented as the . lengthened shadow of the individual at work — has been the pattern maker of institutionalized modern life. It is also the masterpiece and the vehicle of capitalism, and if we can discover the processes of its evolution we will throw much light on society's institutional crystallization in the modern age. Though such an analysis cannot be attempted here, one feature of corporate life as it has exhibited itself thus far stands out very clearly.

This feature is a dynamic quality which has expressed itself in growth. This growth extends first to national limits, and then reaches out through cartels to other nations. In its early stages, it proceeds by competition operating in a laissez faire manner, and in its later stages it grows by elimination to near-monopoly. The view advanced in this study is that the frontier has been a prime contributing factor which made possible this dynamism. The frontier increased manyfold the room over which European people could move, and the body of wealth which they could acquire. The physical facts called for motion and volition. As long as there was room, more work than men, more material than machines, the process of expansion was socially and politically safe. In the very dynamics the people could have a maximum of freedom, political and economic, for the boom was such that all could live, many could prosper, and government could look on while men had their way. The result is that a whole civilization evolved in this atmosphere of expansion with institutions adapted to it.

The question naturally arises: What will happen to the

habits and institutions when there is no more room? We have come recently to boast of a global economy without thinking of its implications, of how unfortunate we are in finding it. It would indeed be more cheering if news should come that by some curious freak of the solar system another world had swung gently into our orbit and moved along so close that a bridge could be built over which people could pass to new continents untenanted and new seas uncharted. Would those eager immigrants repeat the processes they followed when they had that opportunity, or would they redress the grievances of the old earth by a new bill of rights designed to protect man from work's imperative institutions? The availability of such a new planet, at any rate, would prolong, if it did not save, a civilization based on dynamism, and in the prolongation the individual would again enjoy a spell of freedom. In the following chapter we shall examine his transit across the four frontier centuries, and as he makes this journey we shall see him in his interval of maximum freedom, as a free atom between two stages of institutional crystallization.

CHAPTER FOUR

THE PARABOLA OF INDIVIDUALISM

IT IS THE PURPOSE of this chapter to follow the individual in Western civilization from the time he emerged from the anonymity of medievalism through a parabola of freedom to the present age in which he seems to be approaching anonymity in the modern corporate culture. It is unfortunately difficult to express what I see in a manner that will not arouse resentment from some group or faction, committed to some ideology. It is not my purpose to do this, but rather to plot the curve of the individual human being with the objectivity of the mathematician. I shall not, of course, achieve my purpose because I am dealing with things too intangible and variable to be caught in mathematical formulas and am compelled to use the most evanescent of all mediums, words and sentences instead of figures and lines.

It is perhaps significant that in modern economic literature the individual is receiving scant attention. He appears as an innocent bystander in the clash and clangor of modern conflict, domestic and international. His name is heard more and his presence seen less in the mummery and ceremonial of modern life than that of any other figure. His is like a face seen in a motion picture, first close up and then from greater and greater distance. Though the features disappear as the figure becomes a part of the larger scene, we still know it is there because we project on the screen the memory of a closer and earlier view. We see it but the person who enters the theater at this juncture could not detect it at all. So it may be with our individualism; what we have left of it may be largely a memory projected. Therefore, the time may be at hand to sketch the biography of the individual.

1. Behold the Individual!

The individual began to appear on the stage as an important actor during the Renaissance. We have evidence of this in paintings that resembled human beings rather than saints and devils, in the sculpture of Michelangelo (whose figures had muscles and bones), and in the very human qualities of Chaucer's unsaintly characters. Men began to be proud of themselves after an age of real or feigned humility; they raised their heads from prayer long enough to see the world, and seeing, they decided it was an interesting place, worthy of further attention. They began to experiment with it, and with themselves, and were so pleased with the exercise that they signed their names to what they created. These were the first tentative steps, taken by a few bold artists and craftsmen whose inner urge was such as to cause them to defy tradition, and to break the pattern of institutions. They breached the walls of authority through which other men, Luther, Columbus, and all the rest, were to escape from their long mental prison onto the high plain of individual thinking and acting. It was one of the grandest moments in human history, this jail delivery of the human mind.

Both Luther and Columbus made use of the new technique of thinking and investigating in launching almost simultaneously two revolutionary ideas. Luther emancipated men — those who followed him — from the bondage of a prescribed religion and logically set them free to find God through their own faith. If he did not himself live up to his logic, it was because of practical difficulties he could not overcome. Columbus, through equally courageous and individualistic action, proved his global theory and in so doing altered the relationships existing between man and land, between man and wealth. He sought the wealth of the Indies, but he brought the wealth of a new and untenanted world and laid it in the poverty-stricken hand of an uncomprehending Europe. Men of the Renaissance delivered the mind, Luther delivered the spirit, but Columbus delivered the body by providing a substance and setting for the three freedoms. That setting was the Great Frontier in which men could think, believe, and labor without finding themselves in conflict with the hoary institutions of an old order. As men moved out to the frontier, the institutional shackles fell away, and as they sent a record of their practices, successful practices of real freedom on which wise men had long theorized, back to the Metropolis, they sent also the abundance of their labor to furnish an essential base on which any sort of freedom must ultimately rest. Thus the frontier wrought in favor of freedom wherever the returning ships bore their abundance.

Wherever the new forces made themselves felt the old order in Europe began to pass away, not rapidly but gradually. Feudalism crumbled fast, the guild system could not hold its members, the cities took on rapid growth, and the church continued to lose its temporal power. The Metropolis of Europe retained many of the old forms, such as titles of nobility, but on the frontiers these passed without benefit of revolution. The frontier made a clean sweep, but the fragments and relics of the old order remained in the old house which in part reminds an observer from the frontier of a museum. The whole process was brought about because individuals asserted and reasserted their freedom; they took it from the church, from feudal lords, from guilds, and eventually from the monarchs, and as the individuals succeeded, the institutions declined.

Individuals obtained recognition of their freedom by fighting and bargaining, or — failing in this — they could run away. This running away was possible because they had somewhere to go. In comparison, Gandhi's passive resistance seems but a poor tool of emancipation. Running away not only gives the runner his freedom, but it works insidiously on the institution from which he flees and in time tends to alter it. It raises wages, shortens hours, and secures toleration for those left behind. The east coast of the United States was largely peopled by those who had run away, to Massachusetts for religion, to Georgia for debt, and to Pennsylvania for the crime of being Quakers. The present conglomerate population of the United States is made up largely of people whose ancestors ran away from persecution or poverty, mostly poverty. Many books have been written about the immigrants and their influence on American history; few have been written on the effect that their departure had on Europe. None would deny that the cutting off of this running away through recent immigration laws is having an effect.[1] Through the eighteenth and nineteenth centuries individuals were fleeing from all Europe, fanning out across the seas on their way to the Americas, to Africa, and to Australia. They were by flight relieving pressures at home, leaving more room and therefore more freedom.

We are now in position to view the emergence of the free man. He seems to appear as through a gap in a mountain chain behind which he had moved through the centuries, a mountain chain of institutions. We see him moving from left to right on a time scale. He has emerged from behind a mountain wall of medieval institutions which have fallen down into a pass or broad valley where he is clearly visible. He lingers in the valley for some three centuries enjoying hitherto unknown vistas of freedom and opportunity. Busied with his work and play, he creates for himself a culture based on the conditions *in the valley,* and he acts as if there would never be any more mountains to hide him, to limit his view, to curb his action. But all the time he is moving forward toward another range — a mountain of modern institutions as high and impregnable in their way as were the medieval ones from which he emerged. As he approaches it, he carries his valley culture, one not suited to conditions that will soon confront him. The question is whether he can surmount modern institutions and remain in plain sight *as an individual,* or whether he is to disappear within the institutional folds. The prospect does not please him because he has come to love the valley where the great world frontier force made a pass to give him an interlude of freedom to work, play, and worship as he pleased.

[1] In September, 1950, I attended at the Ethel Barrymore Theater in New York Gian-Carlo Menotti's powerful play, *The Consul.* The theme is the frustration and tragedy resulting because of the difficulty experienced by people seeking to flee from persecution and tyranny. It is made obvious that the consul's office stood between people somewhere in Europe attempting to escape to somewhere in the New World. The play could not have been written and would have had no meaning prior to the closing of the frontier as represented by laws cutting off free immigration. In the United States the laws began with the Chinese exclusion acts of the late nineteenth century but became really effective as applied to Europe after World War I. To a greater or less extent other frontier countries such as Australia and South Africa followed the American pattern. All over the world the bars went up. It is against these bars that the stark tragedy of *The Consul* breaks.

2. *Institutions for an Institutionless Society*

This pass to freedom, this broad valley, owes its existence to the fact that the old institutions were either left behind or were disintegrated by frontier forces before new ones had organized and grown to their present dominating position. The disintegrating forces of the frontier had to wear down and destroy before the integrating forces of civilization could rebuild. It was in this institutionless interval that man had his moment of greatest liberty. He was virtually camping out, and he adapted his economy and politics to camp life.

Finding himself really free, man tried to guard against the limitations he had escaped by enacting laws and adopting constitutions. He seemed to think that he had achieved freedom by his own efforts and did not realize that it had come to him largely through a condition where nearly every factor of existence favored it. At any rate he wrote a prescription for old ailments from which he had about recovered, one designed to keep off the germs of absolutism and mercantilism, but in reality it was the climate and not the medicine that gave him health. He did not see, and could not be expected to see, that, out of his new condition, one of abundance and freedom, germs of new institutions as menacing as the old ones lay hidden — that his sojourn in the valley was of the nature of a long vacation from supervision and control.

The above figure which visualizes a single man on his way across a broad valley between two mountain chains is an oversimplification. It is a mass of humanity, a society, some dying as others are born, making the journey; it is civilization in transit across the centuries of the Great Frontier. If we can view society in this manner, we are in position to understand a little better some of our present perplexities, not a few of which grow out of the fact that Western society is now leaving the valley of the Great Frontier and is getting well into the foothills of the mountain chain that lies ahead of them, the mountain of modern corporate institutions. The long sojourn in the valley of the Great Frontier has had its effect on the society, and has given birth to ways of doing things that were quite practicable and successful there. Gradually these successful practices resolved themselves into what may be called — for want of a better name — institutions for an institutionless society. That expression would be an awkward one if it did not express so well the exact situation in which people who move into a frontier find themselves. Such institutions as were adopted were of the loosest sort, giving the very maximum of liberty to the human particles making up the society. This looseness prevailed in reference to economic regulation, political regulation, and religious regulation. It prevailed in reference to all regulation. This general laxity and absence of regulation was an effect, an expression of the desire of the individual to conduct his own affairs in whatever way he thought best, with as little institutional restraint as possible.

The perplexities that beset the individual today arise from the fact that he is now leaving the valley of institutionless freedom and entering the foothills of the great corporate institutions into which society is crystallizing. He is nonplussed at the restraints laid upon him, and he chafes at the restrictions which he formerly did not know. Like the reluctant ox, he comes slowly to the yoke, but he comes nevertheless.

Unlike the ox, man is articulate, and to put it mildly he quarrels a good deal about what is happening to him. In his dilemma he finds it necessary to place the blame on something familiar to him and to propose strange remedies, alien to all that he has known before. In short, he turns on his institutions and begins to question their efficacy, and he begins to ask questions of himself.

The American people, like others, have always complained about something, but in recent years there has been a change in the object of criticism, and in its character. For example, people have objected strenuously to the way economic affairs were managed, but only recently have they doubted the principle of economic procedure. They have always criticized the men who held public office, but not until recently have they questioned the democratic principle. They have sought to correct the evils in economic life by providing more economic freedom, and to remedy the defects of democracy by more democracy. It rarely occurred to any critic to propose a revolution by substituting a new set of institutions for those that had served so well. Usually the proposal has been to put a new set of men in charge of the old institutions rather than to put in a new set of institutions. It is this faith in institutions that now seems to be weakening.

In current economic literature one does not have to read far to find predictions that modern capitalism, which involves our entire economic system, is on its way out. The reasons given for its contemplated demise vary with the bias and knowledge of the writer. Even the most conservative men, those whose every interest is tied up in the capitalistic order, reveal deep concern over "the way things are going." Many of them avoid the task of thinking the problem out by blaming the government and its officials for features that displease them. They see such liberal governments as that of England going socialistic; they see the government of the United States doing things that affect seriously the economic order, substituting strange social practices for the old capitalistic one. In short, they see the economic world they knew in the process of falling about their ears. Some of them, in desperation, begin to doubt the principles on which they once depended, and to advocate the restoration of the old order by the strong hand. Others, favoring the change, advocate faster progress along the road to complete social control. They, the extremes, agree only in the conviction that the old principle on which previous action was predicated must be changed. The one tends toward capitalism by compulsion; the other would destroy it.

The case is not much different in our attitude toward democracy. Throughout the nineteenth century we were ardently democratic. Underneath the surface manifestations, the froth and foam of boisterous politics, the current of democratic faith ran strong, deep, and, as I shall show, almost silently. The people were so confident that the people could govern that they raised no question about it. They thought they could mend any deficiencies by more democracy, extension of suffrage, referendum, recall, secret ballot, and runoff primaries. It never occurred to many that there could possibly be anything wrong with the principle on which they acted. Here again there has been a not too subtle change. One does not have to go far to find some quite respectable people expressing doubt as to whether democracy can do the job. If it were not so we would not have the numerous loyalty oaths now required of public servants. Propaganda agencies have been formed to promote doubt, questioning, and scepticism. These cells of democratic distrust are well known, and are receiving considerable attention. They are no great menace because they can be dealt with, but what cannot be detected and isolated is that vague penumbra of silent misgiving which permeates public opinion, and is leading to a good deal of whistling in the dark.

It is a mistake to lay the blame for this defection and doubt of cherished institutions on foreign ideologies. Such ideologies are not new; they have always been outside the gates in some form. If they are making inroads now, it may be, it probably is, because democracy is suffering from a weakened internal condition, and with its low resistance the foreign germs more easily take hold. The very logic of democracy implies that it must maintain itself amidst all ideas and ideologies, not by force or compulsion, but by its internal vigor and good health. Unlike contrary systems, democracy's doors must always be held open with the confidence that it will be able to deal with all who enter. By its very nature — which is the negation of force — democracy must be held together by its own *esprit de corps,* by the abiding confidence of its members in its methods and ultimate objectives.

Reference was made above to the early silent current of democratic faith and to the later whistling in the dark. An examination of the literature of democracy for a century and a half seems to indicate that the better democracy worked, the less was said about it. Throughout the nineteenth century it might almost be called a silent force, "too deep for sound or foam"; during the twentieth century it has become highly vociferous, almost blatant. The merits of democracy are being proclaimed on all sides, from the pulpit, the school rostrum, the political platform, and in all the magazines. Why so much noise about something everyone is supposed to desire, something once so natural and so generally accepted that little comment was made on it?

An illustration of this crescendo of democratic comment is furnished by articles appearing in the best magazines from 1850 to 1950. *Harper's Magazine* used the word "Democracy" in the titles of articles only four times prior to 1917, and none of these is concerned with the efficacy of the system. The word did not appear in titles from 1899 to 1917. Between 1917 and 1929, six articles carried the word, and what is of importance is that four of the titles imply doubt as to democracy's efficiency, success, or vitality. Robert W. Bruère inquires, "Can Democracy Be Efficient?" Frank I. Cobb asks, "Is Our Democracy Stagnant?" Will Durant queries, "Is Democracy a Failure?" The best that Charles A. Beard can say is that "Democracy Holds Its Ground." From 1930 to 1950 *Harper's* published seventeen articles with some form of the word in the title. Harold J. Laski deals with "The Elite in a Democratic Society." Stanley High asks, "Is Japan Going Democratic?" Avis D. Carlson inquires, "Can the Schools Save Democracy?" Stanley High wonders about the President in "Roosevelt — Democratic or Dictatorial?" Peter Van Dresser wants "New Tools for Democracy." H. Schewarsky and John McJernett are alarmed at "Democracy's Crisis in France." Roy Holton thinks "Debt Threatens Democracy." Alden Stevens sees "Washington: Blight on Democracy," and Gerald W. Johnson deals with "Overloaded Democracy."

A reading of these titles, without reference to the contents of the article, could drive the mind inexorably to the conclusion that democracy is the sick man of the Western World, overloaded, blighted, in debt, in crisis, in need of new tools, threatened with dictatorship and an élite, and in need of salvation by schoolteachers and school kids! Inefficiency, stagnation, and possible failure are suggested if not affirmed. There is little doubt that each author thought he was defending democracy, rendering a service by pointing out something in need of correction. It is when we bring their titles together that we get the full impact and the deeper significance of what they — unwittingly, no doubt — are doing. In spite of themselves they are creating grave doubts in the minds of the people as to the merits of a form of government about which people of a prevous century had little question. They are not advocating a change in the principle of government, but they are undermining the unconscious loyalty of the people and preparing them to consider some alternative system, to exchange a known evil for an unknown one. Their purpose is to bolster up democracy, but in the long range they may be heralds of its deterioration.

A further indication of the growing tendency to talk more and more about democracy may be found by examining the appearance of the term in Poole's *Index* and in the *Reader's Guide* to periodical literature. From 1802 to 1892 "Democracy" appeared in titles 154 times, less than twice annually. From 1890 to 1949 inclusive, it appeared 1669 times, an average of 27.7 times annually. It reached an all-time annual high of 190 in the critical year of 1940–41. Its appearance by decades is interesting showing that reference to democracy seems to rise in time of crisis.

Number of Times "Democracy" Appeared in Titles
in Periodical Literature

1890–1899	59
1900–1909	135
1910–1919	233 (World War I)
1920–1929	164 (Postwar Boom)
1930–1939	449 (Depression)
1940–1949	619 (World War II)

3. The Puzzled Individual

Let us return to the individual whose course we are tracing as he makes his way toward the farther end of the valley of the frontier. It is there that he is showing his dissatisfaction and begins to doubt the institutions such as capitalism and democracy, which he and his fellows in turn abuse or praise. As he approaches the modern corporate world — a world of order and regulation — he finds that the loose institutions of the institutionless frontier no longer function as they did. They no longer guarantee him that maximum liberty he enjoyed when he was free from both economic regulation and government control. We need not wonder that he is perplexed and uncertain as to what course he should pursue.

Let us try to catch this individual looking at himself and asking himself questions as to his role. What economic opportunities are open to me in which I may achieve a competence and something besides for a rainy day and old age? Can I hope under present conditions to set up a business and succeed in competition with the powerful competitors around me? If not, and I seek employment at a salary or wage, who will be my employer, whose "man" will I be? Are employers as a class increasing or decreasing in number? If I become an employee, on whom shall I depend for protection, the government, the labor union, or the generosity of my employer? Can I remain free and independent of all these? If not, is it because they are so much more powerful, so much stronger than I? If I enter into a relation of dependence to one or more of these, what becomes of my independence? Can I be independent and dependent at the same time? What am I in this crystallized society, this corporate world, a determining power or a usable pawn?

The individual is compelled to answer many of these questions in a way that adds little to his ego. He is curbed on all sides by corporations or government agencies or labor unions, or associations, and the chief choice left to him is a choice of curbers. Actually the same individual is often caught by more than one. For example, the laborer works for a corporation, belongs to a labor union, and is subject to all sorts of government regulations. When we compare his freedom with that of the man on the frontier of America in the eighteenth and nineteenth century, we can easily see to what extent institutional restraints have caught up with him. The whole psychology of social security is tied up in this situation. No greater thrill comes to the individual than that of providing for himself, making his own way, solving his own problems. It is when he finds so many of the gates to opportunity closed, so many avenues blocked that he seeks security in the arms of the institutions. The popularity of the Beveridge plan in England, the reliance of the Germans on the promises of Hitler, and the acceptance of Americans of the New Deal social security are all manifestations of the spirit of resignation which seems to be supplanting a former spirit of personal risk-taking and daring. It is not that people are no longer willing to take risks, but rather that they are overborne by a sense of futility in striking for what seems unattainable.

What we are seeing here is man's increasing loss of faith in things he formerly believed in almost without question. His growing skepticism touches the economic system, capitalism; the political system, democracy; and, most important of all, it touches himself. Alongside of this general loss of confidence goes in many quarters a general disregard of religion. Perhaps the spread of education, the growth of science, and a general acceptance of the theory of evolution have undermined the old orthodox faith which permitted man to surrender himself to an unseen power and receive inner assurance of spiritual security regardless of what his physical condition might be. This seems to be particularly true of the Protestants, whose creeds required considerable intellectual effort to understand, and whose mode of salvation required the most vigorous individual initiative. If men are quitting the democratic way, giving up their individualism for security, it need surprise no one if they set off in vast numbers for an authoritarian church whose salvation is administered rather than worked for. He who accepts social security from the state is logically prepared to accept soul security from a church, both on terms requiring little in the way of individualism and initiative.[2]

If man is losing faith in himself and in his most cherished institutions, the fact is one of far-reaching consequence. It may be noted that the things he is losing confidence in are those which have most glorified the individual — capitalism, democracy, and Protestantism. Those people who have turned away from capitalism and democracy have turned to totalitarian forms where the individual becomes a part of a mass, gives up his identity — ceases to be an individual. To put the matter another way, the growing loss of faith has tended to break man loose from his moorings and safe anchorage, and to set him adrift where he is willing to grasp at anything offering safety. This change-over makes for a state of temporary confusion and affords an opportunity for such strong men as have shown up in the various countries with panaceas for the common man. But here we must return to the uncommon man — the frontier individual.

[2] The influence that the new wealth of the frontier had in secularizing society, making it worldly, is a subject worthy of investigation. It is quite certain that in America the use of public lands to subsidize education had the effect of secularizing the schools. See Chapter Twelve, Section 3.

Let us observe him at the point when he is beginning to show loss of confidence in himself and in his institutions. We see him hesitate in his uncertainty, and begin to examine the baggage he carries with a view to discarding that which no longer seems useful to him. In this case the baggage he carries is his institutions and practices. He debates with his companions, who are likewise affected, as to what shall be kept, what discarded, and what altered. Some would throw over capitalism, some would alter the imperatives of democracy; others would do away with corporations or abolish labor unions. Still others would turn back, bemoaning the fact that they ever left the valley; they are homesick for the old days. These last constitute a very powerful group, men who succeeded by their own efforts, who have become established, and they view the dissatisfaction of their brothers with mixed alarm and disgust. They shout encouragement to those who falter; they yell imprecations at those who fail. But if we examine their antecedents, we are likely to find that most of them long ago abandoned the principles they teach, principles of individual action, and that they are successful because they have acted for corporate groups, blocks of human beings who have yielded their property and in some measure their own will to a power much greater than an individual. They retain their individualism only because they *lead* a group, not because they *act* as individuals.

It is not the function of the historian to say what view is right and which is wrong. For the historian there are only facts and tendencies, to be recorded and charted as best he can. It is his function to point out that mankind — as seen marching from the conditions of the frontier where the individual was everything into a highly institutionalized state where the individual counts for much less — seems to be caught in a serious dilemma. It is this dilemma that makes men hesitate with uncertainty, falter and stumble. The effects of this loss of confidence are manifest in three places, in the mass of individuals, in the institutions, and in the single individual.

Viewing these indecisive people as a marching herd, we see them no longer moving with accustomed unity. The herd wavers, recoils before obstacles, and tends to become stubborn and recalcitrant. The members are no longer of one mind.

Some wander away, some try to turn back, and eventually like a cattle herd on a dry drive they may become crazed and march as thirst-blind cattle do into the flanks of those who try to guide them. What we have in a cattle herd is the loss of unity, of the herdlike quality, because of the suffering, the dilemmas, of the separate members. The bad effects are compounded by numbers and may result in mass frenzy, a stampede among cattle, a revolution among people. The surviving great democracies are nowhere near this stage, but the most casual conversation with thoughtful persons will reveal the deep apprehensions and uncertainties.

The institution itself is somewhat like the road or trail that the herd follows. If the herd turns back, refuses to follow the trail, time soon mantles it with grass and trees. It ceases to exist. So it is with institutions; they must be *used* to exist. Any wavering, wandering, or turning back tends to blur the road, creates troublesome detours, and in time obliterates a path that was once so plain. The studied efforts now being made to create public opinion favorable to various economic, social, and political institutions indicate clearly that someone feels the efforts and expense are necessary. Some nations have come to the point of prescribing "good" institutions, but such prescriptions cannot be imposed on a democracy except by persuasion of either the emotions or the intelligence. The most durable institution is one that men support by instinct, almost unconsciously. It may be, therefore, not wholly a good sign that we are becoming so conscious of our democracy.

It is the individual, the central figure in this story, who in last analysis determines the action of the mass and the fate of the institutions which constitute his culture patterns. Here in him we must seek the clue which gives insight not only to individual psychology but to institutional fate as well. If enough individuals have a feeling of uncertainty, of frustration, this is soon reflected in all institutions. If the attitude of distrust is carried to the extreme, it means the doom of those institutions, such as capitalism and democracy, which are based on buoyant optimism and the conviction that success and fortune lie ahead, and can be reached without help. It means the growth of other institutions more authoritarian in character, which take the risks and responsibilities and give in return a sense of security. All large institutions, such as universities, industrial and commercial organizations, have members who carry on the routine and bury all personality on condition that they be let alone. They constitute the army of satisfied and timid souls who are not willing to take a chance, bet on themselves, back their own ego by disputing authority or asserting leadership. They know that it takes a low bush to stand a high wind.

But what of the individual who still wants to be one? Suppose he wants to strike out for himself, be independent, take a long chance for a large reward. Here we enter disputed ground, for many will argue stoutly that there are still opportunities great enough to satisfy the most ambitious. There is no doubt that opportunities do exist by which the individual can rise to affluence and power. In the United States there are enough examples of men who do this to make the argument plausible. But the same thing has been true in all ages; even in the medieval period of highly stratified society an individual could by his talents come to the top. The church itself, one of the tightest organizations of that time, was in a sense the most liberal because it permitted persons of talent to rise, but they had to be exceptional. Since we are here following social trends, we must keep our eyes on the great social body, on the mass of quite ordinary people, not on the exceptions who may be skillfully used to disprove a rule.

The existence of individual opportunity in the present world is purely factual. We can agree that it still exists, but we are likely to differ as to the degree. Do opportunities for individuals, acting as such, exist in as great number as they did fifty or a hundred years ago? Can as many individuals out of a given population aspire to own property, establish their own business, or achieve success in the professions as was the case two or four generations back? The answers to these questions can be got from statistics, and perhaps the sociologists have compiled them. The broad answer is found in the rolls of tenant farmers, in the decrease of home owners, in the concentration of wealth, and a corresponding diffusion of poverty.

When we turn to those who make an outstanding success as

measured by affluence and power, we find that they have in most cases obtained a place on special terms. They have not in the majority of cases achieved it by acting as individuals in the old way, but by attaching themselves to some powerful organization, a hierarchy, and rising within it to leadership and authority. Even those who establish independent business in a highly lucrative field find it difficult to maintain their business as an individual enterprise. If their big competitors cannot eliminate them, break them, they come with such offers of price and position that the individual sells his business and either retires or accepts a place in the larger company. The result is that in the past sixty years in the United States the number of concerns engaged in many lines of standard manufacturing has constantly declined.

So much for the factual side of opportunity. There is also a psychological side, and for our purpose it is almost as important as the factual. The psychological question may be posed thus: What do people *believe* about the existence of opportunity? Do they honestly believe that jobs are becoming more abundant or less plentiful? Are parents optimistic about the future of their children, confident that they can establish themselves in an independent business, acquire a home, and lay aside without bureaucratic aid a competence for old age? If people really believe in the future, in an abundance of opportunities, why do they postpone marriage, restrict the size of the family, and accept the implications of social security? The opportunity may really exist, but if people do not believe it exists, then they react almost as if it did not. The result is an increasing timidity, a decline in aggressiveness, a willingness, however reluctant, to accept what seems inevitable. Here is a social situation which makes it possible for the corporate organizations, labor unions, government bureaus, educational institutions, and perhaps the stronger churches to gather their recruits and to bind to themselves the allegiance of persons fleeing from the old individualism. It is a situation which gives the few bold leaders their opportunity to lead, carry out programs, develop organizational loyalties, in short to command an army noted more for its docility than for its courage.

The situation is most favorable to the dictator who seems to rise from the cemeteries of dead hopes and aspirations. Whether we approach the subject of the old-style individual opportunity factually or psychologically, we find little room for enthusiasm, for buoyant expectations, for optimistic outlook. The facts and the psychology coincide in causing more and more people to face the future with grave concern.[3]

Turning back to the individual, let us, if possible, enter into his psychology and reproduce as best we can his own feeling about his aspirations and his opportunities. What does he *want* to do? What is he *able* to do? Is there a gap between which he cannot bridge? If he fails in his aspirations and in his repeated efforts, what are the effects on him, and how are they made manifest?

He wants to do now, and in the future, what he was able to do in the past, act as an individual in achieving success. He would own his farm, establish a business, write a book, magnify his importance. In frontier countries such as the United States, we have seen how this urge to individualism turned in to economic channels, to making a fortune through work. Almost the whole society was polarized toward financial success. The economic was the main stream, and those who wrote books, painted pictures, developed philosophy, or looked on

[3] World War II has offered strange evidence bearing on that most troublesome problem, steady employment. It brought a boom and provided work for all, and it did this while the worst depression in history was in progress. Now everyone hates war and what it brings, but thousands of people in England and in America received from it a thrill and stimulus that they could not conceal, the thrill of being in demand, of being useful, of exercising muscles and mind, of having a job and some money in their pockets. People dare not applaud war as such, but secretly millions probably deplored peace. This is the first war in American history — and it may be unique in modern history — that did not promise to settle the gravest issues confronting the combatants. Many can still remember the feeling of assurance in World War I that if we could only defeat the Kaiser, all would be well. The mad enthusiasm of November 11, 1918, with its banners, its horns and whistles, its joyful ecstasy, attested to our confidence in the future and our thanksgiving for a chance to take up where we left off. That was just what we hoped to avoid in the second war — taking up where we left off: that, above all, people wished to avoid. Hence the misgivings when the question was asked, What will happen after the war? The peace and the defeat of Hitler brought no such spontaneous outburst as did November 11, 1918.

living as the art of leisure, moved in eddies and often wound up in the backwash. In short, frontier individualism turned in the direction of least resistance, to a quest of material things. Men moved out like children hunting for Easter eggs, each for himself, each anxious to find more than his companions found. The frontier was a land in which Mother Nature had hidden many Easter eggs, many prizes. Just as the children hunt after the Easter eggs have all been found, so do men with an Easter egg psychology. Of course, the children lose interest if the hunt avails nothing, and eventually they turn to other games. Perhaps a few stubborn or stupid ones continue to look. So it is with men in search of fortunes. When the gap between their aspirations, desires, and their realization and fulfillment is too great, they are bound in the long run to lose interest, and perhaps to lose faith in the rabbit.[4]

Let us assume that there are still plenty of Easter eggs. Even so the child finds that the method of hunting them has changed, and this change has taken away much of the fun and prestige of gathering them. Somebody organized the children, and made the hunting of Easter eggs an efficient business. The children move under strict orders and comb every inch of ground thoroughly. They actually gather more eggs, but the eggs are not theirs. They belong to the organization: they must be turned in to the organization, and each child receives a token which is like that of the other children. He may admire the great pile of Easter eggs, but he knows they are not for him. He wants to have the ones he found by his own efforts, to admire, to caress, and to exhibit. They would be good for his ego. It will take expert management on the part of the organization, and perhaps some compulsion, to hold the children to the game — which has now become drudgery. Gone is the spontaneous outburst of pleasure in the individual hunt, competition, and achievement. This parable of the Easter eggs illustrates the present plight of the individual. When he acts as an independent individual, he finds few prizes; when he acts in the organization, which has taken over most of the territory, he does not act as an individual with the old freedom.

4 Since the advent of high income taxes, it is quite common to hear men say: "There is no use in my making any more money."

4. The End of Frontier Individualism

The dilemma of the modern man is due to the persistence of his psychology, the last piece of baggage to be discarded by the traveler faced with new conditions. The modern man cannot divest himself of his desire to act in the old way; but he cannot succeed by acting in the old way. The result is an offset between his desires and his possibilities. The cogs of his mind do not engage with reality, and therefore he is out of gear. Despite all his efforts, nothing happens, he does not get forward, for the reason that he is living in the realm of unreality, a land of remembered things. He is trying to harness the dreams of yesterday, of the frontier, to the machines of today and tomorrow.

What goes on in the man's mind as he witnesses the futility of his efforts? What are the effects on him of his failure to achieve practical results? What, he wonders, are others saying of him? Some are saying he does not work, or that he does not work hard enough. Others are saying he is impractical. A few believe he is worthless. He senses their thinking, and secretly wonders whether some of them may be right. Learned men speak of him as an example of the cultural lag, of the psychological split, of frustration and neurosis.

Franz Alexander, director of the Institute of Psychoanalysis in Chicago, deals at length with this frustration. He says in effect that, as the individual moves forward in time, he finds himself possessed by a succession of emotions and interests. He finds it necessary constantly to throw off the old habits and attitudes in order to make way for the new. Through various social and political compulsions he represses the old, drives them under the surface, makes them at least dormant, for they are always lurking in his psychological background. This submergence of the past is repressive, and if successfully carried out permits a normal development because the balanced individual is constantly adapting himself to realities that are present. If, however, the individual finds it impossible to make the adaptation required, he retreats to safer ground, away from reality. In this retreat he disengages himself from present reality and lives in a world of daydreaming or phantasy. This is called *regression.* "The discrepancy between traditional attitudes and changed conditions results in a withdrawal from reality into phantasy life. Action is now replaced by phantasy." [5] If this phantasy becomes chronic, a permanent abode of a mind disengaged from the present, it amounts to *fixation.*

It is thus that many American people remember frontier life, its romance, its freedom, its opportunity. For them it has become a fixation, and many of them wish they could return to the "good old days." They represent the cultural lag, the failure to make a necessary adjustment. "This longing for the past is as a rule intensified in times of social change and insecurity like our own." [6]

If there are really in progress changes from an age of rampant individualism and of personal risk and responsibility to one of institutional order and authority, they will bring the maximum of pain and suffering to the people of the United States who have made the outstanding success of the individualistic period. In the United States was built a society on the theory that the individual is paramount, above all class and rank. Moreover, this society turned practically all its energy into the economic channel, with the result that the United States made the most spectacular success of capitalism, building more fortunes and greater fortunes than any other country in the world. This means that the philosophy of economic individualism is more deeply entrenched in the United States than in countries which went less far in their devotion to wealth. England's individualism is muted and mild in comparison with America's. Germany made little progress in that direction and easily yielded to totalitarian promises. The Latin countries, both in Europe and in America, expressed their individualism in other ways than the economic. The Latin-American countries have not glorified work and business as the North Americans have. Therefore, if totalitarianism comes to subordinate the individual, it will come hardest among the people who made the most of individualism, the Americans of the United States. To resort to psychological terms, they will find it extremely difficult to repress their old habits and at-

[5] Franz Alexander, *Our Age of Unreason* (New York: J. B. Lippincott Co., 1942), p. 137.
[6] *Ibid.,* p. 192.

titues even after they have moved into another stage of existence. Their great success as frontier individualists results now in fixation, a frontier shelter under which they seek safety by regression. If we may judge by the following quotation Alexander thinks we are retreating to the medieval period.

> The history of Western Civilization can be regarded as an interplay between two opposing principles of organization and individualism, with an ever-changing equilibrium between the two. Since the Middle Ages, an increasing emphasis upon the individual has been clearly noticeable. . . . In the last five hundred years, there has been an emancipation of the individual and emphasis on freedom and social mobility with more far-reaching, yet less permanent and less rigid specialization of social functions. The present trend toward a bureaucratic corporate state, fascist or communist, appears to us a regression toward the Dark Ages. In the corporate state the emphasis is again on the state and the single individual becomes an insignificant, dependent part of the social superorganism.[7]

Alexander is perhaps correct in his longer view, which takes in all Western civilization. My view is a shorter one, limited to modern times and to the United States. Here it seems that though the American regresses from corporateness, the reality in which he now finds himself caught, yet he does not go back to the medieval position of which he knows little. He stops with the frontier, the reality of yesterday which has become the unreality of today. His fixation at present is frontier individualism and not medieval corporateness.[8]

An example of the American retreat to the frontier is found in American crime. As already pointed out, disregard of the law was a common frontier trait because each man was in effect his own law. This self-dependence worked very well where men had moved so far as to outrun established law, but it became awkward when civilization caught up with them, and informed them that their mores and ideals had become "lawless."

---

[7] *Ibid.*, pp. 273–74.

[8] It would seem to me that corporateness is the present reality to which we cannot adjust, and that our frustration drives us back to the age of individualism, not to corporateness. Why should we regress from one form of corporateness to another form when our drive is to get away from it in all forms? What we revolt against is our drift into corporateness.

The great majority of young men are still reared with ideals of individual initiative, endurance, self-reliance, and courage like their pioneer forefathers, but when they grow up they are exposed to a world in which opportunities for individual initiative, bravado, and individual accomplishment are extremely limited. . . . The old ideals are alive but their realization becomes daily more difficult. One escape from this dilemma is criminality. . . . Driven by an inner need to be successful through personal initiative, the individual resorts to a pathological form of individualism and adventure, — crime.[9]

Modern frustration of frontier ideals has resulted in greater social damage than that arising from crime, greater because it is more subtle and affects more people. I refer to an increasing neurosis. "In our own day," says Alexander, "neurosis has become the rule and the well-adjusted person the exception." [10] This neurosis arises among men and women engaged primarily in an economic struggle, and because nearly all American adults are so engaged, the incidence of neurosis is high. The fierceness of the economic struggle is intense in America, and therefore neurosis arising from that cause is great. The most common cause discovered by the specialist in emotional disturbances is "relentless competitiveness in any given field." Even though people want to stop, to rest, they are driven forward by the fear of being left behind, of appearing soft, of not being real men. America is full of these torn and distracted people. In the following moving passage the physician to these patients tells how they look to him.

After long hours of daily work, spent listening to the suffering victims of these unsettled times and trying to extract sense from the . . . variety of sincere self-revelations, a . . . vision appears before the eyes of the pondering psychoanalyst. The analyst sees his patients — physicians, lawyers, engineers, bankers, advertising men, teachers, and laboratory research men of universities, students, and clerks — engaged in a Marathon race, their eager faces distorted by strain, their eyes focused not upon their goal, but upon each other with a mixture of hate, envy, and admiration. Panting and perspiring, they run and never arrive. They would all like to stop but dare not as long as the others are running.

9 Alexander, *Our Age of Unreason,* pp. 302-3.
10 *Ibid.,* p. 168.

What makes them run so frantically, as though they were driven by the threatening swish of an invisible whip wielded by an invisible slave driver? The driver and the whip they carry in their own minds. If one of them finally stops and begins leisurely to whistle a tune or watch a passing cloud or picks up a stone and with childish curiosity turns it around in his hand, they all look upon him at first with astonishment and then with contempt and disgust. They call him names, a dreamer or a parasite, a theoretician or a schizophrenic, and above all, an effeminate. They not only do not understand him — they not only despise him but "they hate him as their own sin." All of them would like to stop — ask each other questions, sit down to chat about futilities — they all would like to belong to each other because they all feel desperately alone — chasing on in a never-ending chase. They do not dare to stop until the rest stop lest they lose all their self-respect, because they know only one value — that of running — running for its own sake.[11]

Actually all these people are running for individualism and their strain comes from the increasing difficulty of finding it. They are running after a particular *kind* of individualism, that reflected in personal economic gain, in professional prestige, in public or institutional recognition of their personal worth. Whistling a tune, looking at clouds, or enjoying the heft and texture of a colored stone might give them a sensory or spiritual satisfaction, but they are not seeking that form of individualism.

> Can a civilization [inquires Alexander] survive where discontent and frustration are so oppressive and extensive and in which men are driven towards a goal of an extinct period, engaged in futile and exhaustive efforts to live up to unattainable standards of individualism? . . . The economic conquest of America is nearly accomplished and the practical exploitation of the basic inventions on a large scale well-nigh exhausted. And even though some technical innovations are still to be expected, the economic field is near to its saturation point and will no longer provide sufficient outlet for creative ambition and so becomes the arena of destructive competition. Are there new frontiers — open territories worthy of the individualistic and productive forces of a great nation? [12]

11 *Ibid.*, p. 310.
12 *Ibid.*, pp. 311–12.

Are there new frontiers? What a terrible question, and with what pathetic eagerness Americans — the most frontier-conscious people — seek an affirmative answer! Is there a human soul? The philosophers tell us that one reason for believing there is a human soul is the universal desire for one. If universal or nation-wide desire guarantees a frontier, the Americans, of all people, will find one. They not only long for it; they search for it. And some claim that they have found it.

The tenor of this discussion is such as may lead the reader to conclude that the individual has had his day, and that he is now in the process of being swallowed up by corporate business, corporate labor, and eventually by the corporate church and the corporate state. There is much surface evidence which can be used to bolster such a view, but we must remember that there are deeper currents which may in the long range of things rise to overwhelm the surface indications. It is very alarming when we see the corporate principle emerge as fascism and nazism in government and as equally objectionable corporate monopoly of both money and labor in the democracies. The individual seems to be pushed down, submerged, and in reality destroyed by the ponderous growth of vast, centrally controlled and directed organizations, associations, monopolies, trusts, and cartels.

Looked at from long range, we find that this very corporateness which frightens us with its threat of domination carries within its bosom a germ, not so much a germ that will destroy corporateness, but one that may eat away its objectionable features.[13] What we object to is not corporateness as such; we object to the submergence of individuality, with its resultant effects on freedom, initiative, and the personal creative impulse. This is equivalent to saying that corporateness as we know it curbs individualism *as we have known it*. It does not mean that corporateness need curb individualism per se, or that it might not actually promote it in quite desirable ways.

We are concerned here with two factors: The first is the sort of individualism we have known; the second is the sort of

13 See John Kenneth Galbraith, *American Capitalism: The Concept of Countervailing Power* (Boston: Houghton Mifflin Co., 1952), for an interesting theory as to the manner in which society is protected from complete corporate dominance by what the author calls countervailing power.

corporateness that we have to deal with. The view set forth here is that the kind of individualism we have known, that which was given its greatest opportunity during the centuries of the open frontier, is well-nigh done for and is definitely on the decline. That kind of individualism, economic in character, arose at a time when men stood in the presence of an unlimited quantity of potential wealth, which could be converted into actual wealth by a man or a family working alone. Throughout the formative period there was always an abundance of work, more than men could do. It was this abundance of work on a superabundance of material that led men along the path of economic individualism and enabled them to adopt political individualism or democracy as a corollary. It is the opinion of J. Franklin Jameson that "political democracy came to the United States as a result of economic democracy, that this nation came to be marked by political institutions of a democratic type because it had, still earlier, come to be characterized in its economic life by democratic arrangements and practices." [14]

By the end of the nineteenth century the facts were changing and the change was brought about by two forces moving in opposite directions. Because of the abundance of work to do and the enormous quantity of materials available to work on, man developed through science machines and power competent to handle the materials. The machines were so efficient that they enabled the man to catch up with the work. Equipped with these powerful machines, a technology predicated on constant expansion, man came rather suddenly to the end of the open space, to the limits of land expansion, to the closed doors of the physical world. Thus did a dynamic economic technology run into a vacuum. Man had through his own ingenuity and industry not only caught up with his work, but he had in a sense also run out of stuff to work on, the stuff of unlimited area. This statement is contrary to much we have heard about this being an age of abundance. In a sense there is an abundance, but it is mainly an abundance of things made available by machines, such as typewriters, motorcars, refrigerators, and food produced by the science of agriculture. This

[14] J. Franklin Jameson, *The American Revolution Considered as a Social Movement* (Princeton: Princeton University Press, 1926), p. 41.

is quite a different sort of abundance from that of the frontier. The frontier offered an abundance of raw materials whereas science and technology give us finished products. The frontier abundance required work, furnished the stuff to work on, and therefore provided employment; the abundance of finished things all around us cannot be had on these terms. This modern abundance does not bring with it the obligation, the duty, or the opportunity to work that the frontier abundance brought. This modern abundance requires money, not work, and it is not concerned with the source from which the money comes. Men who make money by management, by manipulation, by speculation, by taking bribes can have more of the gadgets of easy living than the man who swings the axe, follows the plow, or stands at the lathe.

The modern individual finds himself caught between the closing frontier and the expanding production of the machine. Having in America, and to some extent in Western civilization, expressed his individuality mainly in work, he finds himself cut off from the frontier where work could always be found and barred by the machine which is doing more and more of the work left to be done in civilization. It is a situation in which he feels quite useless, baffled, and defeated.

5. The Prospect of a Corporate Individualism

The question we come to now is whether the individual can recover his individualism. An answer to this question has been attempted by John Dewey, and may be found in a book which attracted little but deserves much attention, entitled *Individualism, Old and New*. What I have called frontier individualism Dewey calls the old individualism. But I believe we would agree that both terms are appropriate. Frontier individualism is now old, a thing of history, something to look back on, representing the "goal of an extinct period." Dewey as a pragmatist is interested more in the present or immediate future than in the past, and he seeks a new individualism which will accord with current and future facts. He believes it will be easier to modify individualism than it will be to change facts, conditions, and physical circumstance. To be specific, it will be easier to provide a new type of individualism within the modern corporation than it will be to eliminate the corporation in the hope, quite forlorn, that the old individualism may be recaptured. In comparison with those who urge their fellows off to all sorts of vague "new" frontiers, Dewey appears as the pragmatist who suggests that we accept what is, adopt what works, what *will* work, here and now, not at the equator, the poles, deep within the earth or in the heavens above. We can no longer flee civilization in search of individualism. If it is to exist at all, or to any social extent, it must find existence possible and desirable within society and not beyond it; it should flourish where people are thickest. The problem is to find "a *new* individualism, as *significant* for *modern conditions* as the old individualism at its best was for its day and place." [15]

Dewey's view here is not so long as mine. He believes that the old individualism arose out of the early stages of the Industrial Revolution when men found it possible to create and acquire wealth as individuals. But the early stages of the Industrial Revolution were the middle stages of the frontier revolution, which had been busy for a long time creating the individualism of that period. It was in the period in which the Industrial Revolution and the frontier revolution overlapped that the individualism of which we both speak emerged. The Industrial Revolution or science caught the spirit of the frontier individual after his character was formed and gave him a tool which enabled him to do all the work that the materials and the occasion demanded. In time the tool and the organizations formed around it overtook the man and wrested from him his own individuality as expressed in his habit of working and acquiring wealth on his own hook. He became lost in the labyrinth of the tool and its enveloping corporation. Dewey does not credit the frontier as an influence in developing this old individualism nor does he point out the consequence of its closing; still he sees the plight of the individual thus cut off. He says:

It is evident enough that the rapid industrialization of our

[15] John Dewey, *Individualism, Old and New* (New York: Minton, Balch & Co., 1930), p. 33. Italics supplied.

civilization took us unawares.[16] Being mentally and morally un-
prepared, our older creeds have become ingrowing; the more
we depart from them in fact, the more loudly we proclaim
them. . . .

With an enormous command of instrumentalities, with possession of a secure technology, we glorify the past, and legalize
and idealize the *status quo,* instead of seriously asking how we
are to employ the means at our disposal so as to form an equitable and stable society. This is our great abdication. It explains
how and why we are a house divided against itself. Our traditions, our heritage, is itself double. It contains in itself the ideal
of equality of opportunity and of freedom for all, without regard to birth and status, as a condition for the effective realization of that equality.[17]

Dewey is in general agreement with Alexander as to the
psychology of the modern man. He speaks of a "split" between
his ideal of action and the set of facts which determine his
action. The individual today is lost, bewildered and confused,
as he feels the old foundations giving way under him with no
new ones on which he can find secure footing. "The significant
thing," saws Dewey in his chapter on "The Lost Individual,"
"is that the loyalties which once held individuals, which gave
them support, direction, and unity of outlook on life, have
well-nigh disappeared. In consequence, individuals are confused and bewildered. It would be difficult to find in history
an epoch as lacking in solid and assured objects of belief and
approved ends of action as is the present." [18]

Despite his confusion and bewilderment, the individual does
have an anchor, something to take hold of, to believe in — if
he will only use it. His difficulty is in getting his own consent to recognize existing facts and forces and seizing with firm

16 If the reader will substitute for "the rapid industrialization of our civilization" the words "the closing of the frontier" in the first sentence, he will
have another and equally rational explanation of the altered circumstances of
the individual.

17 Dewey, *Individualism, Old and New,* pp. 16–17.

18 *Ibid.,* p. 52. The struggle of American philosophers with individualism
is an interesting one. Josiah Royce, William James, and John Dewey were all
concerned with it. William James glorified the individual in *Pragmatism.*
Dewey found the individual in trouble, and undertook to save him. If he fails,
his book. *Individualism, Old and New,* will appear as a quaint philosophical
exercise.

hold the opportunities that *they* offer. By doing this the individual would bring himself in harmony with what is possible, in the present situation; and by establishing harmony, he would achieve a new individualism as precious and as practicable as the old was in its best days. This sounds quite sensible in principle, but when we come to carry it out in detail we find almost insuperable mental obstacles. The survival of the old ideals in men's minds creates in them a psychological unwillingness to make such a complete about-face. In effect the memory of the old not only blocks the purposeful adoption of the new, but it persuades man that the new is positively an evil thing. In short, the new individualism must make its way against the greatest of all barriers, those intangible blockades of the human mind. It can, Dewey believes, make its way because it comes with the facts of modern life, and facts in the long run are the greatest imperatives.

The essential facts of the present cling around applied science, the tools and technology which are quite adequate to do the work formerly distributed among individuals. It was in doing this work, and doing it for profit, that men expressed their old individualism. In those old days the individual was the center, the single economic cell, the major agent in producing wealth and profit, a pecuniary culture. As the function of working was gradually taken over by the tools and technology furnished by science, the tools became the center, leaving the man pretty much out of it. As work became mechanized, men became corporatized, if that word may be used. Corporateness has extended in every direction, into all forms of business, into the professions through associations, into churches, into amusements, into education. Its influence is today as pervasive in America as the frontier influence was a century ago. Corporateness is now the primary fact and the dominant force in modern life, and whatever men are to have of individualism they must come at by making terms with a corporate world and not a frontier one. These are the essential facts which men are so loath to accept. For a half-century Americans have been taught that corporateness is an evil, something to be condemned. They have insisted on making laws to curb, check, or destroy it, but they have steadily become more corporate. It is futile for people to argue any longer or to declare that they will not have corporateness, for it has them completely surrounded. Those who refuse to come to terms with the facts are described as follows:

> Individuals are groping their way through situations which they do not direct and which do not give them direction. The beliefs and ideals which are uppermost in their consciousness are not relevant to the society in which they outwardly act and which constantly reacts on them. Their conscious ideas and standards are inherited from an age that has passed away; their minds . . . are at odds with actual conditions. This profound split is the cause of distraction and bewilderment.
>
> Individuals will refind themselves only as their ideas and ideals are brought into harmony with the realities of the age in which they act.[19]

The new individualism, therefore, must come harmonious with the corporate structure. We are now in the stage of realizing that a little corporateness is a dangerous thing, dangerous to those who resist it or remain outside it. Let us therefore all enter into the corporate house and put it in such order that the individual may live there, if not happily at least tolerably. After all, corporations — I use the term broadly — are composed of human beings, and the question is whether they shall serve the individual or be served by him. The new individualism will arrive when corporateness comes to serve society rather than master, crowd, and drive it.

The question is how can the corporation be brought into the service of society in a more direct manner. Many corporate spokesmen are ready to say that corporations already serve society, and that they could not long exist if they did not. They do serve society by providing the goods and services that society requires, and certainly they are more considerate of the public interest than they were in the not too distant past.[20] The

---

[19] Dewey, *Individualism, Old and New*, p. 70.

[20] The change in public attitude toward modern corporations is being reflected in books which seem to say that after all corporations are not so bad as we once thought. See Peter F. Drucker, *The Concept of the Corporation* (New York: The John Day Co., 1946). Galbraith's *American Capitalism* is a highly original contribution to this attitude. The corporations themselves are undertaking to give the public an understanding of their role as evidenced by educational conferences, such as those held by Standard Oil, Du Pont and others. The Corning Conference is described in Eugene Staley, ed. *Creating an Industrial Civilization* (New York: Harper and Bros., 1952).

fact remains that the business corporations have not had this service as their main function: Their main function, the goal they must always keep in mind, is that of making a profit. When they make up their balance sheets at the end of the year, they are judged, and judge themselves, not by the good they have done, but by the money they have earned above all their costs. The prospect of profit is what drives them to their exertions, expansion, and development.

This is the same motive that drove the old individuals; but we have seen that as these are gathered into collective groups they tend to yield up their personal initiative to that of the group — of the labor union, the bureau, or the association. They cease to act as individuals as they once did; they may still cling to the profit motive as a desirable thing, but the opportunity to act is cut off in every direction by the institutions which guarantee them a measure of security but at the same time restrain them from seeking extra profit on their own initiative.

Here we come to a divergence of attitude between the individual and the business corporation. While the individual has moved away from the profit motive, seeking security in the collective group, the business corporation retains the profit motive in full force and exercises initiative, takes risks, and seeks aggrandizement in the old way. It has succeeded in carrying over into the corporate age which it has helped to create the ideals and the motives of a previous age in which the profit motive was the animating force of the whole society. The rugged individualists of the late nineteenth century — we need not name them — were in perfect harmony with the society in which they operated because every individual in that society was acting as they were, and hoping to follow their examples. The rugged individualist has now disappeared within the business corporation; the little fellows have before them no such living examples, and have given up all expectation of being giants. Personality has been submerged by organization on all sides. But what remains in the business corporation is the old motive of profit, the old method of competition, the old philosophy of a free and unfettered world. In a sense the business corporation has institutionalized the old individualism and is seeking to preserve it especially for itself as a survival from an extinct period.

Survivals of an extinct period are usually relegated to museums by a society that no longer has use for them. Whether or not the profit motive which flourished in the period of the old individualism can be retained, or preserved, by the business corporation remains to be seen. Dewey maintains that it must be given up because it is out of harmony with the corporate age, an anachronism. The maladjustment is due to the retention of the profit motive by one group to the exclusion of the others. It is not due to corporateness, which is here to stay, but to the elimination of so many human beings from full participation in corporate benefits. Corporateness is now the big show and every man and woman ought to have a ticket to its pageants or some part in the performance. Only in this way can the *new* individualism and the worthwhile life of a shared culture be achieved.

It is unfortunate that the words "a shared culture" carry an unwelcome connotation. But by shared culture Dewey means much more than is realized by those who shy at words. He is in search of a harmonized society, and he believes that the people — all people — can find harmony only when they live in accord with the realities around them. "In a society so rapidly becoming corporate," he says, "there is need of associated thought to take account of the realities of the situation and to frame policies in the social interest." In short, the new individualism will emerge when we think corporately and frame policies which will make this corporateness function in the interest of people rather than in the interest of a few who use it for pecuniary gain. When corporateness functions in this way, opposition to it will cease because it will receive not only the conscious but also the unconscious approval of the public just as the old individualism did in the old days. People approve of things they share in, which is another way of saying that they approve of a culture of which they are an essential part.[21]

The term "shared culture" we might like to avoid because it stirs up emotions which obscure the processes of logical

[21] The public school system is an excellent example of a shared culture. It is conducted without profit in the interest of all the people. The approval of it is almost universal and most of its supporters would be surprised to learn that it is a "shared" or socialistic culture. It was not always so. Another example may be found in the highway system.

thought. The capitalistic culture of the frontier cultivated ideals antagonistic to the idea of a shared culture as applied to wealth.[22] The ideal was that each man was supposed to take what he could, and what he took was his. It must be remembered that this ideal arose in an exceptional time in human history, a time when there was such an abundance to take that no limit need be placed on either the amount taken or the methods used. The frontier culture was after all a shared culture in a rough sense because everyone had a right to carry off all he could pack from the frontier storehouse.

No one ever thought of calling this program socialism — this program of helping everybody get a start through frontier bounty. The reason they did not think of it was that the government started with the property from scratch and distributed it in such a way as to cause the individual to feel, erroneously, that he earned it. Every farmer, every railroad magnate, every holder of patent monopoly or beneficiary of a protective tariff honestly believed that he was earning all he got by the sweat of his brow or equivalent perspiration of his nervous system. It was quite proper to share the wealth as long as it was frontier wealth, as long as the government could furnish it to A without asking anything from B. It will not be easy to lead people to see that the frontier made a shared culture a practical thing.

Since the close of the frontier, and regardless of prejudice, the democracies have gone a long way toward recognized socialism. Therefore we need not take offense at Dewey when he says:

> We are in for some kind of socialism, call it by whatever name we please, and no matter what it will be called when it is realized. Economic determinism is now a fact, not a theory. But there is a difference and a choice between a blind, chaotic and unplanned determinism, issuing from business conducted for pecuniary profit, and the determinism of socially planned and ordered development. It is the difference and the choice between a socialism that is public and one that is capitalistic.[23]

[22] In a capitalistic culture men objected historically to sharing their private wealth. They had no such objection to sharing public wealth as witness their acceptance of free homesteads, free gold claims, free grass, subsidies to railroads and other enterprises, and a protective tariff.

[23] Dewey, *Individualism, Old and New*, pp. 119–20.

The new individualism must be found by accepting corporateness as a reality, just as men accepted the frontier, and then working out the new individualism within the corporate frame. To do this the pecuniary element will have to be got rid of, and science and technology will have to be turned loose to work in the interest of and for the benefit of mankind. This is about as far as Dewey's socialism goes. His theory of a shared culture implies that if society can produce an abundance, then society should share it.

How can individualism flourish in this situation? What will be its rewards? It is obvious that the rewards will not be primarily economic. The way the new individualism may be arrived at is illustrated in the following examples.

The first example is that of a man employed by a corporation chartered by the state, a university. Its function is that of education, and in order that its members may be free to perform their duties they are in some measure freed from pecuniary consideration. They are given reasonable security of tenure and a salary on which they can live. Nearly the whole expense is paid by the state. Now within this corporate structure the man finds it possible to work out his own individuality without regard for profit. He teaches classes, yes, but in addition he amuses himself by playing with ideas, by watching the procession of society through time, and trying to analyze the causes which have brought it to its present state. Eventually he puts these ideas on paper and finds a publisher who is willing to take a chance. The book appears and the fresh new copy is opened with a satisfaction entirely apart from any pecuniary gain anticipated. In time there are reviews, some favorable and some unfavorable, and perhaps occasionally comes a letter bearing a strange postmark. This scholar has reached out and touched someone in New England, in Old England, or in some other distant land. To him this is not a bad life, and in it he finds the room for developing the individualism that he has always wanted. He has had fun in finding a new truth, in developing a philosophy, in saying things in a better way than they have been said before.

If the publisher sends him a check, that is fun too, not so much from the position of the decimal point but as a sure sign that he has done something that people approve. And it does not disturb him that he is bound for life, though voluntarily, to a public corporation conducted on a public nonprofit basis. It so happens that the public approves of the corporation, the university, which has no balance sheet and must therefore be socialistic in character.

Another example may be found in our system of public roads. Today these roads have been taken over by another corporation, the State Highway Department. Citizens give up their frontier individualism which consisted of determining the way the roads should go, of constructing and maintaining them, in order to have modern and efficient highways so necessary for the civilization of technology. The public has also given its complete approval to this social, nonprofit corporate body, and the approval is so complete as to be almost unconscious.

What opportunity exists within this corporate socialistic and publicly approved enterprise for the expression of individualism of the new type? A friend of mine furnishes an example. This man is a landscape architect who has had broad experience in private service. He gave this up and took a place in a Highway Department on a moderate salary. His task was to develop the roadside so that the soil would be preserved, so that farms adjacent would not erode, so that wild native flowers and native shrubbery would have on the highways a preserve on which they could grow undisturbed for their aesthetic and cultural value. Trees were planted in such position as to exert a psychological influence on drivers, slowing them down at dangerous places, giving them a sense of security where it is needed. Parks and rest grounds were designed where motorists and weary transport drivers could pull off for sleep. In short, this man applied his art to public highways, and made them so attractive that men came from all over the nation — came to observe them and to adopt his methods in other states.

It would seem that the new individualism proposed is related to avocations or hobbies as distinguished from vocations. The installation of early retirement systems combined with increased longevity makes necessary the development of avocations or hobbies which will absorb the interest and prolong the usefulness of the increasing number of retired people. Comment is often made on the fact that after retirement many able men, cut off from their accustomed economic struggle, fail rapidly with enforced idleness. They no longer belong, and unless they have developed an absorbing hobby, they lose their grip completely. The fortunate few who escape this fate do so by developing a new individualism. I know of one man whose leisure was spent in the observation of nature, as a field naturalist. When he was nearly seventy, he was freed from the exactions of his job, and used the time to write a book which had been maturing throughout a long and busy lifetime. The book was well received, and put him in touch with kindred spirits throughout the English-speaking world. He got a tremendous lift from the experience, which is making the years of his retirement the most enjoyable of his life.

The case of the field naturalist is useful in a discussion of the new individualism. Let us assume that because of technology, which does more and more of the work, enforced retirement will be pushed back from the age of sixty-five or seventy. How important it will be for the individual at that age to find an outlet for his creative energy! Few men at fifty are cut off from employment, but we have seen that with the growth of corporateness, more and more men are cut off from the exercise of initiative and from the exercise of their creative energy. They may hold jobs for which they receive the customary pay, but they are after all only half employed. It is for that part of them which is not employed that the new type of individualism is needed. To the extent that corporateness takes away the old frontier individualism, where every man was employed to the limit of his capacity, it should compensate him by providing conditions favorable to the development of another type.

There is some hope for the new individualism. It must be confessed, however, that its achievement will not be easy. The business corporations are going to find it difficult to give up the profit motive under which they have done so much. They will disregard the admonition of the philosopher, even so distinguished a one as John Dewey. A renunciation of the profit motive will come slowly, as it should, partly from within and partly from without, but it seems to be on its way.

Since our primary concern is with the individual, we may well inquire as to what will be expected of him if he is to achieve a new status. What must *the* individual do in order that he may have a new individualism in a corporate world? The examples given of the author, the landscape engineer, and the field naturalist are examples of exceptional men, educated, trained to use their minds, to observe what goes on around them. Is it possible in any society to bring any considerable number of men up to such a level, to educate them so that they can employ themselves in an advantageous manner? The answer is probably no. The alternative is to find other levels of self-employment which will enable other men — a great many men — to find an outlet for such kinds of creative energy as they may have. It is quite clear that to achieve the new individualism the greatest initiative is going to be required from all hands. The frontiersman developed his form of individualism because all the forces operating around him were favorable to it. This is not true in a collective society such as we are coming to have. In a society where security is guaranteed and obedience expected, it is going to require a sheer act of will on the part of the member to work out a new individualism worthy of the name. The number who do it should be about equal or proportional to the number who made fortunes under the old system.

The attempt has been made to follow the individual as he made his transit across the Great Frontier. We saw him emerge from the obscurity of medieval corporate life into the broad valley of the frontier where for a long interval he acted increasingly for himself, both in economics and in politics. As he leaves the frontier, we see him returning again to a corporate life of the modern type. It was in the interval between, that we saw him detached in a noncorporate state. In that interval he acted on a highly individualistic basis. Such institutions as he had were of such loose structure that they sat lightly upon him, hardly restrained him at all. In the later period we see him entering another corporate world and we note his confusion and frustration because he is as yet poorly equipped for corporate living. His path between the two corporate worlds across the centuries of the Great Frontier describes the parabola of freedom and individualism now designated by the philosopher as old.

CHAPTER FIVE

THE GENESIS OF MODERN DYNAMISM

IN THE PRECEDING CHAPTERS the view has been advanced that the character of the modern age is due in large measure to the fact that it had a frontier setting, that it grew up in an economic boom induced by the appropriation and use of frontier resources, and that its institutions were designed and modified to meet the needs of a booming society. If this be true, then the whole modern age would appear to be an abnormal one. By its very nature a boom is a temporal thing, something out of the ordinary run of life, an abnormal state of affairs which is destined to end when the forces that caused it cease to operate. Though this truth is obvious, people do not bear it in mind, even in the briefest periods of unusual prosperity. They act as if the "good times" are permanent, as if the abnormal activity is the normal thing. It seems that their whole psychology is quickly affected, leading them into extravagances they would not ordinarily think of indulging. In short, ideas and institutions begin to form themselves around the boom conditions; the boom itself begins to make history, institutions, ideas, to form a culture complex.

Historians and philosophers have constantly sought for a principle of unity in human affairs, something around which events formed themselves. The popularity of such terms as renaissance, reformation, industrial revolution, and democracy attest to man's desire to find a master key to complex human relations. Men speak of progress, or of what has happened, and seek to explain it through the operation of a bundle of forces covered by some such abstract term as renaissance, reformation, the industrial revolution, or the age of science. I am offering the frontier as a new category, and suggesting that modern history be looked at as the Age of the Frontiers.

This new category does not supplant any of the old ones, but it may be entitled to a place beside the most important of them. That depends on whether an understanding of it illuminates the age considered. It is no simple undertaking to pick up a word which outside of one country has little meaning, and clothe it with substance, significance, and connotation until it takes its place among the most meaningful in the language. Any attempt to develop such a sweeping concept must make its way against the inertia of preconceived ideas, and the effort cannot succeed unless it fits into the facts as they have developed. If the idea of the Age of the Frontiers has any validity, it will not be difficult to show how the frontier was related to the contemporary forces which form the commonly accepted categories of thought about the past. For some of these categories the frontier will furnish a setting; for others a motive; and for one or two the conditions that made their growth possible and important. At its least, the frontier was a single factor in human affairs for four important centuries; at its best, it was an influence so great as to make itself felt by all of them. In either case it is worth considering.

It is often stated that the outstanding characteristic of the modern age is its dynamic quality. Serious efforts have been made to discover the origin of this dynamism, to find the force that propelled Western society from its lowly state of 1500 to something a little short of world dominance four centuries later.[1] In the present chapter the frontier will be examined as a possible source of modern dynamism. The story begins in the first section with the breakup of medieval society under the impact of new forces of which the frontier was an important one. We proceed to examine the vertical flow of property and to note the effect of Things. Finally, we arrive at the human motive for all the coming and going, the essence of what men were striving for, and in this motive we may have found the throbbing heart of a dynamic society. It was not

[1] Lawrence Dennis, *The Dynamics of War and Revolution* ([New York:] The Weekly Foreign Letter, 1940). As the title of this book indicates, Dennis attributes the dynamic quality of the modern age to war and revolution.

war or glory or heaven, but it was a material gain that was sought and most easily found. This brief explanation may make clear the intent of the sections of the chapter: "The Advent of Modern Dynamism," "The Vertical Pulsation of Wealth," "The Dynamic Effect of Things," and "The Rise of Capitalism."

The two succeeding chapters are a continuation of the subject of dynamism as related to capitalism. "Frontier Windfalls" had peculiarly dynamic effects in getting capitalism on the road and were particularly potent in the first two centuries of the frontier. In time they created too much excitement and expectation, causing men to overreach themselves. The crisis which ended the age came with the opening of the eighteenth century and is treated under the heading of "The Three Unwise Bubbles." Out of the crisis of the bubbles came a new attitude toward the frontiers, and a new instrument, credit, with which the broken ranks of finance could reform and continue for two more centuries the dynamic quest for gain.

1. The Advent of Modern Dynamism

If we examine Europe before 1500 we find ourselves in what is commonly called the medieval age. Now almost anything one says about this period is subject to dispute and exception, but we are not too far wrong in saying that the medieval period when compared to the modern seems static. Certainly society was stratified in well-defined classes — nobles, churchmen, and common people. Commerce was limited largely to the community, and industry had hardly begun its marvelous growth. It was an age in which the individual counted for little, his identity being lost in organizations and in the class to which he belonged. Feudalism still exercised great power, and where it was passing away in politics and economics, it was still dominant in social life. In short, society was fairly well frozen in its tracks of custom and convention.

The population of Europe was relatively stable, numbering perhaps one hundred million, a figure which had obtained in 1300 and that did not change materially until the middle of the seventeenth century. If the figures be correct, then no considerable dynamic quality issued from an increasing population.

Moreover, the land area available to Europeans had not changed, no new increment had been added since the Roman period. Men tilled the same acres century after century, and the idea of expanding this area was one that could hardly have entered their heads. The coming dynamic age did not receive its impetus either from an increasing population or from an expanding land area *within* Europe. Therefore the propelling force may be sought for *outside* the Metropolis.

The medieval world was broken up and the modern age was ushered in by a series of revolutionary changes which began before the Great Frontier was opened, and continued in succession as it was exploited. The Renaissance preceded the opening of the frontier; the Reformation was contemporary with it; while the commercial, industrial, and democratic revolutions appeared in the midst of the boom which new wealth engendered. The revolutions appear historically against the background of an expanding physical world, and can never be fully understood when considered apart from their setting.

The frontier differed from the other ingredients in that it was the most corporeal. The Renaissance dealt with ideas; the Reformation dealt with the spirit and things of the spirit and was other-worldly; the scientific and industrial revolution was concerned with methods, a manner, a way of doing; the democratic revolution dealt with the individual as the most important factor in the realm of politics, law, and government. The new land was more tangible than any of these, a thing of substance, of *things*. It was land, timber, game, cattle, soil, grass, and minerals. It was not an idea or an institution, but it was substance on which these broke and reformed.

Each of the revolutions shook off some impediment, lifted some burden that the old order had tolerated. The Renaissance emancipated the human mind and set it free to range the universe. The Reformation freed many men from the thraldom of an authoritarian church institution. The scientific and industrial revolution lifted the burden of human labor and made effort more productive. It took the harness off the human horse and put it on inanimate horsepower. The democratic revolution gave men the privilege of participating in the shaping of their politics and government. The frontier had some part in all these emancipations. It enlarged the field in which the human mind could operate, enabled men to make rendezvous with new stars. It reinforced the worth of the individual which Martin Luther contended for in religion. It furnished an abundance of things for men to buy and sell, and for science and the wheels of industry to work on. It was in the wilderness, on the frontiers, that men found nature working with them to throw off the shackles of political domination and reshape governments to their own liking through their own acts. The frontier served as the matrix of the modern world; it furnished the setting, supplied the physical substance, and paid the freight on almost anything belonging to human freedom, and on much that belonged to human welfare. It made modern dynamism possible and profitable. Without it Europe could not have been the dynamic society it was from 1500 to the present time.

In studying the various aspects of modern dynamism, it is necessary to bear in mind that we are examining a social phenomenon which resulted largely from the introduction of a new ingredient into the historical stew. It is important to remember that a stew is a blended composite of many things, and that each affects all the others. Our business now is to examine the effects that the frontier ingredient had on what was already present, such institutions of the old order as the church and the state.

A stew, though containing many elements, is usually dominated by one. This principal ingredient takes possession, as it were, and goes off in its own direction, carying all the mixed flavors in its train, dominating and giving character to the whole. Modern civilization is just such a stew, and though it has many ingredients and flavors, its salient potency is due to its dynamic quality, its flashing vitality, its amazing energy which has led it to the ends of the earth. Whence came this energy, this primary force? If we can answer this question, we can come close to discovering the peculiar genius of the age. My answer is that the energy of the people of the Metropolis was a response to the stimuli of the material wealth of the frontier, wealth which not only affected everything present in the society, but nourished the energy that sought it. The motor that converted this latent energy into activity was the desire of men to appropriate the wealth and adapt it to their own uses. The combination of frontier wealth and metropolitan desire to have it carried modern civilization in the direction of materialism and determined the specialized character of the age. Inherent in the combination was the dynamic quality of which we speak. The dynamics grew out of the simple fact that the people with their desires were in one place and the things desired were in another. In bringing them together, the idea was to *go* and to stand not on the order. In the *going* dynamism was implicit and inevitable.

Our first task is to show how the frontier was related to certain institutions with which it has not ordinarily been associated. Our second task is to follow it as a specializer which demanded new institutions suited to its special needs. In the first instance we shall deal with its effects on the church and the rise of the absolute monarchs in Europe. In the second, we shall turn from men to Things, and show how they were related to the commercial and industrial revolution and to the rise of the modern financial order of capitalism.

The question of the extent to which the frontiers affected religious practices and church organization in the modern age cannot be answered until much research is done. The discussion here will be limited to one phase of religious development which, without doubt, is dynamic in character. The missionary movement is dynamics operating in the field of religion. Paul, the Apostle, furnished an impetus to it when he urged his hearers to go preach the gospel to all creatures. When the frontiers were opened, the missionaries had about done their job; they had run out of nations. Europe had become Christendom, and if every individual had not been converted, all had at least received an invitation to confess or to migrate. Luther introduced, or gave impetus to, the divisive forces with the result that Christendom split into rival camps and entered into a series of religious wars which plagued Europe for more than a century. During this time many factions that found life intolerable in Europe set off to the frontiers. Each faction carried with it the idea of extending the blessings of a particular Christian creed to such natives as might be found. A congeries of "new nations" appeared to the missionaries, who — as later history shows — were not slow in moving out into the untouched fields. The Protestants in North America talked sternly to uncomprehending Indians about their soul salvation, talked with the Bible in one hand and a rifle in the other. The Quakers at one time took over the whole Indian policy of the United States, with results which were often amusing, sometimes tragic, and always irritating to hard frontiersmen who had their own notions about dealing with the red men. The Catholics in Mexico and South America lighted their candles on old Indian altars and wrote lengthy reports to their superiors reflecting their dangers, devotions, and hopes. Several of the mendicant orders which had been established before the discoveries took up the task of carrying on the missionary work. Among these were the Franciscans, Dominicans, Carmelites, and Augustinians. The Jesuit order was established by Ignatius Loyola in 1534, and with its rigid discipline and military organization was well adapted to the frontier missionary task which it undertook with great zeal. The Pope took notice of the frontier problem and on September 6, 1493, Alexander VI issued the bull, *Dudum siguidem omnes,* in which he called attention to the need for missionary effort in order that occupation of the new country might have justification. The total effect of this opportunity to expand the dominion of God must have been enormous. And the effects were not limited to those who were converted, but reached back into the metropolitan center and altered the character of the institutions there. For example, the spiritual business in the New World was sufficient to lead Gregory XV to create the *Congregatio de propaganda fide* on June 22, 1622, consisting originally of thirteen cardinals. Under its auspices colleges of *Propaganda Fide* (Propagation of the Faith) were set up in Rome and in many of the overseas colonies for the training of missionaries who were to work in the heathen lands.

The relation of the frontiers to the emergence of the modern national states, and to the supremacy of the monarch within the state, is another subject which awaits investigation. We do know that the national states were not far advanced when the discoveries were made. Spain had achieved some unity through the union of Castile and Aragon. France had not progressed far; England and Scotland were separate kingdoms. Germany and Italy had not begun unification. Everywhere monarchs were struggling for supremacy with their feudal lords. It is significant that the first states to emerge as strong national powers were those that had colonial empires, that is, frontiers in the new lands. We do know that this royal drive toward national unity and a centralized government was a dynamic thing, depending on work and war — on getting things done. The king was playing a tough game with a set of nobles who were contesting every step he made. The church was sometimes friendly, sometimes antagonistic, depending on the interest of the church politicians. Protestantism favored the new nationalism, but Catholicism was usually opposed with the result that its influence on national history tended to diminish as the modern nations gained power.

In this contest of forces, where did the frontier throw its weight? Did it serve to enhance the power of the king and enable him to become absolute or did it act on behalf of the nobles? It seems obvious that frontier possessions increased both the power and the prestige of the king. The new territories, wherever they might be, belonged without question to the sovereign.[2] His claim to them was far better than the claim any feudal lord might assert. Moreover, such possessions increased the kingly prerogative by requiring him to exercise it in a realm where no other could act. First, the frontier increased the king's wealth, notably in the case of Spain where the sovereign demanded usually a fifth of the American treasure, and if hard pressed he took more. This wealth was very useful to the king in paying professional soldiers who were his bulwark against local disturbers; it enabled him to pay the

---

[2] Viola F. Barnes writes, "Colonial charters carried to America the basic conception in English land law of the time, that the king was the ultimate owner of all the lands he ruled and the only person who was always lord and never tenant." See Viola F. Barnes, "Land Tenure in English Colonial Charters of the Seventeenth Century," in *Essays in Colonial History Presented to Charles McLean Andrews by His Students* (New Haven: Yale University Press, 1931), p. 4.

national debt and gave him the wherewithal to launch other frontier ventures and prosecute foreign wars.[3]

The possession of the frontiers probably added more to the king's prestige than it did to his wealth. The mere fact that he had such extensive claims to territory, however worthless or expensive it might be, inevitably lent glamor to him. He found himself loaded with grave new responsibilities which required the deliberation of the best minds. He and his advisers had to decide what policies should be followed in India, in the Americas, in the South Seas; and the necessity of making such decisions, dealing with global affairs, must have developed latent administrative and executive powers, and called for a bureaucracy that headed up in the king. The constant exercise of such powers gave the king and his ministers confidence in their ability to rule.

It took bold men to go to the frontiers, and if they returned successful, they were of importance. The best evidence of their importance was an audience with the king, and they were content with nothing less. They looked to the court for their support, for titles and preferment. They had been about the king's business, and so far as they were concerned, the old feudal lords would have perished from neglect. Where was the feudal lord that would bring the king the ready cash that Cortez brought to Charles V, that Francis Drake brought to Elizabeth, or that William Phipps brought to the court of James II? Kings, being human, were always glad to see these frontier roughnecks come in, and despite their manners did everything possible to make gentlemen of them. If, as Keynes says, enterprise was afoot at this time, the frontier afforded the stimulus and made the prize awards.

Often in the study of frontier processes we find in the United States a clear example of what we are discussing, and to it we

---

[3] For a discussion of the influence of American treasure on the Spanish sovereign, see Earl J. Hamilton, *American Treasure and the Price Revolution in Spain, 1501–1650* (Cambridge: Harvard University Press, 1934).

John Maynard Keynes states that Elizabeth paid the entire national debt of England with her share of the booty brought in by Drake, and that she had a considerable sum left. See John Maynard Keynes, *A Treatise on Money* (New York: Harcourt, Brace & Co., 1930), vol. II, pp. 156–57.

turn to see whether the frontier favored or hindered the growth of a centralized government. When the thirteen colonies freed themselves from England, each colony considered itself a sovereign state, and the idea of a strong centralized government was almost as repugnant to these little commonwealths as it was to the feudal powers of Europe. It so happened, however, that the new "nation" came into possession of extensive territory lying beyond the borders of the thirteen states, between the Appalachian mountain chain and the Mississippi River, constituting the American frontier.[4]

The possession of this extensive domain probably did more to strengthen the central government in its earlier and weaker days than any other single factor. It gave the central government an exclusive function, one that could not be disputed by any state. The separate states might resent, and even block, federal action, but not one of them could perform the function it vetoed. All the states had an undivided interest in the frontier, and since it was an indivisible interest, action could come only through common consent as represented in the central government. The frontier offered no opportunity for any state to aggrandize itself by building up its power beyond its own borders; the frontier aggrandized the central government only.

In time new states were carved from the frontier territory and entered the Union as equal partners. They did not come, however, with quite the separatist attitude held by the original thirteen. The central government was the creature and creation of the original thirteen, but the new states were themselves the creatures of the central government. Not one of the thirty-five new states, with the possible exception of Texas, entertained the idea that it could stand alone, or that it was more important than the government that created it. There was often some murmuring about states' rights, but the talk was characterized by doubt and lack of assurance.

If the possession of the frontier strengthened the hand of the central government in the United States, it must have likewise

---

4 The influence of frontier land on the formation of a strong national government is indicated by the fact that the states having claims voluntarily relinquished them, and those who had no claims refused to agree to the Articles of Confederation until the lands were given up.

strengthened the sovereigns in England, in France, and in Spain. The fact that the European nations' frontiers lay overseas confuses the problem but does not change its character. And so it appears that in the early period the frontiers everywhere added strength and prestige to the central governments, at the expense of the feudal lords and feudal states in Europe and at the expense of the separate states in the American Republic. In the next section we will follow the method used by the sovereign in disposing of the acquisitions.

2. *The Vertical Pulsation of Wealth*

In this section we shall be concerned with one of the strangest phenomena in modern history, one that goes far in explaining the dynamic character of the Frontier Age. The situation which gave rise to the phenomenon was the acquisition by the sovereigns of Europe of all the real estate in three new continents and a large part of a fourth, and the subsequent distribution of that landed property to the people of the Western World. This vast acquisition and distribution of land would probably make any age in which it occurred dynamic; and, when we come to consider the singular manner in which the distribution was made, we gain an insight into the nature of some very important modern institutions designed to serve the society on such an occasion. Perhaps we can see that these institutions are closely tied in with the unique circumstances attending the acquisition and distribution of so much land.

In examining the distribution it is well for us to think of property in motion, flowing from one owner to another. Of course, where land is concerned it is ownership, titles and deeds that are in motion, and not the land itself. We are accustomed to thinking of wealth as in motion, and we say it "circulates," meaning that it moves from hand to hand among the people of a society. For the present purpose it will be convenient to call this the *horizontal* motion of wealth. It is that other motion of wealth which claims our attention, the *vertical* movement which has not been taken much into account by economists or historians. It is this vertical motion of wealth,

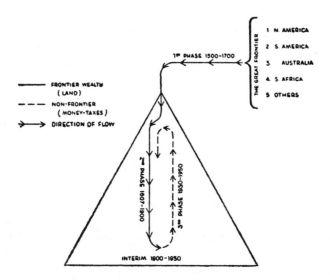

THE VERTICAL FLOW OF WEALTH IN THE WESTERN WORLD
AFTER 1500

1st phase. Acquisition by sovereign — 1500–1700

2d phase. Dispersion by sovereign to the people — 1607–1900
        Interim — 1900–1930

3d phase. Acquisition by sovereign from the people — 1930–1950

The triangle represents the modern state with frontier possessions.
The sovereign at the apex represents the government. The solid line
indicates the flow of frontier wealth, mainly land, and the arrows the
direction. The broken line represents the situation since the world
depression when the sovereign began to take wealth in the form of
money or taxes.

as represented in land, that accounts for the strange phenomenon alluded to above.

Three factors are involved in this vertical motion, and they
are land as the rough equivalent of wealth, government as the
sovereign representative within the state, and the people as
private individuals. It seems that throughout the modern age,
and perhaps in other periods as well, property has moved pre-

dominantly in one vertical direction as distinguished from its horizontal or circulatory movement. It has either moved upward from the people to the sovereign or downward from the sovereign to the people. In other words, there has been something resembling a pulsation of wealth vertically between the public authority and the people as well as the circulation among the people.

This vertical motion of land or wealth in the period under consideration has gone through three phases. In the first phase, extending from 1500 to about 1700, the land was flowing out of the frontier into the hands of the European sovereigns. In the second phase, beginning about 1607 and lasting down to about 1900, this same land was in motion from the various sovereigns to the people. In the third phase, which is the present, wealth, though not in the form of land, is flowing from the people to the sovereigns. Each phase is overlapped by the one that follows and finally eclipses it. This pulsation has gone on in this manner and about on this schedule in all nations of the Western World which held large frontier areas and in all nations formed in frontier regions. Despite the universality of the phenomenon, it is in its first two phases unique.

It was the exceptional manner in which the European sovereigns acquired the Great Frontier that enabled this rhythm of wealth to get under way. Before 1500 property in the form of land had little movement horizontally from hand to hand or in a vertical direction. Such institutions as primogeniture and entail were designed to keep property out of motion. The kings were not yet powerful, and were struggling with the emperor, the pope, and their own nobles for supremacy and were uncertain of the outcome. Then the kings received on exceptional terms a windfall of land from the Great Frontier, an advantage which none of the others had. Up to that time the scales had been fairly well balanced among the contestants, but when the discoverers threw three new continents and a large part of a fourth into the kings' side of the balance, the results were not long in doubt. The kings marched straight on to absolutism over their opponents, and it so happened that they reached the high point of their power at about the time their undisputed possession of the frontier regions was at its zenith. In the seventeenth century the Great Frontier was a vast royal domain in the hands of the kings of Europe.

Lest some reader may think that history repeats itself, and that some basic law is about to be drawn up on the dynamics of wealth, it should be remembered that the acquisition of this extensive royal domain was a windfall of the first magnitude, unusual in every way. First, the kings did not get this land by taking it away from their subjects or their neighbors. It did not come to them vertically to create ill will among those who lost it, nor did it come by war with neighbors. It came horizontally, sideways, from the outside, and therefore its royal acquisition created no offense domestically and not too much among immediate neighbors. This meant that the lucky monarchs received the land under the very best auspices, but since they got all such land in the world such favorable auspices cannot be hoped for again. Therefore, the first phase, in which the sovereign acquired his royal domain, is not likely to be duplicated, nor for that matter the second.

The second phase (1607–1900), involving the disposition of the royal domain, was directly dependent on the first phase and would have been impossible without it. Having all this rich land, the king had to decide what he should do with it. Since he could not possibly use all of it himself, he had several choices as to its disposition. He could give it to the emperor, to the pope, or to his nobles, but these were his old enemies, and he would have been a fool to strengthen them in this manner. Then there were the people, to whom he could give the land in the hope that they would work it and give him a part of the proceeds so that he could hold his advantage over his powerful opponents. It would no doubt be to the king's credit, especially in a democracy, if we could say that he decided on a rational basis to divide the royal domain with his little people and give them a chance they had never had before. There is no evidence to show that any king made any such calculated decision, but as things turned out the little people wound up with the major portion of the former royal domain in their hands anyhow. Though the king might make large grants to the nobles, to the discoverers, to the chartered companies, and he did all of these, the nature of the land was such that it could only be developed and made to pay through a lot of hard work; and of the willingness to work it seems the little people had a virtual monopoly. At any rate the sovereign began to alienate the frontier land and it began to drift down into the hands of the people, leaving the church and the emperor out of it, and the nobility only feebly and temporarily represented. This was the second phase, the long phase, in the vertical movement of wealth.

Since this period of descent lasted for the three important centuries, from 1600 to 1900, we need to examine the influence the vertical flow of wealth may have had on the sovereigns who distributed it, on the individuals who received it, and on the institutions devised to facilitate the process. Because we are dealing here with a gigantic movement of wealth, we shall be involved in consideration of economic practices and theories.

The first thing to note is the easy terms on which the sovereign set the frontier property flowing. He never exacted more than a token price, and in general he gave the land without price to those who were willing to run and cry out for it. In giving property in this manner, the sovereign furnished many individuals a stake, what Damon Runyon called a *taw*, enabling them to enter into the capitalistic game and plump for more. If the player lost his taw, the generous sovereign would give him another so that he could continue playing. The wealth was falling gently all around, like the pennies from heaven in the song, and the only thing the individual needed to do to get a share was to turn his economic umbrella upside down. As for the sovereign, he put the broad foundation under the bourgeois class, of whom he was to hear more.

In its vertical descent from the sovereign to the people the land passed through a twilight zone giving rise to a very curious process of acquiring property and to some strange antics on the part of those who got it. In this twilight zone the title to the property still rested with the sovereign, but the property was "claimed" by the individual. The claim endured until the necessary legal steps could be taken alienating the land from the sovereign and making it the private possession of the individual. The word *claim* has become so embedded in American phrase as to have lost the charm and excitement of its original meaning. It had great vogue from the time the European discoverers drove the first stake and raised the first flag in the New World until the homesteader drove the last peg on the last free quarter section. The practice of claiming began with kings and was taken up by the people; and in the United States during the last two centuries, claims were so numerous and merchantable as to serve as a medium of exchange. There were land claims, silver claims, gold claims, timber claims, grass claims, and water claims. As used on the frontier, a claim was not a title, but was the nearest thing to a title, marking a stage in the transfer of public or royal property into private hands. The right and the privilege of claim was a broad one, applied to many things besides land and water. The bee tree was claimed by the man who found and marked it, the deer by the man whose bullet brought it down, the maverick by the man who roped and branded it. In every case an individual act of volition, marking, branding, driving a stake, proclaiming in some way that the property was no longer in the public domain, was required.

The derivation of the word "claim" is not without interest because in its wide use on the frontier it reverted to its ancient meaning. In Middle English it was *claimen,* from Old French, *clamer,* which is related to Latin *clamare,* meaning to cry out or call. This for the verb. The noun, as in mining claim or land claim, has as its first meaning "a demand of a right or supposed right; a calling on another for something due or supposed to be due." The obsolete meaning of the noun is "a loud call; a shout." This ancient meaning was resurrected on the frontier when some man, after a stiff race or a search, drove down a stake and shouted to all the world, *"This is mine!"* All down the ages, for four centuries, the wild call of possession rang across the seas, first in the name of the monarch and later in the name of the people. Through the forests, along the rushing rivers, reverberating from the cliffs that concealed the minerals, rolling over the prairies and plains to the horizon it rose and fell as men rushed from the centers of civilization, running a race in which at the end the runners proclaimed a prize. The word "proclaim," more significant than the shorter form, means *to cry out before*. It comes from *pro,* meaning before or forward, and *clamare,* to call or cry out. Hence property was acquired by crying out before. Thus it was that, through running and proclaiming, wealth which had been owned by no European, king or man, became royal and then private and capitalistic through acts of appropriation, giving rise to the most extreme and undiluted form of dynamic individualism that the world has yet seen in civilized man. It was only during the period of the open frontier that men could come into possession of real wealth on such easy terms, by running, squatting, pre-empting, and crying out. It was the method used in the gold rush to California in 1849 and in the Oklahoma land rush of 1889 and 1893.

The following passage from a recent book describes the manner in which a quarter-section of land was obtained in the Oklahoma rush to the Cherokee Strip in 1893. I myself remember the excitement incident to this rush that ran throughout the community of West Texas in which I lived. The story is told by Billy McGinty, one of the participants: [5]

> I've seen many a danged thing happen in Oklahoma. . . . But, nothing, nowhere, compares with that big stampede back there in '93 — a thousand pawing, bellowing humans tearing out at the pop of a gun to lay claim to six hundred million acres. In all my days of riding, I never rode harder and for less than I did in that one hour.
>
> . . . I reckon there's no sound I hear louder than that of the smashing wheels and the pounding hoofs of that "git-there-first" race into the Cherokee Strip. . . .
>
> *September sixteenth is the day. . . .*
>
> I had already slipped over into the Strip and picked out the place I aimed to file on. A hundred and sixty acres on the bank of Camp Creek; land sloping down so pretty you could run furrows . . . smooth and straight as . . . ribbons. . . . I'd sow seed and reap money. Then I'd find me a spry girl and raise myself a crop of kids on that stretch. . . .
>
> Day of the Run, I beat the roosters up. . . . By eight o'clock, four hours till starting time, men and horses were packed in so close lightning couldn't have cut them loose. . . .

[5] Billy McGinty, "Plow Fever," in Harold Preece, *Living Pioneers* (New York: World Publishing Company, 1952), pp. 190–204, *passim.*

Behind the saddles were the wheels; five miles of 'em waiting to tear out into that Promised Land. . . . I saw every contraption that's rolled since Noah put rubber tires on the Ark. . . .

Row after row of old buckboards . . . were loaded with lank-looking hillbilly families from Arkansas and Missouri. Flocks of young 'uns, from toddlers in diapers to boys . . . sprouting their first fuzz, peeped over the sides. Heavy democrat wagons were loaded with plows and seeds and drouth-blistered old farmers who would stake out hell for a chunk of land. . . .

Worn-out surreys and victorias rested on their tired wheels with their worn-out drivers. . . . .

Light spring wagons that needed just one horse . . . were lined up alongside buggies new-greased in the axles . . .

But it was now eleven o'clock and . . . you couldn't hear yourself think. The riders were being pushed by the wheels trying to move nearer the line. The soldiers on guard bawled at us horsemen. . . .

Men cursed and snarled at each other like dogs. . . .

Eleven forty-five. Our horses were pawing and pitching as the wheels crowded close to their hoofs. . . . .

Eleven fifty. Ten minutes until hell would break. . . .

Eleven fifty-nine. And now the talk was like the buzz of wild bees starting to swarm, as the official starter stepped on the line. He had his watch in one hand and his gun in the other. . . .

He fired one shot in the air. Wheels cracked! Whips popped! Hoofs thundered! The Run was on.

. . . Horses' hides were raw red from being whipped to make them run faster. Drivers were standing up in wagons and buggies, lashing their own teams and those of other men when they crowded too close. . . . Just before we reached the creek, I jumped off at the stretch I had picked out.

I grabbed rocks and sticks to mark off my hundred and sixty. . . . I cut a branch from a cottonwood and stuck my bandanna on it. For the law said you had to put up some kind of a banner when you had finished staking a place. . . .

Then I stood up and looked out over that first piece of ground that I had ever called my own. . . .

"You're somebody now, Billy," I said to myself. "You got the finest horse, and you staked the finest claim. You outrode 'em all and, by thunder, you'll outfarm 'em all."

Billy was so absorbed in the immediate tasks that it was four o'clock before he looked at his watch. "Four hours since the start of the Run," he said, "and I'd seen calves take more time to get birthed than a country."

Billy McGinty lost his land to a claim jumper, but that is not the important matter. The important thing is that this run is the last dramatic episode in the long story of the dispersion of frontier land. Today the idea of getting title to a valuable block of real estate by outrunning other people to it seems absurd, yet for three hundred years valuable property could be and was acquired in that way in all the continents of the Great Frontier.

If experts were assigned the task of framing a set of economic institutions that would be appropriate and useful to a society in which the sovereign was sifting an avalanche of wealth down on a people, such a society as Billy McGinty represents, they could not do much better than adopt the institutions and practices that came into use during the three centuries of frontier land dispersion. Their first task would be to set up a general economic system suitable to the handling of an ever-increasing, continuously augmenting volume of wealth. Capitalism is just such a system, doing best in an expanding economy, so the real experts tell us.

In such a situation free competition is an acceptable method of moving property horizontally, of letting it circulate among the people. The property is coming down so fast and on such easy terms from above as to make squeamishness about how it is handled seem picayunish. Regulations are unnecessary, and under the circumstances could not be enforced. Actually, these same circumstances affected the character of competition, made it much less severe than it would be, and is, in a closed society. In appropriating public property, that which was coming vertically, men competed in quite a different manner than they do when engaged in taking property away from one another. In taking wealth from the frontier, they were not depriving another individual of it. They were acting on parallel lines as in a quarter dash, but they were not blocking and tackling one another. There were no personal opponents. The process is illustrated in the Oklahoma land rush where men lined up and set out for a quarter-section, each man bent on taking from the government. Once the stakes were driven down on the claim, the situation changed and the claimant was ready to trade and barter and get the better of his fellow man. In taking from the government there was a good deal of co-operation mingled with a very special kind of competition noted for its mildness.

As long as wealth was falling from above, competition could go on among individuals without resulting in monopoly. Competition and luck would give some men more than others, but no man and no group of men could establish a monopoly in land as long as the sovereign was able to keep up the free or nearly free dispersion. The frontier always had something for him who had been crowded out by a competitor. Therefore free competition did not need to be curbed on the charge that it led to monopoly. In fact, it was a situation in which nobody need be restrained, and this led to the ready acceptance of the logical economic philosophy of laissez faire.

Once the vertical descent of property ceased, as it did with the closing of the frontier, the whole economic system began to be transformed. The only manner in which property could be obtained now was through competition, for the only property in motion was that moving horizontally among individuals. The government or sovereign could no longer sweeten the game or provide a stake for the losers. Therefore competition could and did proceed toward monopoly, leading to the demand that competition be curbed, monopoly forbidden, and laissez faire abandoned. Thus it appears that the experts would find that the appropriate economic system for a society in which the sovereign was continuously dispersing wealth among the people would be that system which prevailed when the Great Frontier was being dispersed.

It would be appropriate at this place to let the experts set up the sort of government that should accompany the economic system that prevailed during the long phase of land dispersion just described. But before doing that, it would be best to look at the third phase in the pulsation of wealth. At this point one general observation may be pertinent, and that is that during such a dispersion the whole tendency of government would be toward liberalism. How could it be otherwise with a sovereign or sovereigns engaged in distributing on the most liberal terms to all comers an estate capable of being cut into eighty million 160-acre homesteads? The mere act of itself would be liberalism, not only in the economic sense, but in the broadest meaning of that term. Democracy as it developed in the frontier countries was merely an extreme form of the liberal movement induced in the Metropolis and out by the dispersion.

With the closing of the Great Frontier about 1900 the vertical flow of property from the sovereign to the people ceased for the simple reason that the sovereign was bankrupt. The monarchs of Europe had given away the royal domain, and the republics and democracies had given away the public domain. They still had scraps of marginal land, but nothing comparable to what they had when the distribution began. To make the case extreme in order to make it clear, we may say that by 1900 the people had everything and the sovereign nothing he could call his own. The long phase in the vertical flow of property had ended and the stage was set for the third phase, the one we are now in, when property is flowing from the people to the sovereign in ever-increasing volume.

There is an instant of pause when a pendulum reaches the limit of its arc and starts back, and so with the pulsation of wealth. The pause lasted about a generation, from 1900 to 1930. Through momentum, property was circulating, and through competition it was collecting in fewer and fewer hands to create private monopoly, but there was little vertical motion in either direction. It took a cataclysm to start the vertical motion again, to start property flowing the only way it could flow vertically, and that was from the people to the sovereign. If the sovereign were taking back the land he gave, the picture would be clear enough. As yet he is not taking the land, but he is taking its equivalent in money.

This reverse flow, unlike the former one, does not proceed on a voluntary basis, not by any means. Though the sovereign, from the absolute monarch to the most liberal democracy, volunteered to give to the people, the people have been reluctant to give to the sovereign. Therefore, a new element, that of compulsion, has entered into the present vertical movement of wealth upwards. Compulsion is the negation of liberty, and if carried far enough will destroy it. Throughout the frontier phase men were *permitted* to receive, to claim; now they are *compelled* to give. Men were willing to compete in acquiring property, but they have never been known to compete in giving it up, and certainly they could never establish a private monopoly by doing so. Through constant acquisition they could and did establish monopoly, but through compulsory loss they will lose that which they would monopolize. Thus it would seem that competition and monopoly may flourish in that stage of society which exists when the sovereign is distributing a great treasure, such as the frontier was, on a free and unrestrained basis, letting it fall vertically.

Political democracy can easily exist in a society where all men are freely receiving because all men are favorable to that process. There is no need for compulsion or force. But all men are not in favor of giving, or of a sovereign that takes. To the extent that the sovereign takes, to that extent he must use force, and to that extent the old democratic principle is not operative. The sovereign today maintains a semblance of democracy only because he takes from the few, and what he takes he distributes to the many. He starts property *circulating* vertically rather than flowing upward into his hands to become static. The many are willing to support the sovereign on condition that they receive a part of what is taken, and since the many have the vote, the sovereign is able to carry out the new program under the guise of democracy.[6]

What changes most when the sovereign gets down seriously to the business of taking is the attitude of the people, and especially of those who are required to give. They were quite willing to co-operate when the government was giving them large bonuses, making them rich. They admired its tolerance and generosity and forgave its inefficiencies. But when the sov-

---

[6] It is clear that if the sovereign kept the property taken, he would become absolute. By redistributing it he prevents private monopoly, bolsters capitalism, and enables a modified form of competition to continue.

ereign reversed his policy of giving and began taking, the people reversed their attitude too. They no longer co-operate but resist, and this resistance makes it necessary for the sovereign to resort to compulsion hitherto unnecessary. The government therefore becomes less democratic, in the nineteenth-century meaning of the term.

The present-day attitude of the individual is that of covering up, concealing, and siphoning off his wealth through trusts and donations — anything to prevent the government from taking it. The contrasting attitudes in the two phases of property motion might be represented by a sculptor or cartoonist who would create two figures, one representing the *receiving* man of the frontier era and the other the *giving* man of the present and future. The first figure, standing in the presence of a benign sovereign, would be eager with an outstretched hand, and would suggest a character possessing aggressiveness, independence, and ingenuity. To him the future is bright and the world is a milk-filled coconut. But when the table is turned, and the sovereign begins to take, the same figure assumes a different mien. Is his hand bearing a gift extended, does he shove to be first, does he scheme to get the better of his fellows in giving? What strange questions these are! What a strange world we would have if men acted in this way, if human nature went into reverse along with the reverse flow of property. Since human nature does not yet work in reverse, it is left to the reader to imagine the attitude of the second figure the sculptor or cartoonist would create.

The idea of man exercising the old attributes of initiative and aggressiveness in giving is a most engaging one and offers a bold novelist an opportunity to try his hand at something new. If society were bent on giving, property would again be in motion and the society highly dynamic. Theoretically men could be just as eager, ingenious, and original in getting rid of property as they were in acquiring it. In the process of giving, competition could return, and men could gamble and take all sorts of chances for the thrill of losing. Uncle Sam, John Bull, and other sovereigns would be bug-eyed with astonishment at such a reversal in human nature as they watched the wealth they once distributed returning so easily into their hands. The novelist who undertakes to portray such a fanciful society must be a complete master of plausibility because the sympathy of his readers will not be with him.

Earlier in this book it was noted that the philosphers and psychiatrists are now concerned with the dilemma of the modern individual. There is talk about the lost individual, and some efforts are being made to find him, give him a compass, and to learn how he happened to be out without one. He may not be hopelessly lost, but he is confused, and his quandary may spring from the fact that he got caught by the backlash in the pulsation of wealth. The present-day middle-aged man came on the scene just before the reversal in the flow of property took place. He caught the tail end of the giving age and the beginning of the taking age, and his dilemma and frustration may spring from the fact that he has been whipsawed. Born into a world of claiming, proclaiming, squatting, and doing generally as he pleased, he was taught that his welfare could correspond roughly to his energy, industry, and intelligence. Now he finds that this is not so, and he feels that the sovereign which once enriched him is determined to impoverish him and that his impoverishment is proportional to that same energy, industry, and intelligence once so rewarding. The rules of the game were changed on him while he was in play; and he has not yet caught on and he by no means approves. His feeling is indicated by the following parody on the Gettysburg Address:

> One score and nineteen years ago, our fathers brought forth upon this nation a new tax, conceived in desperation and dedicated to the proposition that all men are fair game. Now we are engaged in a great mass of calculations, testing whether that taxpayer or any taxpayer so confused and so impoverished can long endure. . . . We have come to dedicate a large portion of our income to a final resting place with those who here spend their lives that they may spend our money. It is altogether anguish and torture that we should do this. But in a legal sense we cannot evade, we cannot cheat, we cannot underestimate this tax. . . .
>
> Our creditors will little note or long remember what we pay here, but the Bureau of Internal Revenue can never forget what we report here. It is for us, the taxpayers, rather to be devoted

here to the tax return which the Government has thus far so nobly spent. It is rather for us to be dedicated to the great task remaining before us — that from these vanished dollars we take increased devotion to the few remaining; . . . and that taxation of the people, by the Congress, for the Government shall not cause our solvency to perish.[7]

We are now prepared to return to the kind of government that accompanies the different phases of the pulsation of wealth. We have already noted that in the long phase of dispersion liberalism made constant progress, and that by the time the sovereigns had completed the dispersion of the Great Frontier all pretense at absolutism was gone. The people had all the property and were supreme. The government had become a mere agent with little or no wealth in its own right. If by a study of the pulsation of wealth during modern times, we should deduce a general law about government, the law would be as follows:

1. If the sovereign owns or controls all the property, during the period he holds it the government assumes an absolute form. This absolutism exists regardless of whether the government is monarchical, corporate, or communistic. There could be no democracy, no capitalism, no economic competition, and no private monopoly in this condition. This state of affairs existed in a peculiar manner among the absolute monarchs of Europe during the sixteenth and seventeenth centuries when they held vast royal domains on the Great Frontier. It has existed recently in the corporate states of Europe and in the communistic states of Russia.

2. If the sovereign for any reason begins to distribute the wealth in such a way that it falls into the hands of the people, as happened during the dispersal of the frontier, there goes along with this distribution such a relaxation of controls that absolutism fades away while capitalism rises, competition among individuals springs up, and a trend toward private monopoly begins. The freedom which is implied in all these activities means that by the time the public or royal property has passed into the hands of the people, the substance of absolutism will have disappeared, the sovereign will be bankrupt,

7 Condensed from *Chemical and Engineering News*, February 25, 1952.

and the people will be supreme. Liberalism or democracy is the political accompaniment of this situation, and it may be the inevitable accompaniment.

3. If all the property is in the hands of the people and the sovereign is bankrupt, then property becomes vertically static. It may circulate, but it has no vertical motion. Therefore a crisis impends. The crisis springs from the tendency of property in circulation to collect in a few hands as private monopoly. The sovereign has no choice in this crisis but to start the vertical flow of property, but since he is bankrupt, there is only one place he can obtain the property he would have move. The sovereign begins taking from the people. If he *keeps* what he takes, he soon becomes absolute, but if he *redistributes* what he takes, or a good part of it, thus starting property circulating vertically, a semblance of the democratic forms can be maintained. Thus it seems that the prevailing character of government as well as the prevailing economic institutions are closely related to the prevailing vertical motion of property. It also seems that if for any reason property ceases to move vertically, a crisis will ensue. It ceases to move vertically if it is all held by the sovereign, or by the people, or by private monopoly.

Critics may look askance at this theory of the dynamics of property as related to institutions and human attitudes, including individualism. They may be loath to admit that capitalism, competition, monopoly, liberalism, and democracy have all been as closely connected with the free flow of frontier land to the common people as I have indicated, and they can no doubt support their argument with evidence. So here is room for debate, but argument opposed to the theory becomes weaker as we proceed from the phase in which the government was giving to that in which it is collecting property for redistribution in order to create a mixed form of socialistic capitalism. And the counter argument becomes extremely difficult, if not hopeless, when all property is collected to become static in the hands of the sovereign who dictates its use. From this point the argument cannot proceed until the opposition answers this question: How can capitalism, competition, or democracy exist in a society where all property is held in one hand?

Thus far we have dealt primarily with the movement in

land in accounting for the dynamic quality of the modern age. In the following section we turn to movable wealth, showing the role of Things as distinguished from land in making the Age of the Frontier dynamic.

3. The Dynamic Effect of Things

When we turn from land to Things, we are dealing with what is movable, and here we can really think of the objects rather than the land in motion. In reference to modern America Samuel Strauss wrote an article for *The Atlantic Monthly*, entitled "Things Are in the Saddle." The author believed that many of our ideas and institutions are dependent on Things and on our system of making them. In the following passage where he speaks of industry, he speaks of it as a provider of Things, and what he says applies not only to the United States but also to Western civilization as well.

> If anything were to happen to industry, there would be first confusion and then decline in all our institutions; our great system of free education for the nation would wither, our organized charity would dry up . . . slums would become fever spots, our roads would fall into decay; more than all, our ideals of political authority would be a heap of jackstraw; we should hold the kind of government the Fathers gave us to be a broken reed.[8]

If only half of what the author says is true, Things are indeed in the saddle.

Certainly Things are more abundant in the modern age than they ever were before. They constitute the substance on which our so-called materialistic civilization is founded; they have enabled it to be materialistic, have made it so. They constituted an important portion of the new ingredient which the frontier added to modern Western civilization. It is the disproportionally large number of Things in relation to the number of people that accounts for prosperity.

The critic may point out that Things are nothing new to man, that he has always had them. True enough. But prior to the modern age man was not embarrassed by their quantity;

[8] Samuel Strauss, "Things Are in the Saddle," *The Atlantic Monthly*, November, 1924, p. 78.

he was often vexed by their scarcity. It is the overwhelming quantity of Things that gives to modern civilization a part of its special character.

Whence came this quantity, this surplus? Surely no one would contend that it came from the Metropolis. Western Europe was poor before the discoveries, and would have remained poor throughout the modern period had the Things of the Great Frontier not been made available there. In order to visualize the situation, let us imagine that all the Things of Western Europe at any given time are collected into one pile and all the Things of the Great Frontier are heaped in another, and then let us measure the size and the value of the two collections. The frontier pile would contain on the lowest estimate five times the amount of the land, more than fifteen times the amount of gold and silver, and the greater proportion of grain, fiber, timber, oil, coal, and base metals. To complete the picture, let us imagine all the Europeans gathered in one crowd, and all the inhabitants of the frontier gathered in another, at any time from 1500 to the present. The European crowd would be as great as its collection of material Things is small; and the frontier crowd would be as small as its collection of Things is great. It is as clear that the frontier furnished the Things as it is that the Metropolis supplied the people, and it was the quantity and richness of the frontier goods that set the metropolitan people off on quests which helped shape the ideas and the institutions of the modern world.[9]

Historians have spoken of the price revolution, the commercial revolution, and the industrial revolution as if they were unrelated phenomena of modern times. Their relation to one another becomes clear enough when we remember that they concern Things, how they were acquired, transported, and fabricated. The upheaval which gave each of these phenomena the honor of being called a revolution was due to some radical change in the *manner* of dealing with Things, which were the chief object of desire and the chief subject of action. Their abundance made the desire reasonable and the action rewarding.

[9] For a discussion of the relation of Things to the form of government, see David M. Potter, "Democracy and Abundance," *The Yale Review*, vol. XL, Spring, 1951, pp. 421–39.

The price revolution was a change in the relation between a relatively stable quantity of goods and services and the increasing quantity of gold and silver made available for their purchase. The commercial revolution is much simpler because it is related to the abundance of Things available. The way people reacted to this abundance was perfectly natural: they went after the Things which they could for the first time obtain and the result of their coming and doing was the commercial revolution.

The problem that confronted them was that of distance — for the frontier, with all its abundance, was not next door to Europe. It was three thousand miles to America, much farther to India and to Australia. The game in the forests of America had little effect on the menu cards of Europe until means could be found of transporting the meat, and so with all else. Moreover, the road to the frontier was a waterway, not a landway, and therefore transportation had to be by ships, making the commercial revolution maritime in character. Ships were redesigned for the open seas rather than for inland or offshore waters. When the English began to contest the supremacy of Spain, they built slim, fast vessels which could strike and get away. The evolution of ocean sailing vessels culminated in the nineteenth century with the clipper ships which were pulled by their bellying sails to all the ports of the world. For what? Because they had a big job, that of moving Things from the frontier to the Metropolis and exchanging them for other Things and people bound for the frontiers. This was the commercial revolution, a term used to designate a changed culture pattern necessary in transporting an abundance of commodities over great distances.

The bringing of abundance to the wharves of Europe was a preliminary step in an economic process which electrified the Metropolis and gave modern society a peculiar bent. At Cádiz, London, and Amsterdam, the ships unloaded hides, timber, hemp, cotton, tobacco — raw materials for food, clothing, and shelter. Something had to be done with all this abundance. Some of the Things were carried directly into the stores and put on the shelves for sale. The local citizens came trooping in to see the new strange goods, to chew the sugar cane from the West Indies, to pinch the snuff, to take away a golden twist of tobacco. Excitement ran along the street, into the houses, and the women came chattering to the market place to see "what the ships brought in." The shopkeeper who was fortunate enough to get a supply, found his place taking on a new life. He must build more shelves, hire an extra clerk, expand his building — and he was justified in doing it.

But much of what came in the ships was not ready to sell. The frontier furnished raw products mainly, and these had to be processed. They were carted off to warehouses, to await manufacture. The skins went to the tanneries to issue later as leather, robes, fur coats. The logs went to shipyards for masts and spars, or to woodworkers who needed lintels and frames for cathedral arches or cottage doors. The hemp was turned into rope for rigging ships and hanging criminals. Because Things had come, men had work to do. And the work followed the Things wherever they went, followed until they were consumed or finally ceased moving.

The influx of goods did not react immediately, at least not in a spectacular fashion, on the methods of fabrication. It takes time to change methods, and to change the psychology of craftsmen, but change was inevitable. All conditions favored the speeding up of manufacture, and finally the invention of machines. Every time the master looked at his stockpile, he was embarrassed by its growth, by a surplus of stuff inside and a growing clientele outside. For the first time in his life he had more business than he could attend to . The urge to expand, to employ clerks and workmen, to adopt improved methods was strong with him. His establishment ceased to be static; caught in the current of moving Things, it became dynamic.

This enlarged business opened up new vistas to the owner. Whereas before he had managed to make a living, but nothing to speak of above that, he now found himself with something left at the end of the year, a profit. Profit he expected little of under the old order, but now he found that by the exercise of initiative, by enterprise, he could have it. The more initiative, daring, and the more luck he had, the greater his surplus of money could be. His transformation from a conservative shopkeeper to an entrepreneur was fairly rapid, not rapid for the individual, but for the society. The individual became something of a gambler who backed his judgment in taking greater risks in the hope of greater gains. With the money he had accumulated by selling his surplus of goods, he bought more goods, sold to more customers, and made more profit. The dynamic businessman had begun his long climb to supremacy. By later standards he was still a small man, but he had learned the secret of converting the great surpluses of Things into profits by the process of widening his circle of customers.

Though the dynamic age is represented as receiving part of its impetus from Things, a consideration of it leads us inexorably to the subject of money. Money is such a dazzling symbol that it has often eclipsed in the public and scholarly mind what it represents. We like to think of money in motion, in circulation, as an important feature bearing directly on prosperity. Of far more importance to society is the fact that *Things are in motion*, passing from hand to hand to gratify men's desires and needs. The money is like a gauge on an engine which records what is going on, a measure of the force that is being exerted within. Unless property flows, money cannot move; but property can move and does move in the absence of money. Still, money of some sort is a convenience, and especially when Things are flowing in great quantity and over great distances as they began to do after the frontiers were opened. Therefore it need not surprise us that money took on added significance, underwent changes, and accelerated the dynamism which made it so necessary.

Let us look into the cash box of the embryo businessman of 1500. It would be small and inconspicuous, and one would have to be deep in the confidence of the shopkeeper to have a look at the few gold or silver coins hoarded against a day of need. If he made shoes, he exchanged them for beef, mutton, chicken, a cloth doublet, or a knife with which to cut leather. Such money as existed circulated through the hands of the big merchants, at the fairs and in the eastern trade, but the amount was small and the rate of movement extremely slow. In the life he had known, the shopkeeper found no great need for a medium of exchange.

It was not until the hypothetical shoemaker found a surplus of hides and leather on hand and a number of potential distant customers clamoring for footwear that he felt keenly the need of an equivalent, some symbol of small compass that would represent hides or shoes as the case might be. Fortunately for him, the frontier had already provided what he needed, a supply of gold and silver running a little way ahead of Things. Keller tells us that "between 1525 and 1825, a quantity of bullion was entered via Spain upon the markets of the world, which utterly dwarfed any former experience of the race." And as for the Spanish coins, he says that they "came really to flood the world, being found in China and Japan, the East Indies, Persia, Constantinople, Cairo, and Barbary." [10] This being true, some of these coins, more than he had been accustomed to having, remained in the shopkeeper's cash box at the end of the year, and were counted as profit. These coins became the center of his interest, the gauge of his welfare. Grudgingly he paid them out for leather and wages, eagerly he recovered them with something over from sales. He much preferred them over the payment in kind to which he had been accustomed.

His profits, real and prospective, gave him confidence, justified him in paying high rates of interest. Thus, money began to "circulate" more rapidly than it had before, circulating to keep pace with the movement of Things. The increased circulation plus the annual additions from the American mines furnished a sufficient quantity of exchange to carry the business on in the initial stages, but in time the hard money became inadequate and substitutes had to be devised. It is interesting to speculate on what would have happened in the realm of money if frontier gold and silver had not preceded frontier goods to Europe. We cannot assume that the goods would not have moved because gold and silver were not available. We must assume that some other medium of exchange would have been devised which would have served quite as

[10] A. G. Keller, *Colonization: A Study of the Founding of New Societies* (Boston and New York: Ginn & Co., 1908), pp. 203, 204.

well. Not to concede this is to say that men would not desire goods or find it possible to have them without giving an equivalent in gold and silver. The all but exclusive use of gold and silver as a medium of exchange appears as a frontier incident.[11]

The historical fact is that money became relatively so plentiful and assumed such an important role that the attitude toward it had to be changed. Medieval ethics taught that there was something evil about interest, but now interest became respectable, and no longer had to be bootlegged. Money on hand represented profit, and since it was the means of making more profit, it was worthy of its hire. Though the absolute amount had increased, the demand had by 1700 outrun the supply. There was never enough of it on the frontiers to balance the Things there, never enough for the chance-takers anxious to gamble for profit. Money therefore became an accepted merchantable commodity.

Money merchants sprang up to meet the demand. There had been bankers before, or rather money lenders, but their role became more important and they themselves more numerous. They had more to bank with, and there was no dearth of borrowers, for a spirit of risk-taking had seized Europe. The evolution and spread of banking is a clear index of the adoption of the profit motive expressed in terms of gold and silver or its equivalent. Those who merchandised in money became the nerve centers of the dawning capitalistic age.

Despite the increase in the amount of money, history reveals that there was not enough to move the commodities, which by the middle of the seventeenth century must have been running ahead of the increased quantity of coins. The bankers had to begin to adopt substitutes, supplementary money, so that there would be enough to go around. One of these substitutes, most

11 Looked at in long perspective the use of gold and silver as a medium of exchange appears as an episode in modern history. The bulk of the metals came from the frontier, were adequate for a time, became inadequate and have now been discarded. Their prominence rose and fell with the opening and closing of the frontier. For a fuller discussion of this view, see Walter Prescott Webb and John Francis Murphy, "The Precious Metals as a Medium of Exchange: A Frontier Incident," in Alceu A. Lima, Edgar McInnis, *et al.*, *Esayos sobre la historia del Nuevo Mundo* (Mexico, D.F.: Instituto Panamericano de Geografía e Historia, 1951), pp. 47 ff.

convenient in local trade, was payment by check. More convenient in foreign trade was the use of bills of exchange, with net differences on numerous transactions paid occasionally in gold or silver. Both checks and bills of exchange had the effect of increasing the money supply. These devices were most useful, but still inadequate to match the flow of Things. Still they indicate the direction toward which the frontier surplus of Things was carrying society. One more discovery the bankers and merchants had to make before they could set off on the high road to capitalism, and that was how to create money, not from gold and silver, but from Things used as collateral.[12]

4. The Rise of Capitalism

Capitalism is that culture complex which, whatever its origin, has grown to maturity with the practice of striving for profit. We have already seen how the flow of Things created a situation out of which it was possible and fairly easy for the judicious man to realize a profit, to turn toward capitalism. Let us now inquire into some special aspects of the frontier which conferred special favors on the profit-seeking class and aided it in rising to a dominant position in the society. So many people now want either to defend or condemn capitalism that some are hard pushed to believe that anyone can speak of it objectively. Moreover, to the modern man, profit seems so desirable, is so generally accepted as a motive of action, that he cannot without intellectual effort bring himself to believe that it was not always so. Yet the historians tell us that medieval society was not powered by this motive. Man does not strive long for the impossible, and the medieval man had such limited opportunity for profit as to cause him to seek other values primarily. He could see no sense in hunting a fortune where so few could find it, in figuring interest where there was so little to bear it and where opportunities were too few to

[12] No claim is made here that banking *originated* in response to frontier needs. The Medicis in Florence had a well-developed banking system which had grown up in connection with the eastern trade. The Fuggers of Augsburg dominated northern Europe, taking mortgages from monarchs, popes, and emperors. This was private banking. Public banking seems to have started in the second half of the seventeenth century.

justify the risk of assuming to pay it. The powerful dynamic of an expanded world had not yet issued its invitation to men to gamble with one another and with nature for prizes of unexampled magnitude.

Again it is unnecessary to argue that capitalism originated on the frontier. That capitalism had long existed in rudimentary form cannot be gainsaid, but we are here concerned with modern capitalism, which differs in degree and extent from prior forms. It may be pointed out that the beginning of this modern capitalism was contemporaneous with the youth of the frontier, and that its growth was unchecked throughout the developmental period of the frontier. This contemporaneity does not prove a connection or an interdependence, but it does establish a basis on which to look for a relationship. The view advanced here is that the frontier furnished the setting for and supplied the matrix from which capitalism grew. It furnished the substance with which capitalism works; it supplied the gold and silver which facilitated exchange; and it gave the room for that constant expansion which seems so necessary in a capitalistic economy.

Adam Smith, a respectable economist, had both the precious metals and the more precious Things in mind when he stated that the discovery of America and of the Cape of Good Hope passage to India "are the greatest and most important events in the history of mankind." "This statement," says Earl J. Hamilton, "may be — doubtless is — an exaggeration; but had he [Smith] spoken of the effect of these two events upon the origin of modern capitalism, one of the most important developments of history, his contention would have been incontrovertible." [13] It was this American treasure, and it alone, that reversed the long descent of prices, and sent them slanting upward to such heights as to constitute a revolution. It was out of the unevenness of the rise, giving an advantage to dealers in Things, that the capitalistic class arose to dominance. How this came about we will now examine.

The economists teach us that the three factors entering into the production of wealth are land, labor, and capital. Capital used in this sense applies to money, to machinery, and to

[13] Earl J. Hamilton, "American Treasure and the Rise of Capitalism (1500–1700)," *Economica*, November, 1929, p. 338.

stocks of goods. It is necessary for us to think not so much of money but of commodities, and think of them *in motion*, moving from one owner to another. And when we think of them in this way, we can see that the primary cause men had for moving them was, and is, to make a profit. The accumulation of profit results in capital, whether in the form of land, money, or Things. We might omit capital in the form of money as a category, considering it as a goal which men are trying to reach by selling what they have to sell; or, if we insist on retaining it in the narrow sense as applied to money, we will need four categories instead of three. Men then have four things which they sell:

1. The use of labor sells for wages.
2. The use of land sells for rent.
3. The use of money sells for interest.
4. Things sell for profit.

It should be noted that only in the last instance is there an outright sale carrying a complete title. In the first three cases it is only the *use* that is sold. It is true that both land and money can be sold outright, but when they are thus sold they become Things, bringing profit or loss rather than rent and interest. Apart from slavery, labor is not subject to transfer of ownership, but only the use of it can be bartered.

At some risk of not being followed, I shall consider the following three categories of wealth which men could use in producing profit:

1. The use of labor could be had in return for wages.
2. The use of land could be had in return for rent.
3. Things could be sold outright for profit.

This chapter opened with the observation to the effect that in the modern period Things are in the saddle. What I propose to show now is how in the general upset in prices due to the importation of American treasure, and to other frontier contributions, those who dealt in Things got an advantage over those who depended on income from land or from rent. Specifically, I will show that the major gain accrued on Things which came in increasing abundance from the frontiers for sale in the Metropolis.

The whole story can be put in a nutshell by saying that in the dislocation of prices after 1500, the price of Things *outran* the price of land use and the cost of labor. This means that the merchant class enjoyed the advantage of relatively cheap rent and low wages while selling their goods at profitable prices. It was those who dealt in Things that reaped profits sufficient to create capitalists. The question is: Who profited most, landlords, laborers, or businessmen? Though precise data are not available, such evidence as we have indicates that in England rents lagged far behind prices. The Knight, in Hales' *Discourse on the Common Weal of This Realm of England* (1549), asserted that landlords were becoming impoverished by the lag of rents, and moaned that "the most part of the landes of this Realme stand yet at the old Rent." [14] There were long leases on which rent could not be raised. "Consequently," says Hamilton, "the landowning class suffered a diminution of income." [15] Therefore, it was *not* landowners or rent-takers as a class who became capitalists.

In the case of wages the data are more abundant. In 1501 the index number of prices and wages in England stood at 95, with the period 1451–1500 as a base. By 1700 the price index had risen to 339, but the wage index stood at 233. This means that while prices had risen 256 per cent, wages had risen only 145 per cent. The situation was similar in France. In 1501 the index of prices was 113, and that of wages was 92. By 1700 prices had soared to 229, or 101 per cent, while wages rose to 125 or 35.8 per cent.[16] This means that during these two centuries actual wages had fallen in respect to prices, and that laborers were *not* to be the capitalists of the new age.

By elimination we have arrived at the door of those who benefited by the upheaval in the price structure. They were men who had Things to sell. The landlords were losing and the laborers were losing, but the third class, the entrepreneurs, were gaining. Hamilton says: "For a period of almost two

---

[14] Hamilton, "American Treasure and the Rise of Capitalism (1500–1700)," *Economica*, November, 1929, p. 350.

[15] *Loc. cit.*

[16] *Ibid.*, pp. 352–53.

hundred years English and French capitalists — and presumably those of other economically advanced countries — must have enjoyed incomes analogous to those American profiteers reaped from a similar divergence between prices and wages from 1916 to 1919." [17] Of the period from 1550 to 1650 John Maynard Keynes observes, "Never in the annals of the modern world has there existed so prolonged and so rich an opportunity for the business man, the speculator, and the profiteer. In these golden years modern capitalism was born." [18]

The way in which the merchant class gained an advantage out of this uneven situation is illustrated by Hamilton in a most interesting manner. In a hypothetical case he has a merchant sell a stock of goods in 1500 for £100,000. He assumes that the merchant has spent £60,000 for wages and £20,000 for rent, a total of £80,000. At the end of the transaction he finds himself with £20,000, or 25 per cent profit on his transaction. In 1600 a similar merchant produces the same amount of goods, but for them he must pay £250,000. Allowing for the increase in wages, his labor cost will now be £75,000; and assuming, incorrectly, that rents did not lag, he would pay £50,000 to landlords. His total cost would be £125,000, leaving him in the till £125,000. Whereas in the first case he realized 25 per cent on his turnover, in the second he realized 100 per cent. As Hamilton observes, "The lag of wages behind prices had quadrupled profits." [19]

The above illustration, and it is only an illustration, shows how the merchant and trading class stepped far out in front of labor and landlords to become capitalists. They got the windfall of the frontier and helped to inaugurate the dynamic age of which they were the heart, the age of capitalism. Says Hamilton:

> The windfalls thus received, along with the gains from the East India trade, furnished means to build up capital equipment, and the stupendous profits obtainable supplied an incen-

17 *Ibid.*, p. 355.

18 Keynes, *A Treatise on Money*, vol. II, p. 159.

19 Hamilton, "American Treasure and the Rise of Capitalism (1500–1700)," *Economica*, November, 1929, p. 356. (Hamilton makes no allowance for original cost of the merchandise. He must assume that it is included in one or both of the items of rent and wages.)

tive for the feverish pursuit of capitalistic enterprise. We find
. . . that during the seventeenth and latter part of the sixteenth
centuries England, France, and the Low Countries were seething
with such genuinely capitalistic phenomena as systematic mechanical invention, company formation, and speculation in the shares
of financial and trading concerns. The developments of this
period, accelerated and fructified by the important series of
mechanical inventions in the last half of the eighteenth century,
were a significant step in the direction of the modern factory
system, with the concomitant developments in commerce and
finance.[20]

The advantage gained by the dealers in Things, incident to
a dislocation of prices, was by no means the only benefit accru-
ing to this class at this time. Another factor relating to wages
contributed an additional increment toward converting the
merchants of the frontiers into capitalists of the Metropolis.
Because the frontiers lay overseas, and at a great distance, transportation was probably one of the biggest items of expense,
certainly a major factor in the cost of commodities laid down
in Europe. This was mainly water transportation, which is always less expensive than land transport. During the two centuries we are considering, the cheapness of water transportation was further accentuated because the wages of seamen were
lower than the wages of land laborers. We have already seen
that in the price rise of the two centuries, wages lagged behind
prices, giving a tremendous fillip to budding capitalists. Now
we find that the lag of sea labor was greater than that of land
labor. For example, in Andalusia seamen's wages actually fell
from 100 in 1500 to a low of 70 in 1530, and then climbed ir-
regularly and leveled off at about 190 in 1570. By contrast the
wages of landmen rose from 100 in 1500 to 450 by 1600, and
usually though not always were below prices. Let us assume
that in 1500 the wages on sea and on land were $1 a day. By
1550 the seaman would be getting $1.40, but the landman
would receive $1.90; by 1600 the seaman would be paid $1.75,
while the landman would be paid $4.50.[21]

20 *Ibid.*, p. 356.
21 *Ibid.*, p. 354, "Table of Index Numbers of Prices and wages of Landmen
and Seamen in Andalusia, 1503–1660." Hamilton points out that in addition

If the contention is true that most of the Things that were bought and sold, and certainly the *additional* things, came from the frontiers, and consequently from overseas, or even from the Orient, the cheapness of seamen's wages must have been reflected in the cost of overseas commodities laid down on the wharves of the Metropolis. It does not follow that this saving was passed on to the consumer or European purchaser unless merchants then were different from what they later became. The relatively high wages in the Metropolis enabled the merchant to price his imports just low enough to cause them to move; the difference he added to his profits. He must have received some benefit from using the least expensive forms of transport carried on by the cheapest of labor.

Thus far we have dealt with the cost of Things, either in Europe or in transit thither. We have said nothing about what they cost at the point of origin on the frontiers. This subject is so important in the rise of capitalism, and throws so much light on the contribution of the frontier to it, that it must be given a separate chapter, dealing with frontier windfalls.

---

to pay seamen received subsistence on shipboard, but this cannot account for the discrepancy between the respective increases. The low wages of seamen relative to landmen throws light on the practice of impressment which had historical consequences. Though the figures given here are for Andalusia from 1500 to 1660, they are probably roughly paralleled by those in other countries, and are doubtless typical of the frontier period down to the nineteenth century.

CHAPTER SIX

FRONTIER WINDFALLS AND MODERN
CAPITALISM

THOUGH the subject is still capitalism and its relation to Things, let us turn now to a factor in it that has not received much attention from either economists or historians. The subject is windfalls. A windfall is something that comes free and unexpected and of good import. During the war I lived a year at Oxford, and what with the shortage of fuel and the prevailing low temperature of the college quarters, I kept circulation going by walking past Christ Church, into Christ Church Meadows, making the circuit by the Cherwell where the unused college boats were moored to await better days, and thence among the great spreading trees to the lower exit. One winter night a great wind blew up to whip the trees and keep everyone indoors. Early the next morning, as I walked in Christ Church Meadows, I saw women and children and old men picking up the dead branches that had fallen from the trees and carrying them away in their arms to build a little brighter their small hearth fires. Here from the windfalls of the stormy night was fuel, unrationed and free. I recalled that Woodrow Wilson gave the origin of the word windfall, saying that in early days poor people were permitted to gather for fuel such wood and branches as might be blown from the lord's trees by the wind. Hence windfall came to mean a chance blessing, a bit of pure good luck. And there in Christ Church Meadows the age-old rite was being re-enacted in the old way.

The frontier was like a great tree constantly casting down on the people of Europe windfalls, benefits which exacted little more than the exertion of getting out early, finding, and carrying away the boon. Just as the windfall in the lord's forest made the peasant's fire brighter and his home more comfortable, so did the windfalls from the frontiers make the whole Metropolis a different place. As William Graham Sumner said, "The very greatest, but . . . least noticed significance of the discovery of America was the winning of a new continent for the laboring class." [1] In another connection, he said, "The adventurous voyagers who began to explore the outlying parts of the Earth in the fifteenth century thought little and cared less about the peasants and artisans at home; but it was they more than any others who were fighting for the fortunes of those classes in the future." [2]

1. The Nature of Windfalls

It is not my purpose here to contend that the whole frontier was of the nature of a windfall for the whole Metropolis; it is not necessary because that is the central theme of this book. I propose rather to give some details to illustrate the fact. The examples chosen lie mainly in the sixteenth and seventeenth centuries, during the time of the price revolution and the commercial revolution. The examples exhibit remarkable clarity in that period for the reason that the best windfalls go to the early comers, and these centuries were the morning hours of the modern age.

The windfalls of the frontier consisted of those commodities which came into the hands of the rising capitalistic class with one or more items of the ordinary cost of production partially or completely eliminated. We must remember that in the period from 1500 to 1700 Things were in the saddle, and it was the business of fetching them that caused the great commercial stir in Europe. We have already seen that the dealers in Things gained an advantage and moved along the road toward capitalism because of the low cost on the frontier, the uneven rise in prices in the Metropolis, and the low cost of transportation by sea. We are now concerned with what things cost at the frontier source and what they cost laid down in the Metropolis. It is at this point of origin that the theory of windfalls applies with particular force.

Leaving aside the land — the greatest of all the windfalls —

[1] William Graham Sumner, *Earth-Hunger and Other Essays*, p. 41.
[2] *Ibid.*, p. 41.

let us consider gold and silver, forest products, furs, and ambergris in a first category, and cattle raising and plantation crops in a second category. The reason for the two categories, separating primary and secondary windfalls, is important and will be developed later. The primary windfalls were those quickly come at, things that could be had with a minimum of investment and little preliminary work. The secondary windfalls involved a long time element of waiting, and often great expense, too great for the endurance of a distant and impatient investor. It was the primary windfalls that gave the impetus to capitalism in the sixteenth and seventeenth centuries and the secondary ones which kept capitalism going through the eighteenth and nineteenth centuries.

2. Primary Windfalls

The frontier treasure of gold and silver described earlier was the outstanding primary windfall, and its story has already been told. The metallurgist of nature laid the precious metals down in the new earth of the Americas, South Africa, Australia, and New Zealand, and in many cases — especially in the Americas — the natives had gathered them. Not even the alchemists' flimsy dreams were invested in them.

The furs that were gathered in Canada to found fortunes in Europe constituted a striking windfall because in producing furs many cost factors ordinarily present in the production of wealth were absent or negligible. There was no time element, no period of expensive waiting for the fur hunters. The animals had grown their pelts on their own time, without expense to anyone, and all the fur companies had to do was to harvest them. It was as if a farmer went into a forgotten field and found a crop of corn matured and ready for the harvest. It was better than that. It was as if the farmer found the corn on land that he did not own, in which he had no investment, where his expenses would begin with the gathering. Also, the fur company's labor cost was negligible because it tapped a cheap labor source in the Indians who gathered the furs. Finally, and this was true of all frontier commodities, transportation was largely by sea, and sea transport is the least expensive known. Thus in the production of furs all the cost factors were greatly reduced, with land cost completely absent.

The low cost of producing furs is illustrated in the history of the Hudson's Bay Company. The story of that company begins in the summer of 1656 when two strange men appeared before the walls of Quebec, then less than fifty years old, accompanied by a band of Cree Indians packing such a quantity of furs as to excite the interest of the populace and the cupidity of the French officials. The older of the two was Médart Chouart, better known as Sieur des Groseilliers or Mr. Gooseberry, a title he got by investing some of his first fur money in a gooseberry patch. The younger man, brother of Gooseberry's wife, was Pierre Esprit Radisson. This pair of adventurers had come from the interior of Canada where they had tapped hitherto unknown sources of beaver and other furs, and the cargo they and their entourage of Crees brought as a result of two years' effort caused the guns of Quebec to salute and the Governor to praise them. But neither praise nor the pride of owning a gooseberry farm could hold them long. After two years they asked permission to make another expedition, and were granted it on condition that they take along two of the Governor's men to look after the official interests. Wanting no supervision, they requested time to consider the proposal and used the time to get a head start into the Canadian wilds. Two years later, in the summer of 1660, they returned with three hundred Indians loaded with furs worth £60,000. They were hopeful that the fortune they brought would blur official memory of their unceremonious departure, but they were too optimistic, and when their penalties had been paid they found themselves with only about £4,000. We are not interested in this injustice, but rather in the fact that two men had, by finding the crop of furs matured and by tapping a cheap source of labor to gather them, in two years acquired nearly a quarter million dollars in wealth. It is also significant historically that the two adventurers, with some insight and more luck than loyalty, switched from serving the French to serving the English and laid the foundations of the Hudson's Bay Company.[3]

We have seen how inexpensively Chouart and Radisson started the furs on their journey to the European market. The

[3] Douglas MacKay, *The Honourable Company* (London: Cassell and Co., Ltd., 1937), pp. 17 ff.

Hudson's Bay Company standardized and refined their methods. The company was represented among the Indians by the *voyageurs* and *coureurs de bois,* men only a little less primitive than the Indians and not much more expensive. These canoemen and woods-runners tied in wtih the *bourgeois,* final representative of the company in Canada. From the time the skin was taken until it reached the factor, all was barter. The Indians received no money for their furs, but exchanged them for wooden tokens, a stick for each "Made-Beaver" or its equivalent. The Indian wound up with a quantity of wooden money which he promptly exchanged for coats, blankets, guns and knives, and trinkets more ornamental than useful. For a gun that cost the company $5 the Indian gave twenty beaver skins worth $150; for a coat he paid twelve skins worth $50; and for a knife he paid in skins about $10.[4]

With a labor force for which the company had no responsibility working on such terms, it would have been strange if large profits had not resulted and capital accumulated. The records of the company speak eloquently of dividends. A share of stock purchased at £100 in 1670 brought its owner in the following fifty years declared dividends of 343 per cent and in addition an undivided profit of £800, a total profit of 1143 per cent, slightly less than 23 per cent annually.[5] The windfall of free land and furs, negligible labor cost, and cheap sea transport must have been an important factor in the Hudson's Bay balance sheet. Similar windfalls of the primary type were found among the full-grown Negroes of Africa, in ivory from the same place, in fish from Newfoundland, and in ambergris from Bermuda. They all came without much cost of production, and they all contributed to the rise of capitalism, these first easy gleanings of the Great Frontier.

[4] Testimony given by Chief Factor Dr. John Rae before a Committee of the House of Commons. The Committee was appointed February 5, 1857. This investigation was the first public scrutiny of the company whose business had been conducted in greatest secrecy, described by Andrew Freeport in a letter to Lord Palmerston in 1857. Of the company, the letter said: "The management of their affairs is inscrutable . . . it is like a commercial tomb, closed with the key of death to all except a favoured few . . . its councils unfathomable and its secrets unknown . . . its revenues are acquired in secret and distributed in silence." — *Ibid.,* pp. 286–90.

[5] W. R. Scott, *The Constitution and Finance of English, Scottish, and Irish Joint Stock Companies to 1720,* vol. II, p. 236, note 3.

3. Secondary Windfalls

Secondary windfalls took up where the primary ones left off, but they came in time to keep the boom going and to promote capitalism to full flower. They involved more work and less luck and were therefore lacking in the spectacular and dramatic. Secondary windfalls were closely related to the land, and while land is productive, it is a stubborn thing, and takes its own time in yielding to man's importunities. It was the plantation, the farm, and the ranch cattle industry that furnished important secondary windfalls of the frontier. In each we find the free or negligible cost factor in production which is necessary under our definition. Our search will be confined to land cost and labor cost. Throughout the frontier land was virtually free, and this despite any law to the contrary. Whether a man wanted to grow cotton or sugar cane, run cattle or cut logs from the forest, he paid little or nothing for land.

What wrecked the investors who sought fortunes from the land was not its first cost, but the period of waiting and the amount of labor involved in persuading it to yield its bounty. The time interval exhausted the patience of speculators and the labor exhausted the resources of the investors who expected quick returns, as colonial history records. The thirteen "plantations" established by England along the Atlantic coast illustrate what happened to investors. All the thirteen colonies missed the quick return because they lay north of the gold and south of the furs in a land where wealth waited on a lot of hard work. By the time the hard work was done, the English investors had been washed out, and the people they had sent over were left to shift for themselves. The English had hit upon a land that barred their passage to India, that yielded no gold, was deficient in furs, and lacked a supply of cheap labor. The natives had little wealth and exhibited a sturdy reluctance to produce any at the behest of their visitors. The failure to find easy wealth or cheap labor resulted in suffering, famines, and death among the immigrants and financial loss to the English investors. The miracle is that the colony in Virginia survived at all, but the significant fact is that the members, in surviving the company, became the landholders and took their first step toward equality and freedom. The discovery that tobacco could be grown as a profitable crop came too late to save the Virginia Company, but it did enable some of the Virginians to survive. The first cargo of tobacco was shipped to England in 1613 after the investors had virtually given up the ghost and the adventurers had become discouraged. Even after the first crop of tobacco was sold, the production increased too gradually to constitute a windfall of sufficient size to return dividends and profits which would enable the company in England to act like capitalists. The financial statement of 1618 shows that the expenditure in Virginia had been £67,124, raised by subscription, borrowing, and lotteries. Scott thinks that the success of the company should be measured by the number of persons planted, and that those present could have been brought over for £16,000, leaving an expense of more than £50,000 "against which there were few assets." In short, from the point of view of a capitalist, the Virginia enterprise may be written off as a loss.[6]

The prosperity of Bermuda is an exception in the northern region and seems to illustrate the value of the windfall. Bermuda was settled in 1612 by a subsidiary of the Virginia Company. From the point of view of the investors Bermuda was a success and Virginia a failure. What made the difference? The English became aware of Bermuda in 1609 when a supply ship commanded by Sir George Somers left England to relieve the distress then so acute in Virginia, and this ship was wrecked on the island. On June 15, 1610, Somers wrote to London about Bermuda, calling attention to its favorable climate, its fertile soil, its strategic position, and the presence of pork on land and fish in the waters. Nothing but the pork needs explanation. More than a century earlier Juan Bermúdez, bound from Spain to the West Indies with a shipload of hogs, was wrecked there; and though the Spaniards had long ago departed, the hogs remained, a fine breed of razorbacks if we may judge from the image of one on the first English coin struck in the New World, the famous "hog money" of Bermuda. As a result of Somers' report, an "under" company, a subsidiary of the Virginia Company, was formed which in 1612 sent sixty persons to colonize the now famous English resort.

[6] *Ibid.*, vol. II, p. 254.

Some writers account for the success of the Bermudians by saying that they profited from the mistakes of the Virginians; they turned to agriculture, wasting no time searching for treasure. The real fact is that the Bermudians found the treasure, and it made more difference in the future of their enterprise than the bad example of the Virginians. The first year they stumbled on a fortune in ambergris!

Ambergris, a waxlike substance, varying in color, is formed in the belly of sick whales. When the whale disintegrates the ambergris remains floating in the water, and was found often in the Indian Ocean. It was valued both as a medicine and as a perfume base, and sold at from 60 to 75 shillings an ounce, say $260 a pound. During the year the colony was founded, some men located a great incrusted object shaped like a man with the head and one arm missing; the object was recovered and brought in by the governor, Richard Moore. It turned out to be almost pure ambergris, weighed between 160 and 190 pounds, and was so precious that it was sent to England in three separate ships. The highest estimate is that it brought between £9000 and £11,000, but the company claimed a value of only £3000. The best authorities think it brought about £6000. Of this windfall, this golden egg laid by some indisposed whale, W. R. Scott comments in this restrained manner:

> The funds derived from the sale of the ambergris, to which were to be added the proceeds of pearls found at the islands, were important in launching the company successfully. Not only did these resources diminish the need for pressing the shareholders to pay up instalments at short notice, but also, when capital was required later, it was readily provided. . . . In 1613 the prospects of this colony were considered much more promising than those of Virginia, and some of the leading members who held shares in both were prepared to continue to contribute to the support of the Somers Islands, rather than of the older plantation. As a consequence of these high expectations and under the stimulus of the success already achieved, as much as £20,000 had been expended on the Somers Islands at the end of 1614, and the population was 600 persons.[7]

Before the impetus given the colony by the ambergris had worn off, tobacco culture was established and the success of the Ber-

7 *Ibid.*, vol. II, pp. 261–62.

muda venture was reasonably secure. It is not necessary to say more of these two companies except to point out that by 1625 Virginia as a commercial enterprise had failed, leaving the colonists in possession of the land without further obligation to anyone but king and parliament. The other company lasted until 1684 when the colony was taken over by the crown, and the Bermudas have remained a British possession ever since. A windfall in Virginia or Massachusetts might have made the difference between America independent and America a dominion.

Thus far, logic has driven us toward the conclusion that a very important element which was nearly always present in a frontier windfall was a low labor cost. It would be low either because a very small amount of labor was required, as in robbing a treasure ship, or because it came at a very small wage, as with the fur hunters when they used Indian labor. The planters had to have a large labor force, but they were in worse luck than the fur traders because their Indians would not go along with a plantation program. The solution the planters hit upon to reduce their labor expense to a minimum was Negro slavery. With free land the planter could not get forward, but with free land *and* slave labor he could make some headway — nothing spectacular but something that would enable him to move toward if not into the capitalistic category.

Outside the plantation belt, the small farm prevailed, and here too the demand for cheap labor was inexorable. In some respects the labor on the small farm was cheaper than slave labor because it did not have to be purchased, being furnished by the farmer and his family. With a farmer a big family was something of a windfall, and was so recognized by Adam Smith. Here we come to a paradox, namely, that while the frontier paid the highest cash wages, as all economists have known, at the same time it had the advantage of the cheapest labor, Indian labor, slave labor, and family labor! With all this labor force working for next to nothing on the vast resources of the frontier, it is no wonder that wealth accumulated in Europe and grew in the hands of those who knew how to manage it. This type of labor must have had great influence in driving prices down in Europe by flooding its markets with commodities in whose production rent costs were negligible and labor costs were a minimum.

Turning from the plantation to the ranch cattle business as developed in the American West, we find a secondary windfall with so many free elements as to almost justify placing it in the first class. It is also of special interest because it came so late, right at the end of the era of free land. In land the early cowman had no investment and no obligation for taxes or upkeep. The feed which his cattle required was also free, a matured crop of grass stretching the length and breadth of the Great Plains. The cowman's novel method of harvesting the crop was the least expensive imaginable for the reason that the cows did the work. In the early days the only capital investment was in the cows themselves and a few horses with which to handle them. The cows not only harvested the grass, but they processed it into beef and hides, and in the trail-driving days furnished their own means of transportation to market. Neither the Indians nor the slaves nor the family labored so willingly or so cheaply in the production of wealth as did the grazing cows. We hear now of wholly automatic methods of production by intricate machines, but these automatic methods have nothing on the early cowman's setup. These old Westerners liked to say that they lived in a land where the wind draws the water and the cows cut the wood, and it was true, as any user of windmills and cowchips knows, but it is not all the story of labor saving. The cowman had the prairie full of automatic machines mowing hay, converting it into beef, tallow, and hides, and automatically dropping annually little machines for replacement and obsolescence.

All this automatic business meant that the labor force on the ranch was excessively small. Fifteen cowboys could tend a range of enormous size and take care of a very large number of cattle. The outside wages of these men was thirty dollars a month plus food that cost probably five more. A crew on a year-round basis would cost the cowman $6300. If he sold 2000 head annually at $15, he would gross $30,000 at a labor cost of 21 per cent. Even if his total expense was 50 per cent, he would still make a profit of $15,000 annually, and at that rate at that period he could rise into the capitalist class. Many did.

It was out of this idyllic situation that the cattle kings sprang up in the Great Plains, that the Scotch and English syndicates added their venture money to that of the Americans, setting up such famous brands as the XIT, the Matador, the Spur, and many others. What happened in the Great Plains also happened in South America, Australia, and wherever grass grew on the free frontier.

With the invention of barbed wire in 1873 open range ranching was doomed to end and the free elements of land and feed were to disappear in the production of beef. By 1890 or 1900 most of the land had passed into private hands, much of it was fenced, and the day of free grass was over. To go into the cattle business today requires such a large investment that none but the wealthy can afford to do it. Ranching still has high social prestige, and offers a good opportunity to bury profits from elsewhere for income tax purposes.

After this brief comparative study of frontier projects, some deductions may be made as to how men of enterprise made their way through windfalls into capitalism. We are of course concerned only with those who made a success.

1. The most significant point is that practically all of the successful ones enjoyed partial or full exemption from one or more of the cost factors which under normal conditions enter into the production of wealth.

2. The success of the enterprise seems to have depended on the presence of the windfall and the degree of the success seems to bear a direct relation to its magnitude.

3. Primary windfalls were those involving little labor and a very short time interval before the strike was made. The pirates, the fur hunters, the ambergris finders, and the early slavers were recipients of primary windfalls. Their success was quick and spectacular.

4. Secondary windfalls, though containing reduced or free elements of cost, involved more prior investment, a considerable labor cost, and a long period of preparation. The plantation is the best example, though the open range cattle business may also fall in this class.

5. Both primary and secondary windfalls contributed to the rise of capitalism, but in different ways. The first acted as a

powerful stimulus in the Metropolis, setting men off in a frenzy of enterprises. Most of the joint stock companies of the sixteenth and seventeenth centuries were thus motivated. This fever subsided by 1720 for the reason that by that time most of the primary windfalls had been gathered in. It was in the next two centuries that the secondary windfalls took over, providing an abundance of staple commodities such as plantation crops and beef for men in the Metropolis to buy and sell. The first two centuries have been called the age of projects; the eighteenth and nineteenth may well be called the age of Things. In the next section we will consider some effects of primary frontier windfalls on national wealth as illustrated in England.

4. National Wealth and Frontier Windfalls

Thus far we have seen how the success of frontier enterprise depended on the fortuitous windfalls, the quick prizes which resulted occasionally from venturing into a chancy new world. Our consideration has been limited to individuals and companies, usually companies of some sort, who stumbled upon gold, ambergris, furs, or grass where the cost of production began with the harvest, and where the harvest, as in the case of furs and cows, was carried on with the cheapest of labor. It is obvious that if a sufficient number of these lucky undertakings originated in one country, and returned their booty and gain to that country, the effect would be reflected in a national prosperity comparable to that of the individual or the company. In other words, the nation itself would be the recipient of the collective windfalls of all its citizens, subjects, and companies. If enough individuals and companies became capitalists, their activities and successes would make the nation capitalistic, too. Therefore, it is pertinent to inquire as to the relation between the new capitalistic states and the Great Frontier. The inquiry will be limited to the period between 1500 and 1720, but some observations will be made on the application of the theory to national boom and prosperity after 1720.

This inquiry begins with the work of John Maynard Keynes on the theory of money and his application of the theory to national prosperity. Keynes develops his theory without reference to the frontier, of which he seems unconscious, but when he comes to apply his theory, he cites examples which are directly connected with the frontier and could not have existed without it. This does not mean that his theory is not applicable to a nonfrontier society, but it probably does mean that the sharpest illustrations are to be found in a society engaged in frontier exploitation.

For convenience I shall call Keynes's rationalization of national prosperity the theory of profit inflation, though that is only the better half of his theory; the other half, applicable to national depression, may just as appropriately be called the theory of profit deflation. The two combined determine the upswing and downswing of a nation's welfare, its boom and depression, depending on which of the reciprocal forces is dominant.

Three factors are involved in the increase of national or world wealth, and they are thrift, profit, and enterprise. Of these thrift is the least important, and may be carried so far as to be an actual detriment to national prosperity. It hoards wealth but does not increase it unless the hoard is made available to the factor of enterprise. "It is Enterprise which builds and improves the world's possessions. . . . If Enterprise is afoot, wealth accumulates whatever may be happening to Thrift; and if Enterprise is asleep, wealth decays whatever Thrift may be doing." [8]

Thrift and enterprise are not directly joined together; they are separated, yet linked, by the third factor, profit, "For the engine which drives Enterprise is not Thrift, but Profit." [9] It is the lure of profit that sets enterprise going, and it is thrift which furnishes the means by which enterprise arrives at its destination to claim profit. Enterprise is awakened by expectation and enabled to move on means furnished by savings or thrift.

The theory holds that the boom comes and capital accumulates to make a nation great at those times when enterprise is receiving the lion's share of profit at the expense of the thrifty, when investment is outrunning hoarding, when prices are out-

[8] John Maynard Keynes, *A Treatise on Money* (New York: Harcourt, Brace & Co., 1930), vol. II, pp. 148 f.

[9] *Ibid.*, p. 149.

running costs, including wages. When such conditions prevail, a nation has profit inflation, and the whole society is buoyant, speculative, and optimistic. A great deal is made of the necessity in this situation for the wages of labor to fall relative to prices; if the opposite is true, and wages rise above prices, we have income inflation, which is likely to be accompanied by profit deflation, or depression. The dynamic is furnished, not by the thrifty savers, but by the profiteers who are bold enough to spend lavishly in order to reap more profit.

Perhaps the abstract case can be illustrated by taking a single individual and letting him operate, as individuals often do, both as a thrifty saver of wages on the one hand and as an undertaker or a spending venturer after profits on the other. It is pretty well known that a wage earner or salaried man rarely grows rich through thrift. He hoards for a time, and then he sees a chance of making a profit by investment, by taking a chance on a speculation. He draws off all or a part of his savings, and throws it into the maelstrom of business chance. He may lose it, but on the other hand he may double or quadruple it, thus building up capital at the expense of his role as a hoarder or a thrifty person. If he grows rich, it will be from profit inflation on his role as a speculator and not because of his role as a wage earner by thrift. In his case to have saved more of his wages would have been to lose the much greater gain. What he did was to divert the results of his thrift into speculative enterprise. Again, the two conditions by which he arrives are identical with the two conditions by which the nation arrives; there must be a reasonable expectation of profit; and there must be available enough cash resulting from abstinence or thrift to set the venture on the road. "Were the Seven Wonders of the World built by Thrift?" inquires Keynes. "I deem it doubtful." What he is asking is: Do men build palaces out of their savings or do they build them only because they have made ventures in which they risked something and gained much? The answer can be found by examining the palace owners on the west side of any modern city.

At this stage Keynes introduces the element with which he is primarily concerned, namely, money, and its role in periods of profit inflation. It is what the suddenly liberated monetary metals do to prices, and not the money itself as wealth, that turns the trick by raising prices above costs and giving opportunity for great profits. He raises the question as to the effect the opening of mines had on ancient civilizations, and he pairs the greatness of Sumeria and Egypt with the new gold from Arabia and the new copper from Africa; he connects the glory of Athens with the flow of new silver from Laurium, and he links the distribution of the accumulated hoard of Persia by Alexander to economic progress in the Mediterranean area. Conversely he suggests that the fall of Rome was "contemporaneous with the most prolonged and drastic deflation yet recorded," and that the stagnation of the Middle Ages may be related to the paucity of metals.[10]

Coming to the modern period, Keynes wonders "how much the Glorious Revolution owed to Mr. Phipps." It is when he proceeds to apply his theory to modern history that he lands squarely in the middle of the Great Frontier, and he does not emerge from it until after 1720, if then. Despite the fact that he does not recognize or name the frontier as a factor, being concerned solely with money, he cites example after example of profit inflation, examples which the frontier furnished him. Witness for instance, his main contention that the influx of American treasure in the sixteenth and seventeenth centuries upset the economic balance, caused prices to outstrip costs, and provided just those necessary conditions he had laid down in the development of his theory for the building of capital. Thrift became secondary to enterprise which got in the saddle, rode off after profits, leaving all else behind. Enterprise was afoot because the frontier furnished the awakening prospect, and savings were sufficient to pay the expenses of the journey. The gigantic operation that ensued resulted in "projects" of all descriptions and the rise of agencies to carry them out. Chief of these agencies were the regulated and joint stock companies which dominated the economic world for two centuries, and sent their expeditions questing in every nook and cranny of the world.[11]

It would be a mistake to assume that for two centuries the whole of western Europe was in a continuous, uninterrupted

---

[10] Keynes, *A Treatise on Money*, vol. II, pp. 150 f.

[11] For a comprehensive treatment of this age, see Scott's three-volume study on *Joint Stock Companies to 1720*.

boom of spectacular proportions, or that all nations were affected at the same time. Though the whole Metropolis was affected, the nations were affected serially, one after another, in the order in which the injection of American treasure entered the national veins to boost prices and to depress wages and other costs. In short, there were ups and downs in each nation, periods of profit inflation followed by those of income inflation or depression. The great upsurge of national wealth comes in the periods of profit inflation, for, to quote Keynes, "it is the teaching of this Treatise that the wealth of nations is enriched . . . during Profit Inflations — at times . . . when prices are running away from costs." [12]

In Spain, on which American treasure first impinged, this period came between 1520 and 1580. For the first forty years, to 1560, wages lagged behind prices, but by 1590 they had caught up with them, and stood very high in comparison with wages in France and England. In France, profit inflation prevailed from 1530 to 1700, and in England from 1550 to 1650. Of this period, the author says: "Never in the annals of the modern world has there existed so prolonged and so rich an opportunity for the businessman, the speculator, and the profiteer. In these golden years modern capitalism was born." [13] Pointing out that Europe was very poor in 1500, the author says: "It is unthinkable that the difference between the amount of wealth in France and England in 1700 and the amount in 1500 could ever have been built up by Thrift alone. The intervening Profit Inflation which created the modern world was surely worth while if we take a long view." [14] Keynes thinks that the *accumulation* resulted from a distortion of the price situation which enabled the enterprisers to pile up their surpluses to capitalistic proportions, and he admits that the upset and stimulus came from the American treasure, a frontier product.

It requires some boldness to vary ever so slightly from the conclusions of the great English economists, yet my own view of modern history impels me to inquire how by a mere seesaw of profit inflation and deflation enormous net wealth could

12 Keynes, *A Treatise on Money*, vol. II, p. 154.
13 *Ibid.*, vol. II, p. 159.
14 *Ibid.*, vol. II, p. 163.

accumulate unless the activity resulted in adding increments from sources *outside* the society under consideration. It is my opinion that the whole Metropolis was enjoying a boom of much greater magnitude and of longer duration than the economist visualized. It was within the framework of this greater boom that his theory is applicable, that the comparatively little ups and downs, the seesawing of inflation and deflation took place. There were little booms and little depressions taking place within a greater and constant boom, the tidal wave of wealth sweeping back on all Europe. All the time, in good times or in bad, increments of wealth were being added to Europe as a whole, and these increments were coming from the frontier to build up the metropolitan storehouse. Enterprise was afoot all the time, but it did better in periods of profit inflation when prices outran costs, including wages, than in times of profit deflation when wages or thrift absorbed too much of the risk money. The periods of national prosperity, as distinguished from general European prosperity, came when one nation enjoyed a temporary advantage of having the factors in just the proper relation to one another. In such instances the progress of the favored nation seemed phenomenal in comparison to that of its neighbors.

From these general considerations of the whole problem let us descend to specific examples used by Keynes to illustrate the application of his theory with particular reference to England. What specifically did Mr. Phipps do that contributed to the success of the Glorious Revolution? And more important for us, *where* did he do it? What did Drake do to stir the enterprise of England to prodigious action? *Where* did he do it? In the simplest terms what both men did was to hit a windfall once removed. Instead of taking the gold and silver from its source as the Spaniards had done, they took it by short shrift after the Spaniards had acquired it, dumped it on England, and precipitated or accelerated the upset in prices which gave a big advantage to the enterprisers who had things to sell.

> For [says Keynes], in the case of England, a large part of the imports of bullion were due to Drake's capture of Spanish treasure ships and many similar exploits by others. These expeditions were financed by syndicates and companies and rep-

resented business speculations, the success and fruits of which supplied a stimulus to enterprise of all kinds. The boom-period in England definitely began with the return of Drake's first important expedition (his third voyage) in 1573, and was confirmed by the immense gains of his second expedition which returned home in 1580. . . . The value of the gold and silver brought back in the *Golden Hind* . . . has been variously estimated by historians at anything from £300,000 to £1,500,000. . . . The effect of these great influxes of money in establishing 'the years of prosperity,' from 1575 to 1587, must have been predominant.[15]

It was the results flowing from the treasure brought by the *Golden Hind* that stagger the imagination. With her part of the booty Elizabeth I paid the whole of England's foreign debt and from the balance left she invested £42,000 in the Levant Company. From the profits of the Levant Company were derived most of the capital used in the formation of the East India Company. The profits from the East India Company constituted "the main foundation of England's foreign connections" throughout the sixteenth and seventeenth centuries. "Indeed," says Keynes, "the booty brought back by Drake in the *Golden Hind* may fairly be considered the fountain and origin of British Foreign Investment." [16] This is a most significant statement because it was England's foreign investments that made and kept her rich, and that had much influence in creating and maintaining her empire. The empire and the flag followed the investments to the far corners of the Great Frontier.

But let us return to the initial £42,000 that Elizabeth invested in the Levant Company to set off a chain reaction of fortunate foreign enterprise. Taking this sum as a base, Keynes calculates that if it bore a net rate of $3\frac{1}{4}$ per cent for reinvestment, that is, at compound interest, it will produce a sum corresponding to the total of British foreign investment at any given later time to 1930. For example, British foreign investment in 1930 amounted to £4,200,000,000, which is approximately what £42,000 would produce at $3\frac{1}{4}$ per cent compounded from 1580 to 1930. A more accurate check can be made for the 120 years intervening between 1580 and 1700

[15] Keynes, *A Treatise on Money*, vol. II, p. 156, note 1.
[16] *Ibid.*, vol. II, p. 156.

for the reason that in 1700 the foreign investment was comparatively simple, the bulk of it being represented by the three great companies, the East India, the Royal African, and the Hudson's Bay. The three had in 1700 a total capital of £2,150,-000. Elizabeth's nest egg of £42,000 would in that 120 years have amounted to £2,500,000 at 3¼ per cent compounded interest.[17] The difference might well be accounted for by foreign investments outside the three major companies. It hardly need be pointed out how the frontier is intertwined in this whole interesting exercise. It furnished the initial capital, the scene of operation of two of the companies, the Royal African and the Hudson's Bay, and it supplied the necessary specie which the East India Company used to tap the sources of wealth in the Orient.

Keynes insists that it was not the treasure itself that was of such importance. Had it been handled as a hoard, saved by thrift, it would have had little effect. It was rather the spending of it in other enterprises, and the stimulus they gave to still others that created the economic ferment and excitement of the age. In the midst of all this prosperity England's greatest literary genius made his entry. "We were just in a financial position to afford Shakespeare at the moment when he presented himself!" says the economist. He adds that Shakespeare died rich, as also did Newton and Darwin, and that during his last years Shakespeare lived high, spending a thousand pounds a year. The poet lived high and died rich because "his active career chanced to fall at the date of dates, when any level-headed person in England disposed to make money could hardly help doing so." The years 1575 to 1620 "were the palmy days of profit — one of the greatest 'bull' movements ever known until modern days in the United States. . . . Shakespeare being eleven years old in 1575 and dying in 1616." Then Keynes suggests a thesis for further consideration, namely, that the outpourings of genius in the arts and letters have coincided with periods of great prosperity induced by profit inflation.[18]

Earlier the name of "Mr. Phipps" was mentioned in connec-

17 *Ibid.*, vol. II, p. 157.
18 *Ibid.*, vol. II, p. 154, note 3. (See section on Literature in Chapter XII, "What the Frontier Touched.")

tion with the success of the Glorious Revolution of 1688, a hundred years after Drake set off the fuse of Elizabethan prosperity. There is no better example of the windfall in history than Mr. Phipps's act of stumbling on a sunken treasure off the coast of Hispaniola in 1687. [19] Phipps was born February 2, 1650, "at a despicable plantation on the river of Kennebeck, and almost the furthest village of the eastern settlement of New-England." [20] His father was a gunsmith and his mother was probably among the most prolific women of history, being the mother of twenty-six children of whom all but five were sons. At an early age Phipps apprenticed himself as a shipmaster, removed to Boston where he learned to read, married, and — according to Cotton Mather — dreamed of becoming a great man.

> He was of an enterprizing *genius*, and naturally disdained *littleness.* . . . He would *prudently* contrive a weighty undertaking, and then patiently pursue it unto the end. He was of an inclination, cutting rather like a *hatchet* than like a *razor* . . . Being thus of the *true temper*, for doing of *great things*, he betakes himself to the *sea*, the right *scene* for such things.[21]

Such are the words of Cotton Mather, and how right he was about the sea at the time William Phipps took to it.

He soon became interested in Spanish wrecks, sunken treasure ships, and determined to find one. In England he gained the support he needed, and by 1683 was given command of a frigate of eighteen guns and ninety-five men. Piracy had become a flourishing business by that time, and Phipps had to quell a mutiny among his men who wanted to forsake the dull task of hunting for sunken treasure for the more exciting quest of what was still afloat in Spanish vessels. At Jamaica he turned off the troublesome crew and headed for Hispaniola with a small company. There "he fished out of a very old *Spaniard* (or *Portuguese*) a little advice about the true spot where lay

---

[19] *Ibid.,* vol. II, p. 151, note 4.

[20] Cotton Mather, *Magnalia Christi Americana: The Ecclesiastical History of New England* (Hartford: First American Edition, Silas Andrus, 1820), vol. I, bk. II, pp. 151ff. The following account of Phipps is drawn largely from this book.

[21] *Ibid.,* pp. 153–54.

the *wreck*." [22] The Spaniard told him it was on a reef of shoals north of Port de la Plata, so named by the survivors of the wreck who dragged some of the treasure ashore there. His search was fruitless, and he returned to England for refitting. There he gained the support of the Duke of Albermarle, who was a friend of Sir Henry Morgan, king of the pirates, and with a better equipment, the fortune hunter again "set sail for the fishing-ground, which had been so well baited." [23]

At Port de la Plata he made a canoe or pirogue of eight oars out of a cotton-tree for use in shallow water. Though the pirogue kept "busking to and again," shifting about; it could find nothing but a reef of rising shoals called the Boilers. The party sent to investigate had given up the search, and were returning to the large ship when one of them, peering into the depths, spied what he took to be a sea feather growing out of a rock. An Indian diver was sent to bring it up so that they would have *something* for the captain. The Indian brought up what he was sent for, but astounded the men by saying that the floor of the sea was littered with huge guns. The Indian was sent down again, and this time he brought up a sow, a bar of silver larger than a pig, and worth some £300. When the news and the sow of silver were revealed to Phipps, he is reported to have said exactly what many men have said when an oil well comes in, "Thanks be to God; we are made."

Returning to the scene of the wreck, which had been marked by a buoy, the men had another remarkable piece of good luck. The coined money, pieces of eight, was stored with the ballast; compared to what was in the bullion room, it had little value. But the diver luckily hit the bullion room; the story is better told by Cotton Mather:

> Now, most happily, they first fell upon that room in the *wreck* where the *bullion* had been stored up; and they so prospered in this *new fishery*, that in a little while they had, without the loss of any man's life, brought up *thirty-two tuns* of silver; for it was now come to measuring of silver by tuns.[24] . . . Thus did

[22] *Ibid.*, p. 155.

[23] *Ibid.*, p. 156.

[24] By previous arrangements, Phipps was met here by another ship under command of "one Adderly of Providence." He took up "six tuns of silver," took to riotous living in Bermuda where his mind became unhinged before his death. A most interesting study could be made of the effect of sudden

there once again come into the light of the sun, a treasure which had been half a hundred years *groaning under the waters:* and in this time there was grown upon the plate a crust like *lime-stone . . . ;* which crust being broken open by irons . . . they knocked out whole bushels of rusty pieces of eight which were grown thereinto. Besides that incredible treasure of plate in various forms . . . there were vast riches of *gold,* and *pearls,* and *jewels,* which they also lit upon.[25]

Having loaded his ship to capacity with what he had lit upon, Phipps set off for England, not daring to reprovision anywhere lest all be lost. He reached London in 1687, the year before the Glorious Revolution, with nearly £300,000 of treasure.[26] At this point we shall have to say goodbye to Mr. Phipps, somewhat regretfully because his career is one of the most exciting in that tempestuous century. Our concern is with some of the results of his frontier windfall, and this brings us back to the sober work of the economist.

The success of Phipps was made to order for Keynes. Here was the sudden injection of specie into the veins of a lagging economy. The stockholders in this quick venture received what is probably the biggest dividend in business history, 10,000 per cent as against a paltry 4700 per cent paid by Drake about a century earlier. The treasure came on the eve of the Glorious Revolution, too late to save the Stuarts but in time to make William strong against the claims of the Pretender. But a far greater effect resulted from the stimulus given to business enterprise, the boom which gathered strength as it moved from one segment of society to another. The profits of this boom, which reached its climax in 1695, offset the losses occasioned by the French wars of William (1689–1697) and "must have been invaluable for the stability of the new régime." The boom thus occasioned ended with the foundation of the Bank of England in 1694, the establishment of the Stock Exchange, and the reform of the currency by Locke and Newton in 1695.[27] It is quite probable that this windfall had much to do with leading the Scotch into the Darien enter-

---

wealth on the human mind. Those who lived through the oil booms have seen many examples of the effect on human morals and mentality.

25 Mather, *Magnalia Christi Americana,* vol. I, bk. II, p. 157.
26 *Loc. cit.*
27 Keynes, *A Treatise on Money,* vol. II, p. 151, note 4.

prise and in driving all classes of Frenchmen and Englishmen mad in their pursuit of the Mississippi and South Sea Bubbles. The story of these three ventures illustrates what happened to three nations who hunted the windfalls after they were gone. They are tragic stories marking the end of a definite period in the growth of capitalism.

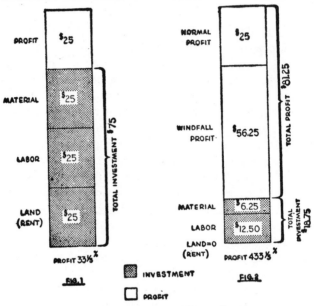

THE "WINDFALL PROFIT"

Figure 1 represents the return of $100, including invested capital and profit, on an ordinary business transaction. The owner finds that he invested $25 in labor, spent $25 for material, and paid $25 rent. The remaining $25 is profit. On an investment of $75, he made a profit of 33⅓ per cent.

Figure 2 represents a transaction that brought the same amount as the first, $100. But this was a frontier operation, and costs were greatly reduced. Labor cost $12.50, material $6.25, and rent nothing. Though the owner comes out with $100, he invested only $18.75, and so he made a profit of $81.25, a return of 433⅓ per cent. Allowing him 33⅓ per cent ordinary profit, there is a windfall profit of 400 per cent, and it was this windfall profit that made capitalists. It is obvious that the abnormal gain was derived from free land, cheap material, and reduced labor cost. These free or reduced elements of cost were present to a greater or less degree throughout the frontier period.

CHAPTER SEVEN

THREE UNWISE BUBBLES

B Y 1700 the windfall dew was off the Great Frontier, and those who ventured for spectacular fortunes after that time are notable for their uniform lack of success. Of course people are slow to realize when an economic game has played out, and their belief that fortunes could still be reaped by following the example of the East India Company, the Hudson's Bay Company, and of a few others less spectacular lured many into the bizarre schemes which culminated in the panics of 1690–1720, panics suggesting that the first phase of the frontier boom was really over.

The three decades from 1690 to 1720 furnish three striking examples that men could no longer find the primary windfalls, and in each case they learned the hard way what is now obvious, that quick windfalls were no longer available. The gold-bearing regions of the Americas were still held closely by Spain. The furs of Canada, and the cheap labor that took them, were a monopoly of the Hudson's Bay Company. The India Companies had appropriated the East Indies, India, and the China coast, all rich in quick goods and teeming with cheap labor. It was into this situation that the Scotch entered with the Darien enterprise, the French with the Mississippi Bubble, and the English with the South Sea Bubble. They were all bubbles, and by 1720 they had all burst.

1. The Scotch Bubble: Darien

The Scotch are a wise people, noted for their logic and learning, but they applied neither to their disastrous undertaking in Darien. A study of the world map should have told them there was in 1695 no place where they could drive either a commercial or plantation wedge without coming into conflict with forces, physical and financial, much greater than any they could command; their knowledge of the past, of history, should have told them that they were but a pigmy among giants, and that their nearest neighbor was their greatest enemy, and that their king was not really theirs, but England's. They knew all these things, separately, but they did not put the parts together and study their implications in relation to what they were about to undertake. They came under the spell of a promoter, as was the case with the other two bubbles, and he stirred their emotions to such an extent that they no longer had use for either their logic or their history.

The man who brought the map and the scheme was William Paterson, whose name is always mentioned in connection with the founding of the Bank of England. Scott says: "The conception of a trading settlement at Panama was originated by William Paterson, the founder of the Bank of England, and it constituted the dream of his life." [1] The Darien region he called "the door of the seas — the key of the universe." Certainly a good promoter can take a map of the world and make Panama or Darien look like the strategic place that it is. A slender thread of land binding two broad continents, separating two wide seas, cannot miss being one of the crossroads of the world. Moreover, Paterson's dream fitted in with the dream of a whole people whose ambition since the Restoration had been to found a Scottish colonial empire. What was needed in the case was a man, and Paterson was the man. When the Scottish parliament met in 1695 Paterson was there with his plan, and I am sure a most convincing map, and on June 26 an act was passed incorporating the Company of Scotland Trading to Africa and the Indies, hereinafter referred to as the Darien Company.

The official title of the Scottish company indicated that it intended to operate in Africa and in the Indies, whether west or east was purposely left vague. Such a program meant im-

[1] W. R. Scott, *The Constitution and Finance of English Scottish and Irish Joint Stock Companies to 1720* (Cambridge: The University Press, 1910–1912; 3 vols.), vol. II, p. 207.

mediate conflict with the Royal African Company of England in African territory and with the East India Company in the Orient, to say nothing of the Dutch East India Company. If the Scots turned to the West, as they eventually did at Darien, and as was Paterson's intention from the start, they would meet the Spaniards in all their fury. As it turned out the rival companies, especially the English East India Company, prepared the victim so thoroughly for the kill that the Spaniards had little need to make it. At the time (1695), the combined assets of the two rival English companies were £1,372,540, though their nominal stock was much greater. The East India Company, incomparably stronger, was the main adversary, and its activities in connection with the Scottish company are all that need concern us.

The basic weakness of the Scottish company was the poverty of Scotland, the fact that the initial funds could not be raised without the help of investors in England and on the continent. "Therefore," says Scott, "the real fate of the venture was decided on the exchanges of London and Amsterdam, and that too before the subscription in Scotland had been completed and before a single ship had sailed to that golden West from which so much was expected." [2]

The plan eventually adopted was to issue £600,000 in stock, allotting half to Scotland and half to England. The books were opened first in England, and by October 29, 1695, the whole stock allotted to England had been subscribed, and when the books closed on November 22 it was oversubscribed by less than two hundred Englishmen, some of whom also held stock in the East India Company. It should be borne in mind that as yet nothing had been paid in; but with the stock subscribed, it could be issued to bring in funds for preliminary operations.

The alacrity with which English investors flocked to the new company alarmed the East India Company, and caused its stock to decline from 93 in September to 50 in October of 1695. The East India Company, having the king and many members of parliament virtually on its payroll, was in position to take effective action. The crisis was presented to the parliament in

[2] *Joint Stock Companies to 1720*, vol. II, p. 214.

December, and a petition was sent to the king, leading him to remark, "I have been ill-served in Scotland." The House of Commons made plans to seize the papers of English subscribers, and to impeach prominent members of the company. This action stopped the Darien Company dead in its tracks, as none of the English money, which was so essential, was paid in, and, according to one authority, deposits already made were returned.

Having failed in London, the promoters returned to Scotland to demonstrate that what the Scots lacked in money they made up in patriotic enthusiasm. The books were opened in February, 1696, and nearly £50,000 was subscribed the first day. "The nobility, the gentry, the merchants, the people, the Royal Burghs . . . subscribed. Young women threw their little fortunes into the stock, widows sold their jointures . . . for the same purpose." [3] Thus encouraged, the company decided to secure the £600,000 in spite of the English by increasing the Scotch quota to £400,000 and picking up the extra £200,000 from subscribers in Hamburg. The Scots did subscribe £400,-000, but the Hamburg plan ran head-on into the strong arm of the East India Company with the result that nothing was realized from the continent. The Darien Company had been completely isolated, and left to stand or fall on capital in Scotland.

Patriotic enthusiasm was a factor in subscribing for stock, but it required hard coin to pay the instalments as they were called. On June 1, 1696, a call was issued for one fourth of the stock, or £100,000, and it was paid to the amount of a little over £98,000. With this inadequate fund operations got under way. Five smaller calls were made later, amounting in all to £170,000, or 42½ per cent, but the total amount paid in was less than £154,000. Thereafter additional funds were obtained only by borrowing.

From the very beginning Paterson had his heart set on Darien, and not on Africa or India. The first expedition set off from Leith on July 26, 1698. All Edinburgh was there, more

3 *Ibid.*, vol. II, p. 216, quoted from Dalrymple, *Memoirs of Great Britain and Ireland.* The facts as to finance are based largely on Scott's work.

seamen volunteered than could be taken, and the stowaways were dragged crying from the holds and ropes of the vessels. "Twelve hundred men sailed in five stout ships." [4]

At last the islands of America hove in sight. There were the Virgin Islands. . . . Then Dorada island, and the coast of Darien! The colony was to be called New Scotland; its capital, New Edinburgh. The flag was the prettiest America was to know for centuries.[5]

The presence of the Scottish interlopers caused a general alarm, and again the English spread their net and drew it tighter on their victims. The Royal Secretary, Sir William Vernon, sent letters to Jamaica and to New England with instructions to give the Scots no aid. The citizens of Jamaica petitioned to have them removed, and the governor apologized to the Spanish governor of Cartagena for their intrusion, and issued a proclamation to the effect that the Scots could have no food from them. In the meantime the Spaniards organized a force to drive them out and besieged the settlement but it was saved by a hurricane. Taking advantage of the only luck they had, the Scots took the initiative and won a skirmish at Tubuganti. When news of this victory reached Edinburgh about June 20, 1700, the city was illuminated with a joyous celebration which lasted all night, but at the time the celebration was held, the Darien settlement had been two months abandoned.

It was March 31, 1700, that the emaciated survivors left for they knew not where, sailing out under the eye of a Spanish fleet of eleven vessels that gave them no choice. Of their five ships only one reached Scotland. One was lost in Darien, one in Cuba, two were destroyed by a hurricane at Charleston, South Carolina, and one reached New York. In the wake of these vessels the sharks picked the bones of more than two hundred dead. The *Caledonia* alone returned to Scottish waters with the story of Darien, and of the nine hundred who sailed seventeen months earlier, only a handful returned. The

[4] Germán Arciniegas, *Caribbean: Sea of the World* (New York: Alfred A Knopf, 1946), p. 257.
[5] *Ibid.*, pp. 257–58.

others were scattered dead or alive from Golden Island near Darien through the Caribbean, and up the Atlantic coast of North America.

Scotland had missed the windfall of the frontier, and soon awakened to hard reality to dream no more of empire. The adventurers had failed to find the windfall of gold for which they looked, and that of the logwood for which they searched. They tried a little piracy, but missed on that, too. Each individual missed the particular thing he went after, and Paterson, the master dreamer, buried his wife in Darien and his hopes in the Caribbean.

The story should close here, and it might were it not for the aftermath, for seeds sown which bore strange fruit in history and in literature. The failure of the Darien Company was an important factor in the union of England and Scotland, the birth of Great Britain in 1707. The Scottish people, feeling that the English parliament and the king contrived their ruin and blasted their hopes for a place on the frontier, exhibited a national fury that knew no bounds. It seemed to them that all the money in Scotland had been lost in Darien, and when the Scottish parliament met in 1701, the members recited the injustices from which they had suffered. Again they told how they had been blocked off from England, how Sir Peter Rycault, with the power of England behind him, had bluffed the Hamburg merchants out of participating; they recalled that the English in Jamaica had refused them food, and that the king himself had ordered his English subjects not to correspond with them, though they were subjects too. The clamor was such that votes could not be taken until at last the shouting subsided from exhaustion. Then memory would stir them anew and men would cry out in their indignation. Accusations were freely made against the English parliament, the king, and the Spaniards. One historian said that when news of the disasters and the part the English had in bringing them about reached Scotland, nothing was talked but war, and a declaration that William had forfeited the crown of Scotland.

King William seems to have realized that the situation

was serious, and that such disputes would continue to arise as long as there were two kingdoms. The solution was a union that would give one parliament, as well as one king, to England and Scotland. In 1700 the king made his recommendation to the English House of Lords, but the jealous House of Commons rejected it. As time went by the tension mounted, and the ghost of Darien returned. Although the Darien Company had lost all its capital, the Scots refused to let the company die. Ships were sent to the Orient to repeat the disaster; one disappeared with all on board, and it was believed that the English had destroyed it; another was seized in the Thames.

Then there showed up in the waters of Scotland a crippled English ship under command of Captain Thomas Green. The Scots seized the ship, charged Green and his officers with the piratical act of having destroyed the ship that had disappeared in the Orient. The infuriated Scots were determined to have their sacrifice of blood; and, though they could not prove their case, they convicted and executed Green along with two of his subordinates, and confiscated his ship, the *Worcester*. It was April 11, 1705. The temper in which the trial and execution were carried out was an indication to the English statesmen that Scotland must be placated. And, since the East India companies had achieved their purpose of destroying a rival, they were willing that it should be so, provided that the Darien Company should be officially recognized as dead.

It was in this setting that the final union of England and Scotland was effected in 1707. Though many factors entered into this union, the most human one perhaps was directly related to the Darien Company, and those who had lost money in it. It is this factor that concerns us here. It is obvious that the most important citizens of Scotland, both in and out of the parliament, had lost their money in the Darien venture, and they blamed that loss on the English. Even if they could get their money back, they would still have no kindly feeling for their southern neighbor, but certainly they would yield much if they could recover a hopelessly lost speculation. The joint commission appointed to bring about the union knew the situation and finally the terms were agreed upon for the merger of the two parliaments on the following conditions:

1. Scotland would give up the charter which kept the now bankrupt company officially alive and made it a legal threat to the monopoly sought by the English companies.

2. England would furnish the funds to pay the Scotch investors all that they had lost plus interest at 5 per cent per annum from the date the investment was made to May 1, 1707. This payment, amounting to £229,482, 15s, 1⅞d, was made out of a fund called the "Equivalent," which the sovereign had at his disposal.[6] Thus was Scotland eliminated as a power on the frontiers. Henceforth she would seek no windfalls.

The settlement offers a striking example of the relation between capitalist enterprise and government. The English India companies used the government to crush an opponent, and once the rival was destroyed and the monopoly made safe, the India companies left the human remains for the government to pick up and mollify at its own expense. This is the sort of governmental interference that the big business of the century did not object to.

There is always something appealing about tragedy, and for some reason those who suffer from it like to tell the story over and over, even to the tenth generation. It has been thus with the tragedy of the South in the Civil War in America; it has been so with Scotland's most exciting bid for greatness. What the losers have lost they regain in literature, and they are al-

---

[6] The total sum paid to Scotland amounted to £398,085 10s. The excess over the amount paid to the investors in the Darien venture was used to retire the Scottish national debt. Here was a double appeal which must have been forceful in placating the Scots and inducing them to take a more favorable view of the proposed Union. George M. Trevelyan says: "There can be no doubt that the 'Equivalent' helped to win for the Union the grudging assent of the Scottish Parliament. . . . The shareholders of the Darien Company, who never expected to see again the money they had lost in King William's reign, were to get back every penny of their capital and five per cent annual interest to boot. Many a Scottish home was the brighter for that clause in the Treaty, which was faithfully and fully performed. By putting his hand into his capacious pocket — a gesture to which he was now gradually accustoming himself — John Bull did something to wipe out, if not the memory of the dead who had been so dear, at least the abiding sense of a still unrequited wrong that the word Darien conjured up in every Scottish heart. The tragic accounts of that company were well wound up . . . its books closed for ever." — George M. Trevelyan, *Ramillies and the Union with Scotland* (London: Longmans, Green and Company, 1932), p. 268. The various factors in the Union are presented by Trevelyan. In my account I have used the one connected with the frontier.

ways looking for retribution by fate, picking out later events which would not have happened had they not made their great effort, seeking to discover the red threads of their disaster in the ironic fabric of later history. Actually, as it turned out, the Company of Scotland was not important, but there has probably been more written about it than about any other company of that period with the exception of the East India Company. Much of this writing, and by far the best part of it, has been done by the historians of Scotland.[7]

It is possible, though by no means certain, that a red thread of the Darien bubble turned up later in one of the delightful adventure masterpieces of English literature. James Balfour, an Edinburgh merchant, ranks as one of the co-founders of the Darien Company, and it was from his papers "which lay for two centuries in a little iron chest in Pilrig House," that Professor Pratt Insh has reconstructed a part of the tragic story. Balfour was a leader from the first, and at various times furnished funds for promoting the company until some stock was sold. He was one of the largest subscribers, putting his name down initially for £1,000; then, at the end, when it was necessary to round out the subscription, he doubled his pledge. He was one of twenty men against whom impeachment was attempted in the English parliament.[8]

If Balfour kept his stock until the settlement was made in 1707, he stood to recover not less than £2,000, nearly $10,000, with accumulated interest for several years, equal to half the original capital. This was no mean sum in Scotland, or anywhere else for that matter, and it no doubt made the Balfour home brighter and maintained the family fortune which provided the leisure for a tubercular descendant when he was wandering over the face of the earth in search of health and material for his stories which have been the delight of several generations. As a boy in Scotland, Robert Louis Stevenson must have heard the stories of the Scottish adventure. We know he sought out the haunts of the pirates, and read extensively

[7] Scott, *Joint Stock Companies to 1720;* George Pratt Insh (ed.), *Papers Relating to the Ships and Voyages of the Company of Scotland Trading to Africa and the Indies, 1696–1707* (Edinburgh: University Press, 1924). Hereinafter referred to as *Darien Shipping Papers.*

[8] The account of the Darien settlement is based primarily on the works of George Pratt Insh.

about them. He must have heard by family tradition of Dorado or Golden Island that lay near the settlement in Darien, a landmark often mentioned in the accounts. It may be a coincidence that he gave a variation of this name as the title of his famous story. According to Stevenson's own account, he began the story in a most casual manner, and without conscious preparation to write it, but preparation he had to have from some source. As his biographer, Graham Balfour, said, "unconscious memory came to his aid." [9] The story as it first appeared was called by the impossible name of "The Sea Cook," but in book form it became the famous *Treasure Island*. Stevenson himself never got away from his ancestors, giving their names to characters in his novels. "I am bound in and in with my forbears," he wrote. Again he said, "I see like a vision the youth of my father and of his father, and the whole stream of lives flowing down there far in the north. . . . And I admire and bow my head before the romance of destiny." [10] Moreover, James Balfour, son of the James Balfour who was active in the Darien Company, bought the estate of Pilrig, and since he was born in 1680, he probably did not buy Pilrig prior to 1707, and he probably bought it with funds realized from the settlement. Pilrig remained in the family until recent times, and it was in Pilrig House that the Darien papers were discovered. Stevenson may never have seen them, but the tragic story they told must have come to him in the family tradition on which he set such store. One other bit of evidence we do know, and that is that Stevenson had not earned a living up to the time he wrote *Treasure Island*, at the age of thirty-one. He says so himself. It was the family fortune which enabled him to travel and to have the leisure in which his writing was done. It may be that the family would have had the fortune anyway, but certainly the sum of approximately £2,000 plus interest which was refunded to James Balfour in 1707 was of service in maintaining the family fortune which gave Robert Louis Stevenson his leisure.

[9] Graham Balfour, *The Life of Robert Louis Stevenson* (New York: Charles Scribner's Sons, 1901), p. 228.
[10] *Ibid.*, p. 1.

There is another red thread of Darien, distinct and authentic, which crops up in the fabric of history two centuries later. It is the connection between the Darien enterprise and the acquisition of the Panama Canal by the United States. As the Scottish ships made their way past Golden Island on June 22, 1699, to any refuge they could find, they not only sowed their dead in the waters of the Atlantic, but they also left the living wherever the ships wrecked or landed. Captain Robert Drummond, writing from New York, described the passage by saying, "Sickness being so universal aboard, and Mortality so great that I have hove overboard 105 Corps. . . . I have buried 11 since I came heire already." This for the *Caledonia.* When the *Unicorn* arrived, it reported having "buried 150 corps by the way." [11]

In the meantime a second expedition got off to Darien, arriving there after the settlement had been abandoned. The adventures of this second expedition furnish raw material for a novel, but we are concerned here with the principal ship, the *Rising Sun.* A Scottish versifier wrote:

> We have another fleet to sail
> the Lord will Reik them fast;
> It will be wonderful to see
> the *Sun rise in the West.*[12]

The second expedition reached Darien in November, 1699, and after many experiences which would be comic if they were not so tragic, was permitted by a Spanish fleet to depart. "The tale of disease and sickness that forms the history of the Second Expedition is, if possible, a more melancholy record than even that of the First." [13] The Scots, who at the time had five ships and two sloops at Darien, surrendered to the Spaniards on March 31, 1700. It was an honorable surrender, and all ships were permitted to depart. Of the seven vessels, only one ship, the *Speedy Return,* and one sloop ever reached Scotland. The

---

[11] George Pratt Insh, *Darien Shipping Papers,* pp. 114–15.

[12] George Pratt Insh, *The Company of Scotland* (London and New York: Charles Scribner's Sons, 1932), p. 179.

[13] *Ibid.,* p. 187.

Rising Sun went to Jamaica and set sail from Blewfields on July 21 bound for New York. A month later, on August 24, the ship anchored outside the bar on the Ashley River in South Carolina for provisions. At that time, according to one account, yellow fever was raging in Charleston, and for this reason the Scots were compelled to remain on board. It was also the season of tropical storms and the *Rising Sun* was still in the harbor when the hurricane struck. An unfinished letter in the Darien collection of the National Library of Scotland begins: "On board the *Ryseing Sun* at Anchor off Ashley River in Carolina, August 29, 1701." (The year was 1700.) The writer says that by midnight the masts, bowsprit, and sails were carried away in the space of three minutes. The long boat and pennace were staved and the flagstaff carried off. The letter ends: "Our men were fatigued with pumping, the water being 6 foot above the keel all the night and the next day after our misfortune and att writing . . . . "

> Thus the letter breaks off. Whether the writer ever penned another line or not, we cannot tell. On the night of September 3rd, the *Rising Sun* was overwhelmed by a hurricane and sank at her anchorage: of all her company there survived only a small group of fifteen, who had been ashore at the time the storm broke.[14]

Among the few who went ashore and were providentially saved was one family which carried the seed of destiny, a destiny curiously related to Panama. Archibald Stobo was a Presbyterian minister, and his services were requested in Charleston at the White Meeting House. Despite the yellow fever epidemic, he had received and accepted an invitation to appear there, and with his wife had come in a small boat to the shore and into the city prior to the storm.[15] The story is best told by Mrs. St. Julien Ravenel as follows:

[14] *Ibid.*, pp. 197–98.

[15] For a fuller account of Archibald Stobo, see George Howe, *History of the Presbyterian Church in South Carolina* (2 vols.) (Columbia: Duffie & Chapman, 1870), vol. I, bk. IV, chap. I, pp. 134 ff. This account does not mention the yellow fever epidemic, but says the *Rising Sun* could not cross the bar to the harbor. Howe lists the names of fourteen people, including Mr. Stobo and his wife, the only woman in the party, who went into Charleston. There are minor discrepancies in the various accounts, but there is general agreement on the main points.

While the epidemic was still raging, in September of the same year a tremendous hurricane struck the town. . . . Outside of the bar the ship *Rising Sun* which had on board the survivors of the unhappy Scotch colony of Darien, was lying at anchor. She was on her way from the Isthmus to Scotland and had stopped for water and provisions. The congregation of the "White Meeting House," hearing that the Reverend Archibald Stobo was among the passengers, sent down to invite him to come up and preach for them on Sunday. He came, bringing his wife with him. They and the boat's crew which had brought them were therefore in Charles Town when the storm arose, and were the sole survivors of the wreck. The bodies of their unfortunate companions strewed the beach of James Island.

It need hardly be said that the congregation of the "White Meeting House" were obedient to the finger of Providence. Mr. Stobo was "called" to the church and proved himself an excellent and influential minister, leaving many descendants in the Province.[16]

It was his descendants and not his spiritual influence that gave Archibald Stobo and his wife their immortality. Their daughter, Jean, married James Bulloch, and their son was named Archibald Bulloch, and his son was James Bulloch, and his son was James Stephen Bulloch, and his daughter was Martha Bulloch, of the Bullochs of Georgia, of course. Martha Bulloch married one Theodore Roosevelt, and their son was Theodore Roosevelt, President of the United States, and so the circle is complete and we are back very near to Darien.[17] It

[16] Mrs. St. Julien Ravenel, *Charleston* (New York: The Macmillan Company, 1922), pp. 35–36.

[17] The line of descent from Archibald Stobo to Theodore Roosevelt is as follows:

Archibald Stobo (b. 167?) (Scotland) and Wife arrive Charlestown 1700.
Jean Stobo (b. 170?)   m. James Bulloch (1701–1780)
Mary de Veaux   m. Archibald Bulloch (1729–1777)
Anne Irvine   m. James Bulloch (1765–1806)
H. & M. Elliott   m. James Stephen Bulloch
Theodore Roosevelt, Sr. m. Martha Bulloch (1834–1887)
Theodore Roosevelt, Jr.

Note the persistence of the family names in the later Roosevelt family, e.g., Theodore had a son named Archibald and F.D.R. had one named Elliott and one named James. Theodore Roosevelt was always very proud of his Southern connections and thought because of his descent from the Bullochs of Georgia that he might be able to break the Solid South of its adherence to the Democratic Party.

was the great-great-great-great-grandson of Archibald Stobo who some two centuries later fulfilled the dream of William Paterson by taking the Isthmus that the Scots failed to take, and uniting the two seas — Paterson's crossroads of the world. Those who love irony and believe in retribution may derive some satisfaction by imagining three Scots, William Paterson the dreamer, James Balfour the financier, and Archibald Stobo the preacher, looking down with grim approval as the Americans reaped the windfall, opened the door of the seas and found the key of the universe, the key that the English had taken from the Scots but never possessed for themselves. The event does indeed reinforce the dry statement by the Scottish historian of the Darien Company who said: "One of the noteworthy features of Scottish colonial projects is that the results they achieved invariably differed widely from those originally aimed at." [18]

It would be easy to assume from the story of the Scots in Darien that their failure was of their own making. In a sense this is true because the whole enterprise suffered from inner weaknesses and mismanagement — which the Scots could not overcome with the means at their disposal. In a larger sense, their failure was a forerunner of things to come, a reasonably clear indication that a phase of the frontier was over. In Darien they sought gold, hunted logwood, and considered a little piracy, but to no avail. The frontier was no longer a treasure-trove of precious metals, furs, or ambergris; the claims had been staked out by the big nations, and the only hope of the Scots was to exist in the interstices with less ostentation than the men of Darien exhibited.

The Scots, acting under the old order of the joint stock company of the seventeenth century, gave an early demonstration that the day of such companies was over, but the significance of their failure was obscured by the confusion that attended it. Their effort must be ranked as the first of three bubbles which burst as a warning to Europe that the quick windfalls were no more in the New World. Of this fact the Mississippi Bubble and the South Sea Bubble furnished further convincing proof.

18 George Pratt Insh, *Darien Shipping Papers*, p. ix.

2. *The French Bubble: Mississippi*

In 1666, Robert Cavelier de La Salle, a well-educated French-man, came to Montreal, where he received a grant of land in the St. Lawrence Valley. Though he was only twenty-three, he turned explorer and soon won favor with Frontenac, the governor. His explorations led him west into the wilderness south of Lake Erie and Lake Ontario, and into the valley of the Mississippi. As a result of a trip to France in 1677, he was given a monopoly of all French trade in the Mississippi Valley. Continuing his explorations, he descended the Mississippi to its mouth, and there on April 9, 1682, he formally took pos-session of the whole valley in the name of Louis XIV, naming the region Louisiana. He determined to establish a string of settlements reaching from Canada to the Gulf, and in 1684 he left France with four ships for the mouth of the great river. The expedition went too far west and landed in Matagorda Bay in Texas. There in the piny woods of East Texas in 1687 La Salle was murdered at the age of forty-four by one of his own men. Though he had failed in his purpose, his activity gave France a claim to one of the greatest river basins in the world, and laid the foundation for one of the strangest aberra-tions of frontier enterprise on record.

At the time La Salle was killed, John Law was a youth of sixteen in Edinburgh, handsome, intelligent, well educated, with a special gift for mathematics. This gift he applied at first to cards, with great success, and later to finance with the most spectacular results. At an early age he went to London, where his way with women and his extravagant habits made him many friends and much trouble. He was saved from his debt-ors by his indulgent mother, but nothing could save him from English justice when on Bloomsbury Square he killed Edward (Beau) Wilson over a woman on April 9, 1694, twelve years to a day from the time when La Salle named Louisiana and pro-claimed the Mississippi Valley the property of Louis XIV. Law escaped to the continent and there devoted himself to gam-bling, the study of finance, and the cultivation of the right people. In order to better understand finance, he became a clerk in the Bank of Amsterdam, then the financial center of the world, and he pursued his studies in other continental countries as well. It was during this period that Law evolved his theory of finance, a theory foreshadowing modern banking practice and government finance. In 1705 he returned to Scotland; after his stay in France and Holland, he was shocked at the comparative' poverty of his own people.

There was nothing farther from Law's mind than a colonial enterprise, and at that date it is doubtful if the word Mississippi meant anything to him at all. He had conceived a scheme of financial maneuver which belonged to a metropolis and not to a frontier, and it is almost an accident, certainly an afterthought and a detail, that the Mississippi Valley became involved and gave its name to what was primarily a banking manipulation. As a matter of fact the part that the Mississippi Valley played in his undertaking was so inconsequential as to excite wonder that the name was used at all. The name itself must have been the reason — in what delightful accents it must have rolled from the lips of the French gamblers in stock!

Because of evil association which grew out of the catastrophe to France resulting from Law's system, it is difficult to present him in his true light as an exceedingly able person with a touch of genius whose real purpose was to make a valuable contribution to mankind. Even a good ship can founder on perilous seas, regardless of its worthy destination. Law's ship, sailing the uncharted sea of high finance, could not make the harbor, and he received all the blame for the wreck. In reality, a more appropriate name for what has come down in history as the Mississippi Bubble would have been Law's System of National Banking, and the Mississippi Valley was actually only a small part of the collateral on which that system was founded.

In essence what Law wanted to do was to use real property, commercial paper, and state promises to pay as collateral for a banking system that would provide an elastic currency in the transaction of business, a currency sufficient to meet the requirements both of business and the nation. It was the elasticity and convenience of paper currency as distinguished from the rigidity and inconvenience of specie, not to mention its scarcity, that formed the foundation stones of his plan. Had

Law lived under Woodrow Wilson he would probably have been one of the founders of the Federal Reserve System of the United States, and his plan as he worked it out, and would have applied it, anticipated much that was incorporated in the Federal Reserve System exactly two centuries later. The best authority on Law's system, Adolphe Thiers, said that Law's error was the assumption, common at that time, that money was wealth, and that lack of money was what prevented prosperity. Therefore, if a convenient and elastic paper currency could be provided, it would be a great boon to national well-being. Thiers, in commenting on Law's reaction to the poor condition in Scotland, quotes Law as saying: "What is wanting to the proprietor to enable him to clear up his lands; to the manufacturer to multiply his looms; to the merchant to extend his operations? *Advances,* that is to say money, to pay for the first materials and the manual labor." [19] He tells how credit may be used as money. "By what means can money be supplied? It is *credit;* it is the establishment of banks which give to paper the value and efficiency of specie." [20]

It would seem that Thiers read an error into Law's system that is hardly justified. In every case, Law envisaged something tangible back of the paper. Note that he spoke of "advances," namely, an extension of credit on a prospect of later profit. He saw, and correctly, that in initiating or expanding an enterprise, it was necessary to have extra funds, advances, credits, to be used until the returns could begin to come in.

The heart of Law's system was to be a bank with sufficient resources to service a whole nation. At any rate, he presented such a plan in Scotland, first in 1700 and again in 1705, only to have it rejected. In the first instance he proposed a company with extensive and inclusive privileges; in the second he proposed a national bank, sometimes called a territorial bank, and set forth his views in a pamphlet entitled "Considerations upon Hard Money." The plan called for a bank to issue notes on loans, on land mortgaged to one half or two thirds of its value, or upon land pledged to sell at a fixed date and at a

[19] Adolphe Thiers, *The Mississippi Bubble* (New York: W. A. Townsend & Co., 1859), p. 19. Italics supplied.
[20] *Loc. cit.*

stipulated price. On the basis of the notes and mortgages received, the bank would issue its notes which would circulate
as a medium of exchange. It is clear that these notes were
issued on the basis of either commercial or land security, and
certainly the margin of safety on land loans seems ample.

Law envisaged a bank that not only would lend money on
commercial paper or security, but that would also take over
other functions. At that time taxes were farmed out to contractors at an enormous cost. The bank would lend the government the necessary money, collect the taxes itself, and eliminate the exorbitant cost. Again he had security. It was also
common to grant monopolies to commercial enterprises operating as chartered companies. The bank would accept these
monopolies, and engage in lucrative commerce. Again the
prospect of profit.

> Combining thus [says Thiers] the profits of a bank of discount
> with those of the administration of the public revenue and those
> of its commerce as a privileged company, it would necessarily
> have an immense capital, which it would distribute in shares
> among which would be divided its profits. In this manner it
> would offer its notes to those who desired a circulating medium,
> and its shares to those who sought a profitable investment.[21]

Failing of success in Scotland, which had been cured of speculation by the Darien Company, Law returned to the continent where he presented his plan to various governments
with a uniform lack of success. Shortly he went to Paris, where
his genius for calculation enabled him to win large sums in
gambling and soon he became the head of the Duclos faro
bank "and never commenced playing without a hundred thousand francs."[22] Being a Protestant, he won no favor with
Louis XIV, but he won so much money from Louis's courtiers,
and lived in such grand style, that he aroused jealousies, and
was invited by the police to go elsewhere. He proceeded to
Italy, expounding his financial system to the rulers and winning money from the courtiers. He was advised by Victor
Amédée of Turin in Switzerland to take his system to Ger-

21 *Ibid.,* p. 26.
22 *Ibid.,* p. 37.

many or France. He now tried Germany, where the emperor was setting up a bank, but failed there, too. Then he returned to Scotland but took the precaution to deposit a vast sum won at gambling, said to have been two million francs, in France.

His bad luck, in banking, broke in 1715 when Louis XIV died, leaving French finances in a deplorable condition. Various expedients were tried, but the debts were so heavy and the situation so desperate that expedients would not work. Into this situation stepped John Law with all the confidence that characterized his whole life, and this time those in authority listened to him. "Law by no means despaired of France, the most fertile and most thickly populated country in Europe, as well as the most industrious." [23] He first won the regent who admired his genius and versatility. Through the regent, the Duke of Orleans, he appeared before the council of finance with a plan (the same one he had had all the time) so magnificent that the timid men could not grasp it. To quote Thiers:

> Law did not propose any half-way measures. He offered his project entire; that is to say, a bank which should discount, should collect the national revenues, should carry on commercial monopolies, and afford, at the same time, a plentiful circulation of paper money and a means of profitable investment.[24]

When this proposal was turned down, Law fell back on a more modest one, the establishment of a bank of discount. He skillfully brushed aside all objections, and on May 2, 1716, was granted a charter permitting him to set up the bank *at his own expense*. There is no doubt Law believed that if he could only make a beginning, even a small one, he could eventually find a way to carry out his bigger plan.

His capital was 6,000,000 francs, twelve hundred shares at 5000 francs each. The wisest provision, in view of an increasing debased coinage, required him to redeem the bank notes in coin of the weight and denomination of the date of the charter, May 2, 1716. This guarantee gave the notes a stability that the coins themselves had hitherto lacked, and made a great

[23] Thiers, *The Mississippi Bubble*, p. 43.
[24] *Ibid.*, p. 44.

appeal to foreigners. A further measure, which must have originated with Law, exempted both the notes and the deposits
from confiscation.

The effect of the bank was not quickly seen, but it was accumulative and in the end magical. The government used
the notes; people found them convenient; and their prompt
payment on demand in specie of standard value — all these
things inspired confidence, and the foreigners resumed business in France. The discount rate was reasonable; usury diminished. "On the whole, at the end of one year, all the results
predicted by Law were, for the most part, accomplished." [25]

The next step was to expand the good effects of the Paris
institution to the provinces. With the aid of the regent, an
edict was issued on April 10, 1717, ordering the tax farmers
and officials of the government treasury to receive the bank
notes in lieu of specie and to redeem them exactly as the bank
did. This resulted in the use of paper in making all payments
and the specie itself tended to accumulate in the bank as a
reserve. Law made the notes more desirable than specie by
providing that each spender should endorse them without liability, making it most hazardous for the thief or finder to use
them because he could be identified. When the notes were
finally returned to Paris, covered with signatures, they were
destroyed and others issued in their place.

The success of Law's bank was phenomenal. Within a year
his notes brought a premium of 15 per cent, while the promise
of the nation of France to pay stood at a discount of 78½ per
cent.[26] Branch banks were opened in five of the large cities of
the provinces, and Law had realized his ambition to have a
bank that was truly national in scope. But he had as yet put
into effect only a small part of his scheme.

Instead of enlarging the scope of his bank, he now proceeded to organize the commercial company, similar to the
great enterprises then so common. He planned to add one
function after another as the company prospered until it included all that he had in mind. Then he would effect a merger
of the banking and commercial enterprises somewhat in the

25 *Ibid.*, p. 47.
26 *Ibid.*, p. 51.

modern manner. In August, 1717, the bedazzled regent issued the edict granting Law all he wanted. Thus entered the Mississippi Valley, the French empire that La Salle founded when Law was sixteen years old.

In 1712, Louis XIV had granted to a merchant, Antonine Crozat, a monopoly of trade in the vast Louisiana territory. Crozat sent over some colonists and carried on some trade, but conditions were such that the undertaking was only an expense, and in 1717 he surrendered his patent. By that date Law's bank was at or near the peak of its success, and Law procured in the Mississippi Valley the opportunity to realize the completion of his design. In August, 1717, he succeeded to the monopoly of trade in all that vast region,[27] hoping to unite the commerce of the great valley with the fur trade of Canada.

In this instance, as in all others, Law approached his problem as a financier rather than as a frontier adventurer seeking a quick windfall or as a well-intentioned colonizer. To him the Mississippi Valley was another piece of collateral which he could put up as security for the "advance" or credit, which he conceived to be necessary to any new enterprise. The advance would be made by investors and speculators in France who would take the shares, hoping to be rewarded by rich returns from the fabulous frontier. It cannot be doubted that the Mississippi Valley was a good piece of collateral, and time has proved its potential. What Law did not realize was that he had come into possession of a secondary windfall — of a part of the frontier where the waiting period for returns would necessarily be entirely too long to be of much benefit to men then living.

The name Mississippi did not occur in the title of the company, and it would be interesting to know by what psychology the word usurped first place in the public mind. The company was capitalized at 100,000,000 francs, divided into two hundred thousand shares of 500 francs each, and these shares were offered to the public. Though Law probably had little real interest in the Mississippi territory, he did know how to use

[27] *Ibid.*, p. 60.

its appeal for all it was worth. The promotion literature emphasized, with justice, the richness of the soil, the abundant resources of this garden of the world;[28] it hinted at the presence of treasure such as Spain had found in Mexico and South America; it was adorned with a coat of arms showing an ancient "river-god leaning upon a horn of plenty." The map maker, the indispensable aid of the promoter, was called in, and as in all booms, the map showed that the new enterprise was right in the middle of production and could not miss.

The next step was to make the new shares palatable to the people of France, and here Law again exhibited his ingenuity by devising a plan which would be a step in the direction of giving him control of the French public debt. The financial situation was so bad that the state's promise to pay was worth about twenty francs on the hundred, and the amount of the debt was 250,000,000 francs in the form of notes. Law agreed to sell his shares for one fourth cash and three fourths in the depreciated state notes *at par value*. These notes paid interest at 4 per cent, not a bad rate when it can be collected. In this manner Law absorbed 75,000,000 francs in notes, relieving their depressed state and causing them to rise, eventually, to par. Since the notes bore interest at 4 per cent, Law had a guarantee of 3,000,000 income which would be used the first year to begin the development in America, and thereafter divided among the shareholders.

Law's bank entered the picture by buying state notes and investing 6,000,000 francs in the colonial venture. Since the shares permitted three fourths payment in depreciated state paper, they naturally sold at first below par, but the combined action of the bank and the company caused the shares to rise and of course the depreciated currency rose also. Another result was that all the hard money of the kingdom was slowly but surely flowing into the bank and coming under the control of Law.

It still remained for Law to acquire the privilege of collecting taxes which were contracted out on such terms as to yield

<hr />

28 For the origin of the Garden of the World see Henry Nash Smith, *Virgin Land: The American West as Symbol and Myth* (Cambridge, Mass.: Harvard University Press, 1950), pp. 123 ff.

the contractors a profit. In December, 1718, the bank was made the Royal Bank, and its notes were made more popular, so popular that the capital stock was increased by ten million francs. Turning back to the Western company, Law executed a maneuver seldom heard of before but very common in modern speculation. This was buying Western shares on margin in anticipation of a continuous rise, which his example, if followed, would bring about. It must be borne in mind that Western shares were below par because they were purchased with the depreciated currency. But Law made a contract to pay 100,000 francs for 200 shares (par) at a fixed future date. He put up 40,000 francs as margin and agreed to forfeit it if the shares did not exceed par at the designated date of final execution. At the time of purchase the shares stood at 300 francs, so that he could have bought them at 60,000 francs. Instead he contracted to buy futures at 500 francs or lose the 40,000-franc margin that he had put up. In short, to use a modern term to describe a common practice, he rigged a bull market. The example Law had set influenced others to buy on margin, and in this way a given amount of capital could be made to purchase a larger number of shares. By April, 1719, the shares were approaching par.

His next step was to unite the two Eastern companies, which were being badly managed, with the Western company, and in the process he picked up the company trading to Senegal. He now had an exclusive French monopoly on the trade of Asia, Africa, and North America. The name of the united company was appropriately changed from the West India Company to the Indian Company, and Law turned to issuing stock on his new collateral. Fifty thousand new shares were authorized with a par value of 500 francs, but a premium of 50 francs was required. This second issue was called the *daughters* to distinguish them from the first, called the *mothers*. The shares could be secured on a down payment of 50 francs, and the balance in twenty monthly instalments of 25 francs each, so that the little fellows could get in and so that the speculator could make a given sum go a long way. The shrewdest provision was one that required the buyer to hold four mother shares before he could have one of the daughters. In the rush to obtain the old shares, they went above par, to 750 francs,[29] and Law won his bet on his futures deal already mentioned.

The opportunity to expand the functions of the Indian Company came because of the financial ineptitude of the government. The regent attempted to meet the crisis by recoining a billion of specie with a new value of 1,200,000,000, a profit of 200,000,000. The difficulty was that the old coins refused to come in to be converted into worse ones. Law offered the regent 50,000,000 francs for the privilege of undertaking the job, and a decree was issued on August 25, 1719, authorizing him to do it. He stood to realize a profit of 150,000,000 francs, less expense. Here was more collateral, and on it Law issued another fifty thousand shares, the *granddaughters*, at the usual par value of 500 francs each which would have produced but half the sum needed to pay the regent. Law solved this problem by selling his shares at twice par, 1000 francs each. The usual easy terms were offered, but five old shares had to be presented to get the privilege of purchasing one new one. To make all the shares seem more desirable, Law announced that a semi-annual dividend of 6 per cent would be paid, a sum amounting to 18,000,000 francs a year. As fantastic as this seems, it would have been possible because Law had a reasonably assured profit on every transaction save the commercial enterprises, where profit was problematical. The state notes brought the company 3,000,000 francs annually, the coinage was profitable, and the commercial enterprises might be.

But one more step remained to make Law the financial master of all France, and that was a contract to collect all taxes, and pay the national debt of about 1,600,000,000 francs, thus freeing the government from its insoluble problem, and making a profit. The interest on the debt amounted to 80,000,000 francs annually, one half the national revenue. There was never money for current expenses, or any to redeem maturing state notes, Law made this offer: The Indian Company would advance the 1,600,000,000 francs to the government, enabling it to wipe the slate clean. The government would in return authorize the Indian Company to issue shares to the public, the purchase of which would restore to the company the funds

29 *Ibid.*, p. 73.

lent to the government. The government would pay the Indian Company 3 per cent interest, an annual income of about 48,000,000 francs for the company, and a saving of around 32,000,000 francs to the government!

In collecting the taxes the Indian Company would realize a profit of 15,000,000 or 16,000,000 francs, which with the 48,-000,000 francs interest paid by the government would give the company a gross profit of 63,000,000 or 64,000,000 francs. This income was sufficient to pay the shareholders an interest rate of about 4 per cent on the shares. There was the added chance of profits derived from the African and East Indian trade and from the magical Mississippi problematical windfalls.

It was the issue of shares on this enormous volume of asssets that led Law into his fatal blunder. The operation of raising 1,600,000,000 francs, turning it over to the government for the payment of the debt, and recovering it by sale of shares was a most delicate one indeed, a transaction involving a considerable lapse of time because the shares could not be sold until the state debt was paid, and the state debt could not be paid until somebody dug up more money than anybody had. The only possible solution was to pay a part of the state debt, issue shares to cover, sell these shares, and with the proceeds pay another portion of the state debt and so on until a complete transfer could be made. But here Law took a short cut which brought his downfall. He had already issued three hundred thousand shares. He now issued an additional one hundred thousand shares, but instead of selling them at par, or even at 550 or 1000, he priced the shares at 5000! We have seen that he had income in sight which would hardly enable him to pay 4 per cent at par, and obviously it would be wholly inadequate on shares at ten times par. What Law did here, to use a modern term, was to water his stock.

The reason he did this was to raise the 1,600,000,000 francs for the government very quickly, and by the sale of 10 per cent of the shares instead of all of them. He would still have nine tenths of his shares in reserve and all his obligations paid! His resources were at this time so enormous that he still might have made it had not the public taken the play out of his hands in such an orgy of gambling as the world had never seen.

The shares were dispensed in such a manner as to whet the public appetite for them; and as the greed increased, the shares rose. Law himself never issued the shares for more than 5000 francs, but the rue Quincampoix, where the speculators formed what amounted to a curb stock exchange, did. With the new issue of shares pegged at 5000 francs, the older ones, purchased at 200, 500, 550, 1000, rose to the same height on the curb. But they did not stop there. The speculators in the rue Quincampoix pushed them on up to 18,000 and 20,000 francs! The total issues of six hundred thousand shares had a par value of 1,677,500,000 francs, but at 15,000 they had a curb value of 9,000,000,000, and no one stopped to inquire as to the soundness of the base on which the whole structure rested. Though Law had not planned on such wild speculation, he seems to have been somewhat affected by what he had done and at any rate he could not now control the situation.

The rue Quincampoix was called the *Mississippi*, and that name has come to be permanently attached to what amounted to a national insanity. It should be perfectly clear that the Mississippi country constituted but a very small part of the West Indian Company enterprises, and even less of the Indian enterprises, and of all of them it was the most questionable. Out of the six hundred thousand shares, only fifty thousand were issued on the Mississippi venture, or 8.3 per cent. Taking the shares at the original price of sale, the Mississippi investment was less than 3 per cent of the whole. The operation was so gigantic that the omission of the Mississippi venture could have made not the slightest difference in the operation.

Why was the name used? This is a question that no one, so far as I have been able to find, has attempted to answer. It therefore furnishes an opportunity for some speculation in connection with the frontier. For one thing, it is a nice name, pleasant to the tongue, pleasing to the ear, and its appeal probably lost nothing of its charm from the soft accents of French lips. Many a Frenchman must have hypnotized himself by repeating it over and over while shaving, and by the time he had finished, he was ready to go out and buy Mississippi stock without realizing how diluted it was. The great river, binding an inland empire, with lakes at one end and a gulf at the other, was flanked on both sides by untouched forests, pristine soil, and perhaps tons of gold and silver hidden in its secret places! There dwelt the ancient river god with his horn of plenty, as represented on the coat of arms of the company, and surely he would richly reward those who trusted in him!

Perhaps another appeal lay in the fact that the Mississippi was far away, a land of romance of which the average Frenchman knew less than he did of any other part of Law's composite enterprises. The French knew about coins and their debasement, about taxes and how hard the collectors were, about the state notes and how worthless they had been until Law came along, but they knew nothing about the Mississippi save what they imagined, and imagination thrives best on little substance and great distances.

It is not germane to our purpose to relate the story of the fall of the House of Law. Once he had made the fatal mistake of watering his shares and suffering the speculators to take over, his fall was inevitable. It was accompanied by all the familiar phenomena of the panic that follows a boom, and as usual the public demanded vengeance. Before the collapse Law consolidated the bank and the Indian Company, as he had had in mind doing, and he resorted to all the stratagems to save the falling structure, but all efforts failed. By 1720 the ruin was complete; the state took back the various privileges it had granted and resumed as best it could its own obligations. In the dissolution, all privileges of the company within France were taken away, but it was left to carry on its monopoly of trade in the West and in the East. The company had no success, and it was finally abolished in 1731.

The public clamor was such that Law was compelled to quit the country, but to the very end he acted with an uprightness not often seen among his successors in speculation and promotion. He saved nothing for himself, made no investments outside of France, and took practically nothing with him when he quitted Paris for Brussels. All of his property in France was confiscated, as was much of that of the Mississippians, as they were called — men who had grown rich in speculation. On March 21, 1729 — three years before George Washington was born — Law died in Venice. His estate consisted of a few pictures, and a ring which he would pawn when the luck of the cards was against him. Though he had lost, he had left a pattern of high finance which lesser men were to follow. He had shown how to take the public into speculation, how to deal in futures, how to rig the market, how to operate on the curb, how to water stock, and he had illustrated the danger of the last two operations.

Needless to say that the word bubble was not of his devising, and it was probably little used until after the blowup. Though we have seen what a small part the distant frontier land played in Law's gigantic operation, the whole speculation was designated the Mississippi Bubble, and so it is known in history.

3. The English Bubble: The South Seas

It is said that small boys around the world begin playing at marbles at about the same time, and it might be said that history reveals them following the pattern endemically in matters of trade and finance when they are men. To tell the story of the South Sea Bubble in England would be as dull as its originator, the stuffy Earl of Harley, was dull when compared to the flashing, versatile John Law. But the game in England, beginning a little later and lasting a little longer, followed closely the pattern laid in France. Since we are concerned only with the relation of these enterprises to the frontier, we shall treat the third bubble summarily.

The South Sea Company was projected in 1711 for the purpose of restoring the public debt. Since the Bank of England was already established, Harley did not have the opportunity of including it in his plan. The South Sea Bubble had its beginning when a group of merchants, as yet without a charter, undertook a part of the public debt, making its profit on the interest received from the government, and on collecting imposts on imported commodities, such as wines, India goods, silk, tobacco, and whale fins. A charter was issued to the group on September 8, 1711, for the purpose of "satisfying the public Debt and for erecting a Corporation to carry on the Trade to the South Seas and for the encouragement of the Fishery and for Liberty to trade in unwrought iron with the subjects of Spain." [30]

The public debt which the incorporators assumed amounted to the tidy sum of £9,471,325, and this now became the obligation of the South Sea Company with the official title of "The Governor and Company of Merchants of Great Britain trading to the South Seas and other parts of America." The college of heralds provided a coat of arms with the legend "From Cadiz to the Dawn," and the map makers were called in to perform their customary rites in promotion.

What the company had done thus far was to refund the public debt at 6 per cent, and take a mortgage on the import duties and other levies to secure it. This rather sure prospect of income was sweetened up with the hope of additional profits from the South Seas enterprise, which was purely speculative. The question arises as to the identity and geographical location of the South Seas, and as to the tangible assets of the company in that far country with the soft-sounding name so appealing to residents in the dour English climate. The South Seas consisted of the waters surrounding South America and western North America and no land at all. Much of the region was still firmly in the possession of Spain. Therefore, the tangible assets of the company were almost nothing, merely a prospect of building up trade in a region from which that trade was officially excluded by Spain. In contrast, so far as the frontier was concerned, John Law did have the heart of North America, a good chunk of real estate which had intrinsic value, but his English counterpart had nothing more than a determination to become a claim jumper in a region to which the British nation laid no claim. Immediately rumor supplanted fact and imagination knowledge. There was much talk of the gold and silver of Mexico and Peru, of trading English manufactured goods to simple Indians for ingots of gold and silver. It was reported that Spain would provide four ports for English trade. The answer to this was the *Asiento* of 1713 by which Spain granted the English the right to send into South Amer-

[30] Viscount Erleigh, *The South Sea Bubble* (New York: G. P. Putnam's Sons, 1933), p. 28.

ica one ship each year. There was a further provision that England could supply the Spanish colonies with slaves for thirty years, and in addition could send one ship, limited as to tonnage and value of cargo, each year provided the King of Spain could take a cut of one fourth the profit, and a tax of 5 per cent on what was left. The first voyage was made in 1717; it turned out badly and the trade was suppressed the following year. It may be said that the frontier assets of the South Sea Company consisted, not of blue sky, but of blue sea.

The company got along very well until John Law's star began to rise in France. Then Harley and his associates, stung by Law's success, began to emulate him and hoped to excel him. Instead of having a mere commoner from Scotland to head the company, the board elected George I as governor, and he accepted the job. In the meantime Harley had been ousted, but there rose up in his place John Blount, son of a shoemaker from Rochester; he had become a scrivener, and proved to be a genius with projects and adept in the art of usury. Withal he was a pious person who carried a prayer book in one hand, a prospectus in the other, and kept the moral implications of the two separated. He became the dominant figure in the board whose members were notable for lack of force and perspicacity.

Blount's plan was to assume the whole English debt amounting to £51,000,000. To the operation of the South Sea enterprise, he would add the banking privileges enjoyed by the Bank of England, and take over the trade monopoly held by the East India Company. The result of this suggestion was that he immediately aroused the hostility of both the Bank of England and the East India Company. In spite of this opposition, Blount was able to put his bill through both houses, and on April 7, 1720, it received royal approval. In order that the law might conform to the bill, £1,250,000 was judiciously distributed to court favorites, ministers, and members of parliament. Though the Bank of England was not strong enough to stop the South Sea Company, it shrewdly increased its liability by compelling it through competitive bidding to pay the government a premium of £7,567,000 for the privilege of assuming the public debt, and to lower its interest rate on the debt to 4 per cent.

It is obvious that with the expenditure for bribes, the extra premium, and the reduced interest rate, there was no chance for the company to make ends meet except by increasing the price of the stock which was exchanged with speculating creditors for the various forms of state debts. Consequently, the board began to maneuver the rise of South Sea stock. In January, 1720, it rose to 128, in February to 184, in March to 380 — this before the law was enacted.[31] All the old drums of promotion throbbed again, and rumors of riches flew from tongue to tongue; the maps and the charts, the plans and the pamphlets were all there. Men recalled that Drake once paid his fellow adventurers incredible dividends on their investment, and that Raleigh had dreamed of a magnificent trade empire. The sound of the South Seas was as soothing to the English nerves as that of Mississippi was exciting to the French, and on both sides of the Channel the people went crazy at the same time. By the end of April, the second issue of stock was made at £400! And a dividend of 10 per cent was declared for midsummer, out of capital, of course. By the end of May the stock stood at 500, and two days later, June 2, it was 890. On June 18, a third issue was put out at £1,000. Six days later it stood at 1050, the peak. Thereafter, the only way was down, and in September it was 150.

As in all such speculations, the frenzy was not limited to the biggest bubble. The air was full of small ones, and for a time their stock rose in sympathy with the South Sea stuff. In Exchange Alley, the counterpart of the rue Quincampoix, men and women bought and sold. As the panic progressed men cut their throats, blew out their brains, went mad, or died of broken hearts. And women too.

The government now picked up where the company left off. Now that it could no longer have money, the public demanded vengeance. Ministers were disgraced, members expelled from parliament, and fortunes confiscated to make restitution. The father of Edward Gibbon, the historian, was left but £10,000 out of a fortune of £106,000 which he had built up.

After the bubble burst, and the people had gone back to work, the South Sea Company, recalling that it had fishing rights, tried its hand after whales in Greenland, but "the Pole

[31] *Ibid.*, p. 65.

Star brought it no greater luck than the Southern Cross. The whales forewarned by the fate of the British public, steadfastly refused to be caught." [32] The company continued to exist until 1854, but confined its activities to the payment of annuities.

4. The Meaning of the Bubbles

We have now followed the story of the three bubbles which characterized the end of the seventeenth century. The Scotch bubble, better known as the Darien enterprise, represents the effort of a weak nation to enter into overseas commercial and colonial activities after the free lands of the frontier had been claimed if not appropriated by the stronger powers. As we have seen, it was wrecked, and Scotland was ruined financially and industrially, more by the East India Company and by the English parliament and the king than by the Spaniards. Actually it never had a chance. The Darien Company was conducted along the old lines of the joint stock company, and it therefore did not involve the Scottish people in a frenzy of wild speculation that was present in the two succeeding bubbles. It belonged definitely to the past, and in the last analysis it failed because the future was against it.

The Mississippi and South Sea bubbles represent a distinct departure from the past and were signal guns of the future. The frontier element was present in both of them, an element carried over from the commercial enterprises of the past two centuries. The frontier constituted an infinitesimally small part of both operations. Very little effort was made to colonize the Mississippi Valley; even less effort was made to trade in the South Seas, and all were of indifferent success as to colonization and complete failures as an investment. The purpose in both cases was to conduct a program of high finance, based largely on state debts, and to make money not out of the frontier but out of the people of France and England, respectively. Since there were no longer quick windfalls on the frontier, the windfalls were sought from people who lived in the Metropolis and who still dreamed of such windfalls as those of Drake, Phipps, and the Spaniards. It is significant that the titles of both com-

[32] *Ibid.*, p. 165.

panies were chosen from the frontier, chosen perhaps — and useful beyond doubt — for their appeal to the imagination and for the connotations and associations that clustered around the Mississippi Valley and the South Seas. It is inconceivable that the public would have reacted in the same manner to such appropriate titles as the French Debt or the English Bankrupt Company, which is exactly what they were. It was this turning from the real frontier where new wealth could be had without taking it away from others to the Metropolis where it could be had only by taking it away from a public which was no less gullible than the American Indians and far less dangerous. that has significance. This was the departure from the old-time stock companies of the commercial age and the introduction of modern high finance with which the eighteenth and ninetennth centuries became familiar.

The two ventures can be best understood in their setting. By 1700 the commercial revolution was over — based as it was primarily on carrying commodities easily acquired from one place to another, finding wealth ready made, or in the hands of natives who traded it for baubles. This does not mean that commodities were no longer carried, but it does mean that the trade had become fairly well standardized, and was under the control of such established institutions as the East India Companies, the Hudson's Bay Company, or the Spaniards. In short, to use an oil boom expression, production had settled down.

The price revolution and the commercial revolution had combined to build up fortunes to capitalistic proportions. Despite all the wars, Europe was far richer both in money and in commodities than she had ever been. There was so much money that the time had come to set up national banking institutions, such as the Dutch Bank of Amsterdam in 1609, the Bank of England in 1694, the Royal Bank of France in 1718, and there cannot be the slightest doubt that not less than 80 per cent of the specie and bullion lying in these banks had come from American frontiers, and what is more, it was still coming. The idea — stemming no doubt from a subconscious memory of a time of barter when there was practically no gold or silver — still prevailed that money was real wealth, not just a symbol of it, and this idea was incorporated in the economic practice of mercantilism. But another process was under way which in time would undermine this article of faith, and that process was the unceasing flow of real wealth, commodities, from the world frontiers into the Metropolis of Europe. It is a safe guess — though I know not what the economists will say about it — that by the end of the seventeenth century the volume of commodities was increasing faster than the circulating medium, and with the production of commodities increasing faster than that of precious metals, the inevitable result would be the existence of more Things than money. That is to say that money would become relatively scarce despite the fact that the absolute amount of it was far greater than it had been. In this relative scarcity men would seek a substitute, some supplementary fund that could be added to the gold and silver so that the amount of money and goods would roughly match.[33]

With money generally recognized as the medium of exchange, with banks established to traffic in it, and with commodities pouring in out of all proportion to the money available for their purchase, it became necessary to canvass the situation and see if the impending crisis could be met by increasing the money instead of permitting prices to fall and running the risk of panic or serious depression. As an evidence that money was growing relatively scarce, we find that governments, notably England and France, were deep in debt and could not meet their obligations, and it is likely that other nations were little better off.

In France it was John Law who conceived the idea of credit, an advance on good collateral in anticipation of future profit, as a supplement to money itself. Anticipated profits in the form of notes could be added to the volume of specie or substituted for it, and thus increase by the amount of the note issue the quantity of the circulating medium. Law has been charged with the error of believing that money was the real

---

[33] The economists have said that according to the "law" of supply and demand, the scarcity of money would result in a fall of prices, and vice versa. This, it seems to me, is another way of saying that the amount of money in circulation and the amount of commodities in circulation must be, or tend to be, roughly equal. The "law" is merely a name applied to the adjustment necessary to establish the balance. If this is not true, then money, whatever it is, is no symbol or equivalent of wealth.

wealth, and that credit, an anticipation of actual money, was its equivalent. The charge is hardly justified, for in every case Law had the idea of founding the credit, or notes, on real collateral. The fact that some of his collateral was too flimsy or too raw to support expectations is another point entirely. His mistake in the end was in watering his stock, issuing too much credit on too little collateral. It is clear that Law conceived of credit as an anticipation of profit, money to be realized from the advance on expectations, a device of making the supply of money equal to the supply of Things.

Over in England Blount imitated Law as best his intelligence would permit, and published two pamphlets under the titles of *Credit* and *Loans* in which he set forth similar ideas on the same subject. Lacking Law's understanding he was unequal to Law's clear expression, and it is believed that the learned pamphlets were written by Daniel Defoe, who had some knowledge of finance as well as of the doings of Robinson Crusoe.

It was the financial embarrassment of the state that gave Law and Blount the opportunity to try out their new theory of credit. It is clear in both cases that there was good collateral for the issue of notes in reason and with regard for the prospect of income that would pay a reasonable interest and in time retire the principal. In the end both men came to rely on the rise of stock rather than a moderate return for profit. They gave up a sound plan of refunding the national debt for speculation where the collateral was nothing more than the cupidity and bad judgment of those who followed the Pied Piper's silvery notes to their own ruin.

The frontier was merely the flute on which the tune was played. There were examples in the past of where the frontier had furnished a quick windfall, and paid investors as much as 10,000 per cent! Mississippi and the South Seas had high psychological value used as a front in speculative schemes designed, or at least operated, in such a manner as to fleece mercilessly the gullible public of the Metropolis. Here was the departure from the legitimate joint stock enterprises of the sixteenth and seventeenth centuries, and the advent of the high finance of the next two centuries, and more. The three bubbles were national explosions of sufficient magnitude to indicate the end of the commercial revolution, and that is why the date 1720 is generally accepted as a year of decision. The joint stock companies had served well as instruments for adventuring after the frontier windfalls, but their day was now over. The title of W. R. Scott's exhaustive study emphasizes this fact, *The Constitution and Finance of English, Scottish, and Irish Joint Stock Companies to 1720*. If further proof is needed, it may be found in observing the date of the demise of the various enterprises. The few stock companies that survived 1720 were the powerful ones such as the East India Company and Hudson's Bay Company, both of which had by this time become established commercial monopolies. The importance of this date is emphasized in another book, James E. Gillespie's *The Influence of Oversea Expansion on England to 1700*. No longer could the Drakes, the Phippses, and the Morgans sail off into the blue seas and return in the course of a few months or years with wealth enough to sink a ship. The wealth was still out there, but it could no longer be had on the old terms. And though the past age was dead, it had left an enormous legacy to posterity. That legacy consisted of great personal fortunes which were available for investing on a long-term basis for slower and surer returns. The day of projecting was over, but the day of devising, inventing, and experimenting with the new lands had just begun. Men at last turned to work on the enormous materials readily available, and in the presence of such an abundance of both stuff and opportunity they had to hurry. It now paid them to hurry, to speed work in every way possible, and it was this urgency which turned them to devising machines to enable them to fabricate the available materials for the ever-expanding body of customers. The stage was all set for the next great economic change, the Industrial Revolution.

CHAPTER EIGHT

THE FRONTIER AS A MODIFIER
OF INSTITUTIONS

T HE VIEW that the frontier acted as a force in modifying old institutions or displacing them with new ones better fitted to the needs of a frontier culture is likely to be challenged by that school which holds that heredity or tradition is the dominant force in shaping institutions. The argument between the exponents of heredity and environment has not been settled, and there is no intention of trying to end it here. This thesis holds only that the frontier, which was always an environment a little on the raw side, acted as a sifter; that some institutions could pass through it without change, some with more or less modifications, and some could not pass at all. The frontier was a soil in which the seeds of all ideas were sown, some to flourish, some to languish, and some to die. It is unnecessary to claim that the frontier originated ideas or institutions, but only that it altered them, often in a spectacular manner. This contention is tenable; it can be proved and illustrated with specific historic examples.

Two classes of examples will be chosen to illustrate the principle of institutional innovation wrought by the frontier. The first group treated will be drawn from the American West, from the Great Plains; the second will be taken mainly from the eastern seaboard. The Great Plains affords some excellent examples of the breaking or bending of institutions by an environment. The region itself is a clearly defined geographic area standing in sharp contrast to surrounding areas. Finally, the history of the region is brief. The whole process of taking the Great Plains region and converting it to the uses of Western civilization went on with amazing rapidity; it occurred right under our eyes, within the memory of a single person, so recently that the contemporary records are abundant. It happened between 1850 and 1900, and most of it fell in the quarter-century 1865–1890.

That the Great Plains did, and does, constitute a special environment is emphasized by the fact that it was the last region of the United States to be taken over by the American pioneers, and this despite the high fertility of much of its soil. It is necessary to explain why the region was rejected, and allowed to remain in the hands of the Indians until the very end, causing it to be appropriately called the last American frontier. It was left to the last because the Anglo-American people had not in all their history had any experience with such a country; neither they nor any of their ancestors from England or northern Europe had ever lived in a land like this, one that was semi-arid and devoid of timber. The English-Americans were forest people, and all their institutions and their instruments were designed for use in a rain-swept land where originally great trees towered above them and the forest kept them company. It was their permanent abode, a fact recorded in such folk expressions as "put the bottom rail on top," "hoe a stumpy row," "out of the woods," and "take to the tall timber." Where except in a recently settled woodland could a "stump speaker" and "log rolling" have originated? When these timber-dwellers moved from the land of much rain into one of little rain, very few of the things they had in hand would work, would solve the problems before them.

Actually, they did not reject the new land, for they tried desperately to take it, but the new land rejected them and their forest ways. Here on the Great Plains they could not use boats, for there were no streams to bear them; they could not build log cabins or rail fences because there were no trees for logs or rails. Their weapons were ineffective against the horsemen of the prairies. Their methods of agriculture were those of the humid country and brought only disaster to those who followed them in the arid land; their plows would not turn the grass-matted sod. Their whole culture recoiled on the border of this strange frontier and before they could take it they had to devise a whole new set of practices from their way of fighting to their way of farming. After 1865 the tide of immigration rolled over the Great Plains time after time, only to break and recede, leaving a few stay-behinds to experiment and devise the instruments and institutions that would work there.

For the sake of clarity it is necessary for us to establish a line on the map separating the eastern woodland from the western plains. The line adopted runs north and south approximating the ninety-eighth meridian, though of course the division is an irregular belt rather than a line. Still the ninety-eighth meridian does symbolize the zone of transition from the woodland to the plain. It was in this zone that the old ideas and institutions began to fail, and it was beyond it that others had to be devised. So much for the general principle. As an illustration of the principle, we will tell briefly the story of a military institution and a weapon, of a livestock economy, of a fence, of an agricultural method, and of a legal system, in each case showing the radical modification effected by this frontier.

1. The Texas Rangers and the Revolver

The frontier weapon of the eastern American woodland was the long rifle, commonly known as the Kentucky or Tennessee rifle. The specimen before me has a barrel forty-four inches long, weighs nine pounds, and carries one ball. The loading of it was a slow and tedious process, involving many operations with powder, wadding, ball, more wadding, small caps, and a ramrod. It was a weapon of considerable range and deadly accuracy, but it was obviously intended for use by a man whose feet rested firmly on the ground, and if he could use a tree for a rest so much the better. Though the rifle originated in Europe, it was improved and developed to its highest perfection in the forests of the United States, and it served the purpose of the hunters and fighters until they emerged from the forests onto the open plains where the Indians met them on horseback in a new type of warfare. The Plains Indians occupying the Great Plains from Mexico to Canada were all bedouins, became superb horsemen, who lived, hunted, and fought on their horses. When the Americans entered the plains, they had to go on horseback, too. They quickly found that their long rifle was no longer a suitable weapon, for with it they were unable to meet on equal terms the mounted Indian armed with bow and arrow. To fight, they had to dismount, leaving the initiative in the hands of the enemy who could come and go at will. What the American needed when he left the forest was a multiple-shot weapon that could be used on horseback, and such an arm he did not have.

The answer to this need was the revolver invented by Samuel Colt of Connecticut about 1830–31, at the time when fingers of immigration were being tentatively extended into the open country. Though Colt was a born promoter, he found it impossible to introduce his weapon or to create any demand for it in the United States, and by 1842 he was a bankrupt. His later success and fame turned on a very small hinge, a handful of Americans who left the United States for the Mexican province of Texas which was being colonized by Stephen F. Austin and other impresarios. Though these Texans were not yet out of the woods, they had come to the very eastern edge of the open country, and from that open country came the merciless raids of the Comanches and Apaches on horseback. To make their situation worse, the Texans did not get on with the Mexicans and before the first Colt revolver was five years old they had staged a revolution and declared their independence in 1836. Though they had declared independence, they could hardly maintain it, for they were desperately poor and few in number. They were pressed on two sides, subject to Indian incursions from the west and northwest and to Mexican raids from the southwest. It was their poverty and their desperate need that drove them to create a fighting institution that was not an army because it was too small and not a police force because its business was to fight a foreign foe rather than to deal with domestic disturbances. The Texas Rangers were few in number because of the Republic's poverty; they were mounted — because both their enemies were mounted. Their effectiveness was due to their velocity, the force with which they struck, and the speed with which they got away if getting away was in order. The Texas Rangers were first mentioned by Austin in 1823, and they were given legal status during the early days of the revolution in 1835. They have existed in some form down to the present time and have the longest history of any similar organization in the world.

The relationship between these Texas Rangers in the bankrupt Republic of Texas and the bankrupt inventor of the Colt revolver in the far-off state of Connecticut is one of the most dramatic examples of the interdependence of civilized culture. The Texans soon learned that San Antonio occupied a strategic position, the best place to keep the small force of Texas Rangers to warn of Mexican invasion or to cut off Indian raids.[1] There at San Antonio was stationed one of those natural fighting men who gain recognition by their ability to manage and lead fighting men. He was low in stature, slight in build, had a complexion like a slightly parched coffee berry, hazel eyes, dark hair, and features of almost feminine delicacy.[2] He had come out of Tennessee as a young surveyor, probably knew Sam Houston who was from the same country, and certainly Andrew Jackson. His father had served with Jackson in the Seminole wars, and had named his son for one of Jackson's generals, John Coffee Hays. He was better known in Texas as Jack Hays.

Captain John C. Hays had with him in San Antonio such characters as Samuel C. Walker, at times Ben McCulloch, the Gillespie brothers, and the droll and whimsical frontiersman Big Foot (A. W.) Wallace. There were probably on an average twenty of these men whose business it was to guard the borders of the young republic.

They were all mounted on the best horses obtainable, and they were armed with the best weapons that could be had, the old long rifles and horse pistols brought by the settlers from the United States. One day — and we do not know the date — a few of Colt's revolvers were brought to this camp where

---

[1] San Antonio is still recognized as one of the strategic cities of America as indicated by the fact that it maintains one of the largest military establishments in the country for both the army and the air force. It lies in the transition zone between the eastern woodland and the Great Plains, though it partakes more of the nature of the plains environment. For a history of the Texas Rangers, see Walter Prescott Webb, *The Texas Rangers: A Century of Defense* (Boston: Houghton Mifflin Co., 1931).

[2] John Coffee Hays was the uncle, namesake, and sponsor of John Hays Hammond, the mining engineer, associate of Cecil Rhodes, and participant in the Jameson raid connected with the beginning of the Boer War.

men lived by weapons and speed alone. It must have been about 1838 or '39, but the records are not clear. Hays seems to have recognized the potential value of the revolvers because he tried them out shortly in an Indian battle, the Battle of the Pedernales and found that at last the Rangers *could pursue the Indians on horseback.* Because the Texans had demonstrated that the revolvers were of practical use in warfare, Colt named the first model the "Texas." His second model he named "Walker" because Samuel Walker, one of Hays's men, suggested changes which greatly improved the weapon. Both these early models are sought after by collectors at fabulous prices. The Rangers had found the weapons they needed; and, had Texas been rich and powerful as was the United States, the inventor would have been on his way to success. But the Texans were too few and too poor to buy enough of Colt's guns to keep him going, and in 1842 his business failed, and he made his living for a time with a medicine show as Dr. Colt. Three years later, in 1845, Texas ceased to be an independent republic and became a state in the Union, and almost immediately war followed with Mexico. This war reunited Colt and the Texas Rangers to their mutual benefit.

Captain John C. Hays was made a colonel and authorized to raise a regiment of five hundred Texas Rangers for service with the army of invasion, their function being to act as spies and scouts. Naturally the handful of experienced men who had served under Hays in San Antonio became his officers in the regiment, and naturally they carried with them the strange new weapons which had already proved so useful to them in Texas. These men, Walker, the Gillespie brothers, Big Foot Wallace, and Ben McCulloch — there could not have been more than a dozen or so in all — were the only ones among the five hundred Rangers who had the new weapons with five or six shots instead of one. Though we have no record of it, we can imagine the clamor set up by the rank and file for the sort of weapons their captains had. Their demands prevailed, and Hays sent an order through channels to Washington for one thousand Colt revolvers so that each of his men could have two!

When the order reached Washington, it was necessary to hunt through New England to find the inventor and to inquire whether he could fill the contract. Colt had no money, no machinery, and not even a model of his gun, but being the promoter that he was, he made the contract, designed a new weapon, and had the guns manufactured by the Whitney gun firm. The thousand Colt revolvers were delivered to Hays at Vera Cruz in 1847. The Texas Rangers, armed with two six-shooters, wore them into Mexico City, and the impression they made was described by General Ethan Allen Hitchcock:

> "Hay's Rangers have come . . . their appearance never to be forgotten . . . well mounted and doubly well armed: each man has one or two Colt's revolvers besides ordinary pistols, a sword, and every man a rifle. . . . The Mexicans are terribly afraid of them." [3]

Here the revolvers were on the proving ground before the whole United States army, and the demand for them was immediate and insatiable.

The Mexican War not only anchored Texas safely to the Union, but it also procured for the United States all the Southwest, all Mexican territory then in the present limits of the United States save one small particle. In this acquisition the United States came into possession of an enormous section of the Great Plains where horsemen prevailed, where the revolver was to play such an important and spectacular role. The Texas Rangers was the first American institution created in response to the plains environment, and the revolver was the first mechanical adaptation to the needs of the country. These two innovations were but tokens of other modifications still to come.

2. A New System of Cattle Culture

The rise of the ranch cattle industry on the Great Plains illustrates the effect of an environment on an economic institution, how a frontier modifies an economic system. The elements brought together in the ranch cattle industry are cattle, horses, and grass and water, and to these must be added men.

[3] Ethan Allen Hitchcock, *Fifty Years in Camp and Field* (New York: G. P. Putnam's Sons, 1909), p. 310.

It goes without saying that all Europeans brought their live-stock to whatever frontier they occupied, and that cattle constituted a part of every rural homestead. But again the situation on the plains was something special where cattle were concerned. The special feature was the existence of a field of grass, a field hundreds of miles long and hundreds of miles wide with practically no trees in it, a natural home for both horses and cattle. It was the *method* of handling cattle in this vast pasture that distinguished the ranch cattle business of the Great Plains from the growing of cows around the farmsteads of the eastern part of the United States.

The Cattle Kingdom had its birth at the spot where men began to handle cattle on horseback on an open range instead of on foot in small pastures and cow lots. This beginning took place in the Nueces Valley at the southern tip of Texas where wild cattle, wild horses, and almost equally wild men were thrown by the exigencies of history into close juxtaposition. Both the cattle and the horses were of Spanish extraction, tough, wiry, and hard to handle. They had been brought in by the Spaniards, and left there by the Mexicans when they retired south of the Rio Grande before the American advance. There the young Americans, mainly Texans, began to handle cattle on horseback and so became the first cowboys. What these first cowboys did was to borrow from the Mexicans their methods, their gear for horses, and much of their terminology, and all these they adapted to their own uses in creating within the Great Plains an institution entirely new to the people of the United States.

From the cattle cradle in southern Texas the longhorns and the method of handling them expanded slowly until 1865 when the conflict between the North and the South ended, leaving the North prosperous and the South very poor. There was a great demand in the rising industrial cities of the North for beef, and as after all wars, prices were high. The Texans, hearing of this distant market, gathered their herds and started them on their own power in charge of cowboys, hired men on horseback, who rode horses as Americans never had and carried six-shooters strapped around their waists. These herds were searching for a market, or for a railroad which would carry the cattle to the industrial cities. The first year' (1866) the herds tried to go as directly to a railroad as possible, their destination Sedalia, Missouri, but to go there they had to leave the open, treeless lands and enter the forests of Arkansas and Missouri where horsemen could not operate. The results were so disastrous that the next year, and thereafter, the herds moved west so as to travel in the open country.

Once the contact was made and the market finally established at Abilene, Kansas, the accumulated herds in South Texas swarmed from the mother hive, some to market and some to stock the new ranches set up throughout the grassland. In ten years the dispersion was complete to the extent that the whole Great Plains region which had rejcted farmers, was occupied after a fashion by this new institution, the ranch cattle industry. From Mexico to Canada, from Missouri to California, everywhere that the trees did not grow, men were living and working on horseback, something not seen to such an extent before in this country. The open range days were ended by the invention of a fence, another mechanical adaptation to an environment, one that enabled the farmer to resume his frontier trek.[4]

3. The Invention of a Fence

When in the perspective of sufficient time, the cultural anthropologist looks back on the pioneer civilization of the eastern half of the United States prior to 1850, and undertakes to select a name for its prevailing culture complex, he may with excellent reason call it a woodland culture. Everywhere east of the plains the great forests towered above the toiling men and women, forming an obstacle and offering an opportunity. The axe, the adze, the frow, and the saw were the tools with which the people worked, the artifacts which may survive to

[4] For the story of the beginnings of the cattle kingdom, see Joseph G. McCoy, *Historic Sketches of the Cattle Trade of the West and Southwest* (Kansas City, Missouri: Ramsey, Millet and Hudson, 1874). The best story of the cattle drives is told by Andy Adams, *The Log of a Cowboy* (Boston: Houghton Mifflin Co., 1931). On the factual side, see Philip Ashton Rollis, *The Cowboy* (New York: Charles Scribner's Sons, 1922).

tell future scholars how to put an ancient forest-dwelling civilization together. Unfortunately the things men made with
these tools, being of wood and perishable, could not last; even
today they are become so scarce as to be sought after by collectors and museums. The log cabins are few, and how to build
them is all but forgotten; yet the log cabin was the symbol of
the frontier woodland home. It was so common, so typical, as
to impress European observers. Those who are familiar with
the language of the deaf know that they have a symbolic or
sign language wholly independent of the written and spoken
word. What they do is to select a salient feature of an object
and indicate it by a single sign, horns for cattle, beard for
goats, wings for birds, and long ears for donkeys. The deaf
who first looked out on the landscape of the forests of America,
saw everywhere log cabins with white smoke issuing from the
chimneys. Being in need of a symbol for the new country, they
adopted the log cabin as most suitable, the name for America.
The sign is made by interlocking the fingers and describing a
circle on a horizontal plane, indicating "log cabins all around."
But the log cabin was only the beginning of the use of trees.
From the forests the pioneers not only made their homes, but
they made nearly everything else they used. The trees
furnished cradles for babies, feed troughs for stock, casing for
wells, hinges for gates, wheels and bodies for wagons, beams
for plows, hives (bee bums) for bees, staves for kegs and barrels, nails (pegs) for hardwood furniture, mast for hogs, and
forage for livestock. From the ashes of the burnt trees came
lye for soap, hominy, and the tanning of hides. Ashes also
furnished potash so necessary for the tobacco beds. Indeed
that was a woodland culture complex of the highest order.

It should be perfectly clear that this woodland culture would
be completely confounded when it entered a place where no
trees could be found for the uses of a people who had come to
depend on them for so much. Had the deaf seen the plains
first, they never could have adopted the sign "log cabins all
around" as a name for America. Since the story of the woodland dwellers' adventure into the Great Plains has been told
in detail elsewhere, it need not be repeated here except to illustrate the effect of a new frontier on an older and different

culture. This brings us to the specific case of the invention of a fence.[5]

The common fence in the eastern half of the United States was made of rails split from the tree trunks of the cleared fields. It was supplemented by the stone wall or rock fence in regions such as New England where there were as many rocks as there were trees. Of rails, the most familiar type was the Virginia worm or zigzag fence, remnants of which still exist in remote parts of the woodland states. This fence, along with the log cabin, made its way west until it came to the Great Plains which it could not enter or cross for the simple reason that there was no material for making it. Also, there were no rocks, especially in the eastern plains which the pioneers first entered. In short, fencing became economically impossible, and without fences there could be no farming because livestock and agricultural crops are mutually exclusive. For want of fencing the agricultural frontier was brought almost to a dead halt on the edge of the plains, and it was unable to move forward until a practical and economical substitute could be found. In the interval before a practical fence was invented, every device imaginable was tried, such as thorny hedges of bois d'arc, cactus, running roses; even mud fences were built to go along with sod houses. None of the substitutes were satisfactory and all were expensive. The fence problem may be said to have been acute from 1850 to 1875, leaving the Great Plains in the hands of the cattle kings of the open range whose story has already been sketched.

The solution in this case was neither borrowed from the Spaniards, as the method of handling range cattle on horseback had been, nor furnished by New England, as in the case of the Colt revolver. The solution, the invention of barbed wire, was the work of a group of farmers living in the open prairies of Illinois near the little town of DeKalb. Their names were Joseph Glidden, Jacob Haish, and perhaps a third, Isaac Ellwood. Joseph, Jacob, and Isaac did not make brick without straw, but they made fences requiring little timber. In

---

[5] This section is based on Walter Prescott Webb, *The Great Plains* (Boston: Ginn and Co., 1931), which tells in detail the story of settlement and institutional change.

1873 the first two began making barbed wire, independently, and each obtained a patent. What they discovered was that a cheap and practical fence, one easy to construct and to maintain, could be made by twisting two wires with barbs spaced at regular intervals, and that three strands of this infernal contrivance stretched tight on posts would keep cattle and crops separated.[6] The success of Joseph, Jacob, and Isaac was phenomenal, and though they started as simple farmers they wound up as millionaires because they had the only fence that could be used in about half of the United States. Barbed wire was shipped into the plains by the trainload, and within twenty-five years nearly all the open range had become privately owned and was under fence. Ranching was converted from the open range into the big pasture type. With the possibility of fencing, the farmers, who had been stalled for a generation on the edge of the plains, resumed their march to the west and began the process of crowding out the cattle men. But the ability to fence did not give them the ability to farm, as they were to find out in that greatest of all experiment stations, trial and error. And that brings us to another example of how an environment compelled institutional modifications.

4. Two New Methods of Farming

The farmers who crossed the ninety-eighth meridian could look at the horizon and see that they had left log cabins and rail fences behind them, but they could not understand that they had left much else, including their methods of handling land and water. Their accustomed methods of farming, so well integrated with forty inches of annual precipitation, were to prove disastrous in a land where rainfall averaged twenty inches, and in years of drought fell to ten or twelve. The suffering that resulted from efforts to farm in the traditional manner, in the only manner they knew, is a tragic story of broken fortunes, broken men, and broken women. In the good wet years the migrating homeseekers moved out like a tidal wave on the ocean shore, but the wave broke on the hard dry years, receded, and left behind the wreckage of the high hopes and

6 *Ibid.*, chap. VII.

illusions. But not all went back; some stay-behinds remained, as on other frontiers, and kept experimenting, adapting, and adopting until something of a solution was found. Out of this experimentation emerged two innovations in agricultural methods.

The solution was irrigation farming in lands where water was available and dry-land farming in the much greater areas where all must depend on the scanty rains. Now irrigation is one of the oldest arts, but it was unknown to the English people and to their descendants who had lived for centuries in the humid woodland of England or the eastern United States. They did not need it, had never practiced it, and any knowledge they had of it was purely academic. It took time and study, and the help of the government to work it out, and in the interval a great many people almost starved to death. Today it is well developed throughout the West wherever there is water to support it.[7]

Dry-land farming is an art that had been practiced by many people, but the name for it and the scientific principles of it remained for the practicing farmers of the American West to create and discover. The theory was formulated and the scientific principles discovered by fumbling farmers in conjunction with the experimenting observers. The basic principle of dry farming consists of storing up water from precipitation and making it available to the growing crops in dry weather. In this sense, the method is the same as in irrigation where the surplus water from streams is stored in liquid form in reservoirs and drawn off through ditches for use as needed. The difference lies in the fact that in dry farming the water is stored *within* the soil rather than in reservoirs, and is fed through the soil by capillary action rather than by means of ditches and flumes. Compared to irrigation, dry farming is a most delicate operation, though both methods are highly technical and exacting in their requirements.[8]

[7] For a discussion of irrigation as developed in western America, see Webb, *The Great Plains*, chaps. VII and VIII, with accompanying bibliography.
[8] For a more extended treatment, see *The Great Plains*, chap. VIII.

The first step in dry farming is to prepare a deep soil bed that will absorb, if possible, every drop of water that falls upon it. The second step is to prevent the precious water thus absorbed from escaping by evaporation into the dry air, and managing the soil so that the moisture will rise by the capillary action to the roots of the growing crops. Rise to the roots but not beyond them. The ideal situation, therefore, is to have the soil bed beneath the surface loose and friable so that it will absorb moisture, yet compact enough so that the moisture can move upward toward the surface. The real art consists of stopping its upward movement just below the surface, before it escapes into the air. This is accomplished by creating what the dry farmer calls a "dust mulch," a sort of soil blanket spread over the surface which is most effective in stopping up the pores and in holding the moisture below, a sort of capping of aurifices or vapor chimneys which exist by the millions in a surface crust. All cultivation, after the initial deep breaking, is for the purpose of preserving the dust mulch. It has to be done after each rain, and done very rapidly, for the thirsty hot winds above suck constantly at the soil.

Simple as these principles are, they were wholly unknown to the farmers from the humid east, and were in fact known to no one at the beginning of plains settlement. Eastern farmers had cultivated mainly to keep down noxious weeds and grasses that would smother the crops, not to preserve moisture which was usually abundant. How and where were these principles discovered? By one account they were discovered first by the Mormons who had migrated to the desert of the Great Salt Lake. For a time they drew water from the Malad River to irrigate their potatoes and other crops, but after a short time the alkali from the water ruined the soil, something the irrigator had to learn, and they were faced with starvation. In desperation, they cleared the sagebrush, planted their potatoes on fresh dry ground, cultivated, waited, and prayed. The potatoes, planted perhaps in subirrigated land in the right kind of soil, amazed them with a bountiful production. Thus the process of dry farming began.

Another account says it began in an accidental manner in

California after the gold rush of 1849. A man planted a field of wheat, and during the early growing season a herd of sheep was driven across the field. Now the sheep did two things very essential in dry farming. By their weight they packed the lower soil so that capillarity could operate; the loose dirt crumpled into the deep tracks to create the dust mulch and to prevent the moisture's final escape. At any rate the drought came and the wheat in the sheep walk withstood it and made a fair crop while the remainder of the field was a failure. Naturally, men observed these strange things and began to try to figure out the principles or reasons behind them. The task was taken up by the students of agriculture, notably Professor E. W. Hilgard of California, and in time the reasons were discovered, the principles formulated and a new science of agriculture was born, one now practiced intelligently in most of the subhumid agricultural regions of the world.

According to the Office of Experiment Stations of the United States Department of Agriculture, the United States government maintains in 1952 thirty-seven experiment stations in sixteen of the eighteen Great Plains states. Of these, twenty-four are experimenting with the management of soils in the dry-land region, and twenty-one are studying soils under irrigation, and one station is conducting a study of windbreaks in fruit farming in Cheyenne, Wyoming.

Accompanying the discovery of the principles of dry farming went the search for new plants adapted to an arid climate, and the development of new varieties of old plants by breeding. The very names of the imported plants which have proved successful indicate their origin in a dry country — Sudan grass, feterita, hegira, Rhodes grass, and so on. From Russia came the red fife wheat, brought in tiny bundles to the plains by the Mennonite immigrants. Special varieties of wheat and cotton have been evolved in the experiment stations for use in the land of little rain. Thus did the American people evolve on their frontier two distinctive systems of agriculture, irrigation and dry farming.[9]

[9] The most persuasive book I know on this subject is William MacDonald, *Dry Farming: Its Principles and Practice* (New York: The Century Co., 1911). See also Elwood Mead, *Irrigation Institutions* (New York: The Macmillan Co., 1909).

5. *A Revolution in the Law of Water*

The final example used to illustrate the modification of an institution by the Great Plains environment is in the field of law. It is generally conceded that the law is devoted to tradition and is exceedingly slow to change its basic principles. In spite of this the Great Plains affords a striking example, not only of modification but also of a complete abrogation of the English common law of water and the substitution of a new one based on an entirely different principle. Let us therefore examine the transit of the English common law of water from England to the humid portion of the United States, where it underwent slight modification, thence into the margins of the Great Plains where it was radically altered, and then into the heart of the Great Plains where it has been abrogated and a new law devised.[10]

By way of explanation, it should be said that each state of the American Union has the right to make its own water law except on interstate streams where the federal government has some right and on international streams where federal jurisdiction is somewhat greater. Also, each state, on being admitted to the Union, adopted as a matter of form the English common law, including the law of water. Now the law, as it had developed in England and as it was adopted by most of the forty-eight states, is known as the law of riparian rights. This law, evolved in humid England, was designed to serve a people who had an abundance of moisture and much running water. This is reflected in provisions of the law designed to restrain one neighbor from diverting water from its natural channel to the detriment of the neighbor below.

The important provision with which we are concerned is that under the law of riparian rights only the owner of the bank of the stream had certain water rights, hence *ripa*. The

[10] Webb, *The Great Plains*, chap. IX. The whole subject is treated in the monumental work of Clesson S. Kinney, *A Treatise on the Law of Irrigation and Water Rights and the Arid Region Doctrine of Appropriation of Waters* (4 vols.; San Francisco: Bender-Moss Co., 1912). See especially vol. I. Also Samuel C. Wiel, *Water Rights in the Western States* (2 vols.; San Francisco: Bancroft-Whitney Co., 1911).

nonriparian owner was excluded. The riparian rights were divided into two classes, natural and artificial. Under natural rights came the use of water for livestock and ordinary domestic purposes, and there was no limit on the amount, necessarily small, that was used in these ways. Artificial rights were those under which the riparian owner could use water, usually but not always by diverting it, for the purpose of turning a mill wheel or for other work. If the owner diverted water, he was required to return it to the channel within the limits of his own land; he could not permit it to damage a neighbor.

The basic principle of the riparian law was the correlative or equal rights of all riparian owners. By this principle each riparian owner had a right to the full and undiminished flow of the stream. Obviously this precluded any possibility of irrigation because water for irrigation is absorbed, leaves the stream less than full flow, and diminishes it by the amount of water drawn off. In a humid country where irrigation was unnecessary and unknown the law worked well enough.

In the eastern states where precipitation was similar to that in England, the changes in the original law were slight, but there were some modifications, giving rise to the Eastern American Law of Riparian Rights. The law moved west as the states were admitted, and by the middle of the nineteenth century it was entering the eastern margins of the Great Plains. Here the states lie partly in the humid region and partly in the semi-arid region, such for example as Texas, Kansas, Nebraska, and the Dakotas. The same is true of the three states west of the Great Plains, Washington, Oregon, and California. Immediately, from the drier portions of these states demands began to be made for a *modification* of the riparian law so as to permit irrigation. This modification was brought about, not by making a new law but by further modifying the old one. This task was performed through the courts by re-interpretation, the argument being that in an arid land irrigation was an absolute necessity, something of a natural right and not an artificial one after all. The courts resolved the problem by substituting the words *reasonable* and *unreasonable* for natural and artificial. If, the courts ruled, A's use of water was reasonable and did not deprive the riparian owners B and C downstream of any benefit, then A could use it for irrigation. This modification, adopted by all the states bordering the Great Plains, is known as the Western American Doctrine of Riparian Rights.

In the central portion of the Great Plains there are eight states, all arid, and here the radically modified riparian law was not radical enough. These eight states have abandoned completely the English common law and evolved an indigenous law on an entirely different principle, the Arid Region Doctrine of Prior Appropriation. In essence this law grants the first water to the first comer, whether he be a riparian or non-riparian owner. Once a given amount of water is granted to him, he may continue to have that amount *as long as he uses it.* Not to use it is to forfeit it. Its use belongs to him as an individual and not by virtue of his owning riparian land. After A, the first applicant, receives his allotment, the next goes to B, the second applicant. "He who is first in time is first in right," is the classic statement of the principle. The Arid Region Doctrine of Prior Appropriation prevails in New Mexico, Arizona, Colorado, Utah, Nevada, Wyoming, Idaho, and Montana.

The manner in which this practice, resulting finally in law, began reminds us of the way in which the principles of dry farming were discovered. To the student of the frontier the story of the arid region doctrine is highly significant, indicating how, in meeting practical situations, solving immediate problems, men develop a workable practice, and later get the practice recognized and incorporated into law. When gold was discovered in California, which had just been acquired from Mexico, the frontier of settlement lay a thousand miles away on the eastern margin of the Great Plains. In 1849–50 the gold rush got under way and thousands of fortune seekers made the plains crossing by the California trail or took the longer water route by the Isthmus of Panama or around South America by way of the Magellan Strait. Here in California, far from the seat of culture, was a society, mainly of men who had outrun the established law and all the courts, men who had outrun their institutions. It soon became a very rough society where men, animated by greed and cupidity, violated the rights of others with impunity. The lucky man who found gold had no means of protecting his discovery, and was often murdered before he could enjoy the fruits of his find. It was a desperate situation in which neither life nor property was safe, and it demanded a remedy.

Thoughtful men decided that some rules must be formulated to give protection to the survivors and to bring some order out of chaos. Meetings were called in the diggings and the miners decided to make and enforce their own rules for mutual protection. The organizations which were set up have been called miners' courts, though they were without any legal status. The members have also been called vigilantes, a term which connotes extra-legal status. At any rate, these courts or committees made rules, tried violators, and administered punishment summarily, the most frequent penalties being banishment or hanging. The procedure was rude but highly effective because there was little delay and no appeal.

One of the pressing needs was to make rules protecting a man's gold claim. The miners' courts decided that the first man to discover a claim and to stake it out with proper dimensions and witnesses should hold it against all comers. The next man must respect the claim of the first so that his claim, which would be second, would also be protected. In short, the miners' courts adopted the familiar principle of first come, first served. So far, so good. The next step is to see how this principle was transferred from a gold claim to a water claim.

This transfer came about quite naturally because water was required for sluicing the soil and gravel from the gold. If a stream was available, the miner or miners would construct a diversion ditch, and bring the water to the place where it was needed. Since water was scarce and streams were often weak, the question arose as to who should have claim to such water as was available. If these miners knew anything about riparian rights, they ignored it, and applied the same rule to water that they had applied to gold, regardless of whether the water went to riparian lands or not. The first man to claim and use the water should have the amount necessary *as long as he used it,* and late comers would have to take their turn. If the water gave out, that was their bad luck.

In the boom conditions incident to the gold rush the population grew so fast that before the end of 1850 California was admitted as a state in the Union, and like the others adopted as a formality the English common law. In the first legislature the question immediately arose as to what should be done with the rough and ready regulations adopted by the miners' courts. Should they be accepted and legalized? The miners were a strong element in the society, and since property rights were already dependent on the rules adopted by the miners' courts, the legislature accepted what had been done as an accomplished fact, and in 1851 gave legal status to their rules, regulations, and decisions. In accepting the English common law in 1850 the state of California had adopted the riparian law of water; but by legalizing the acts of the miners' courts in 1851, it had adopted an entirely different principle, that of prior appropriation. As it turned out, the older law, that of modified riparian rights, finally prevailed in California, but in the meantime the new law was taken over and developed into the Arid Regions Doctrine of Prior Appropriation by the eight states of the truly arid region.

To sum up, the English common law of riparian rights came to the eastern United States where it was modified into the Eastern American Doctrine of Riparian Rights. In the nine states flanking the Great Plains east and west it was further modified by substituting reasonable and unreasonable for natural and artificial uses into the Western American Doctrine of Riparian Rights. In the truly arid states the English common law was abridged completely in favor of the Western American Doctrine of Prior Appropriation. Surely no clearer proof can be found that, as Clark Wissler has remarked, institutions do approach an environment hat in hand. They approached the frontier with the same respect.

The argument here is that the frontier modified human institutions. In the Great Plains region, which has been chosen for a case study, we have seen how the frontier compelled the adoption of a special military institution and a weapon, the revolver; how it led to the borrowing of a new method of handling livestock and built the economic institution of the cattle kingdom; how it led to the invention of a practical fence; how it introduced irrigation and discovered dry farming; and finally, how it revolutionized the law of water. Many other examples could be cited, but these would seem to be sufficient to prove the point.

Some may argue in contradiction that the case of the Great Plains is too clear; that though the modifications, about which there can be no dispute, did occur, they were made in response to the needs of a subhumid land and not because the land was a frontier. The basic fact is that the land was a frontier to which the adjustments were made. Its arid quality, setting it off from the older region, did make for radical change — for clean breaks with the past, and for sharp definition. But surely one should not reject an example because it is clear-cut and unequivocal, because it illustrates the principle under consideration. As yet there are few studies of the effects of frontier environments on invading cultures, but it is probable that when the details have been worked out, the scholars and the world in general will be amazed at their number and meaning and at the light such studies will shed on modern civilization. It has often been said that America acted as a melting pot in which the conglomerate people of Europe were fused into something different from what they were. The frontier everywhere was likewise a melting pot for institutions and ideas, fusing old ones that would not function into new ones that would. The samples taken from the Great Plains are after all very small samples, a mere detail in a far greater canvas. Let us now turn to a reverse situation, namely, the destruction of old institutions by the frontier.

6. Primogeniture and Entail

Two European institutions that failed to survive in America, and throughout the frontier, were primogeniture and entail. Though the two differ, they are too closely related to be treated separately. Both date back to feudal times, and were used in general to preserve the integrity of the feudal estates. In a period when land was the chief form of wealth, both primogeniture and entail were applied primarily to it, applied when land was relatively scarce. In fact, it may be that investigation will reveal that wherever and whenever land is scarce in relation to population, the equivalent of primogeniture and entail will tend to appear in some form. Conversely, wherever and whenever land is abundant and relatively free, there can be little excuse for the existence of either of these institutions. It is obvious that when these two legal practices were transferred from the scarce lands of England to the wide and vacant domain of the New World, they tended to melt away in the immensity of space. Since rules of inheritance were already grounded in law, and since law is notable for its inertia, bound as it were by its past, it would be too much to expect the old laws to yield to the new circumstances without a struggle, but in the end they must yield if they are to conform to the desires of the society. The English law of inheritance was confronted in the wilderness of the frontier with a higher law of nature. Men may divide and struggle for this law or that, but oftentimes nature tips the scale for the final decision.

Here we are again faced with the problem of the relation between institutions and environment, and their respective influence on conduct in a society. In the introduction to his lecture on "The Revolution and the Land," J. Franklin Jameson said that in the time of Dickens the first question Americans asked of European visitors was, "How do you like our institutions?" At that time Americans sincerely believed that their institutions, especially those of democracy, were their most notable possessions, and were soberly regarded by Americans as the source of their prosperity. Later historians, says Jameson, have not been idle, and they have come to see that the average man "has been more occupied with making a living than with any other one thing."[11] The historians have come to doubt that the political institutions are more important than economic

[11] J. Franklin Jameson, *The American Revolution Considered as a Social Movement*, p. 40.

phenomena. "The doctrine which underlies the present lecture is that political democracy came to the United States as a result of economic democracy, that this nation came to be marked by political institutions of a democratic type because it had, still earlier, come to be characterized in its economic life by democratic arrangements and practices." [12]

The basic fact about primogeniture and entail is that they came to the thirteen colonies with law, precedent, and history behind them. Hardly had they arrived before they found themselves on the defensive against the more powerful forces that were eventually to destroy them. The story of the legal struggle is long and complicated, involving as it does tangled arguments in each of the thirteen colonies. The lawyers fought hard on both sides, but for those favoring the English practice it was a retreating action. The proponents of change found precedent for some of their contentions, both in England and in some of the colonial charters, but in the end the change went much further than the English precedent or the charters justified.[13] The situation was described by Chief Justice Tilghman of Pennsylvania as follows:

> Every country has its Common Law. Ours is composed partly of the Common Law of England and partly of our own usages. When our ancestors emigrated from England they took with them such of the English principles as were convenient for the situation in which they were about to place themselves. It required time and experience to ascertain how much of the English law would be suitable to this country. By degrees, as circumstances demanded, we adopted the English usages, or substituted others better suited to our wants, till at length before the time of the Revolution we had formed a system of our own.[14]

[12] *Ibid.*, p. 41.

[13] For a detailed account of this struggle see Richard B. Morris, *Studies in the History of American Law* (New York: Columbia University Press, 1930), chap. II. This study is confined to the seventeenth and eighteenth centuries and contains extensive bibliography of primary sources. For a brief account of the situation following the Revolution, see J. Franklin Jameson, "The Revolution and the Land," *The American Revolution Considered as a Social Movement.*

[14] Quoted from *Poor* v. *Greene*, 1813, 5 Binney 554 in Morris, *Studies in the History of American Law*, pp. 12–13.

The part the frontier had in making these changes is set forth so clearly by Morris as to justify a lengthy quotation:

> In the seventeenth century American law was born. It grew amid the surroundings of the American frontier which nurtured self-assertion and independence. By its very isolation from established centers of culture, the frontier created of necessity a culture peculiarly its own. . . . In the western movement of the American population new frontiers were established which fashioned the political and social institutions of the old along characteristically independent lines adapted to their conditions. From the new frontiers emanated new social currents which reacted on the older settlements. This frontier process, which has been called the "American great first cause," brought about in the field of law the scrapping of what Professor Paxson has called "Englishism." [15]

Against this background of the frontier let us observe the two metropolitan institutions. Primogeniture is the principle by which a father's estate is inherited by the eldest son, to the exclusion of other sons and daughters. It is said to have entered England under the Norman kings, and to have developed there and been maintained in the interest of the landed estates of the greater nobles, whose strength it was important for the king to preserve. The legal process by which the recipient, or lord, came into possession of the land was that of entail. He could not divide the land during his lifetime, nor at his death, but was required ordinarily to pass it on intact to his first-born son. The point seems to be that the land was more important than the individual and must be maintained without regard to human justice or equity as we would view it now. Actually, the occupant possessed the land without owning it.

Though this was the prevailing law in England, it was not universal there, and it was not so arbitrary in application as it sounds in theory. In 1285 the barons succeeded in having the statute *De donis conditionalibus* passed which limited the line of descent to those specified in the grant. In an effort to gain the right of alienation, legal devices known as common recovery and fine were invented, but these procedures were both

[15] Morris, *Studies in the History of American Law*, pp. 17–18.

expensive and cumbersome. Primogeniture was not applied throughout England. In the county of Kent, for example, *gavelkind* inheritance, by which the property was divided among all the children, prevailed, and in some parts of the realm descent was by borough English law, which endowed the youngest son on the ground that he was less able to provide for himself. Another modification was that of partible inheritance through which the eldest son received a double portion of the estate. All of these English practices were appealed to by one side or the other in the various colonies prior to the Revolution.

The New England colonies took the lead in opposition to primogeniture and entail. For one thing, the rugged terrain discouraged large holdings. Also grants were ordinarily made to the corporate community rather than to individuals, and the corporate community was inclined to grant land to individuals in small quantities rather than in large blocks. Morris says: "The seventeenth century in New England witnessed a conscious attempt to depart from the archaisms of English property law and to cultivate with solicitude a more democratic tenure and rule of succession to satisfy the desire of a frontier community for an equitable property distribution in the family." [16] When Massachusetts began to colonize the region beyond her charter boundaries, the General Court abolished much of the English feudal law pertaining to inheritance as set forth in 1641 in the Body of Liberties. One historian remarks that "Massachusetts intended by this declaration to modify English land law to fit frontier needs." [17]

Primogeniture and entail held on longer in the South than in New England, and were especially favored in the tidewater region where large holdings were common and economically advantageous. The story cannot be followed in detail, but it was the same story of retreat. It required the shock of the Revolution to finish what had been well begun. Jameson, in

[16] *Ibid.,* p. 95.
[17] Viola F. Barnes, "Land Tenure in English Colonial Charters of the Seventeenth Century," in *Essays in Colonial History Presented to Charles McLean Andrews by His Students* (New Haven: Yale University Press, 1931), p. 35.

commenting on the large landholdings in the manorial estates of Virginia and the patroons of New York, observes:

> But all this was . . . a European system transplanted to the New World. It was not native here, and in some respects it was not natural, nor well suited to American conditions of life. . . . The English system of land-tenure had well enough served the uses of America thus far, perhaps, but it would not serve them much longer. Its hold upon America was loose. If anything should occur which should administer a great shock to the entire social system of the country, it would dislodge and shake off from the body politic, as an outworn vesture, such institutions as no longer met our needs. Now this is just what the Revolution did. . . . There was no violent outbreak against the land-system. . . . But in a quiet, sober, Anglo-Saxon way a great change was effected in the land-system of America between the years 1775 and 1795.[18]

What Jameson is saying is that many old English institutions were withering on the tree in the frontier soil, and therefore when the shock of the Revolution came they fell because they had been weakened by conditions and general disapproval. An analysis of the four changes in the land system made as a result of the Revolution will reveal that all of them were made in the interest of the individual man, the common man, all in the direction of economic opportunity for more people. The changes were as follows: (1) All royal checks on the acquisition of land were abandoned. (2) Quit rents were abolished. (3) All restrictions on cutting timber were abolished. (4) Large Tory estates, such as the Penn estate in Pennsylvania, the Wright estate in Georgia, and even the Fairfax estate on which George Washington was surveyor, were confiscated, broken up, and sold in smaller tracts to less powerful people.

Primogeniture and entail survived the Revolution in some of the states, but they died of delayed shock wherever they had survived. Primogeniture had been abolished in Pennsylvania and Maryland and entail in South Carolina before the Revolution, but they still existed in some form in the other ten states.

[18] Jameson, *The American Revolution Considered as a Social Movement,* pp. 47–49.

Jameson says: "In ten years from the Declaration of Independence every state had abolished entails excepting two, and those were two in which entails were rare. In fifteen years every state, without exception abolished primogeniture and in some form provided for equality of inheritance, since which time the American eldest son has never been a privileged character." [19]

Profesor Jameson marvels that the thirteen legislatures acted with such unanimity in making the same changes in their land laws. He thinks such uniformity must have had a common cause. "Democratic land-tenure," he says, "was a natural thing in a new country like America, and made its way at once when the political revolution loosened the ties of old habit." [20] He is of the opinion that the political revolution carried within it the seeds of a social revolution, and in that respect was not unlike the French Revolution. I am inclined to differ with him as to the ultimate cause. It is my opinion that the French Revolution arose from the fact that the people did not have enough, and resolved to take from those who had much. The American people had an abundance, had long been enjoying it in spite of king and parliament, and were determined to keep it. They did confiscate some Tory estates, but what they took from the Tories was infinitesimal when contrasted with what lay all about them. It was as Herman Melville said, "Your nation enjoyed no little independence before your Declaration declared it." [21]

The social revolution was well along a century and a half before the American Revolution got under way. It began when the first colonists entered the forests; its preliminary battles had been fought, and many of them won. The frontier was the fifth column of liberty. The American Revolution was a result springing from the exuberance of success whereas the French Revolution was a result springing from the desperation, failure, and frustration of a people. The revolutions were alike in

[19] *Ibid.*, p. 57.
[20] *Ibid.*, p. 58.
[21] Herman Melville, *Mardi and a Voyage Thither* (New York: Harper and Bros., 1849), vol. II, p. 240.

shaking off practices which were outworn and unsuited to the society. The American Revolution accelerated the speed but it did not change the direction the American people were traveling; the French Revolution reversed the direction that both the people and the government had been traveling for generations. It was this reversal that made the French Revolution so catastrophic in contrast to the mild and even tenor of its American predecessor.

So much for the abolition of primogeniture and entail in the original thirteen colonies up to the time of the Revolution. With the grant of western lands to the central government, some provision had to be made as to inheritance in the new country. The second paragraph of the Northwest Ordinance of 1787 provided that intestate estates should be distributed among the children in equal parts. It was also provided that real estate could be conveyed in fee simple, excepting only that of the French inhabitants whose laws or customs of inheritance would be respected. Of these provisions Donaldson observes: "This statute struck the key-note of our liberal system of land law, not only in the States formed out of the public domain, but also in the older States. The doctrine of tenure is entirely exploded; it has no existence." [22]

As the frontier advanced across the country, and the new states were admitted, the principle of equal division of the property among all the heirs was generally followed. Thomas Jefferson resorted to irony in making either partible inheritance or primogeniture look ridiculous to the American people. On October 12, 1776, he introduced into the Virginia legislature a bill enabling tenants in tail to convey property in fee simple. Two days later a bill was introduced reforming the land laws and abolishing entail completely, and this bill was enacted with such speed as to leave little record. The attack on primogeniture came later, and the practice was not abolished until 1785. Edmund Pendleton opposed the land reforms and tried to retain the double portion for the eldest son. Jeffer-

[22] Quoted from Joseph S. Wilson in Thomas Corwin Donaldson, *The Public Domain, Its History, with Statistics*, H. Misc. Doc. 45, part 4, 47th Cong., 2d Sess., 1884, p. 158.

son defeated him by the very frontier argument that such discrimination could not be justified unless the first-born son could eat a double portion and do twice as much work as his brothers. In a more sober vein he wrote: "The repeal of the laws of entail would prevent the accumulation and perpetuation of wealth, in select families, and preserve the soil of the country from being daily more and more absorbed in mortmain. The abolition of primogeniture, and equal partition of inheritance removed the feudal and unnatural distinctions which made one member of every family rich, and all the rest poor." [23]

In cases arising after the Revolution, the judges usually brushed aside the old arguments in favor of American practice. Mr. Justice Noah H. Swayne of the United States Supreme Court said in December, 1866:

> Before the Revolution, some of the colonies had passed laws regulating descent of real property upon principles essentially different from those of the common law. . . . With the close of the Revolution came a new state of things. . . . The equality of the legal rights of every citizen was a maxim universally recognized and acted upon as fundamental. . . . In the United States the English common law of descents, in its most essential features, has been universally rejected.[24]

Associate Justice James L. Worden of the Indiana Supreme Court observed in the November 1861 term:

> The feudal policy of tieing up estates in the hands of a landed aristocracy, and which has much to do with the doctrine of shifting descents, as recognized by the *English* canons of descent, is contrary to the spirit of our laws, and the genius of our institutions. It has been the policy in this State, and in this country generally not only to let estates descend to heirs equally, without reference to sex or primogeniture, but also to make titles secure and safe to those who may purchase from heirs upon whom the descent may be cast.[25]

[23] H. A. Washington (ed.), *The Writings of Thomas Jefferson* (Washington: Taylor & Maury, 1853), vol. I, p. 49.
[24] *Bates* v. *Brown*, 5 Wallace (U.S.) 716.
[25] *Cox* v. *Matthews*, 17 Ind. 371.

In Michigan, Associate Justice Flavius L. Brooke remarked in 1916: "The common law touching descent of estates has never obtained in Michigan." [26]

These cases are typical of the American attitude and the general practice throughout the country.

We may now turn briefly to the career of primogeniture in Europe and in the New World nations outside the United States. In Europe Adam Smith condemned primogeniture as contrary to the real interests of a large family. In France, Montesquieu stated that it should be abolished among the nobles. France abolished entails in 1792, but Napoleon later re-created them. Primogeniture was also abolished, but was restored in 1826. Both entail and primogeniture were later abolished. The German states overthrew entails and primogeniture after the French Revolution, but restored them upon the fall of Napoleon. Prussia and others abolished them in 1848, but again they were restored. They were again abolished in 1919. The story is much the same in Italy.

Returning to the frontier, we find that in Canada the English accepted the French system of partible descent, the eldest son under certain circumstances receiving the larger share of an estate. In Australia and New Zealand large estates were the rule, but it seems that free alienation was the accepted practice. The socialization of the land prevented a natural development, but primogeniture was not abolished in Australia for the reason that it never existed. In South America the revolutions were generally followed by the abolition of entailed estates. Chile took the lead under Bernardo O'Higgins in 1819. It is quite probable that the practice followed in the United States had some influence in revising the land systems, both in Europe and in Latin America.

In this study reputable authorities have been quoted to the effect that the modifications were made in the land laws of the United States in response to frontier needs. These authorities have emphasized that the Americans wanted a more democratic

[26] Concerning *Shumway's Estate*, 194 Mich. 251.

system of land distribution than that afforded by the English and European practice. It is quite probable that the American people wanted land more than they wanted democracy, and in this they probably differed not one whit from their European cousins, for land-hunger was a universal hunger in all Western civilization. What distinguished the Americans and other frontier people from their cousins in the Metropolis was that they wanted land in a place where they could have it. Once all of them had or might have a piece of land, equality was a reality and democracy came easy. William Graham Sumner is one of the few thinkers who has recognized the situation.

> It is [he said] the opening of the new continents and the great discoveries and inventions which have made this modern age. . . . The chief source of new power, however, has been the simplest of all, that is, an extension of population over new land. If a half-million proletarians in Europe should inherit each an estate, no one would think it any mystery that they were not proletarians any more; why, then, should it be a mystery that they are not proletarians when they have inherited an estate in America or Australia by going to it? [27]

It may satisfy the lawyers to attribute the loosening of land monopoly by primogeniture, partible inheritance, entail, or by other means, to their own arguments or to the decisions of the judges with democratic inclinations; it may satisfy the historian of the Revolution to attribute the change to the shocks of the conflict. But the force that made the abolitions possible was a higher law which exerted a constant influence in one direction. The higher law was the physical fact that the relation between land and man on the frontier was such that there was no longer any reason for either primogeniture or entail. There was so much land that it could not be monopolized, and in the absence of monopoly, the former poor could not be prevented from inheriting from nature a little piece of the earth.

[27] William Graham Sumner, *Earth-Hunger and Other Essays*, Albert G. Keller, ed. (New Haven: Yale University Press, 1913), p. 163.

In that situation all rules to the contrary were inevitably swept aside.

It is reasonable to assume that the higher law, which is a ratio, actually has little regard for the individual, and that it will have no hesitation in reversing itself when the ratio is reversed. It so happens that for a period of four hundred years the facts have seemed to favor the economic, political, and spiritual freedom of the individual. In that period the higher law has overruled the law of land, insisting that land should be inherited equally, that it should not be bound too much by entail, and that ordinarily men should own it in fee simple, to buy, sell, and divide as they please. It should be observed that this higher law is neither sacred nor divine, but it abides in circumstance, conditions, in a relationship between the amount of land and the number of men to share it. When that relationship changes, the "law" of which we speak will also change, not out of respect to decisions and precedents, but in spite of them. The law resides in final analysis in a ratio and that ratio is an irrevocable thing.

For four hundred years the land-man ratio, though changing from decade to decade, was always of the same character. But with the closing of the frontier, the *character* of the ratio changed in that men became more numerous than land was abundant. As population increases, land will become relatively less abundant, and if that happens, as it apparently will happen, then it will be impossible and perhaps wholly impracticable to continue the present law of equal inheritance, fee-simple ownership, and the right of unlimited division by sale or inheritance. If it turns out, as Professor Jameson observed, that political democracy came into being because economic democracy already prevailed, and if the main support of economic democracy was the free ownership of land in an agricultural society, then the interesting question arises as to whether political democracy can be maintained once economic democracy has departed.[28]

28 If we assume that in Europe in 1500 $\frac{L}{M} = 24$ acres, we can see that with the land increase from the frontier $\frac{L}{M} = 24 + x$ acres. The *plus* diminished as population increased so that since 1930 $\frac{L}{M} = 24 - x$ acres, and that x grows ever larger. It was the change from *plus* to *minus* that marks the change in the *character* of the ratio mentioned above.

Since the character of the ratio between land and man has recently changed, and since it was the character of the ratio that liberated the land policy of the Western World, it is not unlikely that the new character of the land-man ratio which promises to obtain indefinitely will now work in the direction of again restricting the land policy of the Western World. In short, the higher law will probably exert its influence in favor of a return to some equivalent of the old medieval principle of primogeniture and entail and an abolition of unrestricted fee-simple ownership.

One reason for this return may be found in elementary arithmetic, and in plain common sense. There is a fixed amount of land and a variable and constantly increasing number of people. By dividing the number of acres by the number of people we arrive at the average amount of land per person. But since the number of acres is constant, and the number of people is increasing, it follows that the amount of land per person is growing constantly less and less. If it is assumed that each person occupies the land, as most of them did in frontier times, no inconvenience will be experienced in the early stages when land was so bountiful as to make it theoretically possible for every individual in the society to have enough on which to live. But this stage is temporary. If population goes on increasing, the time will inevitably come when the land portion for each person is too small to furnish an independent subsistence. The law then will have no choice but to take cognizance of the accomplished fact, and by the necessary legal ratiocination the judges will conclude that land has become more valuable than people, and that its preservation must once more be given primary consideration. As that time approaches, the present ideas of equality of inheritance, of fee-simple ownership, and of unlimited right of division will go down before the silent necessity of the higher law. If our present social and political institutions are unable to adapt themselves to the new situation, they will go down, too. In fact, they are already bending under the pressure.

The above paragraph sets forth an abstract principle with reference to the entire Western World, the Metropolis of Europe plus the Great Frontier. The same principle may be illustrated by a specific small example, that of a single family in possession of a specific area of land. Let us assume that the family consists of four children and that the estate consists of 4800 acres. The parents die intestate, and by the law of equal inheritance now prevailing, each child would have 1200 acres, which is still sufficient to support a family. But let us suppose that each heir has four children and that they inherit equally. Each will have 300 acres. If one of these heirs has three children, each child will inherit 100 acres, but another generation of four children will reduce the acreage of each to 25 acres. Obviously within four generations the estate will have been cut up into tracts so small that no family can make a living on it by ordinary farm methods. In effect, the value of the original estate is being destroyed by division, a process that is actually going on in this country and in any country which follows the law of equal inheritance. It cannot go on indefinitely without grave consequences.

The results of the endless subdivision of the land by sale and inheritance are becoming dimly apparent. The scholars, who have made a study of the system in the United States, are murmuring their apprehension. After having followed with approval not wholly concealed by their objectivity, the repudiation of the undemocratic European practice of primogeniture and entail, American scholars are somewhat reluctant to follow through to the logical conclusion, which is that eventually unlimited subdivision of land — in the name of democracy, equality, or any other human consideration — was well enough in its day of free land; but in a closed society, such as we now are approaching, it may become a social danger. With the following paragraph Morris ends his excellent chapter on the colonial law governing land:

> This study cannot be concluded without mentioning the telling argument against too great distribution of realty which has been drawn from modern agricultural experience. In Canada, partible descent worked such excessive subdivisions that a royal edict of 1745 was necessary to restrict this practice. The disregard of this edict when Canada came under British control was the subject of much criticism by the attorney-general. Similarly the establishment of egalitarian inheritance in France has resulted in the division of agricultural lands into relatively small hold-

ings, and in this way has prevented the effecting of greater economies by large-scale production. . . . A similar situation exists in India. In Roumania alienation and subdivision of the land of the peasants have been restricted within definite limits in order to avoid the undesirable effects resulting from equality under the civil code. Recent studies indicate that the large plantation and the tenant-farmer are supplanting the smaller freehold in the New South; and that throughout the United States there has been in recent years an appreciable increase in the total acreage operated by tenants. Whether these agrarian readjustments will necessitate a change in our rules of succession is a problem of the future.[29]

It requires some courage on the part of an American citizen to discuss the prospect of a reversal of the law of equal inheritance and a return to a system as unpopular as that of primogeniture and entail is. Still the prospect, though remote, is here and will be examined.

The ranchers and farmers represent the segment of society in which a need for the preservation of an adequate land unit must eventually appear, but it would be a mistake to assume that they would accept such an undemocratic principle of their own volition. They love their children too, and desire to divide the inheritance equally among them. They would bitterly resent any other arrangement, and can never be brought to accept it until they are compelled to do so by the utter failure of freedom and equality which they prefer. Only suffering will induce them to change.

Though the need for the change will arise among the small farmers, the demand for it will not be of them. The prescription may be expected to come from students of agricultural problems, whose knowledge is broad enough to enable them to view the whole scene, to understand the causes of the agricultural distress, and to point out the inevitable consequences flowing from a continuing division of land by the law of inheritance or by any other means. Of course, the scholar cannot, dare not suggest a return to primogeniture and entail, for those

[29] Morris, *Studies in the History of American Law,* pp. 124–25. This was written in 1950.

words have connotations which would prejudice the case in a democratic society. He must find some new bottles for this bad old wine, and he must put attractive labels on the bottles to make the contents palatable. What must be prescribed is a plan that will preserve a land unit sufficient in size to support the family of the person chosen to possess it, and at the same time deal justly and equitably with the co-heirs who are excluded from possession.

The hypothesis advanced here — that the free and abundant lands of the frontier constituted the main factor in removing restrictions on the alienation of realty in the New World, and eventually relaxing these restrictions in the Metropolis — is likely to meet two contrary arguments. The first is that primogeniture and entail would have been abolished had the frontier lands never become available, that they would have been withered by the enlightenment and rooted out by the revolutions in any case. Leaving aside the possibility that the frontier was a potent influence in both the enlightenment and the revolutions, the obvious reply is that this contention cannot be refuted historically because it is not an historical argument. We can never do more than guess what would have happened in history if it had been otherwise than what it is. We do know that both primogeniture and entail were on their way out in the American colonies long before the Revolution occurred, that they have disappeared in all frontier countries, and that they have never returned in any frontier nation. We also know that they disappeared much later in European nations, and that they have returned there in several instances after their abolition.

The second argument deserves careful consideration. It is to this effect: If the presence of the frontier led to the abolition of primogeniture and entail, now that the frontier has gone we should expect the equivalent of these institutions to reappear in some form. That is exactly what ought to happen, and there is some evidence to indicate that it is on its way in the country where it will be least expected and most bitterly opposed. The United States is about the last place where we would look for such return. The idea of equality is too strongly imbedded in American sentiment, as well as in law, to permit a parent or a court to favor one child to the exclusion of the others. Any denial of the absolute right of property is repugnant to every citizen. Moreover, there is still such an abundance of land in America that it, as distinguished from a person, need not yet receive special consideration. Realty is common enough to be bought and sold at will.

The present situation is clouded and complicated by the fact that in modern times other forms of wealth have come upon the stage to sit beside the land. These more liquid forms such as bonds, notes, stocks, and cash have been superimposed on land, which formerly was the chief asset of estates. Such liquid forms of wealth are easily divisible, and little or no value is lost in division. Therefore there is no reason to expect any demand to arise for the equivalent of primogeniture or entail in any other realm than that of land. As a matter of fact, through corporate control the actual forms of wealth in stocks have become indivisible. The stock of the corporation may be divided indefinitely, but the form and the function of the actual body of wealth remains intact. It would seem absurd for a group of heirs or stockholders to cut up a corporation and each take a piece of it off for his independent use, yet that is exactly what is happening to the land.[30]

Difficult as the task of finding a modern equivalent for these discarded institutions seems to be, one such plan has been prepared by a group of scholars in the Columbia University Seminar on Rural Life, and is set forth by Leonard Hastings Schoff in a small volume with the title, *A National Agricultural Policy: For All the People of the United States.*[31] The stated purpose of the book is to formulate "A bold and concrete program aimed to eliminate unprofitable farms and relieve the American taxpayer of the burden of maintaining full farm production."[32]

30 Adolf A. Berle and Gardiner C. Means, in their book, *The Modern Corporation and Private Property*, dwell at length on the fact that control of the corporation is a thing apart from stock ownership. See chap. I, pp. 6–7. (New York and Chicago: Commerce Clearing House, Inc., 1932.)

31 New York: Harper and Bros., 1950.

32 The quotation is from the jacket of the book.

The six million American farms fall into three groups:

1. 3,500,000 farms — 58.33 per cent — average 40 acres.
2. 2,400,000 farms — 40 per cent — average 222 acres.
3. 100,000 farms — 1.67 per cent — average 3640 acres.

It is the first group that constitute the farm problem. The 40-acre farm is too small to mechanize or to support a family. Therefore, it is in this area that reform is recommended, reform designed to prevent the subdivision of land into such small and economically unsound units. In order to make this reform, the law of equal inheritance of land should be changed and a return made to the equivalent of primogeniture and entail. So runs the argument.

The authors propose the "Farm-Family Life-Trust Agreement," which should for convenience be called the Columbia Plan. The problem is to devise a plan that will preserve the farm intact by transferring it to *one* heir, the one who will operate it. This transfer must be made in a way that will excuse the recipient from buying out his brothers and sisters, and yet do it in a way that is equitable to them. This sounds as if it would be extremely difficult, but on paper it is surprisingly simple.

Let us assume that Farmer Jones dies and leaves a farm worth $40,000 and that he has four sons, A, B, C, and D. Each son has a $10,000 interest in the farm, but since it is not to be divided, it goes to A. Theoretically A owes his three brothers $10,000 each, but he never pays anything on this principal unless the land is sold. He pays his brothers 4 per cent interest anually as long as they live. When a brother dies, his part of the debt is canceled. If all three brothers die, A owns the farm intact. The plan is justified on the ground that the farm cannot be divided without destroying its value, that there is but one good family living on it, and that the brothers who go into commerce or industry or the professions have, according to past history, a better go of it than the one who remains on the farm. It may be pointed out to the authors of the Columbia Plan that if the brothers would invest the $400 they receive in life insurance, each one could create a $10,000 estate with something in cash left over.[33]

What is involved in the above proposal is a shift of emphasis from the individual as the most important factor to the land as paramount. This is a complete reversal of a long-established practice, legal and social, of putting the rights of the individual above all else. But we should not take the plan too seriously. It is inconceivable that this thinly disguised equivalent of primogeniture and entail could have received serious consideration, even in a college seminar, when the frontier was open and a homestead could be had from the government for the asking or a quarter-section purchased for a horse, a gun, or a pair of boots. The significant point is that we have made a full circle, returning to the principle of an unfree land system. The prospect of change is still remote, as the scholars admit, but the need for it may in time become too great to be ignored, and make of the scholar in his study a practical and far-seeing man.

This chapter began with the inquiry: Did the frontier modify institutions? Did it contribute materially to the creation of new institutions and in some instances to the abolition of old ones? Six specific cases, all taken from the United States, have been examined. Five of them were selected from the last American frontier, the Great Plains, where physical conditions were so imperative as to compel clean sharp breaks with the past. In these five cases we centered attention on the new creation, on what *became* rather than on what *was*. In the realm of war we witnessed the rise of a peculiar military organization, the Texas Rangers, and the adoption of a new weapon for mounted men, the revolver. In the economic field we saw the rise either by adoption or invention of three methods of production hitherto strange to the American people, the methods of open range ranching, of irrigation, and of dry-land farming. In the domain of technology we find that

---

[33] I am indebted to Mr. Charles Zivley of Austin, Texas, for this practical suggestion. It is not a part of the plan advanced by the Columbia scholars. The amount of cash the brothers would have after buying insurance would vary with the age at which they took the insurance.

barbed wire, so essential and practical where all traditional fencing material was absent, is truly a child of the plains. The change in the law of water is the most startling innovation because something old and honored, namely, the English common law, retreated slowly from the original English riparian system to the Eastern American riparian system, to the Western American riparian system, trying to satisfy the needs of people in new conditions. But retreat was not enough; the forces of change were so strong as to compel the unconditional surrender of the English common law in favor of the revolutionary law of prior appropriation.

In conclusion a word should be said about "new" institutions. It is probably an axiom of history that every institution devised in modern times has replaced or supplemented an older one. Therefore, such terms as "new" institutions or methods are used with the understanding that they were new only to a specific time and place. Man has been tinkering with methods and institutions for a very long period, and he has built up in the historical lumber room an arsenal of discarded institutions, some of them very old and practically forgotten. When he gets in a jam where the equipment he is using no longer works, he goes to the lumber room and digs up something that will work. This is the reason that the historian who has an uncommon knowledge of the antiques in the historical attic is often disconcerting to those who proclaim something new, especially in institutions. For example, the open range method of handling cattle, the principles of irrigation, and the practice — if not the name and theory — of dry farming are as old as recorded history. They were nevertheless new to the Anglo-American people when they entered the Great Plains. The Texas Rangers were the *posse comitatus* in modern dress. The six-shooter and barbed wire, new gadgets made practicable by technology, replaced or supplemented other weapons and fences. In the examples of modifications cited from the Great Plains, more emphasis was placed on what was introduced than on what was cast aside, but in dealing with the law of inheritance the emphasis was reversed. Attention there was centered almost wholly on the destruction of the law of primogeniture and entail rather than those on the principle of equal inheritance which followed. In all examples the impelling force behind the change was of frontier origin.

CHAPTER NINE

THE FALLACY OF NEW FRONTIERS

A NYONE WHO SUGGESTS that the closing down of the frontier poses a serious problem to society has to answer this question: "But, aren't there new frontiers being opened up as important as the old one?" Often the idea is expressed in an emphatic statement rather than as a question. Today "new frontiers" are being conjured up in every direction, and it is the purpose of this chapter to examine them and to compare them with the real thing. We shall proceed by inquiring as to the variety and nature of these new frontiers, by noting the categories into which they seem to fall. The last part of the chapter will examine the so-called scientific frontier with special attention to what science has done thus far with the most important of the earth's resources, stored energy as represented by the fossil fuels.

1. The Nature of New Frontiers

The first thing that strikes the student of these "new frontiers" is their number, variety, and heterogeneity. When the various claims for the existence or prospect of new frontiers are gathered together, the observer notes a miscellaneous assortment and wonders whether they partake more of the nature of panaceas than of cures for the loss of the physical frontier. The frontier experience from 1500 to, say, 1900 was without doubt among the most memorable adventures mankind has had in modern times. On the rim of the Metropolis, always at its yonder edge, the beacon fire of the Great Frontier was luring men outward, stirring them to mighty deeds, achievements, and sacrifices. This was indeed a heroic period, heroic for the individuals and the nations involved. People love their heroic periods, make legends about them, and vaguely hope that they will come again. Looking back on such an age, people are filled with nostalgia, suffer a cultural lag, and begin emotionally to live in the past. They — and this applies with particular force to Americans whose historians have made them conscious of the frontier past — are plainly homesick. They want the old thrills, the remembered adventures, the quick fortunes, the numerous opportunities, and the easy freedom they once had or believe they had. In this state they build in their plaintive imaginings unreal images of new frontiers.

This psychological process has never been better described than by one of the first American historians, Pedro de Castañeda de Naçera, who accompanied Francisco Coronado in his search for the Seven Cities in 1540–42. This chronicler kept a careful record of the expedition and wrote it up in a manner not often surpassed. Anyone reading his lucid account of Coronado's journey through the Far West knows that everybody on it suffered, and no doubt each Spaniard wished many times that he had remained safe in Spain where he could drink good wine and see women dressed in something besides dirty buckskin. The survivors finally returned home, Castañeda with them, and as they loafed and looked back on their American experiences, they began to embroider with their imaginings the actual experiences they had had. But they could not fool Castañeda, the chronicler, because he had made a record as he went; and he, no doubt, read his documents and grieved at the lack of historicity on the part of his companions. Their tales finally became too much for him, and so he wrote an introduction to his account and described how men felt who had lost a frontier:

I always notice . . . that for the most part when we have something valuable in our hands, and deal with it without hindrance, we do not value or prize it as highly as if we understood how much we would miss it after we had lost it, and the longer we continue to have it the less we value it; but after we have lost it and miss the advantages of it, we have a great pain in the heart, and we are all the time imagining and trying to find ways and means by which to get it back again. It seems to me that this has happened to all or most of those who went on the expedition which, in the year . . . 1540, Francisco Vasquez Coronado led in search of the Seven Cities. Granted that they did not find the riches of which they had been told, they found a place in which to search for them, and the beginning of a good country to settle in, so as to go on farther from there. Since they came back . . . their hearts weep for having lost so favorable an opportunity.[1]

This passage seems to describe how today Americans consciously and Europeans and others unconsciously look back on the experience of the race with the Great Frontier. They did not prize it highly when they had it in their hand; and the longer they had it, the less they valued it. But now that they have lost it they also "have a great pain in the heart" and indeed are busy "imagining and trying to find ways and means by which to get it back again."

The great pain in our heart we are now trying to alleviate by following the mirages of new frontiers. On the broad flat plain of monotonous living we see the distorted images of our desires glimmering on the horizons of the future; we press on toward them only to have them disappear completely or reappear in different form in another direction.

A moment's thought should convince a reasonable person that the Great Frontier has practically disappeared, and it is doubtful that any new frontier can be compared with the old one in magnitude, in influence, or in importance. Nor is there much probability that mankind can within the foreseeable future hope to discover a comparable equivalent. Therefore, most of the talk about new frontiers may be thought of as nostalgia. Man, in his vain search for the lost ingredient, is like the individual trying to recapture the exciting and pleasurable experiences of his childhood. He may return to the scene of them only to find it radically changed: the old swimming hole muddy, the hills shrunken, and the valleys less green. The man has not returned to the scene of his youth but only to the place where it was. And so is it with the frontier to which man cannot return. He may go to the place where it was, but it is not there when he arrives. Instead of emptiness he finds homes

[1] George Parker Winship, "The Coronado Expedition, 1540–1542," *Fourteenth Annual Report of the Bureau of American Ethnology, 1892–1893* (Washington: U.S. Government Printing Office, 1896), pt. I, p. 472.

and people; instead of forests he finds farms or stumps or burnt-over land; instead of fertile land lush with the duff and compost of thousands of seasons of leaf-falling, he finds eroded gullies, denuded hillsides, and deserts on the march. He is not free to ride the divides that form the watersheds, to fish in the streams or to take game, or to build a log cabin, or to live by a campfire in solitude. "Memory of the thing behind sometimes plays tricks on hope for the thing ahead," says Bowman.[2]

Unable to find a frontier, and having such a keen desire for it, man builds up the illusion that it must exist somewhere. He is seized with hallucinations and substitutes them for reality. He sees new frontiers, entirely too many of them. Their multiplicity and diversity indicate a lack of consensus as to the existence of the one, which none could doubt. An analysis of a collection of these new frontiers shows that the individual imagines one lying ahead of the direction of his interest. It should be noticed that the new frontier is always *ahead* of him; he is never in it. For example, the businessman sees a business frontier in the customers he has not yet reached; the missionary sees a religious frontier among the souls he has not yet saved; the social worker sees a human frontier among the suffering people whose woes he has not alleviated; the educator sees the ignorance he is trying to dispel as a frontier to be taken; and the scientists permit us to believe that they are uncovering the real thing in a scientific frontier. The prophets of new frontiers may deceive themselves and would deceive us. What they have done, unconsciously no doubt, is to recognize the human desire for a new frontier and capitalize on it as a slogan with good sales quality. But as yet no Columbus has come in from one of these voyages and announced: "*Gentlemen, there is your frontier.*" The best they do is to say it is out there, and if you think hard enough and have faith enough, and put in a little money you will surely find it. If you watch these purveyors of substitute frontiers, you will find that nearly everyone wants you to buy something, give something, or believe something. Unlike Columbus, they bring no continents and no oceans, no gold or silver or grass or forest to you.

[2] Isaiah Bowman, *The Pioneer Fringe* (New York: American Geographical Society, 1931), p. 5.

It is necessary to remember that the frontier experience is a unique one in modern civilization, and the word unique means something singular, existing by itself, without counterpart. There is no plural for frontier. As defined in this study, it was an empty land, a vacancy inviting occupants. By no stretch of the imagination short of total catastrophe can we visualize vacant lands of such magnitude on this earth as the frontier offered, nor can we visualize such a generous ratio of land or of wealth in proportion to population as existed for more than three centuries after the vacant lands were found.

2. *The Kinds of New Frontiers*

An analysis of an extensive file of "new frontiers" reveals three fairly well-defined classes, geographic, socio-economic-political, and scientific. The surviving geographic frontiers comprise the lands rejected by the pioneers of the eighteenth and nineteenth centuries, lands that are still rejected by the twentieth century. In nearly every example the land designated has some handicap that makes its occupation very difficult for the individual on anything like the terms on which he occupied the temperate zones. Isaiah Bowman published a book in 1931 entitled *The Pioneer Fringe*. The "fringe" is significant, and though the author maintains that good lands are still available, he calls attention to the fact that they are found in isolated pockets and often can be had only on special terms. "Most of the pioneer land of today," he says, "represents a growth at the *fringe* of settlement." [3] Again he says:

> No pioneer area is a broad unbroken belt. It is, rather, a series of scattered patches and strips loosely disposed in belt-like form beyond the fringe of present settlement. Taking a world view we see the pioneer lands in a rough zonal arrangement, each continent having its share. A world map shows a belt in each temperate zone and a large number of "spots" still in the pioneering stage. It shows two similar zones of subtropical development of which the southern has by far the larger extent. [4]

[3] *Ibid.*, p. 7.
[4] *Ibid.*, p. 58.

The use of the words "fringe," "belt," "scattered patches," and "spots" shows that Bowman knows what he is talking about. He says: "It is precisely because the remaining pioneer lands are of the less desirable sort that they make their challenge to science and government. When there is the best to choose from in the way of location and soils a government need not concern itself with settlement so much as with law and order." [5] Bowman reveals his own feeling by saying: "We no longer look upon pioneering as a mere outward thrust of a virile stock, for all stocks have lost their old-time pioneering virility. Or, if the virility is still there, to exercise it in the old way would be foolish and even suicidal." [6] Bowman does not talk of "new frontiers" because he knows the nature of the fringe lands where pioneering still goes on.

It is mainly in the magazines that we find new frontiers, and they are divided between the reading matter and the advertising. Under the classification of geographical frontiers, a writer seizes on Alaska. Governor Ernest Gruening, in an article entitled "Go North, Young Man," says: "There still is a frontier [in Alaska] . . . an area nearly as large as the United States east of the Mississippi." This region has seventy-five thousand permanent inhabitants, free land, mineral wealth, and great forests.[7]

From the subarctic Alaska the frontier hunters move to the torrid regions of the Amazon. Here is the "world's biggest and wildest frontier." The author assures us that the region is capable of supporting hundreds of millions of people, but the title of the article, "They're Bringing Hope to the Valley of Death," gives a macabre touch to an otherwise idyllic scene. Even the hardiest pioneer is likely to shy at the Valley of Death and put off going there to the very end.[8] A like-minded author, in a similar country, tells us that in British Guiana and Venezuela "a new and richer frontier . . . awaits Yankee pluck and ingenuity. . . . Somewhere . . . there is a great deposit of dia-

---

5 *Ibid.*, p. 51.
6 *Ibid.*, p. 80.
7 Ernest Gruening, "Go North, Young Man," *Reader's Digest*, January, 1944, p. 53, condensed from *Future*, December, 1943.
8 Hernane Taveres de SA, "They're Bringing Hope to the Valley of Death," *Saturday Evening Post*, December 11, 1948, p. 20.

monds which might rival that of the South African Kimberley." [9]
Ethiopia is hailed as the "Land of the Fabulous Frontier," a
wild and woolly kingdom, "a last frontier, magnificent in its
vastness, its rawness, the savage impact of its beauty." It has
350,000 square miles of land, stands of timber, virgin veins
of precious minerals, and verdant grass lands.[10] The fleeting
game is next sighted by Gaskill Gordon in "Liberia, a New
Frontier." He warns the pioneer that he can't have his daily
paper or his movie. "But for people who can take it like
pioneers, here is a new frontier, with opportunities hanging
from every bush." It is "an almost untouched treasure house,
with gold, diamonds, pearls, rare hardwoods, and rich iron
ore." [11] In "Oceans of Opportunity," Warren E. Atherton reveals a new frontier among the Pacific Islands, a vast treasure
land of natural resources.[12]

Coming closer home we find several frontiers within the
United States, some of them geographic only in that they are
given a specific location in some section of the country. They
may be classed as socio-economic. General Robert E. Wood,
while serving as director of Sears, Roebuck and Company, discovered a new frontier on the Gulf Coast. "From Mobile to
Brownsville," he tells us, "you can see thousands of examples
of a throbbing new frontier," and he clinches his discovery by
telling about the sale of property in Houston at $2000 a front
inch! [13] Another author, ranging through Texas, discovered
among the forests of oil derricks in the Permian Basin the
"Boom Towns of the New Frontier." [14] And still another bold
Columbus stumbles on a "Surviving American Frontier" in

[9] Talcott Powell, "New Frontier for American Pioneers: Tropical South
America," *Reader's Digest*, July, 1937, p. 59.

[10] Temple Fielding, "Land of the Fabulous Frontier," *Reader's Digest*, June,
1947, pp. 1–4, condensed from *The Christian Science Monitor*, May 10, 1947.

[11] Gaskill Gordon, "Liberia, a New Frontier," *Reader's Digest*, October, 1948,
p. 94, condensed from *The American Magazine*, July, 1948.

[12] Warren E. Atherton, "Oceans of Opportunity," *The American Magazine*,
April, 1945, p. 34.

[13] Robert E. Wood, "The Gulf Coast, Our New Frontier," *Reader's Digest*,
September, 1948, pp. 17–20.

[14] Clarence Woodbury, "Boom Towns of the New Frontier," *The American
Magazine*, September, 1948, p. 24.

the Southern Highlands in which he sees one of the oldest and most primitive cultures of the United States. There he finds the leveling-off process characteristic of the frontier, but he does not venture to tell us how level a frontiersman can get.[15] Then *Fortune*, to which any frontier would be exotic, enters the list and in the Missouri Valley finds "the lost frontier" which has now been found, "recreated" by the building of dams.[16]

A casual examination of all these "new frontiers" will reveal that each has limitations. Some are too hot and some are too cold, some too dry and some too wet. And some are pretty well guarded by cyclone fences and legal barricades. As a resident of Texas I should hate to try to stake out a claim in Houston, along the Gulf Coast, or among the oil derricks of the Permian Basin on the same terms that my father staked a land claim in what turned out to be an oil field in West Texas when I was a boy.

Advertisers have a very severe case of frontieritis. Even some modest Texans believe in it. A Houstonian inquires through *Fortune*, "Have you staked your claim yet? The Golden Southwest is the Industrial Frontier of America!" [17] A big insurance company takes a full page in a big weekly to point out "Frontiers of Responsibility." On the upper half of the page is a picture of the Oklahoma Land Rush of 1889 where real frontiersmen were running like hell for a free quarter-section; the lower half descends to reading matter advertising the necessity of "a well-conceived insurance program." [18] The Institute of Life Insurance uses a page in American newspapers to proclaim that "Today's American 'Frontier' is right on your own MAIN STREET!" The statement is proved by citing the cases with appropriate pictures of a shipping clerk, a drug clerk, and a woman who built a business with a bread recipe.[19] All of them no doubt bought insurance. An aircraft concern which we will call the Flyeasy takes a full page in *Time* to say that it has "A

15 C. M. Wilson, "Surviving American Frontier," *Current History*, May, 1931, p. 189.

16 *Fortune*, August, 1949, pp. 59, 65.

17 *Ibid.*, February, 1949, p. 166.

18 *Saturday Evening Post*, October 22, 1949, p. 95

19 *San Antonio Express*, September 12, 1949.

great 'new equalizer' for the business frontier." Samuel Colt and his revolver, reputed to have made little frontiersmen equal to big ones, appears at the top, followed by a sleek plane poised over a great city, and a photograph of the "pioneer in aeronautics, who produced the Flyeasy as a modern 'equalizer' in business transportation." The switch comes at the end with the suggestion that orders will be taken for those who want to set off for the new frontier in a Flyeasy.[20] A tube manufacturer takes a full page in *Fortune* to say that "Men with Vision See New Frontiers" in electronic engineering, provided they use Blank tubes.[21] In these advertisements, it is not difficult to discover the mental working of the authors. Subconsciously they know that the American people are interested in the frontier and would like to have it back. They use it as something with pleasant associations, and then assure the prospective purchaser that he may have it back if he will buy life insurance, aircraft, or electronic tubing. I am at a loss, however, to account for the last example, that of Fifth Avenue's "largest underneath fashion specialists," who want the ladies to "be right in front with the easy to don 'Frontier' Bra" at $1.59 each or $3.00 for two! [22] In advertising, the frontier has no confines.

3. The Scientific Frontier

We come now to the most notable of all the new frontiers. The scientific frontier deserves major attention because it is the most plausible, the most respectable, and may well be the most pernicious. It is not difficult to discern the technique of a blatant advertiser who promises a frontier because he usually gives it away down at the bottom of the page that he wants to sell you something. The geographic frontiers also speak for themselves. Even a pioneer has sense enough to know that the Amazon has a jungle, Alaska a blanket of snow, and the plains and steppes have recurring droughts. He knows, or can easily find out, that there is probably something the matter with most

20 *Time*, August 11, 1947, p. 60.
21 *Fortune*, July, 1943, p. 50.
22 *New York Sunday News*, October 23, 1949.

of the unoccupied spaces of the earth, else more people would be there. But the frontier of science requires more discernment, holding as it does enough of truth to make its representations plausible.

The prestige of science has been built up to such proportions that the layman dares not quibble with it, and perhaps the historian should be wary. For many it is shrouded in mystery which only those white-frocked men of the laboratory can understand and interpret to the believing. The real scientist, often an indifferent interpreter, is prone to remain silent; actually he is busy with his specific project, is often for the most part a piece worker, a highly trained technician; and is either unaware of or indifferent to the social results flowing from what he does. The university faculties are bristling with these busy little men, luxuriating in the bounty of the institution, of industry, and of the research foundations. They have too good a thing to spoil by disclaiming credit for what they have not yet accomplished. It would seem that they do not protest enough.

In fairness it must be said that few scientists of high repute have been promising the world a new frontier. But some of them have come close to it. An outstanding example is Dr. Vannevar Bush, director of the Office of Scientific Research and Development. I refer to his book entitled *Science, the Endless Frontier*.[23] This volume contains a "Report to the President on a Program for Postwar Scientific Research." The report was prepared in response to a request by the President of the United States. In his letter of instruction, dated November 17, 1944, President Roosevelt, who had considerable knowledge of words, fell into the frontier trap. Among other things he said: "New frontiers of the mind are before us, and if they are pioneered with the same vision, boldness, and drive with which we have waged this war we can create a fuller and more fruitful employment and a fuller and more fruitful life."[24] Dr. Bush evidently took his cue for the title from Mr. Roosevelt, but the vision is his. He sees the new frontier and he

[23] Vannevar Bush, *Science, the Endless Frontier* (Washington: Government Printing Office, 1945).
[24] *Ibid.*, p. ix.

thinks it is the duty of the United States Government to perpetuate it. He says:

> It has been the basic United States policy that Government should foster the opening of new frontiers. It opened the seas to clipper ships and furnished land for pioneers. Although these frontiers have more or less disappeared, the frontier of science remains. It is in keeping with the American tradition — one which has made the United States great — that new frontiers shall be made accessible for development by all American citizens.[25]

And so, out of the scientific hat, Dr. Bush pulls what everybody is looking for, an *endless* frontier. If what he envisages turned out to be really a frontier, and endless to boot, one that will not quit as the old one did just when we get geared up to it, then we will really have something of great value. But if he and other scientists are deceiving us, or remain silent while we deceive ourselves about science, then they are rendering a disservice to society which may not be easily overlooked.

Let us subject the new and "interminable" scientific frontier to a little analysis to see how it compares with the old terminable one. Three series of questions need to be answered.

1. What are the elements with which science works? Do these elements have limitations, and if so, what are they?

2. What are the achievements of science up to the present? Under what conditions have these achievements been made? Has applied science or technology left the earth as a piece of property richer or poorer than it was?

3. Granting that science can provide a new frontier, on what terms is the bounty of the scientific frontier to be made available to the people? Are its productions to come to people on the same terms as the wealth of the frontier came to them? If so, what are the implications? If not, what are the results? These three inquiries will be pursued serially.

The elements with which science works are physical elements, substance. It may be argued, with astronomy as an example, that space is an exception to the above statement. Sci-

[25] *Ibid.*, p. 6.

ence does take space into account, but it can do no more than that; it cannot change space's form, make things of it, or alter it in any way as it does the tangible earth-elements. Therefore we may say that the practical applications of science to human service are limited as the earth's elements and its envelope of air are limited. Insofar as this is true, science is circumscribed and subject to the earth's limitations as to area, substance, and quantity. It has not and for the present at least cannot add to the sum total of what is already here. Science is limited in that it has a finite amount of material to work on, and its marvelous role in the modern age has been that of changing the form of the materials and making the desirable ones available in increasing quantity for the uses of man. The skill with which science has performed this function has misled us into the assumption that science can contribute to mankind unlimited benefits without regard for substance. This is a false assumption and appears as such when we look at the whole picture.

The two contributors — that of the frontier and that of science — differ in kind. Science makes what *is present* available by changing its form and position; the frontier added something extra to what was present; and in doing so it extended the base on which even science rests. Science is intensive where the frontier is extensive; science digs deeper into the acre, whether of soil or mineral, but the frontier added more acres. Science makes more *finished* materials available, but the frontier provided more room and more *raw* materials. Both have made great contributions, but they are complementary rather than supplementary; and only the frontier has added to the sum total of things in the absolute.

By way of illustration, let us consider an acre of land in terms of what it will produce, and assume that science can, by intensive methods of cultivation, double or quadruple the normal production of the acre. The acre would then be equal to two or to four acres, as the case might be, and production would be increased in the same ratio. If from the frontier an extra acre is added, science could apply the same intensive methods to the second acre that it did to the first, and in that case the total production would, after science had done its best, be doubled by the presence of the extra acre. Some argue that science has made its contribution by developing the third dimension. This is admitted, but it may be pointed out that, in the matter of acres or area, depth is its only dimension; it has added nothing to length and breadth. The frontier, on the other hand, has come in three dimensions, though it has emphasized length and breadth more than it has depth. Depth, the chief field of science, is now about all that is left for development.

We turn now to the second series of questions which has to do with the achievements of science, the conditions under which the contributions were made, and the price the earth has paid for them. There is no doubt that the achievements of science have been remarkable, but they were made under the most unusual circumstances. The unique conditions prevailing up to quite recent times enabled applied science to operate in all three dimensions. The frontier made so much area available as to render it unnecessary for science to go in search of depth. Thus it happens that science, as applied through technology, has up to quite recently been destructive so far as the sum total of the earth's resources is concerned. If you could hold in your right hand the earth in miniature as it was in 1500 or 1600 and in your left hand the earth as it is now, which earth would you consider richer in resources? Or preferable as a desirable base of future operations? On the first earth you would have the Great Frontier, the natural forests, the clear streams, the virgin soils, and the precious metals intact. On the second earth you would have stumps, foul streams, eroded soils, and outside of Kentucky a depleted store of precious metals. As a manager of real estate, applied science has done a bad job and has left the land in a worse state than it found it. If technology does to the third dimension what it has already done to the first two, the earth will be poor indeed.

Two achievements of science impress us as wholly beneficial. Science has increased the wealth, the conveniences, and the comforts of mankind in the Western World in a most remarkable way, and it keeps on doing it. In the second place, it has through medicine and sanitation, decreased pain and suffering, but at the same time it has raised the limits on the increase in population. Through medicine it has postponed death and through technology it has made living for many attractive. These achievements would be even more laudable if science could guarantee them in perpetuity, but unless science does this, the combined effect over a long period may lead to catastrophe.

The increased production of food and other essentials of good living came about during the period when the frontier countries were pouring their windfall bounty into the centers of population. What science and its servant, technology, did was to speed up the rate at which resources already in existence could be utilized. In short, it speeded up the rate of destruction of the forests, the minerals, and the soils without creating any of these things. It taught us how to skim the Great Frontier for immediate benefits, using up the capital along with any increment of interest it may have added. Therefore the benefits are temporary and will end when the process of destruction is complete. The following observation by Bernard M. Baruch bears on the current situation:

Because of the great abundance of the earth's resources we have taken them for granted. But now, over most of the globe . . . we are face to face with a serious depletion of "resource capital." More than one country is already bankrupt. Such bankruptcy has wiped out civilizations in the past; there is no reason for thinking we can escape the same fate, unless we change our ways.[26]

The problem created by the current destructiveness of applied science would be serious enough with a stable population, but science has given us instead a population that is expanding with explosive force all over the world. Applied science has thus accelerated two forces moving toward each other on the same track. Can its new frontier — its third dimension — enable a constantly increasing population to prosper, or even to

[26] Introduction to William Vogt, *The Road to Survival* (New York: William Sloane Associates, Inc., 1948), p. ix. See also R. O. Whyte and G. V. Jacks, *Vanishing Lands* (New York: Doubleday & Co, 1939); Fairfield Osborn, *Our Plundered Planet* (Boston: Little, Brown and Co., 1948).

live, on a fixed body of land of constantly decreasing resources? That would indeed be the endless frontier.

4. Science and Energy: An Example

There is still another approach to applied science, one through which the limitations of technology become apparent. Let us consider energy, that power which enables science to apply the principles it has discovered to the production of wealth. Though we are concerned here with the sources of energy which have been most useful in making modern civilization what it is, we may before examining these glance briefly at the entire supply available on earth. The scientists tell us that the fountain head, the source of all energy, is the sun, and that the stored-up supply which we have been using is nothing more than accretions built up in the coal beds and oil deposits over a long period of time. The energy available in plants is put there by photosynthesis brought about by the sun. The wind and the waves move because heat from the sun produces a disequilibrium in these elements. In short, without the sun there would be no energy and no life on the earth. Having established this point, we may now proceed to examine the various categories of energy which are practically or theoretically available.

The chief sources of energy apart from living things are as follows: (1) the sun; (2) moving water, such as waves, ocean currents, and inland streams; (3) the wind; (4) nuclear fission; and (5) fossil fuels such as coal, petroleum, shale, and tar sand. Historically these five sources of energy fall into two classes: (1) those which have been used extensively in building our modern civilization, and (2) those which either have not been brought under control or have not been found practicable to any considerable extent. Historically, we are concerned with those which *have been used* rather than those which *may have a future use*. The only sources of energy which have thus far played an important role in the destiny of Western Civilization, the only ones of which man is as yet a complete master, are running inland water and the fossil fuels. How important the others may be we are not prepared to say, though there is extensive scientific literature of a somewhat speculative nature on the subject.[27] It is not an exaggeration to say that modern industrial civilization has been built on two sources, running water and fossil fuels. Therefore our problem narrows down to a consideration of the total supply of these two sources of power.

The two sources differ fundamentally in character, and in order that we may understand their bearing on the future it is important to note this difference. The power derived from running water, while limited in quantity, is reasonably permanent. Once water power is developed to its maximum, it may be maintained indefinitely at or near that level, a fact which may be of vast importance in the future. The fossil fuels are likewise limited in quantity, but they are expendable, can be used but once. To use them is to destroy them utterly. M. King Hubbert [28] tells us that these fossil fuels required five hundred million years to accumulate, and that any accumulation during the next 10,000 years will be negligible. "Hence," he says, "we deal with an essentially fixed storehouse of energy which we are drawing on at a phenomenal rate. The amount which remains at any given time equals the amount originally present less that which has been consumed already." [29] This means that the amount of fossil fuels is historically an absolute, that the fuels are irreplaceable, and that with their use and destruction the amount remaining is the original quantity less that used. With time the amount of fossil fuels remaining approaches zero, which is to say that the energy on which civilization is now based is also approaching zero. It is not a question of *whether* we are approaching zero, but only of *when* we arrive there.

When we arrive depends on the total amount of fossil fuels existent and the rate of utilization. The known total amount is enormous, and has been estimated by the geologists and

27 See Farrington Daniels, "Solar Energy," *Science*, January 21, 1949, vol. CIX, pp. 51–57.

28 M. King Hubbert, "Energy from Fossil Fuels," *Science*, February 4, 1949, vol. CIX, pp. 103–09. Hubbert is Associate Director of the Shell Oil Company. His illuminating article on which the above paragraphs are based should be widely read and pondered.

29 *Ibid.*, p. 105.

mining engineers.[30] They tell us that "the estimated initial supply of energy stored in fossil fuels is of the order of 50×10^{18} kilogram-calories, of which . . . 0.7×10^{18}, or 1.5 per cent has already been consumed." [31] We may not understand the higher . mathematics, but we can derive some comfort from the fact that only 1.5 per cent of the supply has been used, and that we still have 98.5 per cent of the original store. This means that the crisis is not immediate.

It is the rate of utilization that will determine the time of depletion of the fossil fuels. In this respect we cannot judge the future by the past because the rate of use is being steadily accelerated. Here we speak of coal, petroleum, and gas, the three forms which have as yet been tapped. Thus far little has been done with oil shales and tar sands, though the amount of them is also estimated. The use of coal as fuel dates from the thirteenth century when it was discovered in Britain that "sea coles" would burn. During the first five centuries the rate of use, though increasing, was insignificant. In the latter part of the eighteenth century use increased rapidly, and in the nineteenth and twentieth it has constantly accelerated. For example, it is estimated that the total coal production for all time amounted in 1947 to 81 billion metric tons, but of this amount, 40 billion metric tons were mined from 1920 to 1947. Since 1900 more than three quarters of the total production has been mined. If we consider that production of coal is tantamount to the destruction of stored energy, we can see the significance of the accelerated trend. Up to the present, we have used 1.5 per cent of the estimated initial coal supply, but we have used 1 per cent in the last half-century. If the rate of use should be stabilized, we would have fossil fuel for a long time. On the other hand, if the rate of use should continue to accelerate as it has during the last century, then the elimination of this source of energy would occur in a much shorter time. Since coal supplies 92.2 per cent of the energy available in fossil fuels, we see how important this fuel is to the destiny of mankind.

[30] Hubbert says, "While the quantities of fuels upon the earth are not known precisely, their order of magnitude is pretty definitely circumscribed." — *Ibid.*, p. 105.

[31] *Ibid.*, p. 106.

The story of oil and its derivatives is much shorter and more extreme than that of coal. This source supplies only 7.8 per cent of fossil fuel energy. Its use dates from about 1850, but its consumption has been so accelerated that we have already used up 5.7 per cent of the estimated total of petroleum and natural gas. Since the tar sands and shales account for only 3.6 per cent of the total energy from fossil fuels, the fact that these sources are yet to be tapped is not highly significant. Petroleum was first produced in Rumania in 1857, and two years later the Drake well of Pennsylvania opened the American fields. "From these beginnings, with only an occasional setback, the world production of petroleum has increased spectacularly, reaching by the end of 1947 an annual rate of 477 million cubic meters (3 billion U.S. barrels)." [32] The total production up to 1947 has been 57.7 billion U.S. barrels, but half of this was produced in the last ten years of the period, and 97 per cent since 1900. The rate of use has accelerated faster than that of coal, and if the production could be stabilized as of 1900–47, the estimated supply of petroleum would be exhausted in about 1000 years. If, however, it were stabilized as of the period 1937–47, the vanishing point would be reached in four hundred years. Since the production (or destruction) of petroleum is still accelerating, doubling about every fifteen years, its life expectancy is thereby cut down to the uncomfortably near future.

Science claims credit, and deserves it, for this vast expenditure of energy, but it likewise must take the blame for the destruction of an irreplaceable resource. A secondary effect of this destruction is the spectacular growth of the world's population, a growth which rises on a curve almost identical with the curve of fossil fuel consumption. It is the power liberated by the destruction of the fossil fuels which has made it possible to produce and move the foods necessary for the increased population. It is estimated that in 1800 each man had available for use perhaps 300 kilogram-calories of energy per day, but by 1900 the amount had increased to 9880, and by 1940 it stood at 22,100. It is this excess energy derived from fossil fuels which has enabled the population curve to rise so precipitately. As Hubbert remarks with considerable reserve, "the develop-

[32] Hubbert, "Energy from Fossil Fuels," p. 104.

ments within the last century, and especially within the last
few decades, are decidedly exceptional." [33] The world population in 1650 is estimated at 545 million, but by 1940 it stood at
2171 million. The most rapid increase has been during the
last half-century, a rate which would double the world population every 100 years. At this rate within 200 years the world
population would be nearly 9 billion, which is about the maximum the earth can support. If such a rate were projected
1600 years, there would be one person for every square meter,
a little more than a square yard. At this rate Adam and Eve
alone could have produced the present population in 3300
years, but if we assume that the human race has been in existence a million years and that the average rate of increase has
produced the present population, then it would require 33,000
years for the population to double. Whether we look backward or forward, it is clear, as Hubbert says, that "Such a rate
is not 'normal!' "[34] and cannot continue.

It is interesting to examine this sudden burst of power with
its comparable increase of population on a long-time scale, say
of 40,000 years backward and forward. On such a time scale
the period of use of the fossil fuels appears as a projection
rising almost perpendicularly and falling almost as fast. "The
consumption of energy from fossil fuels is thus seen to be but
a 'pip,' rising sharply from zero to a maximum, and almost
as sharply declining, and thus representing but a moment in
the total of human history." "Yet we cannot turn back; neither
can we consolidate our gains and remain where we are. In
fact, we have no choice but to proceed into a future which
we may be assured will differ markedly from anything we have
experienced thus far." [35]

For those who want a ray of hope along with the realities,
Hubbert says that though the exhaustion of fossil fuels is inevitable, it will still be possible to stabilize the population at a
reasonable figure and by the use of other available forms of
energy, such as sunshine and running water, maintain an industrial civilization, but in order to accomplish this and to

33 *Ibid.*, p. 105.
34 *Ibid.*, p. 105.
35 *Ibid.*, p. 108.

avoid a *débâcle*, we must not be caught in a cultural lag and continue to deny the physical facts which are before us.[36]

The physical facts we are concerned with here pertain to the Great Frontier, to the fact that it made available the greatest proportion of the fossil fuels and the water power, and of the other forms of energy which are being used by man. The following table shows the percentage of coal, petroleum, and water power furnished by the continents of the Metropolis and of the Great Frontier. The Great Frontier must share as a factor in the abnormal, exceptional pip in the curve of fossil fuel energy and of population because it furnished about 55 per cent of the fossil fuels and furnished food and room for a vastly increased population.

VISIBLE FUEL AND POWER RESERVES — 1937 [37]

	Coal and Lignite	Petroleum	Water Power
Frontier			
North America	51.0	39.8	9.2
Middle America	.1	1.6	2.4
South America	.6	12.8	11.3
Africa	4.0	.2	41.0
Oceania and Australia	.6	—	.9
Total	56.3	54.4	64.8
Metropolis			
Europe, excluding U.S.S.R.	11.1	1.2	9.2
U.S.S.R.	27.3	11.3	11.8
Asia, excluding U.S.S.R.	5.3	33.1	14.2
Total	43.7	45.6	35.2

This examination of the use of energy, and its probable future, reveals clearly the role of science as a "creator of new frontiers." Science has shown us how to capture the fossil fuels, where they are hidden, and how to use them. It has added

---

[36] *Ibid.*, p. 109.

[37] The above figures are derived from U.S. State Department, *Energy Resources of the World* (Washington, D.C.: Government Printing Office, 1949), Table 14, p. 52; Table 40, p. 83; Table 62, pp. 120–21.

nothing to the original storehouse, but has accelerated the destruction of what is there. It has created nothing, but has been a spendthrift and wastrel of the world's stored energy. Its profligate use of the fossil fuels is a fair example of similar use of other resources such as iron and the less common and less used minerals, of the use of timber, and of soils. Technology has given us the luxuries and comforts in a riotous holiday in which we can eat and breed, but all the time it is sawing off the limb on which it complacently sits, on which civilization rests.

Whether science can in the nick of time harness the source of all energy, the sun, and use it in a practical way as it has used the fossil fuels, remains for the future to determine. It is making some progress in that direction, but it still has a long way to go. Failing this, and with the exhaustion of the fossil fuels, it must fall back on water power which it knows how to use or it must open up other sources of energy such as the atom may furnish.

It is not fashionable to find fault with science. Therefore let us praise it by granting that it can provide a new frontier, one that will really be endless. We now assume that science, despite the laws of physics and chemistry and the progressive exhaustion of resources for which it must take some blame, will open up a package containing all the blessings the frontier offered and more. Not a substitute, but something superior to the original.

When and if this happens society is going to be very curious about how this new treasure is handled, and curious about the terms on which the people will share in the new bounty. Will the products of this scientific frontier be distributed to the people on the same terms as the wealth of the old frontier was distributed — that is, on a free basis? It makes no difference whether the answer to this question is an affirmative or a negative, the answer is fraught with grave consequences. If the products of the scientific frontier are to belong to the sovereign to be distributed to the people on the same easy terms that the land and its wealth were distributed, then modern capitalism based on technology must be sacrificed. If the confiscated products of the scientific frontier are distributed to the people on a free basis, there could be no direct profit, and where there is no profit there can be no capitalism. The result would inevitably be some form of socialism.

If, on the other hand, the better things for better living through science are to be made available, as now, for a fixed and profitable price, then those who own the techniques will hold a monopoly and thereby destroy free enterprise and opportunity. If the products of science are to be sold at a profit, we would have a departure from the method used in distributing frontier wealth. If the sovereign should own the products of the scientific frontier we would have socialism or worse. If the sovereign is not to own these products we will have some form of monopoly capitalism toward which we have been tending. In either case we would not have the traditional form of democracy with its concomitant of free enterprise and profit economy.

This analysis reveals from another angle the peculiar character of the frontier age, an age that was abnormal and exceptional in many respects. The physical situation was such that, in the presence of the frontier, capitalism and democracy could exist side by side, but when we penetrate below the surface we see that in reality the frontier subsidized both of them in a way we may not like to admit. It must be remembered that the sovereign, that is the state, originally owned the frontier, and that during all the time that democracy and capitalism were making their rapid progress the sovereign was dispensing the frontier to the people and to the capitalists with a lavish hand and on practically a free basis. Had the sovereign had a full treasury of gold and silver or a full granary from which to make bread to hand out in these centuries, we would not have the slightest trouble in seeing that the gift was a subsidy. What the sovereign had in the frontier was land, and because a considerable amount of work was involved in digging it up for the minerals, or clearing it of timber for farm homes, and because the process of dispensing it went on over a long period of time, everybody concerned lost sight of the fact that the proceedings were extraordinary and that the greatest dividend in the history of the world was being declared to people who had made no considerable investment.

When we consider the magnitude and the significance of the

Great Frontier in its historical role, we cannot do other than suspect that the "new" frontiers of which we are hearing so much may represent wishful thinking. It is as Coronado's scrivener said more than three centuries ago. We once had a frontier, and the longer we had it the less we valued it; but now that we have lost it, we have a great pain in the heart and we are always trying to get it back again. Hence the cry for new frontiers.. It would seem that thoughtful persons are bound by their obligation to say that there is as yet no new frontier in sight comparable to the one that is lost. The scientists should take more note of what is being done in their name and assist in warning the public not to expect everything from science. Science can do much, but to paraphrase Isaiah Bowman, it is not likely soon to find a new world or make the one we have much better than it is. If the frontier is gone, we should have the courage to recognize the fact, cease to cry for what we have lost, and devote our energy to finding solutions to the problems that now face a frontierless society.

CHAPTER TEN

WHAT THE FRONTIER TOUCHED:
THE SCIENCES

THE FRONTIER HYPOTHESIS presented in this volume has implications which could not be traced out in a lifetime. They can only be suggested. Therefore this survey on what the frontier touched will have fulfilled its purpose if it suggests lines of investigation which will fairly test the validity of the idea that the Great Frontier has had a profound influence in making modern civilization what it is. It is the opinion of the writer that when the inquiries have been made, the Great Frontier will take its place as a factor of the first magnitude in modern history. This factor should rank with others which have been long accepted, such as the Renaissance, the Reformation, the American and French Revolutions, the Industrial Revolution, and the World Revolution now in progress. The purpose of this study has been to point out a star in the firmament of forces operating on modern culture, leaving to others the task of checking by all means and methods whether the star is there, discovering its various aspects and characteristics, and determining the ramifications of its influence.

In the preceding chapters attention has been concentrated on making the Great Frontier visible, and in showing its influence on those aspects of Western civilization which seem to stand in the forefront of our thinking. A special effort has been directed toward relating the frontier to those things it affected most: to the rise of the individual and his temporary supremacy over institutions; and to democracy and to capitalism, both of which expressed the individual's paramount importance in government and in economics.

These, then — the individual, democracy, and capitalism —

form the main avenues leading off from the Great Frontier like spokes in a wheel. But there are other avenues to be followed, and there are all sorts of feeder trails which open up vistas to the intellectual explorer. In the course of many years of study and inquiry as to what the frontier has meant to Western civilization, more of these trails have been seen — some of them most alluring — than could be followed. Some have been marked and commented on in passing, but others have as yet hardly been mentioned. This chapter and the two following may be considered as consisting of a system of signboards set up to mark the entrance into these untraversed trails of the Great Frontier. Where the trail has been followed for a short distance, the information gleaned will be set down and in some instances a guess will be risked as to what may lie ahead. The process followed is not unlike that followed by the first physical explorers who marked clearly enough the trails they followed and often guessed at what lay beyond, where the river headed, what sea it finally reached, and all that. They made mistakes, many of them, but they added something to the knowledge of a new country, and they gave hints to those who came after to work out the details and finally to make a map that was accurate and illuminating. And so it is with the student who attempts to perceive and tell the meaning of the successes and failures in an area so vast as to thwart the best effort of any single explorer.

He who reads these signs will soon see the basic assumption implicit in this study, namely, that the frontier influence has been pervasive in our modern culture, that hardly anything has escaped it. The problem therefore is to find the point of tangency, or the common segment between the frontier force and other contemporary forces, ideas, and institutions: How they were related, whether they were at war or peace with one another.

Some of the fields of knowledge which have indubitably been affected by the opening of the Great Frontier are set down below. For convenience they are divided into two classes: scientific, pertaining to the physical world, including its flora and fauna; and the humanistic, pertaining to man and his activities.

I. Sciences:
1. Astronomy
2. Geology and Geography
3. Botany
4. Zoology
5. Anthropology
6. Darwin and the Theory of Evolution

II. Humanities:
1. History: Modern Dynamics and Progress
2. Economics
3. Government and Law
4. Language
5. Literature, Art, Education, and History

If we look at the subjects listed under sciences, we can readily see that they derived from the Great Frontier a completeness which they never could have attained until the whole world came under scrutiny. Not until then could the various scientists have in hand the information which would enable them to compare, classify, and describe the facts pertaining to a given subject. Prior to the advent of the Great Frontier, knowledge was hemispheric and not global. Until then the facts were not available. The first two or three centuries of the modern period were spent in observation, but toward the end of the eighteenth century observation had proceeded to the point where classification and systematization could begin and could proceed rapidly. By that time theories based on deductions from observed facts and phenomena were advanced, and, what is more important, they could be tested in the broad laboratory of the world. It is no wonder that in this period, rationalism emerged to threaten every tenet of faith. And why not — when men everywhere were proving so much that they formerly disbelieved as to cause them to bring all beliefs into question.

The findings of the observers in these scientific subjects from astronomy to anthropology tended in the same direction — toward the conclusion that all natural phenomena could be explained by natural causes. The astronomers held the stars in their orbits by the laws of physics, the geologists read in the rocks the long record of the slow processes of the earth's construction, the zoologists found that life forms graded almost imperceptibly from one to another, and the anthropologists could for the first time see societies of men in every stage of culture from the most primitive to the most advanced. This accumulation of knowledge, gathering of data, went on in the separate fields, and reminds us of the mania of the collector who wants to add one more book, or butterfly, or fossil, or skull, or doorknob to what he already has. This piling up of data or specimens made for disorder and confusion, and must have led the more intelligent collectors to see that some method of classification was necessary, if for no other reason than to keep all collectors from being drowned by the results of their industry. Classification and systematization, once under way, enabled one scientist to talk to another and be understood, each to profit from the investigations of others.

The man who taught the world how to classify specimens and to designate genera and species was Carl von Linné or Linnaeus, who was born in Sweden on May 23, 1707, and died on January 10, 1778. Linnaeus made the indispensable contribution which enabled the observers and collectors to manage their ever-increasing materials by devising a system of classifying and naming living forms, a system which with some modifications is still in use. He adopted Latin as the language of scholarship and the binomial system of naming plants. The first name indicates the genus and the second the species. Though this system was first applied in botany, it was later extended to zoology and anthropology, to all life forms. The importance of the Linnaean system as a necessary step in advancing knowledge can hardly be overemphasized. The device adopted enabled the collectors to put what they collected in some order, and in the end this order prepared the way for the deductions which classification is bound to suggest. Linnaeus made it possible for all the life sciences to run a base line through the respective studies; he gave the life scientists a place to take off from and to come back to in their thinking.

The man who performed a similar service by running a base line in geology was Sir Charles Lyell, who lived from 1797 to 1875, nearly a century after the Swedish botanist. Lyell's most notable work was *The Principles of Geology*, in three volumes, published in 1830–33. He performed for the students of fossils a service similar to that performed by Linnaeus for living forms. He had observed in penetrating the various geological structures that the fossil forms still represented in living forms became fewer and fewer in proportion to the extinct forms.

The base line was the deepest strata in which current life forms appeared at all. Here was the place of beginning for the study of "recent" life in the geological sense. Lyell invented or adopted a nomenclature for the three divisions of this "recent" period. The oldest was given the name of *Eocene,* meaning "dawn of recent." Above that was *Miocene,* "less of recent," and finally *Pliocene,* or "more of recent."

This method of naming life forms — plant, animal, human, and fossil — all seems very simple, as simple as the discovery of the New World or the law of gravitation. It may be simple when once done but it was not easy for a collector of specimens to hit upon. The fact that nearly a century elapsed between the time Linnaeus devised his system and Lyell brought his into use indicates how slowly men make their way toward the knowable but as yet unknown. What these men did was to prepare a system which would prove most useful for all who sought to investigate in the different fields. It was possible now for the collectors to arrange their collections in series. As yet they did not know that the series was ascending, that higher life forms evolved with time, that one form merged gradually into succeeding ones. But nevertheless this story of ascending life forms was plainly evident in the very arrangements of the fossils, plants, animals, and men. Unconsciously, the scientists were sketching the outlines of a great masterpiece of truth which was not yet apparent to any of them. They were making a pilgrimage without knowledge of their destination, making it almost without purpose other than to collect, name, and classify. Though the investigators were on the right track, following it as if by an instinct for truth, they were not able to draw the grand conclusion, to see whither their science was going, or why. It remained for Charles Darwin and Alfred Russell Wallace to perform this service, to bring the powerful lenses of insight into focus, and to furnish the collectors, classifiers, and systematizers their goal and destination. If Linnaeus and Lyell and others, even the astronomers, were running *base* lines for their respective sciences, it was Darwin who put in the big trunk line of evolution for which all the other lines became feeders, giving the world a *system* of science with a definite goal.

It is only when one surveys the evolution of the various

sciences, especially the life sciences, that Darwin's importance becomes clear. He came like a commanding general among a miscellaneous collection of irregular troops under local leaders some of whom were trying to bring a little order into their discipline; but for the most part there was no harmony, no common purpose, and no definite objective. Darwin was immediately recognized as the commander-in-chief, and he soon created an army by pointing out the task ahead and convincing even the most skeptical that in matters pertaining to life forms evolution is the base line. Linnaeus had shown how to name and classify material, and Lyell had established the point of departure for the study of fossil remains. The botanists quickly recognized the Darwinian principle as their guide, and Lyell also gladly accepted it and incorporated it in his later works.

Once Darwin had raised the banner of evolution, the period of fumbling was over, and many subdivisions of the basic sciences showed up to become separate disciplines. Biology, which had to wait on the microscope, was one of these late comers. Zoology and anthropology came to be separate fields. The army of Darwin has continued to grow and his concept of evolution is so generally accepted that it has excluded all other theories. Evolution is one of the assumptions mentioned by Oswald Spengler upon which the superstructure of the modern life sciences is being erected. If this assumption of evolution could be pulled from under these sciences today, they would fall down in confusion.

What does all this have to do with the Great Frontier? There is no indication that either of Darwin's important precursors was directly influenced by the frontier. Linnaeus did his basic work in Sweden, Lyell in England. In later life Lyell traveled a great deal, and visited the New World, but he had made his important contributions prior to his travels. Though these men must have been stimulated by the general ferment, the frontier influence on them was indirect. It was Charles Darwin whose genius was touched off by the frontier. He had as a youth a natural interest in botany, entomology, and geology, but had shown no great promise up to the time he was invited to go on the voyage of the *Beagle*. The ship left England in December, 1831, while Lyell's *Principles of Geology* was being published, and did not return until October, 1836. Darwin was the naturalist with a party of surveyors, and a roll of the ports of call shows that the whole party was concerned with the new lands. The ship touched at the Cape Verde and other Atlantic islands, and then went around the coast of South America, touching at various islands, including the Galápagos; then it went to Tahiti, New Zealand, Australia, Tasmania, Keeling Island, Maldivés, Mauritius, St. Helena, Ascensión, the Azores, and many others. Darwin observed and made notes constantly, and on his return began the slow process of editing and publishing. He was in constant contact with Lyell, and dedicated the second edition of his journal to the geologist.

Darwin has given testimony that his whole future was determined by what he observed on the voyage of the *Beagle*. In the year 1837 he wrote: "In July opened first note-book on Transmutation of Species. Had been greatly struck from about the month of previous March on character of South American fossils, and species on Galápagos Archipelago. These facts (especially latter) origin of all my views." [1] Victor W. von Hagen said, "This young man would initiate an epoch in science. And the Galápagos would be its crucible." [2] It is not difficult to see how the frontier — the real crucible — furnished the spark which enabled Darwin to make his synthesis. Here on the frontier he found lands where nature had worked for ages almost untouched by man — who has a genius for mixing things up. Darwin himself noted that life on the Galápagos was similar to that on the mainland of South America, but at the same time the island specimens differed slightly from those of the mainland and from island to island. He also observed that as he went south on the continent, one form of life was displaced by a closely allied one. Here was the stuff suggesting some form of evolution, though just what it was Darwin had not yet seen. He tells us also that he made a step forward by reading Malthus's *Essay on Population* in 1838, and Malthus drew heavily on his knowledge of geography and the distribu-

[1] *Encyclopaedia Britannica*, vol. 7, p. 66.
[2] Victor Wolfgang von Hagen, *Ecuador and the Galápagos Islands* (Norman, Oklahoma: University of Oklahoma Press, 1949), p. 212.

tion of man in making his own analysis of the relationship between man and land.

The story of the relation between Darwin and Wallace is often told. It is only necessary to say that Alfred Russell Wallace, who was younger than Darwin, came independently and contemporaneously to the same conclusion that Darwin had reached as to the origin of species. In February, 1858, while ill in Ternate, Wallace had that flash of insight which brings understanding of complex problems. He, too, had been reading Malthus's *Essay on Population* when "there suddenly flashed upon . . . [him] the *idea* of the survival of the fittest." Without waiting to recover, he wrote out his views, and sent them to Darwin, of all people, suggesting that if Darwin thought well of what he had done, to have it published. Darwin's book on the *Origin of Species* was all but complete; he had shown sketches of his idea to various scientists, but nothing had been published. Darwin made an abstract of his work and sent this, with Wallace's paper, to Lyell with a request for advice. Both papers were read as a joint paper before the Linnaean Society on July 1, 1858. It was Charles Lyell, the geologist, and Joseph Hooker,[3] the botanist, who advised this procedure. The incident shows the close connection existing among these early scientists — Linnaeus, Lyell, Hooker, Wallace, Darwin.

But the point of emphasis here is that Wallace was also a traveler to the frontier. He became a beetle collector as a student, and at the age of twenty-five set out on an expedition to the Amazon. In 1853 he published his *Travels on the Amazon and Rio Negro*. Then he went to the Malay Archipelago, where he made notable studies of the varying forms of life between Asia and Australia. It was there that he hit upon his theory of evolution. It is certain that Darwin drew his inspiration from the frontier because we have his word for it; it is equally certain that Wallace did not draw his from the Metropolis because all his interests had been in the new lands, east and west.

It seems probable that the theory of evolution would have

[3] Sir Joseph Hooker was assistant director or director of Kew Gardens from 1855 to 1885. He traveled extensively and published numerous books on botany, his most notable being the monumental *Genera plantarum*, based on the collection in Kew Gardens.

come had Wallace and Darwin never lived. Collectors were going all over the world, bringing their specimens home to Europe. There the classifiers were arranging them in order, and the order in which they were arranged would seem to speak so plainly of gradual evolution that some thoughtful person was bound to see it. The fact that two men hit upon the idea independently indicates that a third one might have hit upon it too. The fact that both of these men derived the evidence on which they based their conclusions from distant lands occupied by primitive peoples, or by none, connects the actual discovery of the principle irrevocably to the frontier.

It remains for the historians of the Great Frontier to examine the many scientific expeditions sent out from England and other countries during the seventeenth, eighteenth, and nineteenth centuries. These expeditions often had practical purposes, but it became the custom to take along scientists to collect and observe. Such men accompanied American expeditions to the West from the time of Lewis and Clark down to the railroad surveys of the mid-nineteenth century and even later, until the whole land was well known. It would be interesting to know several things about these scientists. What enabled them to have the leisure for such "useless" labor? Darwin's funds came from his mother's people, the Wedgwoods, makers of pottery. They were merchants, profiting from the general boom in Europe. What was the purpose of the *Beagle's* voyage? Where did the money come from to pay the expenses of the *Beagle's* five-year tour of the world? In many cases the government sponsored the expeditions, but something made it possible for the governments to spend money in this way. The government was taking a little of its profits from the general boom and seeding the land with scientific observers. Until the middle or end of the nineteenth century London was the capital of the new culture. When Audubon had completed his collection of bird paintings in America he had to take them to London to find patrons and publisher; when George Catlin had made his collection of paintings of Indian life, he had to do the same thing. Long before this John and William Bartram had threaded the forests of America studying botany, but they looked to England and the Continent for understanding and appreciation of what they were doing. The frontier itself had little use for scientists, gave them no recognition, but it furnishd them stuff to work with, and it helped supply their patrons in Europe with the wealth that enabled them to be patrons. The result was that from all the distant lands the specimens of plants, animals, and fossil rocks poured in a steady stream into the Metropolis to fill the gardens and museums and to act as a constant challenge to scholars and thinkers.

The general discussion of science has led us to consider Darwin and his precursors Linnaeus and Lyell apart from their subjects. We shall now turn to the various subdivisions of science to see how they were affected by the frontier.

1. Astronomy

A casual reading of the history of astronomy fails to reveal that the frontier had any direct effect on the mathematicians who were busy figuring out the mysteries of the solar and stellar systems. It is true that during the seventeenth and eighteenth centuries astronomy made much progress in the hands of Descartes, Kepler, Newton, Halley, and others. In 1671 a national observatory was set up at Paris and another in Greenwich five years later.

The discovery of the Great Frontier did have two effects on astronomy. First, it enlarged the visible heavens as it enlarged the earth. The scholars shut up in Europe had access only to those stars visible in the Northern Hemisphere, but now the whole southern half of the earth was a platform from which to view new constellations. As Camões has Da Gama say in *The Lusiads:*

> We had discovered earlier in our way
> A new star set in the new hemisphere.[4]

The inspiring view of the firmament from the frontier platform gave impetus to investigations, furnished new data to

---

[4] *The Lusiads of Luiz de Camões,* canto V, stanza 14, Leonard Bacon Translation — the Hispanic Society of America, New York, 1950.

check old theories, and promoted the formulation of new ones. The navigators who visited the Southern Hemisphere made such observations as they could of the new sky, and the results were published in Nuremberg as early as 1603 in a celestial atlas showing twelve new constellations. The magnitude of the contribution of the Southern Hemisphere to astronomy is indicated by the distribution of the constellations. They are distributed in three bands as follows:

North of the Zodiac	30
Within the Zodiac (path of sun and moon)	12
South of the Zodiac	48

Out of the total of ninety constellations, forty-eight are *south* of the Zodiac, and therefore could have been little known prior to the opening of the frontier. The comparative youth of the southern heavens is clearly indicated by the internal evidence of the names given to the constellations. There is not a name suggestive of the Christian religion either in the Zodiac or to the north of it. This would seem to mean that the constellations were known and named by the ancients. South of the Zodiac we find *Ara* (the altar), *Crux* (the cross). We also find constellations named for things unknown until the modern era, most of them connected with the new science: *Microscopium* (microscope), *Octans* (octant), *Sextans* (sextant), *Telescopium* (telescope), and finally *Indus* (Indian). The invention of the reflecting telescope by Newton in 1668 and its later refinements further extend the realm of astronomy in both hemispheres.

The problem of navigating the oceans gave impetus to the perfecting of instruments that would be useful. The most important information for the navigator was to know his exact location, and to have at hand the means of determining it. The astrolabe, known to the ancients, could determine time and latitude, but not longitude. It was not displaced until the sextant was invented by John Hadley in 1731 and adapted to navigation by Captain Campbell in 1757.

A second effect of opening the frontier was the practical one of furnishing a need for the information being gathered by the astronomers. It was one thing to traverse the familiar shores of Europe and northern Africa, where every port was known, and where inquiry could be made of local inhabitants. It was quite another to set off on a voyage of months or even years where inquiry was impossible. In such a voyage a mistake in reckoning could make the difference between life and death to all concerned.

2. Geology

In geology as in astronomy the general theories were worked out in Europe, mainly in England. The basis for the modern concept of geology owes much to James Hutton (1726–97), who in 1795 published his *Theory of the Earth, with Proofs and Illustrations*. His style of writing was so difficult that his work attracted little attention until it was popularized by John Playfair in a volume entitled *Illustrations of the Huttonian Theory* (1802). Hutton's basic idea was that the geological forces at work at present are not different in character from those of the past and that, therefore, the forms of the past can be explained by agents which are still present. In 1807 the Geological Society of London was founded with the program of collecting and examining facts rather than arguing over theories. It remained for Sir Charles Lyell (1797–1875) to systematize the study of geology by publishing *The Principles of Geology* (3 vols., 1830–33), which went through many revisions and editions. As stated above, he invented the nomenclature for the geological ages on the basis of the proportion of current life forms to extinct ones in rock strata. The influence of the frontier on him came through Darwin, and is reflected in the later editions of his *Principles*. In his *Antiquities of Man* (1863) he accepted wholeheartedly Darwin's theory of evolution.

There can be little doubt that the expanded world stimulated the study of geology by offering broader fields for investigation, and an opportunity to check the universality of deductions made by scholars in Europe. Geography follows the pattern of geology, except that the information was gathered more rapidly. The constant improvement of the maps from 1500 onward indicates clearly enough that detailed and accurate information was supplanting guesswork and imagination. It was Alexander von Humboldt (1769–1859) who attempted a synthesis based on his own wide travels to all parts of the world, and on information made available to him by other travelers. In his *Cosmos*, published in five volumes from 1845 to 1862, Humboldt viewed the world as a whole, one of those ambitious undertakings which could not have come much earlier because of lack of information, and does not come later because of the too great abundance and complexity of materials.

The science of geodesy was purely speculative until it was faced with the necessity of measuring the earth accurately. For example, it became a matter of practical value to know exact latitude, but it was impossible to determine this until the shape of the earth was really known. Was it a sphere or an oblate spheroid flattened at the poles? If the latter, then a degree of latitude would vary in length, being shorter at the equator and longer near the poles. The dispute over the two theories was finally settled by the French Academy of Sciences which sent one expedition to Lapland and another to Peru (present Ecuador) to make accurate measurements. The expeditions left France about 1735. The Lapland party finished its work promptly, but the Peruvian expedition did not return until 1743. The experiment proved the oblate spheroid theory. The Peruvian expedition had a measuring rod made with great care, and it remained for a long time the standard of length used in geodetic work. This is the "toise of Peru," a stick six French feet in length, approximately six feet five inches English measure.

When the world was small there was no need for an international date line, but with world travel after 1500 such a line was necessary. It was based on Greenwich time, approximately 180° away. Greenwich itself is associated with astronomy and geodesy as is no other place in the world. There the Royal Observatory was established in 1675 for purely practical purposes, "the advancement of navigation and nautical astronomy."

The international date line had no reason to exist until men began to roam the world, but once they did, it was both a necessity and a convenience. There was another line which men began to cross in going to the frontier, and that was the line separating the Northern and Southern Hemispheres. It was not necessary for nations in conventions to establish this line because it was established in nature, by the rotary motion of the earth and its relation to the sun. It seemed necessary, however, to have some sort of ceremony when the equator was crossed, a sort of acknowledgment that the neophytes were entering a strange realm. Crossing the line signified a passage from the Christian to the pagan world. The ceremony antedates knowledge of the equator. Some accounts say it was instituted on ships passing by the Pillars of Hercules on voyage from the Mediterranean to the Atlantic. Another account says the ritual was designed to propitiate Neptune who had been expelled from Christendom, and had retired below the equator where he still ruled.

The present-day practice could not have been adopted until after the discoveries, but it was taken up soon after. Jean de Léry in his *Voyage fait en la terre du Brésil* describes a ceremony that took place at the equator on February 4, 1557, but there is no mention of Neptune. In the seventeenth century mention of baptism at sea is frequent. The first mention of Neptune was in 1702.[5]

3. Botany

The opening up of the New World unfolded such a wealth of new plants that the task of gathering and classifying them required centuries. Many ships returning from foreign ports brought collections for European gardens, and resulted in the setting up of the famous national botanical gardens. Their location and date of establishment indicate how general and widespread this interest in plants was. The system of classifying plants had been devised by Linnaeus, and with later modifications it enabled the herbalists and botanists to make an index of the plant kingdom. The work of Darwin furnished the direction for experiment and investigation, extending

[5] Those interested in the ceremony of "crossing the line" may consult Robert Chambers, *Book of Days* (2 vols.; Edinburgh: W. and R. Chambers, 1873), vol. II, p. 653, and Leland P. Lovette, *Naval Customs, Traditions and Usage* (Annapolis, Maryland: United States Naval Academy, 1939), pp. 42–43.

backward into geology and forward into plant breeding and adaptation.

The famous botanical gardens were begun as private gardens, usually where herbs were grown for medicinal purposes. John Gerard's garden in Holland and John Bartram's in Philadelphia are two of many. Four famous European botanical gardens in order of their establishment are as follows: The garden at Pisa, Italy, founded by the Grand Duke Cosimo de' Medici in 1543; Jardin Royal des Plantes Médicinales, Paris, 1635; Chelsea Physic Garden, London, 1673; der Staatliche Botanischer Garten und Museum, Berlin, 1679; the Royal Botanic Gardens, Kew, London, 1759.

Though Kew was founded late, it is the most important, for here were concentrated the plants gathered from all parts of the empire and of the world. It is said that Kew bears the same relation to botanical science that Greenwich does to astronomy and navigation. It was from Kew that the plants of the New World were distributed to other regions, often with marvelous practical results. Kew transplanted the production of quinine from South America to India in 1860. Sir Henry Wickham got the Para rubber plant seeds from South America in 1875 which were used to establish the rubber industry in the East Indies. Kew published the *Index Kewensis*, which lists alphabetically every plant name known. Of more than three hundred botanical gardens, Kew is the most important and may be called the international botanical garden of the world. There may be many reasons for this, but one important one is the fact that England was penetrating all the frontier countries and bringing their floral offerings to Kew.

4. Zoology

Modern zoology is really a post-Darwinian subject. This does not mean that from antiquity men had not been interested in animate things but the study was mainly physiological with the background assumption that God had created the various forms out of nothing. Darwin's theory of evolution placed more responsibility on chance and less on divinity to account for all forms on a developmental basis. It was the task of the zoologists to discover the various steps in the process, and to find in the animal kingdom, living or fossil representatives of each step in a series. For example, the horse was found to be one of the most highly specialized animals in the world with jaws superbly formed to eat the grasses and with feet and frame adapted to running swiftly over the prairies. His ancestry has been traced through the fossil records back to the little eohippus, a four-toed little fellow about the size of the coyote. According to the poet, he decided to be a horse, and so he began to develop his jaw and to lose his toes until he had nothing left but his middle fingernail on which to continue his earthly course. Now the zoologists, given the eohippus at one end of the line and the horse at the other, had a most absorbing and not too difficult task of filling in the gaps. They assumed they knew what the intentions of the little eohippus were; and more important, they knew what their own purpose was.

It was when the scientist applied this same principle to the sacred animal, man, that he ran afoul of religion. It might be all right to reduce the horse to an ancestral eohippus, but when man's possible connection with the most ridiculous of all animals was pointed out, the implications were bitterly resented in some quarters.

Whether the scholars were studying plants, animals, or man himself, the frontier contributed one indispensable thing, a wealth of specimens spread over the entire range of life from the lowest to the highest forms. *Comparative* studies became possible and profitable, especially in anthropology, which was an offshoot of zoology. It has been remarked that the *Index* of Kew gives the names of all known plants with their classification, and a notation of the first mention of each in literature. It would be possible for a scholar to run through this list and separate the species and varieties found in the New World from those found in the Old. There is little doubt that by far the greater number of plant forms today were found in the frontier countries.

A study has been made of the animal kingdom, and though it is by no means conclusive, it is probably representative. In an unpublished paper entitled "Animals New to Europeans after 1492," George D. Hendricks made a study of wild mammals, excluding those of universal distribution. He found that Wendler's *Animal Encyclopedia* lists more named animals than any other source available. Also, Hendricks used the common rather than the scientific names for the practical reason that it was only under the common names that he could find the date at which the animals in question became known. This part of the information he obtained largely from *The Oxford English Dictionary* and some other standard works, such as F. E. Beddard's *Mammalia*, R. Lydekker's *Wild Life of the World*, Alfred Russell Wallace's *Geographic Distribution of Animals*, and A. Heilprin's *The Geographical and Geological Distribution of Animals*. After excluding domesticated animals and others with almost world-wide distribution, Hendricks had left a list of 142 animals found in the various continents known in Europe prior to 1492. Within this number were 17 animals found in the other continents. The Europeans were also acquainted with 105 animals in the other continents which were not native to Europe. Of these North America furnished 2, South America 0, Africa 62, Australia 1, and Asia 40. In other words, Europe was acquainted with 247 wild animals prior to 1492. In the New World, or the expanded world, Europeans discovered 510 new varieties of animals which they already knew. North America furnished 115; Africa, 134; Asia, 143; South America, 93; and Australia, the most remote, 25. Of animals totally unknown to Europe prior to 1492, there were 547. North America furnished 65; South America, 106; Africa, 178, Australia, 84; and Asia, 114.

Of the 1304 animals listed by common name, 1057 or 81 per cent were furnished by the non-European lands, and of these 547 were unknown in any variety in Europe prior to 1492.[6] These figures, while not infallible, reveal to what extent the frontier enlarged the zoological horizon. A similar study of plants would show comparable results.

[6] George D. Hendricks, *Western Wild Animals and Man*, chap. I, "Animals New to Europeans after 1492." The animals considered by Hendricks in this study are the mammals.

CHAPTER ELEVEN

WHAT THE FRONTIER TOUCHED: LAW, GOVERNMENT, AND ECONOMICS

1. Law and Government

A STUDY of the effect of the frontier on law could probably throw considerable light on modern jurisprudence in Western civilization, and to some degree would modify legal philosophy. There is reason to believe that the frontier may eventually be recognized as a force ranking next only to that of the Roman and German in making modern law what it is. The root and the stem of modern law is either Roman or Germanic, but much of the flower and fruit as we know them today bear a strong frontier flavor.

Law may be thought of as a rationalization and an enactment into formal rules of those practices which have been found expedient and useful in human relations. This means that law grows in response to the imperative conditions to which human beings must become adjusted; and it is at this point of adjustment that the frontier enters as a factor in shaping legal rules. Law, like other institutions, changes — or, as we often say, "grows" — because a new problem presents itself for solution, a new need is felt. In time the solution is found, and the remedy is enacted into law. Theory follows tardily with justification and explanation, and philosophy puts together that which was always united.

The opening of the Great Frontier flooded the Metropolis with new facts. New situations were created, and for many of these there were no rules of conduct, or precedents, or codes. It would be impossible to list more than a fraction of the legal problems that the advent of the Great Frontier placed before the lawmakers, but it is possible to give certain large categories about which there can be little dispute. Three of these categories have to do with the new land, the new people, and the new seas.

Very suddenly Europe came into possession of three continents it had never heard of before, and it became acquainted with a fourth which it had known only in part. In addition there were thousands of islands, and numerous archipelagos which in time became European real estate. How could the lawyers establish titles, prepare abstracts, and arrange succession for so much real property? There was no recognized law by which this could be done, and the result was a series of world conflicts which began in the seventeenth century and lasted down to quite recent times.

Though most of the lands were assumed to be vacant, they were nearly all occupied sparsely by primitive people in various stages of development. These people differed among themselves in color, language, and disposition, but as a group they probably differed more from Europeans than from one another. Actually at the time of the discoveries Europe had some unity — more perhaps than it has today. For example, all Europeans professed Christianity, and their unity of religion was expressed geographically as Christendom. The vernacular languages were not yet completely differentiated, and the universal language of scholars was Latin, which was understood by the educated everywhere. In the broad sense Europe was a community with a common historical background, a common language, and a common religion. And much of Europe's contacts had been prior to 1492 with people equal or superior to them in civilization, however different in culture and religion.

After 1492 foreign contacts became radically different in character from what they had been before. On the Great Frontier the Europeans found a different breed, the Negroes of Africa, the Indians of the Americas, the Bushmen of Australia, the Maoris of New Zealand, and the Polynesians of the Pacific Islands. Not one of these knew the Europeans' God, their alphabet, or their law. There was practically nothing to go on in dealing with them.

It may be argued that the Romans were in contact with and were finally overwhelmed by just such rude barbarians. Admittedly, the invaders of the Roman Empire were barbaric, but at that point similarity disappears in the comparison. The Germanic tribes, and even the Mongols, could enter Europe

overland whereas there is no record that any primitive people
from the Great Frontier ever entered Europe, or attempted to
do so as invaders. The seas protected Europe from all frontier people, but they did not protect the frontier people from
the Europeans. Quite the contrary. The barbarians from the
East proved themselves stronger than the Europeans, but the
barbarians of the frontier were in all cases weaker. Rome had
to compromise with the Germans, but the Europeans were
throughout in position to dictate to the New World aborigines.
The invading Germans participated in the making of medieval
law, engrafting their institutions onto the Roman, but the
business of making law for the frontier was a function exercised exclusively by the Europeans. Their task was not to
compromise, but to find a law that would enable them to live
with their European neighbors and with their Christian con-
science.

What were the lawyers and theologians going to do about
these simple people who were helpless in their hands? Were
they to be treated as nations with whom to make war and
peace? Was their individual freedom to be respected or were
they to become slaves and servants for no other reason than
that they did not know the Cross, write Latin, or respect the
Roman and Germanic law? And what of their souls? Did they
have such appurtenances? What of their property? Should
they have any?

In respect to these natives the subject of property rights was
one of major importance. As we have seen, property had been
and was a scarce item in Europe, and whatever litigation occurred over it was confined to relatively few, but the Great
Frontier was nearly all property. Leaving aside the land, which
in time was confiscated, there remained the personal or tribal
property. The Indians had in places collected a great deal of
gold and silver, and it was a grave question whether this and
other forms of movable wealth should be taken by force or by
ordeal of contract in exchange for rum, mirrors, fine-toothed
combs, and sleazy cloth. Even after the natives had lost their
land and their gold, there remained many legal problems as to
distribution among the victors.

Another category of problems had to do with the rules of the
sea, the highroad to the Great Frontier. Did the sea belong to

one nation and exist exclusively for its use, or did it belong to none with all free to use it at will? Was it a public highway or a toll road? *Mare liberum* or *mare clausum?* For centuries lawyers had busied themselves with the question of whether there should be an open or closed sea, but the question had never demanded an answer so imperiously as it did when men were determined to reach the Great Frontier by the highway of the ocean.

Looking at the Great Frontier as distinct from the Metropolis, it appears that the situation called for extraordinary development in the law of land, the law for primitive people, and the law of the sea. Obviously, these are big fields and would have been complicated enough if Europe had had political unity tantamount to its cultural unity. Though Europe had cultural unity, it was divided into a community of political and usually antagonistic states. It was this antagonism, rivalry, and competition which made the Metropolis as a whole so cruel and merciless in its dealings with the people of the Great Frontier.

Again, however, necessity dictated that despite their mutual hatred the European nations must find a meeting of minds in order that all might not be lost in bitter conflict, a way that would enable the nations to get on in the common task of exploiting the treasure.[1] There must be some rules of the road. In short, the nations had good reason to agree among themselves as to a live-and-let-live procedure, and these agreements have come to be known as international law. Those who have not given the matter thought may contend that international law was common in the Metropolis prior to the rise of the frontier problems. In a sense this is true, but the equivalent of international law among the factions within the Metropolis was not international but universal, not an affair of states, but an affair of the Church of Rome. For example, the task of ameliorating the horrors of war was a function of Christianity. Obviously the church was most effective only within Christendom, where it had one foot in each warring camp. On the fron-

[1] George Wolfskill points out that the immediate force driving toward the formulation of an international law came from the commercial companies rather than from the nations. See "The Role of the New World Frontier in the Theory of International Law," unpublished Doctor's dissertation, University of Texas, 1952.

tier, where one party was Christian and one heathen, the church could not function as it did in the Metropolis. As a practical matter on any expedition to any frontier anywhere the church's power decreased as the distance from the Metropolis increased. If an expedition was sent out by Spain, it was up to the Spanish crown and not to the church to support it and to defend it, let us say, from an English buccaneer or an Indian war party. Force has always been a factor on the frontier, and it was the state and not the church that was prepared to use force. Also the revolt of Luther had split the church, and there was little more unity among the religious sects after 1520 than there was among the states. In short, the relations between nations were becoming secularized, more temporal and less spiritual. The church had lost within Christendom because of its growing disunity and it had not succeeded geographically because it had found no common denominator between heathen tribes of the frontier and the civilized tribes of the Metropolis. In both cases it fell to the temporal powers to work out a new basis for dealing with one another. The new basis was to be secular and national rather than religious and universal.

International law enjoys two very large areas exclusive to it, the domain of war and the domain of the sea. International law implies the existence of independent and sovereign nations. Therefore we may look for the joint beginnings of international law in the modern sense at about the time the national states began to emerge from feudalism, and to escape the jurisdiction of the church. This is the assumption of the scholars and jurists, and is reflected in the literature.

It is generally assumed that Hugo Grotius (1583–1645) is the father of modern international law, and that its principles were first set forth in his *De jure belli ac pacis* in 1625. The facts are that according to the literature on international law Grotius marks the end rather than the beginning of the first phase in modern development. Preceding Grotius was the famous Spanish School of International Law, and in reality Grotius, though Dutch, was, in a sense, the last member of that school. His contribution was to put an end to theoretical discussion as to whether there should be such law. It was the Spaniards who laid the foundations on which Grotius built.

Their contributions were such as to lead the students to speak of the Spanish School of International Law. The first of that school, the real pioneers, were Francisco de Victoria, the Dominican theologian, and Francisco Suárez, the Jesuit.

Francisco de Vitoria, or as he is better known, Victoria, was born about 1483, a hundred years before Grotius. If that date is correct, he was a lad of nine when Columbus set off to the frontier. He was educated for the priesthood and on September 7, 1526, became *prima* professor of sacred theology at the University of Salamanca. It was the custom in those days (as distinguished from these) to submit current problems to university thinkers for such light as their knowledge might shed. The Spanish government had in its lap at that time a large number of difficult problems incident to the discovery of America. What attitude should be taken toward the new lands? How should the natives, the Indians, be dealt with? Were they to be treated as subjects or separate nations? What of their gold and silver? These were some of the problems that Victoria lectured on, and his lectures were so popular that he was asked to repeat them to a larger audience. He did this in his *Relectiones*. What these lectures meant is set forth by James Brown Scott as follows: "In the year 1532 Victoria prepared a series of readings on the relation of Spain to America, then recently discovered; many well-informed persons there are who look upon these readings as having founded the modern school of international law, of which Grotius was the most illustrious member, and his treatise the culmination of the Spanish school." [2] In another place Scott says of Victoria: "He dealt in fundamentals and his fundamentals are the funda-

[2] James Brown Scott (ed.), *The Spanish Origin of International Law: Francisco de Victoria and His Law of Nations* (Washington: Carnegie Endowment for International Peace, 1934), p. 3. In the Preface to this volume Scott makes a statement as of 1932 about the *Classics of International Law*, a series designed to make available the most notable contributions to the subject: "The publication of the *Classics of International Law*, to which the three volumes of *The Spanish Origin of International Law* are to be as an introduction, was proposed and begun a quarter of a century ago, in order to show that international law is not a thing of treaties or conventions but the result of centuries and centuries of experience, and that it comes to us from the Golden Age of Spain as the result of the discovery of America." — Preface, p. xii.

mentals of the system of international law for which he is responsible; and they are the fundamentals in which is implicit, if not expressed, the newer international law beginning with the individual, to end with the international community." [3]

Victoria's fame as the first international lawyer and as the father of modern international law comes from two of his *Relectiones*, one on the Indians and the other on war. We do not have his written lectures, because he probably spoke from notes, but his prestige was such that his students wrote down what he said and preserved it. It is not the purpose here to deal at length with Victoria, or with the great Spanish School of International Law, or even with the law itself. One purpose is to suggest that Victoria was a pioneer in the first school of international law, a fact admitted by legal authorities from Grotius on; but the main purpose is to show the occasion and the subject which led Victoria to make his contribution in response to a concrete problem arising on the Great Frontier. In the Americas the Spaniards had found a people whose status they — the better of them — were trying to determine with some justice. As early as 1494 a commission had been set up in Spain to study the Indian question, but little came of it because of the greed of the *conquistadores*. Here were people beyond Christendom, without private property, and with much wealth. What attitude should Spaniards take toward them? In attempting to answer the question, Victoria found himself involved in a consideration of the subject of war, for war was also a reality on the frontier; he also saw that war was different in character from that known in Europe. The new Spanish possessions presented a concrete problem the solution of which led Victoria to lay down the principles of justice to all which form the philosophic basis of modern international law. It was not in spinning a theory but in offering a just way out of a difficulty that led Victoria to his conclusions, to a law applicable to all nations, heathen as well as Christian. It was therefore in consideration of the Indians — children of the frontier — that Victoria laid down the principles upon which the superstructure of international law was later to be erected.

[3] *Ibid.*, p. 95.

It was in consideration of the plight of these primitive men that he dealt with the following subjects: 1. Title by discovery, 2. Ambassadors, 3. Compulsory acceptance of Pacific settlement, 4. Conscientious objectors, 5. Intervention, 6. Letters of Marque and Reprisal, 7. Booty and Prize, 8. Neutrals, 9. *Temperamenta*. In his consideration of *Temperamenta* Victoria intervened on behalf of the individuals, noncombatants. "These *temperamenta* [says Scott] were designed to mitigate the harshness of war . . . in the absence of a court between the nations. The creation of such a court is not the least contribution of the successors of those first Americans to whom Victoria extended the Law of nations." [4]

Lest the connection of Victoria seem too patent, the opening passage of his lecture which has been given the title "On the Indians Lately Discovered" is quoted:

> "Teach all nations, baptizing them in the name of the Father and Son and Holy Spirit." This passage raises the question whether the children of unbelievers [the Indians] may be baptized against the wishes of their parents. . . . The whole of this controversy and discussion was started on account of the aborigines of the New World, commonly called Indians, who came forty years ago into the power of the Spaniards, not having been previously known to our world. This present disputation about them will fall into three parts. In the first part we shall inquire by what right these Indian natives came under Spanish sway. In the second part, what rights the Spanish sovereigns obtained over them in temporal and civil matters. In the third part, what rights these sovereigns of the Church obtained over them in matters spiritual and touching religion, in the course of which answers will be given to the question before us.[5]

From this introduction it is not difficult to understand that Victoria was considered a great teacher, and that his students numbered at one time a thousand less or plus one. A man who could present the subject so clearly and with such economy of words would be a great teacher at any time. We may also be struck with the magnitude of his topics, and a little study of them should show how it would be possible to derive the prin-

---

[4] *Ibid.*, p. 286. For a discussion of the nine subjects listed, see pp. 283 ff.
[5] *Ibid.*, pp. i, ii.

ciples of justice as between the Spaniards of the Metropolis and the Indians of the Great Frontier from a consideration of the propositions laid down. And having derived those principles from a consideration of the rights of the primitive Indians in the presence of the conquering Spaniards, we would have arrived at a law between nations throughout the world, an international law.

There is little doubt that Victoria would have been recognized as an extraordinary man and teacher in his day had he never lectured on Indians or war. He never would have lectured on Indians had the New World not been found; he probably would not have lectured on war either because war in Europe was generally between Christians — within the Christian commonwealth, largely a family affair in which certain rules of the church were theoretically observed. In that sort of war there would have been precedents and authorities of long standing but for frontier war with Indians there were no precedents and no authorities. The subject had to be considered *de novo*. He might have been ever so famous as a teacher, yet had Victoria not given these lectures pertaining to the frontier, he would have remained just another learned medieval theologian. His name would not head the list of the founders of modern international law. His would not be the first of the Spanish School of International Law, nor would it be the second in the comprehensive series entitled *The Classics of International Law*. Certainly without these lectures he, together with his successor Suárez, would not have been honored by a meeting of the Association Internationale de Francisco Vitoria et Suárez held in Oslo in August, 1932, four centuries from the date of the lectures. It was the touch of the frontier that gave to the theologian of Salamanca his international immortality.

An examination of the masters of international law would seem to suggest that they showed up mainly in those nations which were facing in a practical way the task of dealing with the other powers of the world. Though it does not appear in the *Classics,* an early contribution to international law was Giovanni da Legnano, who wrote *De bello, de repraesaliis et de duello*. This work was published in Bologna and was written about 1390, just at the time when Italy was dominant in world trade. The Spanish School of International Law flourished from the time of Victoria to that of Hugo Grotius, the sixteenth century, which was Spain's century of world supremacy. At the end of the sixteenth century England was still a relatively weak power, although she had prospered by piracy and buccaneering and had dealt a deathblow to Spain in 1588, a necessity preliminary to the founding of an overseas dominion the basis for which was laid during the reign of James I. It is suggested that the principal contributions to international law have been made by or in defense of nations which were struggling for a place on the seas with stronger powers. As we shall see presently, that was the case with Grotius when the Dutch were contending with the combined power of Spain and Portugal. It is reasonable to assume that the dominant state would have no very practical need to devise principles of international law for the reason that its interests would be best served by the absence of it. In this connection it is significant that England is not represented in the *Classics of International Law*. As the series stands, thirteen authors are represented in the titles, and of these England is represented only by Gentili, an Italian in exile. If England's supremacy on the sea can be dated from the Armada in 1588, there was obviously no real need for England to expend any legal energy in trying to provide for her own welfare there. It will be noted that she attained her position nearly two decades before Grotius made his law case which resulted later in his classic contribution. The English might have made out a case against the Spanish prior to 1588, but did not, and after that time it was not necessary. The cases after that were made probably by the weaker nations against England, the stronger one.

This theory that international law was developed by second-rate powers contending with first-rate powers is supported by the fact that the American, Henry Wheaton, is represented in the *Classics* with his volume, *Elements of International Law*. This publication appeared in 1836, just twenty-one years after the War of 1812 closed. It will be remembered that one cause for that war was the fact that England was violating what the Americans supposed to be their right to freedom on the seas.

The elapsed time was just about sufficient to enable Wheaton to do the research and write his book, keeping in mind the practical difficulties the Americans had had with both England and Napoleon. As a matter of fact his whole career was such as to cause Wheaton to think of the seas and the right of weak nations to be there. From 1815 to 1819 he was justice of the marine court of New York, and later reporter for the United States Supreme Court. He entered the diplomatic service in 1827, serving first in Denmark and then in Prussia. He published a *Digest of the Law of Maritime Captures* in 1815, the *Elements of International Law* in 1836, *Histoire du Progrès du Droit des Gens en Europe* in 1838 and translated into English in 1845 as *A History of the Law of Nations in Europe and America*. In the meantime he published the *Right of Visitation and Search* in 1842. Both his experience and the titles of his books show that he was concerned with the sea, and with the sorry role the United States had played with the strong powers during the Napoleonic era. In seeking a solution, he produced his classic work. With the theory as to the relation of international law to the needs of second-rate powers, let us turn to Grotius.

Though some may dispute Victoria's claim as the founder of international law, none would argue against the importance of Hugo Grotius. What has not been emphasized is that Grotius, like Victoria, made his contribution as a by-product of his effort to solve a specific problem which had arisen on the distant frontier. Grotius was born in the Dutch town of Delft on April 10, 1583, a century after the accepted date of Victoria's birth in Spain. He took the law degree at Leyden and entered practice as an advocate. At the age of twenty he was made historiographer of the new States-General, and it was his combination of law and history that enabled him to make his contribution. It was in 1603 that Grotius received this appointment. In that year James had taken the throne of England. The year before, on March 20, 1602, the Dutch East India Company had been formed by the States-General to assist in the war of independence and to combine the various Dutch companies trading to the East in order that they might contend with the Spaniards and Portuguese and cease to compete among themselves. Portugal and Spain had been united in

1581 and their combined strength had enabled them to break up the carrying trade which the Dutch had built up between Lisbon and northern Europe. The Dutch decided to organize and fight their way through the Spaniards to the East Indies. Their first expedition set out in 1595 under a Lisbon merchant named Cornelius Houtman, who used a book of sailing instructions prepared by Jan Huyghen van Linschoten. Though the expedition met with many disasters, some of the ships returned in 1597 with a valuable cargo and report of good prospects in the East. As a result many companies were formed known as "Van Ferne," meaning of the distant seas. By 1602 as many as sixty ships had set out, and, being soon beyond the law, they not only fought the Portuguese and others, but also fought among themselves. In these tumultuous circumstances the young Grotius began his legal career.

It was to put an end to this chaotic situation in trade that Jan van Oldenbarneveldt took the lead in the move by the States-General to combine the numerous companies into the Dutch East India Company; granting of the charter for the company was in effect an assertion of the independence of the Dutch from the Spaniards. The company was to act as a government in the East, prosecute the war for independence, and regulate trade. It was capitalized at 6,500,000 florins and naturally was in need of a bright young lawyer with good connections. It was quite natural for Jan van Oldenbarneveldt to give young Hugo Grotius a job with the new company. The two had long been closely associated. When Grotius was only fifteen, Oldenbarneveldt took him to the court of France on a diplomatic mission. Both were captured by Prince Maurice of Nassau in 1618; Oldenbarneveldt was sentenced to death and Grotius to life imprisonment. Through the ingenuity of his wife, who had come to share his prison, Grotius escaped in a box of laundry and sought refuge in Antwerp and later in Paris, where he arrived in April, 1621. Between that date and 1625 he completed his famous book, *De jure belli ac pacis.*

There would seem to be nothing in this story that would connect Grotius with the frontier, or to make his famous classic in any way dependent on it. It must be remembered, however, that it was Oldenbarneveldt who had helped form the Dutch

East India Company in 1602, and that Grotius became attorney for that company in 1603, doubtless through Oldenbarneveldt's influence. We have seen the conditions attending the formation of the Dutch East India Company and the hazards of overseas trade. Actually Grotius' whole future and his reputation as the father of international law hinged on a case he was assigned to defend shortly after his employment. A captain of a Dutch East India ship by the name of Heemskirk captured a treasure-laden Portuguese galleon, as was the custom in those days, in the Straits of Malacca. This act no doubt pleased the merchants and traders, but it outraged the religious element in the Netherlands, and action was brought against Heemskirk. Grotius was assigned to defend Heemskirk, and the company too, no doubt. It was up to him to justify a private company in taking a prize on the high seas. The point on which he concentrated his defense was an attack on the Portuguese and Spanish claim that the eastern seas were their private property and that the Dutch had no business being there. In his argument Grotius contended for the free sea, and from this point it was a logical step to consider the general problem of war and peace.

His study of the Heemskirk case resulted in the composition by 1604 of *De jure praedae*, or law of prize. This document, being the property of the corporation, was not published at the time and lay unknown for 260 years. It was discovered in 1864 and published in 1868. It is true that one chapter of *De jure praedae* was published by Grotius in 1609 under the title of *Mare liberum*. Here he set forth his theory of the free seas, a general theory which could not be objected to by his company. Just as in the case of Victoria, we may see in the following quotation that Grotius was dealing with a specific problem which arose in connection with the frontier lands, though in this case the lands lay to the east instead of to the west of Europe. In the first paragraph of his commentary in the *Mare liberum*, Grotius says:

> My intention is to demonstrate briefly and clearly that the Dutch — that is to say, the subjects of the United Netherlands — have the right to sail to the East Indies, as they are now doing,

and to engage in trade with the people there. I shall base my argument on the following most specific and unimpeachable axiom of the Law of Nations, called a primary rule or first principle, the spirit of which is self-evident and immutable, to wit: Every nation is free to travel to every other nation, and to trade with it.[6]

De jure belli ac pacis, published at Paris in 1625, is the book on which Grotius' fame rests, but the interesting point is that this book was but an elaboration and development of the Law of Prize which he wrote for a specific purpose in defense of Heemskirk in 1604.

This brief sketch of Grotius reveals what often happens to an author who is looking for one thing and stumbles on something much bigger, an idea so magnetic that he cannot divest himself of it, for it will give him no rest, and yet so large that he cannot develop it without years of thought and study to mature it, test it, and trace out its numerous ramifications. In writing his defense of Heemskirk, Grotius got the germ of his idea for the Law of War and Peace, but the immediate task in hand had to be done, and so he produced the Law of Prize. Only one part of this was he willing to publish and that was the chapter on the Free Sea, the *Mare liberum*. There are two probable reasons why he did not publish *De jure praedae* in its entirety: one is that it may have been against the policy of his client, the Dutch East India Company; the more probable one is that he realized he had something important and he preferred to wait until he had gathered the evidence that would make his work on the subject definitive. The fact that he kept the manuscript of *De jure praedae* through all his ups and downs seems to indicate that he set considerable store by it. This is speculation based on probability. But there is no speculation needed to show that Grotius, like Victoria, had a specific task, a concrete question to answer. In both cases the ques-

[6] *Mare liberum* has been translated as *The Freedom of the Seas* by Ralph van Deman Magoffin and was published by the Carnegie Endowment for International Peace in 1916. The above quotation appears on p. 7 of this translation and on p. 159 of Scott's *The Spanish Origin of International Law*. Scott is of the opinion that Grotius derived his theory of the free seas from the Spanish authorities, Victoria and Suárez. Grotius gave credit to Victoria, but seems to have slighted Suárez.

tion lay over the seas, to the west for Victoria and to the east for Grotius. Both questions were of the frontier, and in answering them both men came to similar conclusions.

The frontier as a factor in the development of international law has been discussed at some length because it is such a clearcut example of that influence. It is beyond the scope of this study to undertake to show the effects of the frontier on law in general as applied within the different nations, and to the different parts of the Great Frontier. It will require much study to show how the frontier modified the English common law in America, Australia, or South Africa; or to show how the Spanish law was changed in the Latin American republics. It has been pointed out in Chapter Eight how the English common law of water, of riparian rights, was abrogated in the arid regions of the United States and how the law of primogeniture and entail broke down in the presence of free land on all frontiers. These are only samples, and probably not exceptional.

In view of the philosophy of history developed in this book, certain suggestions can be made as to where, in what fields, students who are interested may search for modifications, abrogation of old laws, and the creation of new ones in response to frontier compulsions. One of these fields has to do with the individual.

The view has been presented that the frontier made the individual important, and that during the three or four centuries of its dominance he made progress toward greater liberty and more freedom. If this be true, then the fact of his progress should be found incorporated in the laws and in the constitutions. As a matter of fact, the constitution of the United States, and especially the Bill of Rights, are plain footprints of the individual's progress toward freedom. The preamble of the constitution — "We, the people . . . do ordain and establish this Constitution for the United States of America" — is a proclamation of human rights without precedent. It is in the name of and on behalf of the individual that the homestead acts, the pre-emption laws, and the exemptions in bankruptcy have been enacted. The whole philosophy behind the antitrust and antimonopoly laws has been developed in his interest. In modern times the laws will reflect that it has been the individual versus the institution — church, state, or business corporation — that has occupied the lawmakers and the politicians. It is only recently that the philosophy and perhaps the need of society, of the mass, has produced legislation on the assumption that the individual needs a guardian and a director; the assumption until recently was that the individual was an entity, revolving in his own orbit, and that all the church or the state or the corporation needed to do was to let him be.

Another field of law that must have been greatly affected by the opening of the frontier was that pertaining to property. Of this at the time of the discoveries there was very little, and only a small fraction of it was in individual hands. It belonged to the church or the king or the feudal nobility; in short property was pretty highly institutionalized and practically monopolized by what Adam Smith called the "superior orders." With the opening of the frontier, such an abundance of wealth percolated into the Metropolis that some of it seeped down to humble people, making them less humble and more demanding. The land itself — most precious of all wealth — could not be brought to Europe, but the people could go out to it, and when they got to the frontier they found it so plentiful and so cheap that every man could be a lord of some of it. In medieval times property and people were all frozen, but with the opening of the Great Frontier both thawed out and began to flow and mingle. The flow of property from hand to hand was a legal matter with legal ramifications too vast to be explored here. All matters pertaining to titles, deeds, abstracts, conveyances, inheritances, dowries, bequests, and wills came in ever-increasing volume into the hands of lawyers and advocates and before judges and juries; and these last two, however reluctantly, had in the long run no choice but to bend the law to the will and convenience of the new owners. Of course, all of these changes tie in closely with the gradual emancipation of the people spoken of in the paragraphs above, for the free flow of property was a part of the individual's emancipation.

With the introduction of the American treasure, hard money became sufficiently abundant to serve for a time as a practical medium of exchange. There must be a vast body of law designed to govern money and to preserve its service for mankind. Concern with money and another body of law on mining which grew apace in the New World gave rise to numerous economic theories which would not have arisen had gold and silver not been augmented from the frontier mines. Actually, the money was only a convenience more useful than before in moving commodities from one place to another, from overseas to the Metropolis. Someday some economist or sociologist is going to concentrate his attention on the *flow of property* rather than on the flow of money as an index to what is going on in a society. When he analyzes society in this manner, he is going to learn a great deal more about it than he has by tracing the movements of milled discs of metal or engraved pieces of paper. The movement of money is but a gauge registering the flow of wealth.

Connected with the increased flow of property, there grew up in modern times a body of law pertaining to commerce and trade. The foundations of these laws were present in the medieval and the ancient worlds, but the practices followed in the past were improved, modified, and standardized because the volume of business was sufficient to justify and to pay for any sort of improvement. Bills of exchange, checks, national banks, letters of credit, and clearing houses became more necessary and highly expedient. Stocks became common, for with all the potential it was possible, as Ted R. Worley has said, to cut the future up into shares and sell it for stock. The stock exchange, futures, margins, rigging and watering all came into existence in a big way at the beginning of the eighteenth century when John Law was cutting up the Mississippi bubble and selling the shares. All these practices have been the concern of lawmakers ever since.

The frontier influence on government, on modification of government, is another subject awaiting re-examination. This discussion can do no more than suggest certain broad areas for inquiry as to how governments reacted to new forces and to the problems posed by the new lands. Central to the whole discussion is authority, or to use a modern term, sovereignty, and what happened to it following the opening of the frontier. Government is a subject of unlimited complications and the student may be easily drowned in the details. Basically, however, it is a simple thing, having to do with people on the one hand and their rulers on the other. In a narrower sense the study comes down to a consideration of where power to rule over human affairs is lodged in a society and how it happened to be there. Once the location of power is determined, it is not difficult to derive approximately the manner in which it is exercised, and thereby arrive at the form of government — monarchy, republic or democracy, as the case may be. There can be little doubt that in modern times at least there is a close relation between property and government. It is quite likely that when we locate the owners of the property in any society we shall not be far from those who exercise the political authority — those who govern, and they govern regardless of any theory to the contrary.

Though the relationship between frontier wealth and government has been developed in Chapter Five, the subject may be reviewed here by way of suggesting fields of investigation. For example, if the theory of the vertical flow of wealth in modern times is valid, there is room for students to examine the effects of this vertical pulsation on governmental forms and practices. The following questions present themselves:

1. Who within the Metropolis was the first recognized owner of the land of the Great Frontier and what power did the ownership confer? How did the administration of the frontier lands affect the administration of the sovereign?

2. Did the monarchs, as the first claimants, retain title to the frontier lands or did they alienate the land? If they alienated it, on what terms?

3. What happened to the power of the monarch as he alienated the land?

4. Was the land alienated placed in the hands of a few large owners or was it dispersed on a broad basis to many people? What effect did the character of the distribution have on government?

5. What form of government was the concomitant of the several stages in the ownership of frontier land?

These are a few questions that lead in the direction of determining the over-all influence of the Great Frontier on the forms and practices of modern governments.

2. *Economics*

A specialist in economic theory, on being asked what effect the frontier had on his subject, expressed a doubt that the frontier had played any part in the formulation of the various theories concerning wealth. What he probably meant was that no economic theorist had consciously dealt with the frontier as an important factor in his thinking. In that sense, the statement may be true, and probably is, because economic theory is supposed to be of universal applicability, and hitherto the frontier has not been treated as a factor in any field of thought in a serious way outside the United States. Since no American has as yet founded a school of economic thought, it is not strange that the frontier has not been given a place in the extensive vocabulary of the economic theorists. The *word* may have been absent, but the *substance* has been present from the time the first shipload of gold was unloaded on the European shore down to the present, during the whole existence of modern economic thought. The purpose here is to call the attention of the economic theorists to the possibility that the frontier may be worthy of consideration as a factor in all that concerns modern wealth. This is done at the risk of suggesting a new "school" of thought in a field which seems already to be well supplied. The multiplicity of the schools indicates that as yet no economic Darwin has shown up to run a base line which will give that unity in economic thinking that Darwin gave to scientific thinking in the realm of living things. It is not implied that the frontier is the base line, but it may be the unknown factor which has thrown a lot of theory out of gear with the facts. And if so it must be taken into account by him who makes the final and generally accepted synthesis which will unify a rather chaotic discipline.

Since no man and no school has established a base line from which to approach the subject and to give it unity, it seems necessary to examine briefly the various schools for the purpose of determining the one that has approached nearest to general approval. *The Encyclopaedia of the Social Sciences* lists the following schools: (1) The Physiocrats, (2) The Classical School, (3) The Marginal Utility School, (4) The Mathematical School, (5) The Cambridge School, (6) The Historical School, (7) The Socialist School, (8) The Socio-Ethical School, (9) The Romantic and Universalist School, and (10) The Institutional School. To the above list should be added the followers of John Maynard Keynes, whose views are dominant in current economic thought. It would be tedious to set forth the theories advanced by these schools, and it is not necessary because they can be read in any library. The purpose is to call attention to their large number, the apparent lack of agreement among them, and to discover if possible the one which has been most influential, which has stood if not all tests, then more than any other.

There is not the slightest doubt that the Classical School has enjoyed, and still enjoys, prestige unmatched by any other. It is the oldest but one, the Physiocrat, which was short-lived and relatively uninfluential outside of France. As for the others, they are all beholden to the Classical School. Some of them owe their existence to the fact that they *differ* from the Classical School, and the first task of each one is to show that Classicists were wrong in greater or less degree. Even if they assert, as none would dare do, that the Classical School was wrong *in toto*, they still could not get away from Adam Smith and his collaborators.

Within the Classical School Adam Smith was the first in time and foremost in importance. He not only is recognized as the founder of the school; but he is also often called — and perhaps not incorrectly — the father of modern economics. He may not deserve the title, but he does have a better claim to it than any other. If this much be true, then our task is to inquire whether the frontier — although he did not know or use the term — was an important factor in his thinking about the wealth of nations and how it might be acquired and managed. Did he deal with the substance of the frontier in formulating his treatise? Were the problems of wealth and its production, of commerce, industry, etc., related to the new countries? Was his theory of free trade and laissez faire based on the European situation prior to the opening of the frontier or was it based on the situation of Europe, and particularly of England, as related to the lands overseas? Would the open economy of Adam Smith have been practical in the closed world of the frontier? Did the frontier contribute partially to the situation which he sought to analyze, to the wealth which he sought to explain, to the techniques he suggested for handling it?

Fortunately we do not have to depend on the commentators to answer these questions because Adam Smith answered them himself. But before letting him speak on the subject let us view the economic environment surrounding him in the third quarter of the eighteenth century. By that time the broadest foundations of the British Empire had been laid, which is another way of saying that England was the largest owner of the Great Frontier, with the possible exception of Spain. Elsewhere the view has been advanced that the Great Frontier was in essence a vast body of wealth, and that its discovery had made wealth available in all forms out of proportion to the people to share it. That meant in last analysis that wealth was so abundant that it could be handled with the greatest liberality, distributed with a prodigal hand. Directly or indirectly the whole Metropolis was its beneficiary, as Adam Smith pointed out; but England, by developing great skill in exploiting it, was by far the greatest beneficiary in all the Metropolis. This was the economic environment, the medium and the climate surrounding Adam Smith at the time he set himself the task of making his analysis.

That analysis led him to suggest certain techniques for handling wealth, techniques which would have been unthinkable three centuries earlier when wealth was too scarce and is unthinkable now when people are too numerous. Free trade and laissez faire cannot exist in extreme form except in situations where wealth, real or potential, is abundant in proportion to population. That situation did exist in an exaggerated degree in England when Smith wrote, and to a lesser degree it existed in other European nations. It was the Great Frontier that furnished the excess of wealth that gave validity to Adam Smith's main contention, namely, that all shackles could with safety be removed from the individual in search of wealth. His analysis resulted in a theory of complete economic freedom which was in keeping with the facts of his day, and for a century more. The theory was good for the conditions then present, good for a century beçause the conditions lasted for a century, but the conditions were exceptional, abnormal, and temporal. The theory took hold because the future was with it, and its acceptance was most cordial in England and the United States where the frontier wealth was most abundant.

What of Adam Smith now? James Maurice Clark says: "The validity of Smith's doctrines for a much later age is perhaps mainly a matter of academic interest. It may possibly be said that, so far as economic behavior is still a matter of free individual choice, much truth remains, although it all needs to be rethought in terms of modern conditions and knowledge, especially of the forces conditioning such free choices." As for his vogue in his day, Clark continues: "In his time as now the world was far from following a 'system of natural liberty'; but then it was moving towards it, while now it is moving away. From an expression of things in process of becoming the doctrines became in the midnineteenth century a bulwark of things existing; from an attack on outstanding vested interests of its day it became a defense of those of a later day. . . . And now it seems a refuge of 'historic homesickness.' " [7] This "historic homesickness" has been treated elsewhere, not as a nostalgia for Adam Smith but for the conditions of abundance of which he thought. (See Chapter Nine.)

Let us turn now to the question of Smith's awareness of the forces with which he dealt. As already stated, he did not know the word but he did know the substance of the frontier. *The Wealth of Nations* is replete with references to the Americas, and to other overseas lands. The following statement, if there were no more, would prove that the frontier as an economic force had not escaped him:

The discovery of America and that of a passage to the East Indies by the Cape of Good Hope, are the two greatest and most important events recorded in the history of mankind. Their consequences have already been very great; but, in the short period of between two and three centuries which has elapsed since these discoveries were made, it is impossible that the whole

[7] See James Maurice Clark, "Adam Smith," *Encyclopaedia of the Social Sciences*, vol. XIV, pp. 113–14.

extent of their consequences can have been seen. What benefits, or what misfortunes to mankind may hereafter result from those great events, no human wisdom can foresee. By uniting, in some measure, the most distant parts of the world, by enabling them to relieve one another's wants, to increase one another's enjoyments, and to encourage one another's industry, their general tendency would seem to be beneficial. . . .

In the mean time one of the principal effects of those discoveries has been to raise the mercantile system to a degree of splendour and glory which it could never otherwise have attained to. It is the object of that system to enrich a great nation rather by trade and manufactures than by the improvement and cultivation of land, rather by the industry of the towns than by that of the country. But, in consequence of those discoveries, the commercial towns of Europe, instead of being the manufacturers and carriers for but a very small part of the world (that part of Europe which is washed by the Atlantic ocean, and the countries which lie round the Baltic and Mediterranean seas), have now become the manufacturers for the numerous and thriving cultivators of America, and the carriers, and in some respects the manufacturers too, for almost all the different nations of Asia, Africa, and America. Two new worlds have been opened to their industry, each of them much greater and more extensive than the old one, and the market of one of them growing still greater and greater every day.[8]

It is possible to comb *The Wealth of Nations* and bring up irrefutable proof that its author did not write the above statement as a generality. His subject was wealth, and it was wealth he had in mind when he wrote the sweeping passage just quoted. Throughout, he talks of "new lands," "new colonies," and he cites examples from the new continents. There are many allusions to the American colonies, and many of his principles are derived from a comparative study of conditions in America and in Europe. In a previous chapter of this work it was stated that the strange paradox of the frontier was that it paid the highest wages and produced the cheapest commodities. Adam Smith knew that and said it this way:

[8] Adam Smith, *An Inquiry into the Nature and Causes of the Wealth of Nations*, Edwin Cannan, ed. (London: Methuen Co., 1904), vol. II, pp. 125–26.

England is certainly, in the present times, a much richer country than any part of North America. The wages of labour, however, are much higher in North America than in any part of England. . . . The price of provisions is everywhere in North America much lower than in England, a dearth has never been known there. . . . If the money price of labour, therefore, be higher than it is any where in the mother country, its real price . . . must be higher in a still greater proportion.

But though America is not yet so rich as England, it is much more thriving, and advancing with much greater rapidity to the further acquisition of riches.[9]

What Smith is saying here is that wealth was accumulating much faster on the American frontier than it was in the English Metropolis. He is saying in principle that, taking wealth as a whole, the frontier as a whole is adding to the sum total the greater increment of it. It would follow that the boasted wealth of the modern age is basically a frontier contribution. Smith thought that the rapid increase of wealth was due to the rapid increase of population, but that the increase in population was made possible by the abundance of food, namely wealth.

When Smith turned to the interest rate and the return on investments, he recognized the exceptional circumstance afforded by the new country, "In our North American and West Indian colonies, not only the wages of labour, but the interest of money, and consequently the profits of stock, are higher than in England. . . . High wages of labour and high profits of stock, however, are things, perhaps, which scarce ever go together, except in the peculiar circumstances of new colonies." [10] In another place he remarks anent the prosperity of new colonies: "The colony of a civilized nation which takes possession either of a waste country, or of one so thinly inhabited, that the natives easily give place to the new settlers, advances more rapidly to wealth and greatness than any other human society." [11] In giving reasons for this "wealth and great-

9 *Ibid.*, vol. I, pp. 71, 72.
10 *Ibid.*, vol. I, p. 94.
11 *Ibid.*, vol. II, p. 66.

ness," the author touches on wages, rent, taxes — and freedom
from oppression by the "two superior orders."

> Every colonist gets more land than he can possibly cultivate. He
> has no rent, and scarce any taxes to pay. No landlord shares
> with him in its produce, and the share of the sovereign is com-
> monly but a trifle. . . .
> In other countries, rent and profit eat up wages, and the two
> superior orders of people oppress the inferior one. But in new
> colonies, the interest of the two superior orders obliges them to
> treat the inferior one with more generosity and humanity;
> at least, where that inferior one is not in a state of slavery. . . .
> The high wages of labour encourage population. The cheapness
> and plenty of good land encourage improvement, and enable
> the proprietor to pay those high wages. In those wages consists
> almost the whole price of the land; and though they are high,
> considered as the wages of labour, they are low, considered as
> the price of what is so very valuable.[12]

It is not our business here to show that the frontier was a
factor that entered into the economic theories of rent, wages,
and interest, not to mention liberty and free trade, which
Adam Smith adduced from his inquiry. That is the affair of
the economist. Rather the purpose here is to show the extent to
which Adam Smith was conscious of new lands, new colonies,
Africa, the Americas, and Asia as well, conscious of them as a
force in the current situation with which he was concerned.

The economist, like so many who followed him, found no
word symbol that would bind together the concept which he
had formed. Hence, when he was writing about economic conditions produced by the Great Frontier, he was forced to use a
variety of terms none of which without a modifier — usually
"new," as "new country" and "new land" — comprehended the
whole of what he had in mind. Naturally, in the forefront of
his thinking was England in the Metropolis; and in the forefront of his thinking about the frontier were the English colonies in America. He did not use the device adopted in this
study of considering all Europe as the Metropolis, seat of civilization, and all the new lands as frontier, the mainspring and
headwater of the modern flood of wealth. He knew so much

[12] *Ibid.*, vol. II, pp. 67, 68.

about both, however, that he probably would have welcomed the advent of a convenient symbol for his well-developed concept.

Though the idea of "mother country" and "colony" stood in his way, he had nevertheless the concept of the unified effect of the frontier on all Europe. The passage in which he sets this forth is rather involved because he was dealing with an involved process in economics. He said:

> The discovery and colonization of America, it will readily be allowed, have contributed to augment the industries, first, of all the countries which trade to it directly; such as Spain, Portugal, France, and England; and, secondly, of all those which, without trading to it directly, send, through the medium of other countries, goods to it of their own produce; such as Austrian Flanders, and some provinces of Germany, which, through the medium of the countries before mentioned, send to it a considerable quantity of linen and other goods. All such countries have evidently gained a more extensive market for their surplus produce, and must consequently have been encouraged to increase its quantity.[13]

Enough has been said to indicate that Adam Smith viewed intelligently and with much understanding the whole world in which he lived. His tentative approach is indicated by the full title of his book rather than by the abbreviated form — *The Wealth of Nations* — commonly used. He considered his work as a quest, a search, and examination of available data to see what their meaning was, and all this is indicated by the title, *An Inquiry into the Nature and Causes of the Wealth of Nations*. He did not intend to be dogmatic, probably had no idea that he was "laying down laws" that would be considered irrevocable, would not have believed that he was founding a school, much less a whole discipline. He was, we are told, surprised at the attention his inquiry received. No doubt he would be astonished to know that intelligent men would expect all his observations on conditions as they existed in the third quarter of the eighteenth century when he was writing to be still valid two centuries later when all the basic conditions had radically changed. He wrote as an observer of

[13] *Ibid.*, vol. II, p. 92.

the then present and the immediate past and not as a seer of the future, although he did occasionally make projections into the future of the tendencies he noted.

The vogue of Adam Smith for a century or more is to be explained by the fact that the conditions he observed in the eighteenth century continued, and in many respects were heavily accented, until the last quarter of the nineteenth century. He did anticipate the future and therein lay his great influence on economic theory. Had his *Inquiry* been offered in 1950, it would have been published by an antiquarian society.

What we seem to need now is another *Inquiry* which will ignore economic dogma and view the world today as dispassionately and intelligently as Adam Smith viewed his world in his day. If such an author could have the awareness, not of what theorists have said, but of what has been and is going on, he might do a volume that would again illuminate the present and anticipate the future until conditions again change. Perhaps he would find it appropriate to be tentative also, and call his work *An Inquiry into the Nature and Causes of the Poverty of Nations*, a poverty which apparently only the remaining wealth of the old frontier can ameliorate. He might even tell us what will happen when the vacant world of Adam Smith's time is completely filled up with people, and the finite wealth which was then just being tapped approaches exhaustion. That is the sort of book that Adam Smith might write were he here to do so. It would not be a popular book, but in time it might be recognized as a great one.

The above discussion seems to lead to the conclusion that economics, like history, has no immutable laws. It is too much circumstanced by history. There is one law for boom and one for bust, one technique for a society of much land and few people and another for a society of many people and little land. There are principles that will work when wealth is increasing and principles that work when wealth is decreasing. It seems that it is always doing the one or the other. Therefore, observations made at one period, and "laws" deduced from them, are not applicable in a later period. It seems that economics, if not a dismal science, is ephemeral, and probably not more scientific than the humanities. If Adam Smith still towers above his successors, it is because he wrote his book with his eyes on the world he lived in and not on what some theorist had said about it. If he is now mainly a subject of academic interest and a refuge for "historic homesickness," it is because he spoke of a world that exists only academically and for which many people grow homesick when they think about it. If the economic theorist, concerned as he is with the present, has done with Adam Smith, the historians should take him over body, boots, and breeches, for he understood better than anyone else of his day that segment of human activity with which he dealt, and within the fabric of his thinking he incorporated a knowledge of the relationship of the new world to the old, of the Great Frontier to the Metropolis.

CHAPTER TWELVE

WHAT THE FRONTIER TOUCHED: LITERATURE, ART, EDUCATION, AND HISTORY

1. Literature

IT HAS ALWAYS seemed to me that literature represents the fragrance of culture, the expression through highly talented persons of the genius of a society. This genius is expressed in other forms, in art, in music, and in architecture, for example, but its literary expression differs from the others in that it can be available to the many instead of the few, and moreover it can be understood by any literate persons without commentary or explanation by a special priesthood. It is self-explanatory. Literature, after the invention of printing, became the most democratic of all the arts, and in a way it comprehends within itself all the others.

Also, literature is an accented and often idealized recording of human experience, like a sketch or painting in which lights and shadows are used for dramatic effect. Literature ignores history's exactitude, but it can rarely, if ever, escape completely that which it ignores, for history is the medium in which it operates, furnishing literature a frame and a background. The main difference between the two is that one is earthbound by its heavy cargo of facts whereas the other travels light, and can soar to the gates of heaven or plunge to hell on the wings of imagination. Imagination! That is the thing which concerns us, for it is the essence of literature, giving it a distinctive quality and a separate place in the categories of human endeavor.

It is important to note, however, that imagination must always have a base to take off from, and a place to land when it returns. Though easily airborne it cannot remain aloft forever; it must begin with facts and must keep touch with them in order to maintain a sense of reality. Therefore, literature

348

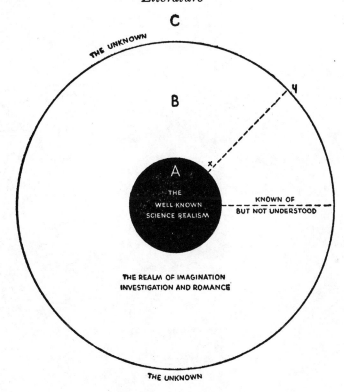

FIG. 1 THE LIMITS OF KNOWLEDGE

The inner circle represents the area of accurate knowledge. The outer circle represents the limits of knowledge. The area B is the region known of but not understood. It is here that imagination has free play, that mystery and romance abound, that inquiry and investigation go on. Gradually the inner circle is enlarged. If it could expand until coterminous with the outer circle there would be no mystery, little room for imagination and nothing to investigate. The greater the distance x–y, the greater the opportunity for the imagination, literary and scientific.

may be thought of as having a factual core of some sort with an extension outward to the unreal and the unknown which can be arrived at only by imagination.

Imagination would seem therefore to be the impatient forerunner of truth, seeking to anticipate other means of attaining it. It must be off to the future before the manuscripts of his-

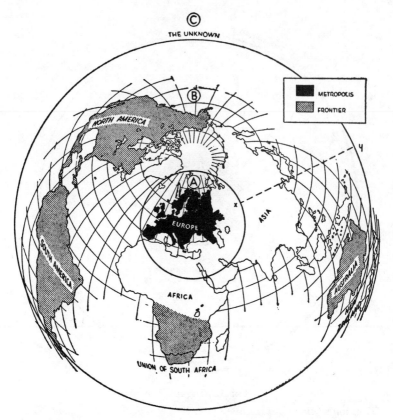

FIG. 2 THE GREAT FRONTIER
Adapted from Harper's Magazine

The principle set forth in Fig. 1 is illustrated for geography in Fig. 2. The inner circle A is the Metropolis of 1500. The outer circle encompasses the earth. In the area B lies the Great Frontier, known of but not understood, for centuries. After the discovery the distance x–y was greater than it was before, has been since, or can be again. The inner circle of accurate geographic knowledge has expanded almost to the outer circle. The area B has been so reduced that little room remains to explore or guess or seek adventure and romance in the unknown.

tory are written, a sort of John the Baptist crying in a recordless wilderness. It outruns the scientist who proceeds but slowly.

The accompanying figure may be useful in showing the realm of the imagination and its relation to the area of well-known fact. The central spot represents what is definitely known; the outer circles encompass what is suspected or known slightly, while all beyond the outer circle is unknown, where the footing for any sort of rational thinking is impossible. The imagination can do little within the dark center where all is known; it can do less beyond the outer circle where nothing is known. Its realm lies in the area between the inner core and the outer circle, where something is known, but not too much. Here in the white space both investigation and imagination operate. Investigation results in the discovery of more truth, and thereby enlarges the black dot, causing it to encroach on the total area. This process has gone on rapidly since 1500 and the realm left to the imagination has been correspondingly reduced. If knowledge should ever become coterminous with imagination, then imagination as we know it, and literature as well, would be drowned in a sea of facts and realism. There would be no romance, nothing to be romantic about. There would also be nothing to investigate. It is hoped that the scientists will not deprive us of something pleasurable and themselves of a job.

Geography offers the clearest illustration of the ideas set forth above. A series of contemporary maps spaced at intervals of fifty years from 1450 to 1850 would tell the story of the enlargement of the black dot of geographical knowledge, and a corresponding reduction of the area on this earth for geographic guesswork and literary imagination. In this case it may be said that so far as map making is concerned the earth now holds few and insignificant secrets. After Magellan's voyage the main landmarks of the world were known. The knowledge for a time thereafter was just sufficient to free the imagination, but not abundant enough to restrain it. The map makers proceeded to do their worst, inhabiting the Great Frontier with fantastic creatures never known on land or sea. But even so, what these early map makers did was not so bad as what the map makers of the late medieval period had done when all the world outside the three continents was a matter of pure fantasy.

"Nothing, I think [says Professor John Livingston Lowes], is harder to translate into terms of our own blasé experience than the pregnant fact that the little pre-Columbian world was literally islanded in the unknown — an unknown, none the less, across which came drifting signs and rumors of some kindred knowable beyond. . . . No documents in the world are more eloquent than the laconic legends of the early maps." [1]

It may be a coincidence, but a curious one, that imaginative literature reached its apex in the modern world in those centuries when the white space in the circle representing the slightly known was greater in proportion to the black space, representing the well known, than it has ever been in the history of mankind. There was in the sixteenth and seventeenth centuries a preponderance of new material of all sorts from geology to astronomy which the world had just discovered but had not yet investigated, analyzed, classified, or understood. Therefore, there was an equally vast area over which imagination could range in search of material and inspiration. Animated by an insatiable curiosity, supplied with enough facts to make a safe beginning, inspired by an abundance of new data, and rewarded with enough success to sustain interest, men of imagination cut their moorings, shook off the formalism of the classical style, and charted new paths leading forward into the Great Frontier. There is hardly a writer after 1550 who was not affected directly or indirectly; many prior to that date were influenced. Taken all together they formed a towhead of genius such as the world has not seen since.

There is another coincidence worth noting about this Golden Age. Above we have looked at imaginative literature as a whole, as something of the Metropolis, as a unit without regard to nations. When we break it up into subdivisions of the growing nationalism, and speak of Portuguese, Spanish, English, and French literature, we find that in general each nation's Golden Age coincides more or less with that nation's supremacy in frontier activity. Perhaps supremacy is too strong

---

[1] For an account of these maps see John Livingston Lowes, *The Road to Xanadu* (Boston: Houghton Mifflin Co., 1927), chap. VII. The quotation is from pp. 116 f.

a word, so let us say that the Golden Age was contemporary with intense frontier ferment. It seems that as the frontier boom got under way in any country, the literary genius of that nation was liberated to become an important part of a triumphal procession.[2]

As is well known, Portugal was the first to tap the secrets of the frontier world; her mariners sought the eastern water route, found the Cape of Good Hope and the way to India. In celebration of this event, Luis de Camões wrote the great epic of Portuguese literature. This is *The Lusiads*, which was written largely in the distant lands and published in 1572. It tells the story of Vasco da Gama's voyage to India, but weaves in the exploits of other explorers and much of the history of the Iberian land. *The Lusiads* not only represents the apex of Portuguese literature, but it stands in a class by itself as a literary celebration of the exploits of explorers, and has been called the epic of commerce.[3] Neglect of it today is to be explained more by the decline of the nation that gave it than by lack of merit in the poem. The spirit of *The Lusiads* is illustrated by the following lines:

> Right onward still the brave Armada stray'd:
> Right on they steer by Ethiopa's strand,
> And pastoral Madagascar's verdant land.
> Before the balmy gales of cheerful spring,
> With heav'n their friend, they spread the canvass [sic] wing . . . .

[2] The case of Italy and its Renaissance development of the arts cannot be related to the Great Frontier. However, Italy had an early outlet to the East, and enjoyed something of a boom because of that contact.

[3] William Julius Mickle, in the introduction to his English translation, says of *The Lusiad*: "If a concatenation of events centered in one great action, events which gave birth to the present commercial system of the world; if these be of the first importance in the civil history of mankind, the *Lusiad*, of all other poems, challenges the attention of the philosopher, the politician, and the gentleman.

"In contradistinction to the *Iliad* and *Æneid*, the *Paradise Lost* has been called the Epic Poem of Religion. In the same manner may the *Lusiad* be named the Epic Poem of Commerce." — [Luis de] Camoëns, *The Lusiad*, translated by William Julius Mickle, bk. I (London: W. S. Suttaby, 1809), p. i.

For a recent translation of *The Lusiads* see Leonard Bacon, *The Lusiads of Luiz de Camões* (New York: The Hispanic Society of America, 1950). The introduction sketches the life of Camões or Camoëns.

Behind them now the cape of Praso bends,
Another Ocean to their view extends,
Where black-topt islands, to their longing eyes,
Lav'd by the gentle waves, in prospect rise.
But Gama, (captain of the vent'rous band,
Of bold emprize, and born for high command,
Whose martial fires, with prudence close allied,
Ensured the smiles of fortune on his side)
Bears off those shores which waste and wild appear'd
And eastward still for happier climates steer'd.[4]

By the lucky discovery of the Western World among other reasons, Spain soon surpassed Portugal as a frontier power, and her Golden Age of literature came a little later, from 1530 to 1680. Within this period fall the literary works of Juan de la Cruz, Cervantes, Lope de Vega, and Calderón. Twenty-one universities were founded in the sixteenth century and five in the seventeenth. By 1532 Victoria had laid the foundation of international law, and just a generation later Suárez formulated its abstract principles. It cannot be said that the literary men of Spain paid much attention to the New World, although Lope de Vega devoted one drama to *The New World of Columbus*. No epic comparable to *The Lusiads* appeared in Spain or any other country. This does not mean that the writers were not influenced and inspired by the general ferment not to mention the prosperity which the frontier had created.

The Dutch were engaged in the twofold task of freeing themselves from Spanish domination and fighting their way to India to participate in the new wealth overseas. The formation of the Dutch East India Company in 1602 marks the rise of the Dutch, who in 1623 settled New York. We have already seen that Grotius was led to compose his masterpiece on international law because he was assigned to defend one Heemskirk, who had captured a Portuguese galleon in the Far East in 1603. The seventeenth is called the Golden Century of Dutch literature, and the four most notable figures — Jakob Cats, Pieter Hooft, Joost van den Vondel, and Constantijn Huygens — died between 1647 and 1687. None of these men seems to

4 Camoëns, *The Lusiad*, p. 11.

have been much concerned with the New World, but they were much concerned with worldly things. Cats made a fortune by draining swamp land, Huygens was a lawyer with a literary sideline, Hooft was from a family of Amsterdam merchants, and the parents of Vondel kept a hosiery shop. Another member of the school, who died in 1618 at the age of thirty-three, was Gerbrand Badero, who must have been of humble origin as he did not have the classical education which the others had; since he lacked this classical training, it is not remarkable that he turned to romantic plays and humorous or satirical poetry. This display of literary talent occurred in the same century in which the Dutch were reaping great profits from the distant lands.

England's period of greatness was the Elizabethan Age, culminating in Shakespeare. The relation of English literature to the frontier is treated at some length in James E. Gillespie, *The Influence of Oversea Expansion on England to 1700,* which should be read by anyone who is interested. This Golden Age coincided with the period when the English sea dogs and pirates were probing the Spanish Main and bringing their booty to London. The English did not yet possess the frontier, but they had made its acquaintance, and were receiving tremendous stimulus to the imagination from the rich prizes found there and the hazardous daring involved in securing them. Keynes points out that the boom, which he attributes to profit inflation induced by the sudden influx of American treasure, lasted in Spain from 1520 to 1590, in England from 1550 to 1650, and in France from 1530 to 1700. He comments on the fact that Shakespeare lived from 1564 to 1616 "when any level-headed person in England disposed to make money could hardly help doing so." He observes the relationship between national good times and literary genius: "I offer it as a thesis for examination by those who like rash generalisations, that by far the larger proportion of the world's greatest writers and artists have flourished in the atmosphere of buoyancy, exhilaration and the freedom from economic cares felt by the governing class, which is engendered by profit inflations." [5]

[5] John Maynard Keynes, *Treatise on Money* (New York: Harcourt, Brace & Co., 1930), vol. II, p. 154, note 3.

Keynes, with his eyes fixed on money and its influence, could well overlook the intangible effects which the conditions favorable to men who would make money might also have on men who make imagination. If literature resulting from imagination is truly dependent on national wealth, on profit inflation, on boom conditions, then the Shakespearean Age should have been as a threshold to a greater literature, for England grew constantly richer until the end of the nineteenth century. Actually England was not so rich in the last quarter of the sixteenth century, but she was in that state of nervous ecstasy which comes with the hint of great things ahead. In the case of Spain, Holland, and England, the Golden Age of literature came in the beginning stages of prosperity rather than after its full realization.

Whether the Golden Age was induced by wealth or by the presence of a little-known frontier is not the primary question with which we are concerned. Our concern is with the impact of the frontier on the human imagination as expressed in literature. Imagination, as the common denominator of all literature worthy of the name, gives us something to take hold of, a unifying element in a chaotic sea of form and content. At least we can ask ourselves what was the subject matter to which imagination was applied in a given period. Having got that far, we can find the subject matter which was frontier in character, and isolate it, put it in a pile as it were and see what it looks like; and then we can set it over against what is left, and if our patience and erudition were sufficient we might eventually evaluate the literature inspired by the frontier and compare it with that on other subjects. That is a task that has never been performed, one which might engage a host of explorers of modern literature for a long time.

Though we wander off from a discussion of imagination into talk about literature, as if it were something apart, we are compelled to return to imagination as the unique quality, the unifying element of the subject. Centering our attention on the frontier, we ask this question: What did the human imagination do with a New World? What record of this imaginative activity has been left us in literary form? We might reverse the first question and ask, What did the frontier do to the human imagination? Was the effect on literature as great as it was on life? If so, then R. B. Cunninghame Graham has attempted to describe it:

There has been but one real conquest worthy of the name — that of the New World. The human race in all its annals holds no record like it. Uncharted seas, unnavigated gulfs; new constellations, the unfathomable black pit of the Magellan clouds; the Cross hung in the sky; the very needle varying from the pole; islands innumerable and an unknown world rising from out of the sea; all unsuspected races living in flora never seen by Europeans, made it an achievement unique in all the history of mankind.[6]

The best that can be done here is to suggest subjects from the frontier around which the imagination of literary men played as lightning plays on the dark crests of the distant mountain. From the list must be omitted historical records such as the books of travelers and reports of voyagers, though these furnished necessary substance for the literary productions. About the following categories there can be no dispute:

1. Primitive man and nature
2. Eldorado
3. Utopia
4. Civilized man in isolation
5. Man in conflict with nature

Around these five subjects the poets and prose writers spun the gossamer tissues of a new literature. But before commenting on examples of the various categories some observations may be made on their general characteristics. The first thing to note is that as treated by literary men each subject overlaps one or more of the others. Another point is that the subjects are wordly in the extreme with hardly a hint of religion in the lot. Neither Dante nor Milton would have been very comfortable in the situation or the societies dealt with. In the third place it is implied in each category that the action takes place between the Metropolis and the Frontier. Primitive man is of the frontier, but is presented as he appears to the metro-

6 R. B. Cunninghame Graham, *Conquest of New Granada* (London: W. Heine-mann, 1922), p. vii.

politan observer. Eldorado was never sought within the Metropolis, but always in the distant lands, and always by misguided individuals from the Metropolis. The point is illustrated in Poe's "Eldorado."

> Gaily bedight,
>   A gallant knight,
> In sunshine and in shadow,
>   Had journeyed long,
>   Singing a song,
> In search of Eldorado.
>
> But he grew old,
>   This knight so bold,
> And o'er his heart a shadow
>   Fell as he found
>   No spot of ground
> That looked like Eldorado.[7]

The first and most important Utopias, those ideal societies usually composed of primitive people who lived pure lives in contrast to the corrupt society of Europe, were always located far from Europe to be observed by the narrator through metropolitan eyes. This is true from More's *Utopia* to Barrie's *The Admirable Crichton*; the point of view is metropolitan, and in most cases from a vantage point not of the observer's choosing. Nor is the case different in those conflicts with nature recorded by the Ancient Mariner. That he was pretty far off home base is evident when he says "we were the first that ever burst into that silent sea." Shipwreck and storm, tempest and mutiny are nasty incidents near home, but when touched by the genius of a Shakespeare, Coleridge, Stevenson, or Melville, and enchanted by distance from the Metropolis, they make wonderful reading indeed.

It is pretty clear that when human imagination concerned itself in a literary way with the above subjects, it was involved with two important elements, adventure and distance. The adventure was always that of the metropolitan in getting to

[7] The present-day search for "new frontiers" reminds us of the search for Eldorado.

some distant place, getting along after he got there, and finally in getting away so that he could come back to the Metropolis to tell his tale and reap the acclaim of his envious stay-at-home acquaintances. There is probably not a record of where an observer of a Utopia, however delightful its society might be, or Robinson Crusoe or the Ancient Mariner, or any other who did not hurry back to the printing presses rather than throw in his fortunes and stay where his adventures were found. Of the Ancient Mariner, Professor Lowes says: "But even the Ancient Mariner returned in the end to the kirk and the hill and the lighthouse top, and however remotely we may for the moment range afield, the ways of the poetic faculty which are our starting point will also be the upshot of our travel's history." [8] One would suspect that of the three things to which the literary traveler returned, his mind was centered more on the lighthouse top than on the kirk or the hill. At heart the modern writer has been full of egotism, an imaginative extrovert bursting with superiority and importance. He had escaped from God and the devil and become the most important thing in his universe, a talented agent whose business it was to prove, through his hero, that the world was a good place to spend a lifetime; it was a place where excitement and interest existed in full measure. He was a little above the Metropolis because he had been to the Great Frontier; and he was much better than the frontier because he came from the Metropolis. This delightful circle of self-aggrandizement often enabled the author to play over his own head, and perform feats of imagination difficult for those who live in less exuberant days to understand.

As we look back on this body of literature formed around primitive man and nature, Eldorados, Utopias, and civilized men caught in nature's traps, we feel the need of a convenient literary term which will encompass the various categories and at the same time convey a notion of their common qualities. We have a rare combination of elements, all tending toward something unusual. Egoism, distance, adventure, an inadequate knowledge of all the facts, a complete ignorance of what may

[8] Lowes, *The Road to Xanadu*, p. 116.

lie ahead and a momentary disregard of the past, all these things form a mixture out of which the tales that emerge cannot escape being romantic.

If we may return to the figure of the circle with its central core of fact, we may again see in the white space outside the core the enormous area in which imagination and fancy could freely play. That white area represents the Great Frontier, distant, slightly known, but not yet explored or half understood. There lay the realm of adventure, there the impossible feats could be performed, there anything could happen. There, on the periphery of the unknown, lay the land of high romance. When the ship set out to an unknown shore, the question was asked with awe: "Where lies the land to which the ship would go?" And as it drew away from the familiar harbor, dipped lower on the horizon and finally disappeared, it was to those left behind the symbol of all that is meant by the word romantic. It made no difference to those on shore what happened to or on the ship, it was romance. The ship might be becalmed or wrecked by storm; the sailor's teeth might drop out from scurvy and his body be scourged by fever and lice — that to the stay-at-home was romance. It made no difference to the shorebound; for the ship — in its departure, its return, and in all between — was a vehicle of romance. We can still get something of the feeling of it by reading the folders put out by steamship companies and travel bureaus, and many of us are still lured away by them on uncomfortable vacations to find what we left at home — at twice the price. But still we deceive ourselves, and in distant places seek romance.

There may be a better term than romantic to describe the descriptions which represented life on the frontier, but there is no other term commonly understood that carries the desired connotations quite so well. Professor Gilbert Chinard has written a cycle of books and a number of articles dealing with exoticism and its influence on France and French literature. In general what he does is to show the influence of things foreign, curious, outlandish, on French culture. Exotic plants, animals, and people were brought into France from the sixteenth century on, just as they were brought into all other European countries. Under the head of exoticism Professor Chinard deals with these subjects that are romantic in their effect. Still exoticism will not quite serve as a substitute for the romantic in this study of the frontier. It will not serve because it is strictly metropolitan in essence. The exotic is not exotic until it is rooted out of its natural habitat, as of the frontier, and set down in another land and another environment where its strangeness can be admired in exotic rapture. "Nothing was so splendid and exotic," said Evelyn, "as the ambassador." Indeed! Exotic to whom? In modern times exoticism would seem to have national limits, and what is exotic to one nation could well be, as in the case of the ambassador, native to another. The romantic is not thus limited, for it overrides national boundaries and is well-nigh universal. The frontier was exotic everywhere in the Metropolis.

The romantic character of the literature of the frontier resulted, not from the import of the exotic into the Metropolis, but in the export of the metropolitan imagination into the frontier. We Americans have never seen ourselves through Indian eyes, though we have had some hints of how we appeared to them. For example, George Catlin, the artist, once took a band of Indians to Europe and the Indians thought the Europeans were a very unusual people. They led dogs about by strings, they drank from strange bottles which went *Chick-a-bob-boo* when the corks were pulled. Noting the many different denominations, Fast Dancer observed that the white man had several ladders all too short to reach heaven, whereas the Indian had one long one which reached up to the happy hunting grounds. The Indians thought it very strange for a fine people like the English to be ruled over by a young squaw such as Victoria was at the time. The substitution of squaw for queen still shocks our sensibilities, but no more than the substitution of a feminine ruler for a masculine one shocked the Indians. Their descriptions of Europe and their mimicry of its people must have struck the Indians who remained in the forests of America as sheer romance.

Even though exoticism cannot be accepted as a term applicable to the impact of the frontier on the metropolitan imagination as represented in literature, it has its uses, and in the skillful hands of Professor Chinard it has taken on tremendous meaning for those who would understand the interaction between an old world and a new one. Some indication of his concept is best set forth in his own words:

> Over three centuries of French literature we have studied the influence exercised by the recitals of voyages to America upon the history of ideas .·We have tried to determine what had been the attitude of the French with respect to the new lands; in what ways their mentality and their sensibility had been affected by the revelations of the great discoverers; how finally one can see appear at rare intervals . . . a promise of artistic expression, a literary or sentimental theme. In this long review we have had to employ the word exoticism in default of a more satisfactory term to designate that which is a variety of exoticism but not exoticism entirely.[9]

It is when Professor Chinard undertakes to analyze the meaning of the term he has adopted that he runs immediately into the frontier for which we have been claiming so much. The difference between his view and our view is that he looks out on the frontier as the source of the exotic imported into France whereas we take our position on the frontier and observe the reverse phenomena, namely, the sweep of the metropolitan imagination across the wide circle of the strange lands, so that metropolitan stay-at-homes can get some idea of what those lands are like. But again let Professor Chinard speak for himself:

> At the very foundation of exoticism there is indeed found an eternal desire to escape from one's own time, from the civilization that surrounds one, to change one's environment. . . .
> In the epochs when the discontent produced by intense civilization has coincided with important geographical discoveries, a new sentiment has appeared: a desire to escape from present conditions, not by taking refuge in the past, but in changing climate. If, under other skies, men who are not familiar with our laws, nor our religion, live more happily, more freely, more easily than ourselves, . . . why not sail toward the Fortunate Isles? The dreamers, the poets, after having absorbed the recitals of discoverers of new lands, have then voyaged in spirit to the corners

[9] Gilbert Chinard, "Introduction," *L'exotisme américain dans l'oeuvre de Chateaubriand* (Paris: Hachette et C^le, 1918), p. v. Translation by John Haller.

of the earth, giving free rein to their imaginations and painting to themselves this recovered Paradise, the conquest of which . . . they left to others more audacious.[10]

The author observes, as we have, that those whose imaginations has been touched rarely remain in the land found so perfect, and if perchance they do remain there, they bring with them "all the inquietudes, all the passions poorly extinguished, all the vague desires of their former existence." As the author says, "They have asked of the new lands more than they could give; incapable of rejuvenating a soul three thousand years old, they have felt pass by them in the solitudes of the forest and on the wind of the savannah a happiness impossible to fix." [11]

Professor Chinard thinks that sentimental exoticism, as distinguished from the picturesque and philosophic types, results from a desire to civilize a primitive people plus a feeling of compulsion to enjoy their simple life, combined with a knowledge that both are a fantasy; longing to live like the *coureur de bois*, need for great space, nostalgia for distant countries, and inability to find happiness anywhere — these are the stuff sentimental exoticism is made of.

It appears that Professor Chinard considers sentimental exoticism as a literary nexus between two worlds, the Metropolis as represented by France and the Great Frontier as represented by America. Every element in his analysis belongs to the one or the other, and the gulf between them is wide. As Chinard observes, "In order for the American exoticism to produce its masterpiece, after a slow incubation of three centuries, it was necessary that, after the philosophic missionaries, the naturalists, and the adventurers, — it was necessary that René discover the New World." [12] To call Chateaubriand's work a masterpiece of American exoticism seems misleading, an intimation that it is American whereas it is strictly French. From our point of view it would do as well to say also that *René* is highly romantic, and for many of the reasons Professor Chinard gives for its being an example of sentimental exoticism. However all this may be, the Chinard studies have

[10] *Ibid.*, p. vi.
[11] *Ibid.*, p. ix.
[12] Chinard, *L'exotisme américain dans l'oeuvre de Chateaubriand*, p. 13.

opened up a new and rich field, and parallel studies of a similar nature for Spain, England, Holland, Germany, and Italy would supply invaluable material for an over-all examination of the literary influence of the Great Frontier on the Metropolis.

Finally, let us look at the five categories, derived from the Great Frontier, around which the metropolitan imagination played with magic literary effect. Literary concern with primitive man and nature expressed itself in what is sometimes known as primitivism, and resulted in the creation of the natural man of Rousseau and others, in the noble savage concept which not only permeated literature but philosophy and political science as well. The study of nature became a cult, and led directly into romanticism as distinguished from the classical forms of literature which emerged from the Renaissance attention to the Greek and Roman forms, and distinguished also from the medieval literature which was concerned with things out of this world. It is not easy to select literary prose masterpieces to illustrate this primitive category, but it is impossible to examine the fabric of general literature of the seventeenth and eighteenth centuries without discovering increased attention to nature, a glorification of the primitive, and the romantic if unreal image of the noble savage. Even the Utopias are pregnant with primeval nature, and through the pages enough noble savages move to show by contrast the ignobility and meanness of civilized man. Even the sophisticated Byron thought there was a pleasure in the pathless wood and a wild beauty on the lonely shore, and this despite the fact that he rarely disturbed such solitudes by his urbane intrusion. Byron was an inveterate romantic, ranging backward in time and outward in space to find things to remind him of his own sentimental sorrow.

The Eldorados seemed to exert more influence on explorers and fortune hunters than on literary men. After all, literature cannot well make a hero of gold or any inanimate object. But, like primitivism, gold forms an ingredient which literary craftsmen have used liberally to give flavor and color to what otherwise might have been a dull dish. It is not difficult to keep a tale going and make activity seem worth while if the promise of gold stands outlined a short way ahead on the actor's horizon. It was the thing that caused Tom Sawyer and Huck Finn to dig a little deeper, on the theory advanced by Tom that the treasure was often found in the last few licks with the pick and shovel, made after all hope had been abandoned. Robert Louis Stevenson knew the value of gold as a literary prop, and used it effectively to keep the adventure going in *Treasure Island* and in other stories.

As we come to the Utopias, we seem to be on firm ground so far as the frontier influence is concerned. The first Utopias, the principal ones, and the most famous ones — those which established the vogue — are on the frontier, both in physical location and in substance. It is against the backdrop of the forest in an environment remote from the Metropolis, among simple and uncorrupted people that these ideal societies had their imaginary existence. Those of the modern period — with which we are concerned — form a cluster caught in the river of time where the currents of the New World and the Old swirled together to fire the imagination of literary and political observers.

The question might be raised as to whether the Utopias belong in the field of literature or that of political philosophy. All are literature in the sense that they are fictional, romantic in the sense that they are unreal and far-fetched, and some of them were political in effect. For example, it is said that the framers of the American democratic government were influenced by James Harrington's *Oceana*, and certainly the various idealistic experiments which were popular in the first half of the nineteenth century drew their inspiration from the books. The climax was reached in impracticality when the three poets, Coleridge, Southey, and Lovell, decided to marry sisters and remove to America to found a Pantisocracy. Fortunately for poetry, and probably for the sisters, the scheme never got far beyond the altar.

Looked at in the long perspective, the Utopias offer evidence of the existence of a point of view and a philosophical concept that is modern. In general they assume that progress can be made, that man can mend his own net without divine assistance; that human perfectibility is attainable and worth striving for. The new abundance of wealth had enabled men to make

real progress in economic affairs. Science and criticism had
eaten away the pillars of superstition and unreasoning faith,
and set men adrift to shift for themselves in a sea of disbelief.
If man could make progress in economics and finance, perfect
a fortune, why could he not also by taking thought improve his
government and perfect a society? If by his own wit he could
conquer the material world, why could he not control and direct himself and his fellows? A little thought would have shown
him the magnitude of the last task in comparison with the first
one. The material world which he was conquering was inanimate and did not talk back or argue or have other plans of its
own. His attack on it was motivated by selfishness and the prospect of personal gain, i.e., progress. But his proposal to master
human society, to make it ideal, was based on selflessness, a
willingness to sacrifice, an abnegation of self-interest, and at
a time when self-seeking was most rewarding. The time for
asceticism is when there is not much to be had anyway, and
whatever may be said of the Utopias, they were a call to asceticism to people who were approaching the groaning board with
huge appetites. Hence Utopias were impractical, romantic, and
wholly out of joint with their times, and with human nature
at all times.

Civilized man in isolation is best represented by Daniel Defoe's *Robinson Crusoe* and Saint-Pierre's *Paul et Virginie*. Vol-
taire's *Candide* would seem to fall between civilized man in
isolation and Utopia. Of the three, one is English and two are
French. All of them were located in the New World. The
classic of this form of literature is *Robinson Crusoe*, the scene
of which was laid by Defoe on an island off the western coast
of South America. Defoe based his story on the narratives of
Captain William Dampier, who wrote three books dealing
with his voyages, the first in 1697 and the third in 1709. It
was on the second voyage that one Alexander Selkirk was
abandoned on the island of Juan Fernández in September,
1704; he was picked up by Dampier on a third voyage commanded by Captain Woodes Rogers in 1709. Defoe was acquainted with Dampier and drew liberally on his writings in
his *Robinson Crusoe* story. As a matter of fact, though Defoe
is remembered for the first volume of *Robinson Crusoe*, he was

one of the most prolific writers of the century and was interested in all sorts of overseas ventures. He wrote promotion literature for Harley in floating the South Sea Bubble, and prior to that had acted as secret agent in persuading the Scots to agree to the Act of Union in 1707 after the disastrous Darien venture. His success with *Robinson Crusoe* grew out of his fluency as a reporter, his prodigious memory for detail, and his thorough familiarity with travel literature. By accident he produced one masterpiece out of scores of mediocre productions which he probably thought as good. He was for the most part a high grade hack journalist and ghost writer. Swift is another writer who drew on Dampier. Willard H. Bonner has shown that Gulliver in his travels tracked the path laid out by Dampier in his voyages, and points out other parallels too close to have been accidental.

We come finally to that category of frontier-inspired literature which deals with man in conflict with nature. A section of this literature is of the sea, which had to play some part in metropolitan experience in the new lands because the sea was the only highway by which the metropolitans could reach their frontier destination. "Only with the eighteenth century," says Bonner, "does the sea occupy a place in English literature at all comparable with its place in English life." [13] It is further observed that English prose turned to the sea in the early eighteenth century, but the poets did not get around to it until much later. To the Europeans after 1500 the seas were as much frontier as the new continents, and mightily did they affect the men of imagination. The literature on the subject is extensive, and it would be impossible to do more here than to relate a portion of it to the frontier.

The most economical method of doing this is to select an example and let it represent the class. Every writer mentions that Shakespeare's *The Tempest* is the story of storm and shipwreck in the Atlantic. "Before Coleridge and the Romantic poets, scarcely anyone . . . wrote poetry filled with the beauty

[13] Willard Hallam Bonner, *Captain William Dampier: Buccaneer-Author*, p. 3.

and mystery of the sea."[14] "The Rime of the Ancient Mariner," published in 1798, represents the poetic imagination of the man of the Metropolis sweeping the frontier seas as does no other work, prose or poetry. Also there is no other character in literature who is caught so starkly in the vise-like grip of nature as was the Ancient Mariner. It would be impossible to say anything original about this piece of literary art because Professor Lowes has said it all in *The Road to Xanadu*. He shows that Coleridge was steeped in travel literature, knew what the ancients thought about geography, and probably borrowed his albatross from Shelvocke's *Voyage*. There is hardly a line in "The Rime of the Ancient Mariner" that does not reflect the most painstaking research on the part of the poet, proof of which is found in his notebooks. The Ancient Mariner is caught in about all the traps that Neptune can lay for puny man and the fragile ship on which he dared to sweep the seas, following in the wake of Magellan and Drake, through torrid calm and storm and frozen waste.

The remarkable achievement of "The Ancient Mariner" is that Coleridge compressed into 144 stanzas the human aspiration to know, the misapprehensions of the past, the daring to investigate at all hazards; and with all this went the ability to track the facts. Such an achievement can be attained only through the application of an all-inclusive imagination to a vast body of digested facts wrought into a simple work of art whose meaning and significance are commensurate with the reader's knowledge. The story is so simple that it is easily understood by a child who is held by its graphic imagery, and yet it is so profound that all its implications cannot be discovered by a mind less erudite than that of the mature scholar. In "The Ancient Mariner" the poet overtook the travelers and geographers and told their story in essence with that economy of words and fullness of spirit which only the poet commands. After dealing with the weird speculation and guesswork of the early map makers, and the fumbling and often tragic voyagers who finally enabled the accurate map of the world to emerge, Professor Lowes inquires:

14 *Ibid.*, pp. 2–3.

What has all this to do with "The Rime of the Ancient Mariner"? Well, here was a route from sea to sea, to which repeated use had given the familiarity of an established type. Ship after ship sailed south into the Atlantic, past the great skull-shaped westward rondure of Africa, across the Line, and down around the jutting shoulder of Brazil towards the Horn. They were driven . . . past the tempestuous headland into fields of floating ice. Once round the cape, they ran before the trade winds towards the Line again, to lie becalmed for days or weeks, under a heaven that was burning brass above them, in a tranced and breathless sea. Beyond which sea . . . we need not follow them. But that vast, sweeping curve, cutting the Equator, with its apex toward the pole, and bending up again from the white terrors of the austral ice to the long nightmare of equatorial calms — that mighty loop thrown around a continent from flaming heat to pitiless cold and back to heat again — not merely translate into living fact the fabulous barriers of the antique maps, but is also the graphic symbol of the track of a host of ships, the absorbing tales of which by the end of the eighteenth century, had been set down in books.[15]

Of Coleridge's log of his ship, which he set down in prose as the route of the Ancient Mariner, Professor Lowes says: "The basic structure of the voyage regarded as a voyage is as austerely true to fact as an Admiralty report. Yet that stark outline . . . is itself a compendium of the premonitory dreams, and the imaginative vision, and the intrepid daring of two-score generations. And now on this frame, as upon a loom, the imagination was to weave another, and this time a magic pattern." [16]

I feel sure that Professor Lowes would not have objected to my seizing on the figure of the loom and the magic pattern, and extending it beyond "The Rime of the Ancient Mariner" to an entire class of literature of which the Ancient Mariner is representative. Any reader of *The Road to Xanadu* will see that the author's primary purpose was "A study in the ways of the imagination," and "an attempt to get at the workings of the faculty itself." That is exactly what we are trying here,

15 Lowes, *The Road to Xanadu*, p. 123.
16 *Ibid.*, p. 125.

to get a glimmering of the relationship between the Great Frontier and human imagination as represented in modern literature. The loom and the magic pattern are therefore useful in presenting a vision of a gigantic literary action carried out on a stupendous scale. One side of the loom is the Metropolis, the other the Great Frontier, and as the shuttle of the imagination flew back and forth between the well known and the less well known it produced a fabric of literature which combined in its magic patterns the elements, the colors, shades, and tones of two worlds, one old and the other new.

In this view of literature as a tapestry woven in the frame of the Old World on one side and the New World on the other — a tapestry three centuries in the weaving — there is something epic. This literature tells the story of how the two worlds got acquainted, and how that getting acquainted was attended with many episodes, much tragedy, some comedy, all combined in a drama magnificent in its proportions. In the course of that drama we see the fusion, the slow mixture and blending of the elements of the old metropolitan culture with the strange new materials of the frontier world. It may be true that, as often said, the Metropolis conquered the frontier but it remains to be seen whether or not the frontier dictated the terms of its surrender. The two are now becoming one, and though contrasts still exist, they are due more to habit, tradition, and inertia than to lack of common knowledge. The period of fusion is about over, the loom is about full, the tapestry of an epoch is almost finished, and in the late weaving it is all but impossible to separate the elements derived from the frontier from those out of the Metropolis.

Let us look at the tapestry and see if we can recognize the episodes of the drama unfolded by literary men and other artists. There Camões celebrates in *The Lusiads* Da Gama's voyages to the East and the greatness of Portugal. He sings the feat of men who conquered the fear of the surrounding seas. Shakespeare's *The Tempest* rages around a new island of the Atlantic, and beyond in distant America the Utopians of More live as people should while those of Bacon's *New Atlantis* carry on their ideal life in a region equally remote. In the Pacific off the South American coast Robinson Crusoe tames his goats

and shows his superiority in a most egotistical manner over
Friday, while across the way in another ocean and in a lower
latitude all sorts of adventures take place around Treasure
Island. The Ancient Mariner makes his way in the frozen
Antarctic:

> The ice was here, the ice was there,
> The ice was all around:
> It cracked and growled, and roared and howled,
> Like noises in a swound!

And later that same ship and its distracted observer stuck becalmed in a still and rotting sea:

> Day after day, day after day,
> We stuck, nor breath nor motion;
> As idle as a painted ship
> Upon a painted ocean.

This is the center of the tapestry, but on the western margin
Leatherstocking moves in his simple way among a group of unreal but highly romantic red men and white women under the
facile pen of Cooper, while Mark Twain deals in more robust
and honest fashion with the doings of Tom Sawyer and Huck
Finn along the mighty river, and Walt Whitman and Herman
Melville sing their faith in the new society. In the realm of art
George Catlin is romanticizing the American Indian, along
with Alfred Jacob Miller and Karl Bodmer, while at a later
time Frederic Remington and Charlie Russell are filling the
popular western art galleries — which were saloons — and the
eastern magazines with representations of a half-imagined and
half-real cowboy life. Nor must we omit John James Audubon
sitting at his easel in the forests to record in lifelike manner
the birds of America in their native haunts as no one else has
ever done. These are only a few of the many subthemes worked
out by the men of imagination, patterns which make details
of the great canvas. Since we are dealing primarily with literature, we must leave to one side the historical pageant, the real
characters who were finding adventure, quick fortunes, and
sudden death among the more enduring men of the human

imagination. But it is important to bear in mind that among the deathless aristocracy of literature did move the real men, pirates knocking over treasure ships, conquistadors searching for El Dorados, Indian fighters, rivermen, freebooters, cowboys, and cattle kings: models and source books for the artists and writers who were making the record in print and on canvas.

As we look at the nearly completed tapestry we cannot fail to see that it belongs to a bygone age, to an era now ending. There is no room in the present world for such as the stuff our modern literature was made of. The imagination cannot play any more with the mystery and uncertainty of a half-known world, for there is no such thing. The map is finished, the roads are surveyed, and all the paths to that kind of adventure are plainly marked and tended. Da Gama would have a score of ports of safe call, and no hope of his voyage bringing glory to his country. Robinson Crusoe would be picked up by an airplane before he could make a pirogue or tame a goat. The Eldorados are sought by geophysicists and men with Geiger counters. The noble savage would be exposed in the next Sunday supplement by a sociologist or anthropologist who had seen him and measured his head both ways. The Ancient Mariner would be thrown out of the court of credibility if he claimed to be the first that ever burst into any sea. Cooper's Indians are drinking Coca-Cola on the reservation, Tom Sawyer would be lucky to escape a camp for underprivileged children, Russell and Remington would be painting horses that would frighten one — pictures that no saloonkeeper would tolerate, Audubon would be teaching ornithology to a few disinterested students and hoping for a grant from a foundation, and Walt Whitman would probably turn his savage genius on the frustrations of the democratic vista.

All this does not mean that with the passing of the frontier the human imagination will not still operate, that literature will not continue to be produced. It does mean that the imagination must make its way henceforth amidst a different set of conditions, that it must operate *among* men and not beyond them, that it must deal with what is well known rather than with what is only vaguely known. No more can the imagination sweep out from the Metropolis into the frontier and spin its fantastic tales of adventure and conquest. Man again has been turned back on himself to find his romance and adventure. If we may judge by current manifestations, literature is no longer concerned with man caught between an old world that is curious and a new one that is excitingly strange. It becomes more and more subjective, and seems to be concerned mainly with whether man is all sex or all psychology.

The end of an age is always touched with sadness for those who lived it and those who love it. That sadness is usually attended with much knowledge, some wisdom, and a sort of jaded sophistication. Neither knowledge nor wisdom brings happiness; more often they bring disillusionment. It would be very interesting to speculate on what the human imagination is going to do with a frontierless world where it must seek its inspiration in uniformity rather than in variety, in sameness rather than in contrast, in safety rather than in peril, in probing the harmless nuances of the known rather than the thundering uncertainties of unknown seas or continents. The dreamers, the poets, and the philosophers are after all but instruments which make vocal and articulate the hopes and aspirations and the fears of a people.

The people are going to miss the frontier more than words can express. For four centuries they heard its call, listened to its promises, and bet their lives and fortunes on its outcome. It calls no more, and regardless of how they bend their ears for its faint whisper they cannot hear the suggestion of a promise. The literary men have already caught up their frustration, and are making it the subject of their art. As yet no masterpiece may have come out of it, but there are fragments of writing which hint at what the human imagination may be able to do with the closed frontier.

John Steinbeck wrote a story entitled "The Leader of the People," about a small boy, Jody Tiflin, who lived on a western ranch with his father, Carl, and his mother. But in this story that family are only props for Jody's grandfather, his mother's father, who is coming for a visit. Carl Tiflin, an unimaginative and practical man, does not like Grandfather, who bores him by telling an old story, of how he led the people across the plains, how long ago they fought Indians, and overcame all the difficulties. Always the same story and Carl cannot stand the prospect of hearing it again.

"Well, how many times do I have to listen to the story of the iron plates, and the thirty-five horses? That time's done. Why can't he forget it, now it's done? . . . He came across the plains. All right! Now it's finished. Nobody wants to hear about it over and over. . . ."

Grandfather overheard Carl say this and of course he was deeply hurt, but not as one would expect him to be. He addressed Carl gently:

"I don't mind what you said, but it might be true, and I would mind that."

Carl, feeling sorry for having been honest, left, and Grandfather later justified himself to Jody.

"It wasn't Indians that were important, nor adventures, nor even getting out here. It was a whole bunch of people made into one big crawling beast. . . . It was westering and westering. Every man wanted something for himself, but the big beast that was all of them wanted only westering. . . . When we saw the mountains at last, we cried — all of us. But it wasn't getting here that mattered it was movement and westering.

"We carried life out here and set it down the way those ants carry eggs. And I was the leader. The westering was as big as God, and the slow steps that made the movement piled up until the continent was crossed.

"Then we came down to the sea, and it was done."

"Maybe I could lead the people some day," Jody said.

The old man smiled. "There's no place to go. There's the ocean to stop you. There's a line of old men along the shore hating the ocean because it stopped them."

"In boats, I might, sir."

"No place to go, Jody. Every place is taken. But that's not the worst — no, not the worst. Westering has died out of the people. Westering isn't a hunger any more. It's all done." [17]

[17] John Steinbeck, *The Red Pony* (New York: The Viking Press, 1945), pp. 129–30.

And so, as we linger in contemplation of the great tapestry of modern literature which .has left us images of what the human imagination did with a New World, we know that it represents a special kind of experience, that it is done, and our last impression as we turn away is that to many of us it was as big as God.

We should take a look at language, as an appendage to literature, to see what effect the Great Frontier had on it. The task would require a thorough knowledge of the principal European languages, and a long and patient study of each of them. Language, like muscles, develops when it has something to do, and, therefore, it may best be approached through the tasks it had to perform. It is quite probable that language growth, by which is meant the introduction of new words and expansion of vocabulary, has taken place mainly in two fields: one is science and the other is the frontier. These are the two big things that modern man has had to deal with, think about, and write about. In the realm of science man has tended to revert to Greek and Latin in an effort to build a vocabulary that could be universally understood; the general adoption of the Linnaean system of naming genera and species is a good example of this reversion to the past for scientific nomenclature. The growth of a vocabulary for science grew out of a combination of terms already familiar to educated people equipped with Greek and Latin dictionaries.

The growth of language in the other area, out on the frontier, was of another sort, for the most part independent of the Metropolis. The explorers, the first finders of things to be named, were not scholars. If they had dictionaries in their luggage, they had no time to consult them, and could have read them with difficulty. It mattered not. They found something new and they had to have a name for it, one on which they could hang a description. Therefore they gave to what they found a *common* name, something of the people, in the vernacular. At the time the New World was discovered, the national languages were emerging and struggling with Latin for supremacy. This is reflected in the writings of scholars who stuck to Latin through Erasmus, and even in Thomas

More's *Utopia*. There can be little doubt that the hosts of men, literate but not highly educated, returning from the frontier with a cargo of new words to describe the new plants and animals and peoples, threw those new words into the balance to turn the scales against Latin and in favor of the common languages. The returning adventurers wrote their reports in Spanish, English, French, or Dutch, thus piling up a volume of literature, vibrant with life and action, which was bound in time to smother the ancient forms under the vernaculars. The scientists might come later to apply Latin names to the new forms of life, plant and animal, but the scientists were late comers, and before they got around to the job, the national languages had found names preferred by the people.

The language grew in all the frontier because there were new things to talk about. In the United States it has grown to such an extent that it is becoming recognized as the *American* language. "These States," wrote Walt Whitman, "are rapidly supplying themselves with new words, called for by new occasions, new facts, new policies, new combinations. . . . The appetite of the people of The States, in popular speeches and writings, is for unhemmed latitude, coarseness, directness, live epithets, expletives, words of opprobrium, resistance." [18]

There was a general borrowing all along the line. For example, the Indians or the natives had a nomenclature of their own, and the first Europeans had borrowed these names, often corrupting them to their tongue's convenience. Skunk, opossum, squaw, papoose, wigwam, caucus, are examples. Again the explorers would see an animal and name it for something its appearance suggested. Such are prairie dog (ground squirrel), horned frog, jack rabbit. The jack rabbit, which is not a rabbit but a hare, was named by American soldiers who, seeing it for the first time, were reminded of an animal with which they had been familiar, and hence jackass rabbit, later shortened to jack rabbit. We have seen that in terms of common names the Europeans had to find words for more than a thousand new varieties and species of animals.

There was also much borrowing as among the European

18 Quoted in H. L. Mencken, *The American Language* (4th ed., New York: Alfred A. Knopf, 1941), p. 74.

languages. If the Spaniards named an animal, and the English liked the name, they borrowed it. The word frontier is an example, coming through the French into English. The vocabulary was also enriched by proper names which had been taken over from the natives. How much more attractive to the ear are Mississippi, Missouri, Dakota, Minnesota, Susquehanna, and Tombigbee than would be some European name with the prefix *New* to distinguish it. Even the name of Chicago — meaning the place of the skunk — may be preferred over New Manchester or New Birmingham. Certainly the Mississippi Bubble, by almost any other name, would have had less sucker appeal in Paris.

The volume of language growth due to the development of science and that due to the opening of the frontier cannot be measured or compared. It may be pointed out, however, that there is a fundamental difference in character. Whereas science has made its additions primarily by recombining or reapplying Greek and Latin words, old and well known to scholars, to new phenomena or objects, the frontier added something entirely original, terms not known to the metropolitan culture. These terms represent the net gain to the dictionaries, and make the languages richer for the poets and for the people.[19]

2. The Arts

The emergence of a modern art in harmony with modern culture challenges our consideration. Throughout this study it has been contended that in a society there must be an over-all harmony among the various institutions, a sort of composition as in painting which focuses attention on the primary force, or forces, dominating the society. The Great Frontier has been one of the dominating forces in Western civilization since 1500, powerful enough to effect changes in all aspects of modern life. The purpose here is to discover how the Great Frontier has influenced art.

We have already seen that in many areas the forces issuing

[19] For the influence of the frontier on the English language see James T. Gillespie, *The Influence of Oversea Expansion on England until 1700*, chap. X, pp. 305 ff. See also H. L. Mencken, *The American Language*, an invaluable source for the derivation of American words.

from the Great Frontier have found themselves in conflict with those older ones from the Metropolis, and in many cases the ancient forces have had to yield something and often much to the barbaric strength of the frontier ingredient. Granting the presence of a new factor, we may visualize a contest, a conflict between the ideas newly emerging from the Great Frontier and those present·in the Metropolis. Viewed in that way, the Metropolis seems to be trying to expand its culture into the frontier, which resents the intrusion and undertakes to develop a culture of its own.

It can perhaps be stated as an axiom that a frontier people assume that their makeshift culture is inferior to that of the Metropolis from which they came until there is definite proof to the contrary. In some cases the contest can be resolved by a war, a bank statement, or a ballot, resolved in such a way as to convince both sides that a solution has been found. But there is no tangible basis for a test of strength in the arts, no way of settling the art issue so that the decision will be accepted by both sides. It cannot be done at the council table. In such circumstances each party goes its own way until the divergence is such as to reveal that each has developed its own art as an expression of its own genius. The fact that one side may deny the validity of the other's art is beside the point.

It is not the purpose here to discuss the arts as developed in the lands of the Great Frontier and contrast them with those of the Metropolis. We can, however, take the United States — the leading frontier country — and try to determine the special nature of its artistic life and the direction it is going. If the investigation reveals a divergence so extreme that the product cannot be accepted by the devotees of European art as art at all, we need not be much surprised. We can only say that, after all, America has developed something of its own, and if what it has developed is art, it is indigenous and American. This independent American "art" will now be examined with a view to showing its relation to the frontier.

For convenience we may differentiate the peculiar art with which we shall be concerned as the vernacular art in order to distinguish it from the long-accepted forms which may be called the conventional or traditional art. The traditional art is European in origin with ideals and practices in harmony with European life. Its canons, laws, and ideals were imported into America (into a frontier society) where conditions were so different as to make it appear as something exotic, unrelated to American experience. This proper art has not been well understood by the people, but it has been maintained and defended by some, most stoutly by such expatriates as Ben Franklin spoke of and as Henry James was. To these art-conscious people, America appeared bleak, ugly, repulsive, raw if not yet rotten. Henry James thus described in negative terms what America meant — what all frontier countries meant to the artists of the conventional tradition:

> No sovereign, no court, no personal loyalty, no aristocracy, no church, no clergy, no army, no diplomatic service, no country gentlemen, no palaces, no castles, no manners, nor old country-houses, nor parsonages, nor thatched cottages, nor ivied ruins; no cathedrals, nor abbeys, nor little Norman churches; no great Universities, nor public schools . . . ; no literature, no novels, no museums, no pictures, no political society, no sporting class. . . .[20]

How in heaven's name could such a country have any art? How can art be built in a cultural vacuum? What can be its nucleus? We shall see later how Henry James let the art of the New World pass him by, so completely that he himself admitted that he could not understand it, nor penetrate its meaning. It was as unfathomable to him as European art was to

[20] Quoted from John A. Kouwenhoven, *Made in America: The Arts in Modern Civilization* (Garden City: Doubleday Co., 1938), pp. 208–9. I am indebted to the above study for what is set forth here about the vernacular and the relation of American art to technology. Though some may differ with Kouwenhoven, his claim that America has contributed to art through technology should not be dismissed except by those who are unwilling to accept as art anything that does not have moss on it. Unless we are willing to concede that art can grow, can manifest itself in new forms, we must conclude that it is finished if not dead. The vernacular is offered as an *addition* to the traditional and not as a substitute. The vernacular is offered as an enrichment of what already is accepted as art. In the discussion, the term functional is used several times. No one should conclude that we are contending that art must be functional to be art. We are only contending that art may emerge from that which functions. The vernacular as set forth by Kouwenhoven in his significant book is an example. The quoted passages are used by permission of the publishers.

Mark Twain. Obviously America could not create an art around a culture which it did not have, and what is more it could not import sovereign, court, aristocracy, clergy, country gentlemen, thatched cottages and cathedrals, and all the rest in order to have something to write about and to paint. Had it done so, it would have been inherently dishonest, and art, whatever else it may be, must have integrity.

Where, then, and in what field could Americans develop an art that would be honest and in harmony with their lives? This is where the vernacular comes in. But the vernacular is only the name for what we are going to talk about. The term itself is interesting and very suggestive here. It comes from the Latin *vernaculus*, meaning born in one's house, native. *Verna*, of which *vernaculus* is the diminutive, means a slave born in his master's house, a native of uncertain origin. It means, as applied to language, something developed in and spoken or used by the people of a particular place, region, or country. Though the dictionary does not say so, the term formerly implied something crude, almost vulgar, as the vernacular languages in comparison with the more aristocratic Latin.

Here in the word's history is something very illuminating about the arts that were to develop in America — vernacular arts. They are native, born in the house, and of uncertain origin. They may never have been slaves to the masters of the old conventional arts of Europe, but they were — and may still be in some quarters — looked upon as bastards in the family of art. Like bastards they have proved themselves quite lusty, able to shift for themselves, and they may eventually procure the papers of legitimacy. The vernacular arts are not quite those of the proper family, but they are sufficient for their own purposes and, as we shall see, they are getting by. They are in short the arts of the whole people, lowly, simple, functional in a high degree.

We are told that the genius of the medieval society was expressed when the people all pitched in to build what was to them the most important thing in their lives, a place of worship, a cathedral. The result was a special form of architecture, vernacular to the Roman tradition but quite appropriate to the medieval society and now accepted as a most respectable class of traditional art. Thus it is that when a whole people

set in to build something that they all want, something they
can all understand, and that will serve their chief purpose,
they are likely to come out in the end with something pregnant
with art. The American people have not seen fit to build cathedrals, though they set great store by those left in Europe, but
they have built nevertheless. And what they have built is as
native to them as the cathedral was to the medieval European.

It is necessary here in order to get at the American genius to
refer to the section in Chapter Two entitled "The Religion of
Work." In discussing the vernacular arts, Kouwenhoven talked
primarily about machines. We accept his machines, but need
to get back of them to their *raison d'être*, the driving universal
desire that produced them. We have seen that the American,
set down in the wilderness of the frontier, was destitute of
most of James's catalogue of cultural blessings, and that he
had gumption enough to turn his energy to what would be rewarding in the environment that held him. What paid off was
not poetry, architecture, painting, or sculpture. Geniuses in
any of these fields would have starved to death on the frontier
regardless of their performance. What paid off on the frontier was work, of one sort or another, work that was *useful* in
the narrow practical sense. Now this compulsion to work was
in itself a democratizing influence, tending to level men, to
unite them in a common experience, to rub out distinctions.
The ideals set up to govern the society were derived from
work, *useful* work as Franklin liked to emphasize. Just as the
whole medieval society wanted to build a cathedral, so did a
whole frontier society eventually come to the point where it
wanted to do a great deal of work; and just as the universal
desire for a place of worship led to the creation of an architectural masterpiece, so did the universal desire to do a lot of
work lead the Americans to create masterpieces which when
put together in machines enabled them to do more work than
all the rest of the world put together. The machines are the
products of that desire, of that attitude, something incidental
to a greater purpose. They were created because there was
material to work on and a material heaven — prosperity — at
the end. Prosperity, born of the abundance around them, was
their goal; the work and the machines were the means of reaching it. They had an opportunity on the frontier which they

did not have in Europe with its castles and kings and country gentlemen, and they made the most of it.

It may be now, though we hope not, that machines mold men and determine what their lives will be; but in the beginning men molded, not machines, but tools, the axe, the rifle, the canoe. They improved these things because they had more trees to cut, more game to kill, and more rivers to navigate than they had ever had before. Nothing but the best was good enough for them.

We have seen that the vernacular is of low origin, that it is not invented but grows bit by bit anonymously among the people. Therefore we find it impossible to determine with certainty who streamlined the axe, made it American so that it would bite deeper into the giant trees and come out with less bind. We only know that in the American forests the axe evolved a lovely form, a gracefully curved handle, a functional perfection which enables it to exert more power than any other manual tool yet invented. It is finished, and it was finished by the American woodsmen and the blacksmiths who served them — nameless men of the people. The American rifle is another instrument that had a similar history. The idea of a rifled gunbarrel came from Germany, but in the forests of Pennsylvania and by the streams of Kentucky it evolved in the hands of gunsmiths until it was the best weapon, and the most dangerous individual weapon in the world. Before it was displaced, it had taken on a grace and beauty which makes the surviving specimens a delight to the eye. Neither the axe nor the rifle developed because men wanted to be artists; they developed because men wanted to cut down trees, shoot game, and because there were trees to cut down and game and Indians that had to be shot. The axe and the rifle are examples of the vernacular art, valuable as examples because they are uncomplicated highly functional folk masterpieces.

With his eye on technology, Kouwenhoven in his exposition proceeds from the simple tool to the complicated machines which surround us today, expounding the rational view that they are also American masterpieces of art. When we follow his analysis, examine his illustrations, we see that by and large the purpose behind the machines and the intricate devices was to get work done. When the machine or the architectural form finally arrives, and it arrives only because it works, we have something that functions, that gratifies the predominating desire of the mass of the people. The resulting art is incidental to the function, not an end in itself. In this sense work is the common denominator of the American masterpieces, from the beautifully functional axe to the great Corliss engine, to the lovely locomotive pulling a hundred freight cars and a million tons of merchandise, to the bulldozer rooting foundations for skyscrapers, tearing down forests, destroying hills to fill up gorges — the great clanging, beautiful, brutal symphony of useful work! The crowds that pause to watch the great wheels turn in a power house, to gaze with rapture at the majestic train, and to gape with awe at the almost human shovels rooting foundations are the devotees of American art, the unselfconscious worshippers at the shrine of the religion of work.

It was pointed out in Chapter Two that the American folk heroes are nearly all workers, and to the industrious crew already mentioned should be added a comparative newcomer, the Jackhammer Man. As he hammers away at tunnels and ports he sings:

> I'm Jackhammer John, I'm a Jackhammer man;
> Born with a Jackhammer in my hand!
>
> I'm a Jackhammer Man from a Jackhammer town;
> I built every port from the North Pole down; . . .
>
> Hammered in the mill, hammered in the mines;
> Been in jail about a thousand times.

Woody Guthrie worked and sang his way across the continent and records his impressions in the Spring issue of *Common Ground* of 1942, in an article entitled "Ear Players." As he sees it, work and singing are closely related.

> Work is the thing. The biggest and best thing you can sing about is work — songs where the very time itself is set to the rhythm of a fast whistling train, or a steamboat lost in the fog, or an air-hammer sucking wind, a horse loping home, the rattle and banging of a red-hot steel mill, or the quiet booming and chugging of a new oil field as you look off across the country.
> Work is the thing. Just learn where the work is: that's where

you'll find real honest American music and songs being made up.

Once we accept work as the common denominator of a people, we need not worry about democracy, for work is a democratizing and at the same time a unifying influence. The people of America did not work because they were democratic, but they became democratic through work. When John Smith ordained that those who wanted to eat must work, he proclaimed a democratic principle and knocked aristocracy out of the saddle. Ben Franklin said, "In short, America is the land of labor." Americans, he said, do not ask of the stranger: *"What is he?"* They only ask, *"What can he do?"* The manner in which the individual American answered that question determined his place in the hierarchy of a working society. The greatest danger to a democratic society is to separate men devoted to work from the privilege of doing it!

But Kouwenhoven tells us that the arts in America have come upon us unawares through a marriage of democracy and technology. It must be admitted that his most compelling examples are derived, with the possible exception of jazz music, from the technological side of the house. From the axe and the rifle, the author goes on to work with that material which was most abundant in America, namely, wood, but here he shifts from the objects made to the machinery that made them. The objects made might be arty in the conventional tradition, but the machines that made them — that did the work — threw off all superficialities and became functional. They would tolerate no foolishness.

The Centennial Exposition, held at Philadelphia in 1876, gave America an opportunity to take stock of itself, and unconsciously furnished the finest example of the contrast between the conventional and the vernacular art. The buildings themselves were in every architectural style, prettied up on the surface at least. There were art galleries and fashion displays, but there was one building known as Machinery Hall where were assembled the latest examples of American mechanical ingenuity. It was not enough that these machines should sit there, to be looked at, like Egyptian mummies in a museum. They were not — at least, not yet — museum pieces. They must still work, demonstrate that they would work. In order for them to work, they had to have power, and to furnish power the Corliss steam engine was installed and all the machinery hitched to it. This engine turned out to be an unheralded masterpiece of the exhibition. It was strictly functional with no overlay of conventional art. It had a job to do, and everything was sacrificed to getting it done. Because it lacked ornamentation, commentators thought the public would not be impressed by it. They admitted, however, that it — like the good workman it was — looked better in motion than idle. Evidently it had been built by men who accepted the canon of vernacular art expressed by William Sellers, who said, "if a machine was right, it would *look* right." The great Corliss engine, weighing 1,700,000 pounds, stunned and fascinated the public.

> People said all the fine things that duty required about the pictures and statues in Memorial Hall, but in the presence of the Corliss engine they were exalted. It stood there at the center of a twelve-acre building, towering forty feet above its platform, not an idealization but an unmitigated fact. Yet to the thousands who saw it, it was more than merely the motive power for the miles of shafting which belted their energy to machines throughout the building.
>
> Consciously or unconsciously, each visitor in his own way testified to its aesthetic impact. . . .
>
> Not often were the technological elements of our environment welded into such a vernacular masterpiece.[21]

Having established his concept of a vernacular art, Kouwenhoven follows it and applies it to the various forms, clearly enough in machinery design, in architecture and engineering, and less clearly in the less practical fields of painting, literature, and music. It seems that the people have been torn between the necessities of the practical and native on the one hand and the ideals of the traditional on the other, and that they have first insisted on overlaying the honest functional features with conventional ornamentation. For example, the pioneers built simple and functional houses, but as soon as they were able they "modernized" them by adding arty features, borrowed from

21 *Ibid.*, pp. 29–30.

without. The engineer and the architect have often been at war, the one sticking to function, the other insisting on extraneous additions to conform to traditional ideals.

Americans have made two important contributions in the field of architecture. One is the "balloon frame" house and the other is the skyscraper. The first was a concession to the hurry of building new homes, mainly in the West; the second is a concession to the use of steel and cement in the place of stone. In Europe the residence was built by the use of heavy timbers, set upright at the four corners of the structure and held together by heavy cross members mortised into the uprights. With the invention of nails the Americans adopted a light form by framing the whole structure with 2 × 4's, doubled at the corners for added strength — the ordinary American frame house, which seems flimsy in comparison with the sturdier European type.

The skyscraper is something else. It was made possible by the use of structural steel and concrete, but in the beginning the architects were not content to leave the buildings in their honest simplicity. They insisted on facing them with heavy stone to give the impression that they were in the tradition. It required the boldest architects and builders to accept steel and cement for what they are, and to build such structures as the McGraw-Hill Building in New York, which proclaims to all that it is what it is — a building of steel, concrete, and glass.

The most striking illustration of the conflict between the traditional and the vernacular is that of the George Washington Bridge in New York, said to be the most beautiful bridge in the world. Its present beauty is what may be called an artistic accident. The bridge was, of course, designed and built by engineers. It is supported by and suspended from two towers 635 feet high. These towers were constructed of the only material that could have done the job, steel beams and girders, open air skeletons outlined against the sky. In the eyes of the architects, this would never do. Therefore the plans required that these towers should be covered with "concrete casing faced with granite." That would make them look just as substantial as they already were, even though neither the concrete nor the granite would be doing any work. The towers were built and the great span put in, a thing of such startling grace and beauty as had not been seen before. Here the people stepped in on behalf of a great masterpiece of art, and thus far have had their way.

[For] as the 635-foot steel skeletons of the towers rose from the shores of the river, something unprecedented happened. The "unexpected" functional beauty of the naked steelwork fascinated people, and there was a widespread popular protest against applying the masonry covering which, according to the original plan, was to be the chief element in the aesthetic appeal of the bridge. So far as the present writer knows [1948], the Port of New York Authority has never taken formal action to abandon the original design, and it is still theoretically possible that the towers will be cased in concrete and stone. The protest which prevented the "aesthetic" treatment of the towers was, after all, almost entirely a popular one, and the time may come when our betters in these matters will decide to go ahead with the design which they believed would best cast credit on our generation's taste. For to many people, apparently, it still seems difficult to believe that pure mathematics and engineering expediency can by themselves produce something beautiful.[22]

The passage conveys one author's belief that the genius of American art is a vernacular which has arisen from devotion to that which is functional, and which because it is functional, receives the approval of the people. If it turns out that most of the acknowledged masterpieces are found in the field of technology, or are related to it as in the case of sculptors who started as stone masons and artists who started as mechanics, then it seems apparent that the Americans have erected their temples to work just as the medievalists erected theirs to religious aspirations.

If the view is correct, then America has its art, separate and distinct from that of the Old World. We need not quarrel as to whether it had its origins here or in Europe; and as to where it developed and flowered there can be no quarrel. Its masterpieces are invading the far corners of the world, wherever automobiles and bulldozers run, wherever assembly lines are installed, wherever work is to be lifted from human muscles and done in quantity and quality unmatched by any

22 *Ibid.*, pp. 248–49.

other people. Unlike all other art, and especially that which Henry James must have had in mind when he made his catalogue of America's desolation, it is singing a song, singing to the common people the song of joyous work.

It is not strange that when Henry James returned to America in the latter years of his life, he was confused by what he found here. The art of America, lacking kings and courts, castles and country gentlemen, cathedrals and manners, and all the impedimenta which the disillusioned expatriate thought so essential to the cultured life, had passed him by. As he gazed at the skyscrapers they were to him "a world of immovably-closed doors. Behind those doors, to be sure, there was immense material for the artist, but he reluctantly concluded that it was beyond the reach of a writer who, like himself, had 'so early and so fatally' withdrawn from contacts which might have initiated him into the life which the skyscrapers symbolized." [23] There are still Henry Jameses in the land who see art as something apart from life, but they have less excuse for their attitude than James had because now a few independent writers with much insight have opened the immovable doors to reveal the genius if not the art of a people. There are some who will hold that axes, rifles, bulldozers, and skyscrapers are just those things and no part of art.

As already stated, the American vernacular is less distinguishable in literature, painting, and sculpture than it is in the strictly technological fields. Still there is apparent throughout the common and practical touch of a whole people, not differentiated into classes. Walt Whitman is the outstanding spokesman of the group in literature, though Mark Twain is also an example. When Carl Sandburg sings of Chicago's stockyards he comes in the vernacular tradition. It is in the treatment of jazz, the American contribution to music, that the ways of the Americans are made plain. Nor need the fact that jazz emerged from the red light district of New Orleans' colored section, conflict with the definition of the vernacular as something of low origin. A jazzband leader said that in jazz "it is every man for himself." The intriguing statement is clarified by Kouwenhoven's analysis, which points out that jazz is

[23] *Ibid.*, pp. 206–7.

a combination of group co-operation and free individual wanderings of the members who compose the band.

> What we have here . . . is an art form which within its own well-recognized limits comes closer than any other we have devised to reconciling the . . . conflict between the claims of the individual and of the group. Everybody in a first-class jazz band seems to be — and has all the satisfaction of feeling that he is — going his own way, uninhibited by a prescribed musical pattern, and at the same time all are performing in a dazzlingly precise creative unison. The thing that holds them together is the very thing they are always flouting: the fundamental four-four beat. In this one artistic form, if nowhere else, Americans have found a way to give expression to the Emerson ideal of a union which is perfect only "when all the uniters are isolated." [24]

This discussion of the vernacular art suggests something important about American civilization. The thing revealed is the seamless quality, an over-all unity, and a harmony of various parts. One would not ordinarily see a relation between a skyscraper and jazz, yet that relationship was perceived by the brilliant French architect who described a Manhattan skyscraper as "hot jazz in stone and steel." Here in America was a classless society, lacking the very bases of art in the traditional sense, that turned out to be homogeneous and democratic in nature, and yet at the same time highly individualistic. Since most individuals were bent on material gain, the society became polarized toward the practical and the useful, toward work, something that all could understand. Therefore the greatest social premium was placed on whatever would speed the many jobs to be done, and the result was the development of the technological masterpieces. In politics the same idea of equality — which is inherent in a classless society — asserted itself in democratic forms. In the prevailing religion, Protestantism, there was also the same unifying influence, equal independence of each from the other, and a direct dependence on God. In economics, in politics, in religion, and in architecture there was the ideal of the common weal; no man was to be

24 *Ibid.*, p. 264.

excluded, and with few exceptions none was to be discriminated against. In each case the goal was clear enough, but the method of achieving it was left to the judgment of the individual. Hence there was co-operation and unity in the general theme, but great variety in the pursuit of it. Therefore, like the members of the jazz band, individuals were continually flouting the thing that held them together. In the end the philosophers arrived to provide a rational basis for such apparently irrational action. The philosophers decided that whatever works is right, and thus the "system" of pragmatism was born to explain the harmony in a society which had long been acting on the pragmatic principle.

When we look at American life in this way, we can perhaps see in its confused and ever-changing patterns a unity and proportion — rough-hewn and rude though it may be — that we have not seen before; we may detect an unsuspected harmony buried from the superficial view by its heavy overlay of apparently irrelevant individual antics. American civilization has pursued its theme like a good jazz band in which every player is all the time eagerly watching for his chance to take off on an unannounced solo performance. He who does may strike high and haunting notes of joy or sorrow or violent protest against what is going on, but he cannot tarry long; he must return after his joyous excursion in independence to merge with the group in the common pursuit of the common theme. Though in American life it has been every man for himself, there has been a deep harmony in the confusion among men who made no assumption about class, who were practical, who were willing to work, to accept whatever would work in their interest. If the results have incidentally led to the production of an indigenous art, men will, in spite of conventional ideals, accept that too. And the measure of the influence the frontier had in leveling artificial distinctions, in making men practical, in turning them toward work, is the measure of the effect of the frontier on American art in its broadest sense.

The discussion of the vernacular took us in the direction of men who built such useful things as bridges and skyscrapers, in the direction of the architect and the engineer. Therefore we may inquire as to how the frontier touched these two professions. The subject can best be approached by viewing the task, and the opportunity confronting the builders of whatever order as a result of the opening up of the Great Frontier, a task extending over four centuries. If in 1500 the architects and engineers could have been told that in the next four centuries they would have the job of laying out great cities like New York, Chicago, New Orleans, Montreal, Capetown, Sydney, Melbourne, of building such capital cities as Washington, Ottawa, and Canberra, not to mention state capitols, they would have been aghast at the prospect. In addition they had to bridge the rivers, tunnel the mountains, construct highways and railroads, build great universities and public buildings, all over the new continents.

Their opportunity was unusual — we might say unique — in two respects. In the first place, they could begin their work on clean and uncluttered ground, where no man had built permanently before. They did not have to compromise with things already done, with buildings established, with vested interests. They had a latitude of choice which they had not had before and which they will not have again. In the second place, they were surrounded by an abundance of material such as men had never known before and never can know again. This material consisted of untouched forests offering every sort of building timber and untouched mineral deposits of iron and other metals. Throughout this age the architect needed to give little thought to economy of building timber, as anyone can see by looking at some of his Victorian productions. Of these things he used all he could and more than he should in the interest of good taste.

For heavier structures he learned to use steel, and in the beginning the iron ore seemed as abundant as the forests. The steel, like the timber, was cheap, and the price of it declined constantly until the turn of the twentieth century. Today every builder knows that the rich iron deposits of the Mesabi Range are approaching depletion, and that American producers are seeking new deposits in Canada and other places. Every architect knows that neither timber nor steel is any longer inexpensive, and he may well suspect that it never will be again. The frantic search for substitutes for both steel and timber in building indicates that the architect's and the engineer's task is changing.

It is when we view the whole construction job of the Western World that we see the architect and engineer riding the crest of the building boom which lasted from the time the frontiers were opened up to the time they closed. The room and the materials were so abundant, employment so generous and the patrons so prosperous that the clerks were always at the drafting boards. The situation was one that promoted the highest form of individual action based on private contract with little dependence on the crafts or on the state.

If this boom is now drawing to a close, we are in position to hazard some observations on what the future holds for the architect and the building profession, to say nothing of what it promises the rest of us.

1. The architect is faced with the problem growing out of a constantly increasing scarcity of natural building materials, especially timber and iron ore. More and more he must seek substitutes in clay, stone, and synthetic materials.

2. Because building materials are less abundant, the price of them is bound to increase in proportion to the scarcity. In the end, unless the architects or others solve the problem, a great many potential clients will be priced out of the architect's office. Actually many have already been.

3. It follows that the architects will design relatively fewer individual homes and more and more communal and institutionalized dwelling places. The architects will deal more and more with apartment builders, and more and more with housing authorities, municipal, state and national. The architects in time will become institutionalized, working for a salary rather than for fees.

4. The architects concerned with city planning will lack the opportunity to build a New York or Chicago or a Washington on clean ground. They have before them a far more difficult task of *rebuilding* the present cities to meet changing needs.

If what I have said here has any validity, it means that the architects and engineers of today, along with the rest of us, stand near the end of a great age of history, the Age of the Frontier. We are poised on the threshold of a new age the nature of which none of us can foresee. We are equipped with ideas and institutions and modes of thinking and acting which arose in response to a unique situation which no longer exists. While we cannot foresee the future, or say how present problems may be solved, we can be quite sure that the future will require us to make many adjustments whether we like it or not. The architect or the engineer cannot escape the net of circumstances in which he is caught, but if he can understand the forces operating on him, on the society, he can do a better job of adapting his means to compulsory ends. Despite decreasing materials, increasing populations, and ever higher costs, he may find a way to design homes and other structures that will give men comfort, beauty and utility, on terms that will preserve the individual's self-respect.

3. Education

To trace out the influence of the frontier on the human intellect as reflected in scientific and humanistic fields would require a study of modern civilization in all its aspects. In this sketch consideration will be limited to those institutions designed to train young people at the elementary, secondary, and college or university levels, limited to the education of youth from, let us say, the age of seven to twenty-five. Our problem is to see whether the frontier contributed anything to the origin and foundation of the elaborate system of public free schools which is now accepted as an integral part of the social order, to the philosophy behind the system, and to the means by which it was established and is supported. The inquiry might be extended to all countries, but for practical reasons it will be confined to the United States, and finally illustrated by the example of one state, Texas. The selection of the United States is advisable because that country led the way in establishing the public free school system which now exists in some form in most civilized countries. Texas offers an extreme example of the application of the principle of public free school origin and support previously developed by the older states and the nation. It is that principle, namely economic support, that will receive chief attention.

Given the concept of political democracy as it developed in

the United States, and the further concept of separation of church and state which is a corollary of democracy, the necessity for a broad and general education of the citizenry is obvious. In proposing a revision of the Virginia Code of Laws in 1781, Thomas Jefferson, after outlining a system of schools from the elementary grades to the university, said that one purpose of the revision was "to diffuse knowledge more generally through the mass of the people." He added that "every government degenerates when trusted to the rulers of the people alone. The people, themselves, are its only safe depositories. And to render even them safe, their minds must be improved to a certain degree. . . . The influences over government must be shared by all the people." [25] Sam Houston said that "the benefits of education and of useful knowledge, generally diffused through a community, are essential to the preservation of a free government"; and Mirabeau Lamar, another president of Texas, who rarely agreed with Houston on anything, believed that a "cultivated mind is the guardian genius of Democracy. . . . It is the only dictator that freemen acknowledge, and the only security which freemen desire." [26] The sentiments expressed by the Virginian and by the Texans were voiced over and over across the nation, and everywhere thoughtful men tried to convince the indifferent ones that schools must, in the interest of the new society, be both public and free.

Once the theory of public education was established, the next problem was the practical one of finding the means with which to found and support a system of free schools that would fulfill the need for educating all the people. Obviously such a system would cost money, a great deal of it, and those with money were not ready to pay for the education of other people's children. Therefore, progress toward free schools was slow and halting, and the story too long to follow here. At the present time, when a social need is keenly felt, the practice is to go to the state capital or to the national capital or to both for a grant. But in those early days money was hard to come by, and it was a part of the freedom the frontier had en-

[25] *Notes on Virginia*, ed. of 1853, Richmond, Va., pp. 157–58 and 160.
[26] These two quotations by two of the presidents of the Republic of Texas appear on all publications issued by the University of Texas.

gendered in the Americans that made them reluctant to pay taxes to the state, and there was no law requiring them to pay any tax directly to the federal government. From what source then could the schools be subsidized *without* taxes, without collecting money from anyone or appropriating money to any educational institution?

The frontier furnished the answer to that question by supplying a school subsidy without imposing taxes. The government owned the public domain, land that had never been alienated, and this land it could and did give generously to encourage public education and get it started. This gift of frontier land was an entering wedge to which no one would object because it could be given without taxes. Once the wedge was driven, and public free schools got under way, taxes would be required, but that was a bridge that lay far ahead and out of sight of most of the people. For the present, then as now, what the government gave, the people would accept, regardless of ultimate cost.

The extent to which lands were given to support schools in the thirteen colonies prior to the Revolution need not be dealt with here except to say that, from the first, lands were used to subsidize all sorts of worthwhile projects, including schools. The part the lands played in making education a function of the state instead of a church affair is worth noting. In all cases the land given *belonged* to the state, and after the Revolution the bulk of frontier land belonged to the central government. There was no desire on the part of informed people, such as Jefferson and others half as thoughtful, to see any church become a landholder such as it was at that time in Europe. The niggardliness of the states and the refusal of the federal government to grant land subsidies to church schools had the effect of hastening the secularization of education and making it an affair of the state and not of the church. If the church instead of the sovereign had owned the public domain in America, the results would no doubt have been quite different.

As a result of the American Revolution the former crown lands became the property of the separate states, and by agreement among them the western territory was transferred to the federal authority. The former crown lands had become a public domain — public, not royal. The extent of the public domain at that time was 406,518.41 square miles or 259,171,-787 acres. Later additions of territory increased the public domain to 2,889,175.91 square miles, or 1.85 billion acres. A trifling portion of this vast domain had already passed into private hands, but the amount was so small as to be inconsequential. It was from this public domain that the public free school system was subsidized, and promoted.

The part played by the public lands in founding free education in the United States is set forth by Senator Lister Hill of Alabama. He says that the American capacity for organization and production is the result of two American aspirations about education. The first was the idea of public support for schools, and the second was the use of revenues from public lands for the support of the system desired. In the following paragraphs he summarizes the role of the public lands in encouragement of education at all levels:

> From the earliest beginnings in colonial times many of the colonies earmarked public lands for the support of schools. The first case was in Virginia in 1618. Colleges started with the aid of land grants in the various colonies include Harvard in Massachusetts, William and Mary in Virginia, Yale in Connecticut, Princeton in New Jersey, and others in South Carolina and Georgia. After the American Revolution, when individual states laid claim to the territories west of the Appalachians, Congress wisely ruled against them, and in 1785 and 1787 passed ordinances which specifically set aside a portion of the public lands west of the mountains for school purposes. Many of the great state universities were started with the aid of these lands. And the policy was greatly extended when the Morrill Act, passed by Congress in 1862 and signed into law by President Abraham Lincoln, established our magnificent system of land-grant colleges, which play such an important part in our public system of higher education — particularly in the South and West.
>
> Out of this farsighted and inspired use of a portion of the national domain has arisen a system of great educational institutions upon which the higher education of a great number of Americans depends. No one can estimate what it has meant to the development and progress of the United States. Along with the application of public funds for free education for all

at the primary and secondary level, it has contributed vastly to that trained competence — in industry, in agriculture, in social organization — upon which our national strength is based: a trained competence, not of a selected few, but of a whole nation.[27]

Colonel Richard Bland, delegate from Virginia, seems to have made the first proposal to the Congress of the Confederation for a land grant by the central government for public education. On June 5, 1783, he proposed that one tenth of the income from territory ceded by Virginia be applied to the support of seminaries, of the civil list, and to the erection of frontier forts, but nothing came of his proposal.

For the next step, or a most important one, I quote Edith Parker:

> The Congress of the Confederation in 1784 appointed a committee, headed by Thomas Jefferson, to make recommendations for a public land policy. The report of this committee was the basis of the Land Ordinance of 1785. Provisions, not contained in the report, were introduced during the debate in Congress, for both church and school support, but the reservation for religion was struck out "rather by the way in which the vote was taken than by design." The influence of New England colonial practices is evident in the Ordinance of 1785, both in the system of settlement adopted and in the school reservation policy. The educational provision reads: "There shall be reserved the lot No. 16 of every township for the maintenance of public schools within the said township." [28]

[27] Senator Lister Hill, "A Bonanza for Education," *Harper's Magazine*, March, 1952, pp. 29–31, vol. 204, no. 1222. Senator Hill in this article sees the American tidelands as a public bounty which should be used, he says, to build up American military defense and to further subsidize education at all levels. The article was written in support of Senator Hill's proposed "Oil for Education Amendment."

[28] Edith Parker, "History of Land Grants for Education in Texas," unpublished Ph.D. dissertation, University of Texas, Austin, 1951, pp. 40–41. I am indebted to Miss Parker for the facts used in this account. Good general accounts of the development of education in the United States are to be found in E. P. Cubberley, *Public Education in the United States* (Boston: Houghton Mifflin Company, 1919); Edward H. Reisner, *The Evolution of the Common School* (New York: The Macmillan Company, 1930), chap. XVI. "Rise of Free Public Schools in the United States"; and Fletcher Harper Swift, *History of Public Permanent Common School Funds in the United States, 1795–1905* (New York: Henry Holt Co., 1911).

Had the principle laid down in the Ordinance of 1785 been applied, it would have meant that one thirty-sixth of the public domain of that day — an area of 80,255 square miles or 51.36 million acres — would have been appropriated, and to this would have to be added the Texas donation.

The Northwest Ordinance of 1787 followed the principle if not the letter of the recommendation of 1785. The third article reads as follows: "Religion, morality, and knowledge, being necessary to good government and the happiness of mankind, schools and the means of education shall be forever encouraged." [29] When Ohio, the first state to be carved out of the Northwest Territory, was admitted, 748,482 acres of land were appropriated for the support of education. This is about 1170 sections, or 3 per cent of the present area of the state. Ohio was in no sense an exception but rather an example of the general policy followed when new states were admitted from the public domain.

The purpose here will best be served by taking a look at the total amount of land appropriated to education in the United States prior to the annexation of Texas. Miss Parker has compiled figures to show that the seventeen nonpublic domain states made land grants to education which by 1845 amounted to 9,999,024 acres. Some of this land was given before the Revolution, but by far the larger part of it was donated after the national land policy had been inaugurated. Prior to the admission of Texas, eleven public domain states had entered the Union, and these eleven received land grants for education totaling 64,629,160.76 acres, or 100,984 sections. Adding the federal grants to those made by states we have total gifts by 1845 of 74,628,184 acres, or 116,450 sections. Following the admission of Texas, twenty states were admitted and in them the land grants for education were somewhat in proportion to their size.

The case of Texas is exceptional for many reasons, but mainly because Texas is the only state admitted after 1800 that

[29] Francis Newton Thorpe, *Federal and State Constitutions* (Washington, D.C.: Government Printing Office, 1909), vol. II, p. 961.

received from the federal government no land grant for schools or for any other purpose save the founding of the Agricultural and Mechanical College of Texas. When Texas entered the Union in 1845, it retained its public lands and therefore had the sole responsibility for formulating a policy for their distribution. As the largest state in the Union, Texas had in its own right an enormous public domain which it distributed with a lavish hand. The extent to which this land was used to subsidize public free education will be noted here. The subject breaks up into two categories: first, the land gift to public education below the college level; second, gifts for higher education as represented primarily by The University of Texas.

The story of the bequest to public education begins during the Republic of Texas, 1836–45, and lasts down to 1898, by which date it was realized that there was no more land to give, no more public domain. The details of the story will not be given because they are set forth in various studies based on original sources.[30] It is well, however, to quote a passage from the address of President Mirabeau B. Lamar to the Congress of Texas on December 20, 1838. He emphasized the size of the public domain and its potential in providing for the needs of the state; he recognized that the public domain would disappear; and he intimated that it could be used to initiate public education without resort to taxation.

A suitable appropriation of lands to the purpose of general Education, can be made at this time without inconvenience to the Government or the people; but defer it until the public domain shall have passed from our hands, and the uneducated youths of Texas will constitute the living monuments of our neglect and remissness. To commence a liberal system of education a few years hence may be attended with many difficulties.

[30] See Frederick Eby, *Education in Texas: Source Materials* (Austin: University of Texas Press, 1921), and *Development of Education in Texas* (New York: The Macmillan Company, 1925); Bascom Giles, *History and Disposition of Texas Public Domain* (Austin: 1940); Edith Parker, "History of Land Grants for Education in Texas," unpublished Ph.D. dissertation, University of Texas, Austin, 1951. Eby and Parker contain extensive bibliographies.

The imposition of taxes will be necessary. . . . Postpone it a few years, and millions will be necessary to accomplish the great design.[31]

To make the story brief, both the Republic of Texas and the state succeeding it adopted a policy of contributing lands to encourage education. Within sixty years from the date Lamar spoke, the chapter closed, and Texas found itself without public domain. It had been scattered to the four winds by sale and by gift.[32]

We may ignore special grants and confine our attention to those grants made to the public schools and to The University of Texas. The following table shows the size of the land grant in acres and the proceeds down to 1950: [33]

	Total Land Endowment for Education (acres)	Land Proceeds
State School System	42,561,400	$218,879,286.72
County Schools	4,229,166	12,387,671.45
Total	46,790,566	$231,266,958.17
The University of Texas	2,329,168	123,101,053.04
Grand Total	49,119,734	$354,368,011.21

In addition the federal government made a donation of 180,000 acres of land outside of Texas for the Agricultural and Mechanical College of Texas. From this land was realized

---

[31] *Journal of the House of the Republic of Texas*, Regular Session, Third Congress, p. 170.

[32] It is very likely that many people will be surprised at the statement that the public domain was closed by 1898. They tend to confuse the sale of school lands with public lands, or with "scrap" sales of land recovered through forfeiture. Miss Parker says: "In 1898 it was discovered that the supply of unappropriated lands of the public domain had been exhausted. . . ." Though each newly organized county was supposed to receive a gift of lands for school purposes, those counties organized after 1898 could not receive such lands, and had to be provided for by recovery of forfeited lands and other exceptional means. — Parker, "Land Grants for Education in Texas," pp. 150 f.

[33] *Ibid.*, p. 292.

the sum of $209,000. The above figures do not include grants amounting to 410,000 acres to eleemosynary institutions. Another feature of the grants is that by constitutional provision the proceeds from the sale of these lands — and by interpretation oil royalties are considered as sales — constitute a permanent fund of both the public school system and the University of Texas. This means that both the public schools and the University have large endowments of which only the proceeds, such as interest and rentals, can be used.

The effect of the discovery of oil appears in the column marked "Land Proceeds." It will be noted that while the University of Texas has received only 2.3 million acres, the public school system has received nearly 46.8 million acres. Despite this great disparity in amounts of land received, the proceeds to the University are more than half of the proceeds to the public school system from twenty times the amount of land. This disparity in favor of the University is due to the discovery of oil on University lands, and oil income is treated as endowment rather than income. The public school system sold most of its lands, and at a time before oil was important in Texas.

The University of Texas presents peculiar proof of the fact that higher education could be initiated and for a time supported by this land endowment. It was thought that income from this endowment would serve to erect a plant without legislative appropriation, without taxation. The appropriation of money for buildings at the University of Texas is expressly prohibited by the present state constitution, which was adopted in 1876. Though the University of Texas has a plant estimated to have a value of more than $72,000,000, or for the main University at Austin of more than $57,000,000, not a building has been constructed with tax money. All were built from the proceeds from the Permanent Fund or landed domain.

Nor is this all. The University was opened in 1883 without benefit of taxes. The endowment had accumulated a fund sufficient to get the University under way, and the institution operated for several years before it was deemed necessary or expedient to go to the legislature for an appropriation.[34] The first legislative appropriation for the support of the University was made in 1889, after the University had been in operation six years. The legislature continued to make grants for operation, although the landed endowment provides a portion of operating expenses, and serves to cushion the shocks of legislative economy. It is probably the landed endowment which makes the difference between a mediocre institution and one that has some claim to rank among the better state universities of the nation.

The evidence that frontier lands contributed to get the Texas public schools started, and to found and operate a university generally recognized as very good in its region, is too clear to need further elaboration. The public schools with a base of 73,110 sections of land, and a university with a base of 3640 sections, much of it underlain with oil, had something on which to build, a stake they could not forfeit, a windfall from the frontier, available only once, which has made both systems much of what they are today.

In concluding this account of land support for public education, a few words should be said about the so-called land-grant colleges of which there are sixty-nine in the United States. There is at least one in each state, and as a group they are commonly spoken of as land-grant colleges. The term "land grant" is significant, implying that land was the foundation on which the present structure of agricultural and mechanical and also military colleges has been erected. It would be more accurate, however, to call them "land-bait" colleges, because the grants were relatively small moneywise. They were large enough, however, to induce the states to set up a system of colleges which are supported partly by state taxation and partly by federal funds.

State interest in agricultural education preceded the action

[34] *General Laws of the State of Texas*, Twenty-first Legislature, Regular Session (Austin: State Printing Office, 1889), p. 74. Also see W. J. Battle, "A Concise History of the University of Texas, 1883–1950," *Southwestern Historical Quarterly*, vol. LIV (April, 1951), p. 395. In 1888 the legislature made a grant of $125,000 to the University. This was a repayment of money taken from the University fund during the Civil War. — H. Y. Benedict, *A Source Book Relating to the History of the University of Texas* (Austin: 1917), p. 353.

of the federal government, and several states made application for federal grants. The nation-wide system of agricultural and mechanical colleges dates from the year 1862 when President Lincoln signed the Morrill Act on July 2. This act provided that each state was to receive from the public domain 30,000 acres of land for each member it had in the Congress, and the proceeds from the sale were to be used in setting up an agricultural and mechanical college.[35] In time each state received such lands, those having no public domain being assigned lands in other states or territories. Actually, the gift was insignificant except in its effects, but it does illustrate the value of the wedge. All told, the grants amount to only 10,860,000 acres, or 17,125 sections, but it was enough to lure the state legislatures along and lead them in some cases to set up the A. and M. system before they established their universities. For example, Texas opened its A. and M. College in 1876, but did not open its university until 1883. The frontier could see more sense in the "useful arts" than it could in the less practical forms of education, and some of the country is in that sense still frontier. The Texas legislature, in order to meet the federal requirement, appropriated money for the construction of buildings, something it is precluded from doing and has never done for the University. But the state constitution makes the A. and M. College a part of The University of Texas, and on that basis the A. and M. College receives one third of the income from the land endowment of The University of Texas. In addition the A. and M. College receives appropriation from the federal government in which the University has no share. Of course, the argument is that

[35] The significance of the grants is indicated by the small amount received for the land. Texas sold its 180,000 acres for 87 cents an acre, receiving $156,000. This sale was made under the carpetbag government in 1871. The funds were invested, and by the time the College opened in 1876, it amountd to $209,000, which is retained as a permanent fund. Assuming that it will produce 4 per cent annually, the College realizes $8360 a year, about the price of one professor or an assistant dean, though in 1876 that amount would have gone far in maintaining the institution with its faculty of six members. The Agricultural and Mechanical College of Texas, like the University of Texas, paid its operating expenses for a time from income on its permanent fund. Kentucky sold its land at 44 cents, Mississippi at 47 cents. North Dakota was more fortunate, selling at $110.90 an acre and receiving a total of $1,323,777.

the University is rich in land and oil. But we are digressing here into the realm of logic and justice in Texas, which in this case is as peculiar as some other Texas characteristics. The purpose is to show how a relatively small gift of frontier land was used to establish a system of education that is nation-wide, closely integrated, and now supported almost entirely by taxation, both state and federal. And it was created and raised by a little wedge of frontier land.

Even when the land grants for education are given in sections, the figures are fantastic, so great that they are difficult to comprehend. In such cases we resort to figures of speech and symbols to convey an idea of magnitude. If we sum up the main land grants to education, ignoring odds and ends, we find that the federal government had by 1932 contributed not less than 134,910 sections of land for educational purposes. Texas contributed 76,750 sections. This is a total of 211,660 sections. If these sections were put together they would make a band eight miles wide around the earth at the equator, with enough sections left over to reach from the Arctic Circle to Patagonia, a remnant 11,500 miles in length.[36] This land was carved from the frontier and could have been had from no other place. It is the base on which has been erected the greatest public free educational system in the world.

The extent to which other frontier countries have used public lands to subsidize and support public free education is not known, but the subject offers opportunities for research in the dominions and in the Latin-American countries. We do know that the frontier contributed to education, not only in the frontier countries, but in the Metropolis as well. A striking example of such use is furnished by Cecil Rhodes who took a part of the fortune he made in the frontier of South Africa and established the Rhodes foundation at Oxford. If we should add the private wealth acquired in frontier enterprise to the

36 The figures for federal grants are derived from the *Annual Report of the Commissioner of the General Land Office to the Secretary of the Interior for the Fiscal Year Ended June 30, 1932* (Washington: Government Printing Office, 1932), pp. 45–50. See also Thomas Corwin Donaldson, *The Public Domain, Its History, with Statistics* (H. Misc. Doc. 45, pt. IV, 47th Cong., 2d Sess. [U.S. 2158], Washington, 1884), pp. 226 ff. The figures given are on the conservative side and do not include any lands given by the states.

public lands we would be able to see the magnitude of the frontier gift to education throughout the Western World.

4. History

It is not inappropriate that history should constitute the final section in the body of this study of the Great Frontier. History is the last observer on the field of past human action, lingers there to figure out where man has been, what he did, and why. History's field is as broad as the trail mankind has made out of the past, and its materials comprise all the records — left purposely or accidentally — that have survived. The historians have charted the main path of civilization back to the time when the written records first appeared, and then with the help of the anthropologists (who are really ancient historians) they push still farther down the fading track.

The historians have discovered that prior to the opening of the sixteenth century a great ferment began on the trail, a ferment which broke up the serenity and certitude of medieval life. The excitement extended to art, literature, politics, and religion, bringing about changes in all these things. But these changes were *internal*, and how far they might have gone without the impetus given by an *external* factor which turned up with the discovery of the Great Frontier the historian can never say. He does know that the external factor was found as a result of the internal ferment that was going on.

Because of the entrance of the Great Frontier, the road broadened out to accommodate what came in over the new trail. As a result the excitement and ferment increased constantly and many of the impulses and tendencies already under way could keep going. No historian can travel the whole long trail, but each must choose some segment and examine it and its relation to the whole. In this book the external factor just mentioned, the Great Frontier, has been selected and an effort has been made to sit at the junction where the new-cut road joins the metropolitan thoroughfare of Western civilization. The experience has led to the conclusion that the road to the Great Frontier is perhaps the most important branch to enter the main highway of Western civilization in modern times.

The hypothesis has been advanced that the opening of this

road resulted in a boom, that modern civilization has grown up in this boom, and that most modern institutions have been affected in a greater or less degree. The hypothesis must be tested in the crucible of other historians and other scholars, subjected to the most rigid criticism. No doubt it will be denied, but denial without proof will have in the end no meaning. On the other hand, some may want to investigate their own segment of history, their own special field, to see what light the frontier hypothesis throws on it. Some may wish to learn how the idea originated and to know what studies have been made and what may be worth making. For the convenience of these the following pages are written.

Fustel de Coulanges is reported to have said that it requires years of research for a moment of synthesis. This moment comes to the investigator without warning, and usually while he is engaged in something remote from, but still connected with, the synthesis. There must be preparation, previous research or experience, all of which have charged the mind for the spark to make connections and give the flash of insight. The first step in my preparation to become a student of the frontier was taken in 1892 when my parents moved to West Texas while that country was still in the frontier stage. I grew up there and all my early impressions were of young families (there were few old people there) struggling with raw nature. Thus it was that I touched the hem of the garment of the Great Frontier, almost but not quite too late. Because my father was a teacher, I had books and became a reader, and as I read I caught a distorted but alluring vision of another world, a world of books, of a room lined with them to the ceiling. At an early age I determined to escape to that other world, to leave the frontier to those more audacious, and eventually the opportunity came. I entered the University with the determination to be a writer, to get as far away from what I had known as I could. This desire to get away from the frontier turned out to be an error, fortunately a temporary one. The frontier had left its mark on me that no university and no desire could obliterate.

Eventually I turned to the frontier as a subject of study, and there I found a body of literature that I could understand, and

I found myself. What I wrote about this subject editors would accept and people would read; what I wrote about other things left them politely disinterested. And so I entered the door leading back to the world I had known. Of course I had no idea of where I was going, or what lay ahead on the book-lined road; but I only knew that it interested me and that what I saw, either in the books or in the field, had meaning.

My first assignment was local in nature, the history of a frontier institution, the Texas Rangers. Before I got through with this, I knew a great deal about frontier life in Texas. In the course of studying this institution, the field broadened out to a region of which western Texas is a part. The second study was therefore regional, and resulted in an examination of the last American frontier, the Great Plains. The book by that title, like the present one, presented a thesis to the effect that conditions on the Great Plains were so different from those in the eastern part of the country as to effect radical changes in the institutions, ideas, and practices that were introduced there from the East. The concept seemed so important to me that I laid aside the Texas Rangers and published *The Great Plains* first.

My third study was national in scope, dealing with the relationship existing among the three natural regions of the country, the North, the South, and the West. It was not originally designed to deal with the frontier, but the frontier intruded itself into the title, *Divided We Stand: The Crisis of a Frontierless Democracy.* It was in writing Chapter VI of this volume, "The Crisis of a Frontierless Democracy," that I had the moment of synthesis resulting in the present book. Any reader who takes the trouble to examine that chapter will see the germ idea for the Great Frontier. I had followed the frontier, and it had broadened out, from the local to the regional to the national, and finally to the whole thing, the Great Frontier.

The concept of the Great Frontier was exciting, but nothing could be done about it immediately because the facts were not in hand. It took fifteen years, 1936–1951, to investigate the ramifications of what was in the beginning only an idea, hardly as yet an hypothesis. It was not until 1950 that an outline of the present volume was made. Some writing was done during a year's residence at Oxford, but only in fragments. Sixteen years is a long time to spend on one idea, on one book, but the idea could not be comprehended or the book done earlier.

Some inquiry has already been made about the method used in the investigation. Until the inquiry was made, I had never given any thought to method or noticed that there was anything special about it. Whatever it is, it resembles that followed in writing *The Great Plains*, which was once examined for method and other things by a group of appraisers appointed by the Social Science Research Council. Though they issued a report about the size of what they reported on, they came to no definite conclusion about method.

The procedure I can give. Equipped with the concept of the Great Frontier, I set up a seminar at The University of Texas in 1938, and have given it continuously when in residence. It has been a leisurely seminar extending through the whole year, not one of these semester affairs where thinking is done in a hurry. It has been more like a camping party whose members range far and wide, individually, to see what they can find during the day. At night they return to sit around a common campfire, exhibit specimens, tell what they have seen and say what they think about it. The seminar table is the campfire and the library is the little-traversed forest through which they range. Like all good hunters, they sometimes bring in very little, but it is surprising what they have turned up with. They have, to paraphrase Henry Adams, dug holes all over the Great Frontier.

What is the method? If I must say, it has been to set up an idea clearly, develop a concept, and formulate an hypothesis, in this case the idea, the concept, and the hypothesis of a Great Frontier. Then the method has been to walk around it, view it from all vantage points, examine all its aspects, and trace out its relationships. Along with that goes the reading of many books on all sorts of subjects, some of which seem to be very remote from the frontier. The driving force behind this activity is the insatiable curiosity as to what the meaning of the Great Frontier has been in modern times.

There are as yet no books bearing directly on the concept

presented here, though there are many on various segments of the frontier, more in America than anywhere else. But out of the seminar has come a series of special studies represented by Master's theses and Ph.D. dissertations. Those completed and some in progress are listed in the last section of the bibliography. These special studies and the accumulated seminar papers would constitute several volumes and are in themselves a record of numerous excursions into many parts of the Great Frontier, intellectual adventures of mutual interest and benefit to all participants. My own obligation to all members of the seminar is real.

When it came to the writing I had the choice of undertaking a definitive study or an introductory one. I chose the latter because it was the only possible choice. One lifetime is too short to follow out the ramifications of the concept of the Great Frontier; the task is moreover too much for one mind. I elected to open a subject rather than to attempt to close it. My task was that of presenting the hypothesis, offering such data as could be gathered, and suggesting lines of future investigation. The decision in favor of an introduction helps explain several features about the method of presentation. The main purpose was to make a clear exposition, to persuade the intelligence with reason rather than to overwhelm it with a profusion of detail. Much of the discussion is abstract, carried forward on the assumption that the probable readers will be sufficiently informed to supply the illustrations. Footnotes are used sparingly, mainly in connection with quoted passages. No special effort has been made to exhibit the use of original source material, but rather to employ whatever was useful in illuminating a broad concept. Actually, when it comes to the Great Frontier, what men have thought about the subject — such men as Adam Smith, William Graham Sumner, Frederic Jackson Turner, John Dewey, and Franz Alexander — is to all intents and purposes original source material. In a few instances the purpose could best be achieved by cutting loose from sources and writing imaginative passages intended to clarify a principle. The story of Jim Brown in Chapter Two is an example.

Other features of the book grew out of the vantage point

from which modern history is viewed, out of the fact that the whole frontier and not a part of it was considered. Such an approach brings familiar things into different focus and often reveals relationships not visible from other positions. In this case, some theories have emerged which remain to be tested. One is the boom hypothesis of modern history, another is the theory of windfalls in modern capitalism, and a third is the theory of the vertical flow or circulation of wealth. The only justification for this invasion of the field of economics lies in the fact that from the vantage point of the Great Frontier the boom, windfalls, and the vertical flow of wealth can be seen with remarkable clarity.

The introductory nature of this volume is an invitation to students in the various fields to examine their subjects with a view to seeing how they were related to the frontier. This chapter and the two preceding are intended to show that there was contact. This section is directed to the historians.

Modern European historians must be depended on to tell us how the Great Frontier affected the various nations, and all of Europe as well. In doing this, they may well free themselves from the concept of colonies and empires, realizing that the Great Frontier was more extensive than any colony or empire, and that it exerted its influence on nonowners as well as on the proprietors.

There would seem to be an opportunity for a re-examination of the causes of the Industrial Revolution. Did it come, or flourish, because men suddenly became ingenious and inventive, or because men had available so much new material to work on that they could make their ingenuity a practical thing? Today in the oil fields of America, and elsewhere, men have developed the most marvelous tools with which to work underground to a distance of three miles or more. Were under-reamers, diamond bits, fish-tailed bits, roller bits, slip sockets, and bulldog spears invented and perfected because men suddenly became ingenious or were they developed because there was enough oil under the ground to bring a fortune and justify any expense that would increase its production? Did Eli Whitney become a famous man because he thought of inserting whirling circular saws between steel teeth to strip lint from cotton seed, or did he become famous because there was a supply of cotton to justify him in thinking about separating lint and seed? The cotton came before the gin, before the spinning and weaving machinery.

American historians have about worked out the details of the American frontier on the basis of the Turner hypothesis. It would seem that the time has come for them to take the lead in encouraging parallel studies in other countries which were also a part of the Great Frontier. Two large categories are obvious. One is composed of those countries where English culture is dominant, Canada, Australia, South Africa, and New Zealand. Canada is well indoctrinated with the frontier concept as developed in the United States, but less has been done in other dominions. Professor W. K. Hancock, in his *Survey of British Commonwealth Affairs*, gives special attention to the frontier with credit to Turner for the concept. He acknowledges, however, that when he wrote his history of Australia (1939) he had not heard of Turner. Professor Fred Alexander of the University of Western Australia, Melbourne, published *Moving Frontiers: An American Theme and Its Application to Australian History* in 1947. Professor Eric A. Walker of Cambridge, formerly of the University of Capetown, wrote *The Frontier Tradition of South Africa*, published as a pamphlet in 1930. He has also written a history of South Africa, and the story of the Great Trek. It is perhaps unfortunate that both Hancock and Walker left their respective countries for the great universities of Oxford and Cambridge, and therefore their thinking about their own frontier countries reaches their own people only through their books.

The second category of frontier countries where intensive studies should be made comprise the twenty republics of Central and South America. These studies must be made by the large and growing school of Latin-American historians, native and foreign. The Latin-American frontier was, in comparison with the Anglo-Saxon, very confused and quite different in character from that of the United States. Once the details have been worked out in the numerous biographies and special studies now being written, students might turn to institutions to see how they were modified and why in their transit from

Spain and Portugal to the New World. There must have been basic changes in church practices and ceremonies, if not in fundamental tenets, and in social, political, and economic institutions. The *mesta* would not work in the New World, the *cabildo* continued to develop there, a new military system evolved, and a whole new culture complex of mining developed.

In the study of the Great Frontier there is room for all sorts of investigation, for biography, for local events, for subjects closely circumscribed. But the nature of the subject is such as to lend itself to the long perspective. Therefore the study of institutions should be rewarding for the reason that an institution is ordinarily something of long duration, a trail showing direction and trend rather than a sign showing mere presence at a given time and place. It is in the evolution of institutions that the processes of history become apparent. Chapter Eight has several illustrations of institutions in transit through time and across geography, from their early origins in the Metropolis to their later manifestations in the distant frontier.

It follows from this that any serious student of the Great Frontier cannot be bound by political lines. He must be ready at any time to cross the borders of his own country, or that of the one he is primarily interested in studying; he must also be ready to break academic fences set up in universities to separate the so-called fields of knowledge. Particularly must he cross the ocean in his thinking for the reason that most of the things he will be thinking about crossed the ocean in some form at some time. Nor must he assume that all the traffic on that ocean was in one direction, or that the flow in one direction was of more importance than the opposite one. Eventually he must see that modern history is of one piece of cloth, woven from the materials of the Metropolis and of the Great Frontier.

CHAPTER THIRTEEN

CONCLUSION

THIS BOOK is based on the hypothesis that the Great Frontier as defined has been one of the primary factors in modern history. The major premise is that the sudden acquisition of land and other forms of wealth by the people of Europe precipitated a boom on Western civilization, and that the boom lasted as long as the frontier was open, a period of four centuries. A corollary of the major premise is that our modern institutions, as distinguished from medieval, were differentiated and matured during a boom, and are therefore adapted to boom conditions.

The evidence tends to show that the frontier closed in the period between 1890 and 1910. It is assumed that the frontier was open as long as there remained extensive areas of royal or public domain which the sovereign Powers had not yet alienated, which had not passed into private hands. It was the constant distribution on a nominal or free basis of the royal or public domain that kept the boom going, and that gave a peculiar dynamic quality to Western civilization for four centuries. It was in this atmosphere and under these conditions that democracy, capitalism, and individualism of the modern type came to their dominant position.

Two well-established facts indicate that the frontier closed not later than the first quarter of this century. First was the disappearance of the bulk of the public lands; second was an increase in population until the density per square mile in the whole enlarged area became by 1930 on average greater than the density was in Europe in 1500. Just at the time the sovereign had no more land or natural wealth to give, he found that he had more people to provide for than ever before. These two facts, really different aspects of a single fact, definitely mark the end of the Age of the Frontier.

There would seem to be little room to doubt that our entry

into a new age, which remains to be named, will be accompanied by basic changes in the nature of the institutions which grew up in the earlier one. The changes should be especially marked in those institutions which best fulfilled the needs of a frontier society. There is one question the answer to which will be of interest to many people, and it is this: Will the boom caused by the opening of the frontier continue now that the frontier has closed? It would be most gratifying to be able to answer that question in the affirmative, but such an answer cannot be given. On the other hand, it cannot be answered definitively in the negative. It can be stated, however, that in so far as it was dependent on an open frontier, on the presence of free land, on a high land-man ratio, the boom must slacken. Whether other factors, such as science may offer, can act as a substitute boom-maker remains to be seen.

Whether the boom continues or ends, Western civilization would seem destined to change. The boom we have had *was a frontier boom,* and the institutions devised and the methods of living adopted were highly specialized to meet that particular type of life. If another force comes in to substitute for the frontier, it will bring with it a new set of needs and will call for a sweeping discard or modification of many ideas and practices. It will be necessary to specialize in another direction determined largely by the nature of whatever factor continues the boom, whatever force dominates the society. We might still have a boom but it would be quite different in character from the one we are accustomed to. It can no longer come from the frontier.

On the other hand, if there is no substitute boom-maker, or one that is much less effective than the frontier was, then we are faced with radical changes indeed. The society we have would tend to go through a process of devolution and retrogression rather than evolution and progress. It would lose much of its dynamic character, just as a boom town does when fortunes are lost there and not made. The game would no longer justify the candle. Rural life would tend to become more important, and city life less alluring. Theoretically society might become somewhat medieval in character, and new ideals would have to be formulated to make that life tolerable. In such a state, the historians and philosophers would view the Age of the Frontier as an aberration, a temporary departure from the normal, a strange historical detour in which men developed all sorts of quaint ideas about property for all, freedom for all, and continuous progress. Our institutions would seem to those people to have been so highly specialized that they could not survive the return of society to a normal state where there was a balance between land and the men who lived on it.

We should not take this long and somber view of what may happen too seriously. It will not happen soon, and it possibly need not happen at all. The world still contains an abundance of wealth, and we are becoming more skilled in its conservation. Even though we are faced with change, much of which we heartily dislike, we shall be better prepared to make the necessary adjustments if we recognize the reasons for making them. In view of this study, here are some changes which are at hand and must be accepted.

Society as it thickens will become more closely integrated and its members more interdependent. Governments will tend to become stronger, using more compulsion in order to meet their obligations. There will be a tendency toward socialization as now exhibited in the United States and Great Britain or toward absolutism as exhibited by the fascist states and by Russia. The loose democracy belonged to a frontier stage of society. The individual will become relatively less important and will tend to lose his identity in a growing corporate life. Food and clothing should in the logic of affairs remain high in cost and go higher as population increases while land becomes relatively scarcer. The passing of free land should be registered by the passing of cheap food. Famine will continue to afflict overpopulated countries, and may return to Europe in spite of science. Capitalism of the nineteenth-century type will decline with the passing of the boom on which it was based. Its demand for area expansion cannot be met much longer. It was constantly fed by the distribution of frontier wealth, by the vertical movement of property as set forth in Chapter Five, and that movement has now been cut off.

England, as the leading frontier country of Europe, has been in decline since the close of the frontier, and will continue to decline as she loses her overseas property. Her leadership of the world was due to her control of the sea and her access to the raw materials of all the Great Frontier. With England cut off from her old frontier resources, it will be as difficult for her to maintain her historic position as it would be for New York if it were isolated from the resources of America.

The United States, the Dominions, and some of the Latin-American countries are still prosperous because of the high land-man ratio and because of technological developments which enable those countries to make their resources quickly available to their own people. The constant increase of population and the progressive destruction of resources, if unchecked, will eventually bring the Americas to the situation that obtains in Europe. When they reach that state, they will no longer talk about the cockpit of Europe because they will have one closer home. The effort to alleviate the hunger of the world, and to bolster up the economy of all nations, is highly commendable, but its prospect of success is quite uncertain. Many times Malthus has been thrown out the window only to re-enter the door with the multitude.

The efforts of the United Nations and the United States to re-establish the collapsed economy of western Europe are being made by working *within* the family of nations, reopening trade among them and encouraging their industries. The expedient that is being used in the emergency is that of pouring the wealth of rich countries into the common pot in the hope that in time the poor countries will revive and move forward on their own power. The program is internal — one of shifting rather than adding wealth. In this program little attention is being devoted to the fragments of the frontier which are still subject to development, and which, because they constitute an external factor, would if developed add new increments of room and wealth to the sum total within the society. Whatever is added by a frontier is a net gain to the society and not a mere shifting of the assets already present.

If the dictators, real and potential, would hold still, and if the United States would spend the money it is spending in Europe and Asia in developing the remaining frontier areas so that they could be used, the net gain to society would be enormous. With this vast sum of money much could be done in opening the Amazon region of Brazil, the interior valleys of Africa, and other regions where conditions are such as to thwart the efforts of individual men. An advance on the Amazon Valley would require an army of skilled technicians ranging from men who know how to operate wood saws and bulldozers to those who know how to fight disease, insects, and crop blight. Such an operation would re-create the boom of the old frontier on a small scale, and would result in a net gain to the wealth of the Western World. But the conditions are such in the Amazon region that the program would have to be carried out as a long-time investment, too long for individuals or even corporations to manage. In the end, the returns, though slow in coming, should be reasonably certain and far greater than any hoped for from the expenditures now being made in the Old World. Those expenditures are of the nature of a doctor's bill, an expense which must be stood for with no expectation of direct recovery or return. The development of the frontier is like the opening up of a land where the patient, once he has become convalescent, may improve in health and prosperity.

There has been some talk of turning the waters of the Mediterranean into the interior of Africa to create an inland sea in what is now desert. Such a sea might affect the climate and make sterile regions productive. The flood waters of the Mississippi are sufficient to convert the Great Salt Lake into a fresh-water sea and a reservoir for irrigation in a land that would be very productive. Such a project is feasible from an engineering point of view, and it could be done with a few billion dollars. These two projects may seem absurd, but it is not absurd to say that the money now being thrown into Europe and Asia would be sufficient to dam most of the rivers of the world and to pay for the other services that are necessary in making latent resources available.

The above discussion serves to reveal the contrast between frontier investments and those now being made in the Old World. For centuries the Great Frontier offered an unlimited outlet for enterprise and investment, and in general the investment paid off with good returns. It paid because it brought added increments of wealth to whatever was already present in the society. The expenditures now being made in the Old World are of a different character. They do not add much to the net material wealth of the world and they do not bring any direct returns to investors. In the first instance capitalism could and did grow rapidly; in the present case capitalism is not growing because its substance is being consumed as rapidly as it is being made available. In the Age of the Frontier western European society lived on the returns from its capital; today the capital is being consumed.

Though there is much talk of new frontiers, a careful examination of those suggested reveals that most of them are trivial, and none will compare in magnitude or importance with the Great Frontier. The most plausible claims are made in the name of science and technology. There is no doubt that science has made and is making valuable contributions to the luxury and comfort of those who have the price, but the tendency is to overrate what science can do.

The fact that we cannot find a new frontier comparable to the one we have had need not make us feel that we are now bereft of a challenge and an opportunity. It does mean that we have a different challenge and perhaps an even greater opportunity for achievement. For more than four centuries we bent our effort toward the conquest and exploitation of the Great Frontier, and we have succeeded perhaps beyond expectations. In making this conquest, we rarely looked back but rather pressed forward eagerly to what was before us. We considered the task Herculean, and we take great pride in our ability to perform it. The task was that of taking a new world and making it over into something of an Old World image. That was what we wanted to do, and that is what we did. The question before us now is whether we can manage what we have so eagerly taken. That is our challenge and our opportunity. We should not be so obtuse as to believe that the means of management are the same as those of conquest, or that frontier institutions will necessarily serve a metropolitan society. Our challenge consists in finding out what modifications should be made, and our opportunity will come in making them. Our inspiration may come from history, in looking back to the early sixteenth century when the lamp was lifted beside the golden door of the Great Frontier to change the destiny of mankind.

ACKNOWLEDGMENTS

I T IS IMPOSSIBLE to recall all the obligations for assistance that have been incurred in developing what is set forth in this volume. Certainly a great deal of credit is due those graduate students who pursued with me the subject of The Great Frontier in the seminar from 1938 to 1952, inclusive. The first chapter in the book appeared in substance in *Harper's Magazine* for October, 1951, and in the following month the chapter on windfalls appeared. *The Southwest Review* published the section on literature in the spring issue of 1952. Shortly after the inception of the idea of the study, I received in 1938 a Guggenheim fellowship for study abroad. In the spring of 1951 the Research Council of the University of Texas made a grant which enabled me to devote a semester to the writing, which was by then well under way. Among those who have assisted in the research and with the preparation of the manuscript are John F. Murphy, Miss Betty Brooke Eakle, Miss Edith H. Parker, Mrs. Mary Joe Carroll, and Mrs. Martha Ann Zivley. To Mrs. Zivley I am especially indebted for the final typing of the manuscript, for checking quotations, verifying references, and in general not taking my word for anything. Professor Carlos E. Castañeda gave aid on matter pertaining to Spanish subjects. The footnotes indicate further obligation to authors quoted and to their publishers. To those quiet and efficient people known as editors who in the great publishing houses work almost anonymously for others, I wish to pay tribute and to thank them for all they have done. For what remains, I accept responsibility.

BIBLIOGRAPHY

CHAPTER I

Alexander, Fred. *Moving Frontiers.* Melbourne: University Press, 1947.

Arciniegas, Germán. *Caribbean: Sea of the New World.* New York: Alfred A. Knopf, Inc., 1946. Translated from the Spanish by Harriet de Onís.

Chevalier, Michel. *Remarks on the Production of the Precious Metals, and on the Depreciation of Gold.* Translated by D. Forbes Campbell, Esq. London: Smith Elder & Co., 1853.

Eakle, Betty Brooke. "The Frontier and Population: A Study of the Influence of the New World on Population Growth," unpublished Master's thesis, University of Texas, Austin, Texas, 1948.

Gillespie, James Edward. *The Influence of Oversea Expansion on England to 1700.* ("Studies in History, Economics, and Public Law," vol. XCI.) New York: Columbia University Press, 1920.

Griffin, Robert, Esq. "The Utility of Common Statistics," *The Journal of the Statistical Society,* December, 1882, pp. 517–46.

Hancock, W. K. *Survey of British Commonwealth Affairs.* London: Oxford University Press, 1940.

Homans, George Caspar. *English Villagers of the Thirteenth Century.* Cambridge, Mass.: Harvard University Press, 1941.

Mood, Fulmer. "Notes on the History of the Word *Frontier*," *Agricultural History,* XXII (April, 1948), 78–83.

New York Times, August 11, 1946, p. 25.

Smith, Adam. *The Wealth of Nations,* ed. Edwin Cannan. London: Methuen & Co., Ltd., 1904; 2 vols.

Sumner, William Graham. *Earth-Hunger and Other Essays,* ed. Albert G. Keller. New Haven: Yale University Press, 1913.

Taylor, George Rogers (ed.), *The Turner Thesis Concerning the Role of the Frontier in American History.* Boston: D. C. Heath & Co., 1949.

Turner, Frederick Jackson. *The Frontier in American History.* New York: H. Holt & Co., 1920.

Usher, Abbott Payson. *An Introduction to the Industrial History of England.* Boston: Houghton Mifflin Co., 1920.

Walford, Cornelius. *The Famines of the World: Past and Present.* London: 1879.

Walker, Eric A. *The Frontier Tradition in South Africa.* London: Oxford University Press, 1930.

CHAPTER II

Crèvecoeur, J. Hector St. John de. *Letters from an American Farmer.* London: J. M. Dent & Sons, Ltd., 1912.

Fairbridge, Kingsley. *The Story of Kingsley Fairbridge.* London: Oxford University Press, 1941.

Franklin, Benjamin. "Information to Those Who Would Remove to America." *Collected Works of Benjamin Franklin.* New York: Macmillan Co., 1907.

Garland, Hamlin. *Prairie Songs.* Cambridge and Chicago: Stone & Kimball, 1893.

Gibbon, Perceval. *Vrouw Grobelaar.* New York: McClure, Phillips & Co., 1906.

Gipson, Frederick Benjamin. *Hound-dog Man.* New York: Harper & Bros., 1949.

Rourke, Constance. *Audubon.* New York: Harcourt, Brace & Co., 1936.

CHAPTER III

Brady, Robert Alexander. *Business as a System of Power.* New York: Columbia University Press, 1943.

Hough, Emerson. *The Way to the West.* Indianapolis: The Bobbs-Merrill Co., 1903.

Kouwenhoven, John A. *Made in America: The Arts in Modern Civilization.* Garden City: Doubleday & Co., 1948.

Lahey, Edwin A. "The AFL Will Absorb the CIO When . . . ," *Collier's Weekly,* September 1, 1951.

Nevins, Allan. *Ordeal of the Union,* vol. II. New York: Charles Scribner's Sons, 1948.

Northrop, F. G. C. *The Meeting of East and West: An Inquiry Concerning World Understanding.* New York: The Macmillan Company, 1946.

Rølvaag, O. E. *Giants in the Earth: A Saga of the Prairie.* New York and London: Harper & Bros., 1927.

Trahan, Mauree P. "American Methodism and the Frontier, 1760–1880," unpublished Master's thesis, University of Texas, Austin, Texas, 1951.

U.S. Department of Commerce, Bureau of the Census. *Statistical Abstract of the U.S., 1949.* Washington: U.S. Government Printing Office.

Wiederaenders, Arthur G. "The American Frontier as a Factor in Protestant Denominationalism in the United States," unpublished Ph.D. dissertation, University of Texas, Austin, Texas, 1942.

CHAPTER IV

Alexander, Franz. *Our Age of Unreason.* New York: J. B. Lippincott Co., 1942.

Dewey, John. *Individualism, Old and New.* New York: Minton, Balch & Co., 1930.

Galbraith, John Kenneth. *American Capitalism: The Concept of Countervailing Power.* Boston: Houghton Mifflin Co., 1952.

Jameson, J. Franklin. *The American Revolution Considered as a Social Movement.* Princeton: Princeton University Press, 1926.

CHAPTER V

Barnes, Viola F. "Land Tenure in English Colonial Charters of the Seventeenth Century," in *Essays in Colonial History Presented to Charles McLean Andrews by His Students.* New Haven: Yale University Press, 1931.

Chemical and Engineering News, February 25, 1952.

Dennis, Lawrence. *The Dynamics of War and Revolution.* New York: The Weekly Foreign Letter, 1940.

Hamilton, Earl J. *American Treasure and the Price Revolution in Spain, 1501–1650.* Cambridge: Harvard University Press, 1934.

Hamilton, Earl J. "American Treasure and the Rise of Capitalism, 1500–1700," *Economica,* November, 1929, pp. 338–57.

Keller, A. G. *Colonization: A Study of the Founding of New Societies.* Boston and New York: Ginn & Co., 1908.

Keynes, John Maynard. *A Treatise on Money.* New York: Harcourt, Brace & Co., 1930.

Potter, David M. "Democracy and Abundance," *Yale Review,* vol. XL, Spring, 1951.

Preece, Harold. *Living Pioneers.* New York: World Publishing Co., 1952.

Strauss, Samuel. "Things Are in the Saddle," *Atlantic Monthly,* November, 1924, p. 78.

Webb, Walter Prescott, and John Francis Murphy. "The Precious Metals as a Medium of Exchange — A Frontier Incident," in Alceu A. Lima, Edgar McInnis, et al., *Esayo sobre la hostoria del Nuevo Mundo.* México, D.F.: Instituto Panamericano de Geografía e Historia, 1951.

CHAPTER VI

Keynes, John Maynard. *A Treatise on Money.* New York: Harcourt, Brace & Co., 1930.

MacKay, Douglas. *The Honourable Company.* London: Cassell & Co., Ltd., 1937.

Mather, Cotton. *Magnalia Christi Americana,* vol. I. Hartford: Silas Andrus, Publisher, 1820.

Scott, W. R. *The Constitution and Finance of English, Scottish, and Irish Joint Stock Companies to 1720.* Cambridge: The University Press, 1910–1912; 3 vols.

Sumner, William Graham. *Earth-Hunger and Other Essays,* ed. Albert G. Keller. New Haven: Yale University Press, 1913.

CHAPTER VII

Arciniegas, Germán. *Caribbean: Sea of the New World.* Translated by Harriet de Onís. New York: Alfred A. Knopf, Inc., 1946.

Balfour, Graham. *The Life of Robert Louis Stevenson.* New York: Charles Scribner's Sons, 1901. `

Erleigh, Viscount. *The South Sea Bubble.* New York: G. P. Putnam's Sons, 1933.

Howe, George. *History of the Presbyterian Church in South Carolina.* Columbia: Duffie & Chapman, 1870.

Insh, George Pratt. *The Company of Scotland.* London and New York: Charles Scribner's Sons, 1932.

Insh, George Pratt (ed.). *Papers Relating to the Ships and Voyages of the Company of Scotland Trading to Africa and the Indies, 1696–1707.* Edinburgh: University Press, 1924.

Mather, Cotton. *Magnalia Christi Americana,* vol. II. Hartford: Silas Andrus, Publisher, 1820.

Ravenel, Mrs. St. Julien (Harriott Harry Rutledge). *Charleston.* New York: The Macmillan Co., 1922.

Scott, W. R. *The Constitution and Finance of English, Scottish, and Irish Joint Stock Companies to 1720,* vol. II. Cambridge: University Press, 1910–1912.

Smith, Henry Nash. *Virgin Land: The American West as Symbol and Myth.* Cambridge, Mass.: Harvard University Press, 1950.

Thiers, Adolphe. *The Mississippi Bubble.* New York: W. A. Townsend & Co., 1859.

Trevelyan, George M. *Ramillies and the Union with Scotland.* London: Longmans, Green and Co., 1932.

CHAPTER VIII

Adams, Andy. *The Log of a Cowboy.* Boston: Houghton Mifflin Co., 1931.

Barnes, Viola F. "Land Tenure in English Colonial Charters of the Seventeenth Century," in *Essays in Colonial History Presented to Charles McLean Andrews by His Students.* New Haven: Yale University Press, 1931.

Berle, Adolf A., Jr., and Gardiner C. Means. *The Modern Corporation and Private Property.* New York & Chicago: Commerce Clearing House, Inc., 1932.

Donaldson, Thomas. *The Public Domain,* H. Ex. Doc. 45, 47th Cong., 2d Sess., 1884.

Jameson, J. Franklin. *The American Revolution Considered as a Social Movement.* Princeton: Princeton University Press, 1926.

Kinney, Clesson S. *A Treatise on the Law of Irrigation and Water Rights and the Arid Region Doctrine of Appropriation of Waters.* San Francisco: Bender-Moss Co., 1912; 4 vols.

McCoy, Joseph G. *Historic Sketches of the Cattle Trade of the West and Southwest.* Kansas City: Ramsey, Millet, & Hudson, 1874.

McDonald, William. *Dry Farming: Its Principles and Practice.* New York: The Century Co., 1911.

Mead, Elwood. *Irrigation Institutions.* New York: The Macmillan Co., 1903.

Melville, Herman. *Mardi and a Voyage Thither,* vol. II. New York: Harper & Bros., 1849.

Morris, Richard Brandon. *Studies in the History of American Law.* New York: Columbia University Press, 1930.

Rollins, Philip Ashton. *The Cowboy.* New York: Charles Scribner's Sons, 1922.

Schoff, Leonard Hastings. *A National Agricultural Policy: For All the People of the United States.* Columbia University Seminar on Rural Life. New York: Harper & Bros., 1950.

Sumner, William Graham. *Earth-Hunger and Other Essays,* ed. Albert G. Keller. New Haven: Yale University Press, 1913.

Washington, H. A. (ed.). *The Writings of Thomas Jefferson,* vol. I. Washington: Taylor & Maur, 1853.

Webb, Walter Prescott. *The Great Plains.* Boston: Ginn & Co., 1931.

Webb, Walter Prescott. *The Texas Rangers: A Century of Frontier Defense.* Boston: Houghton Mifflin Co., 1931.

Wiel, Samuel Charles. *Water Rights in the Western States.* San Francisco: Bancroft-Whitney Co., 1911; 2 vols.

Bates *v.* Brown, 5 Wallace (U.S.) 716.

Cox *v.* Matthews, 17 Ind. 371.

In re Shumway's Estate, 194 Mich. 251.

CHAPTER IX

Atherton, Warren E. "Oceans of Opportunity," *American Magazine,* April, 1945, p. 34.

Bowman, Isaiah. *The Pioneer Fringe.* New York: American Geographical Society, 1931.

Bush, Vannevar. *Science, The Endless Frontier.* Washington: Government Printing Office, 1945.

Daniels, Farrington, "Solar Energy," *Science,* January 21, 1929, CIX, 51–57.

Fielding, Temple. "Land of the Fabulous Frontier," *Reader's Digest,* June, 1947, pp. 1–4, condensed from *Christian Science Monitor,* May 10, 1947.

Fortune, July, 1943, and February and August, 1949.

Gordon, Gaskill. "Liberia, a New Frontier," *Reader's Digest,* October, 1948, p. 94, condensed from *American Magazine,* July, 1948.

Gruening, Earnest. "Go North, Young Man," *Reader's Digest,* January, 1944, p. 53, condensed from *Fortune,* December, 1943.

Hubbert, M. King. "Energy from Fossil Fuels," *Science,* February 4, 1949, CIX, 103–9.

New York Sunday News, October 23, 1949.

Osborn, Fairfield. *Our Plundered Planet.* Boston: Little, Brown & Co., 1948.

Powell, Talcott. "New Frontier for American Pioneers: Tropical South America," *Reader's Digest,* July, 1937, p. 59.

San Antonio Express, September 12, 1949.

Saturday Evening Post, October 22, 1949.

Taverse de Sa Hernane. "They're Bringing Hope to the Valley of Death," *Saturday Evening Post,* December 11, 1948, p. 20.

Time, August 11, 1947.

U.S. State Department. *Energy Resources of the World.* Washington, D.C.: Government Printing Office, 1949.

Vogt, William. *The Road to Survival.* New York: William Sloane Associates, Inc., 1948.

Whyte, R. O., and G. V. Jacks. *Vanishing Lands.* New York: Doubleday, Doran & Co., 1939.

Wilson, C. M. "Surviving American Frontier," *Current History,* May, 1931, p. 189.

Winship, George Parker. "The Coronado Expedition, 1540–1542," *14th Annual Report of the Bureau of American Ethnology, 1892–1893,* pt. I. Washington: Government Printing Office, 1896.

Wood, Robert E. "The Gulf Coast, Our New Frontier," *Reader's Digest,* September, 1948, pp. 17–20.

Woodbury, Clarence. "Boom Towns of the New Frontier," *American Magazine,* September, 1948, p. 24.

CHAPTER X

Chambers, Robert. *Book of Days.* Edinburgh: W. & R. Chambers, 1863.

Hendricks, George D. "Animals New to Europeans after 1492," *Western Wild Animals and Man.* Seminar Report, University of Texas, 1950.

Lovette, Leland Pearson. *Naval Customs, Traditions, and Usage.* Annapolis: United States Naval Academy, 1939.

von Hagen, Victor Wolfgang. *Ecuador and the Galápagos Islands.* Norman, Oklahoma: University of Oklahoma Press, 1949.

CHAPTER XI

Clark, James Maurice. "Adam Smith," *Encyclopaedia of the Social Sciences,* vol. XIV. New York: The Macmillan Co., 1931.

Scott, James Brown (ed.). *The Spanish Origin of International Law.* Washington: Carnegie Endowment for International Peace, 1934.

Smith, Adam. *An Inquiry into the Nature and Causes of the Wealth of Nations,* vols. I and II, ed. Edwin Cannan. London: Methuen & Co., Ltd., 1904.

Wolfskill, George. "The New World Frontier and International Law," unpublished Doctor's dissertation, University of Texas, Austin, Texas, 1952.

CHAPTER XII

Annual Report of the Commissioner of the General Land Office to the Secretary of the Interior for the Fiscal Year Ended June 30, 1932. Washington: Government Printing Office, 1932.

Bacon, Leonard. *The Lusiads of Luís de Camões.* New York: The Hispanic Society of America, 1950.

Battle, W. J. "A Concise History of the University of Texas, 1883–1950," *Southwestern Historical Quarterly*, April, 1951, LIV, 395.

Benedict, H. Y. *A Source Book Relating to the History of the University of Texas.* Austin: University of Texas Press, 1917.

Bonner, William Hallam. *Captain William Dampier: Buccaneer-Author.* Stanford University: Stanford University Press, 1934.

Camões, Luis de. *The Lusiad,* vol. I. Translated by William Julius Mickle. London: W. S. Suttaby, 1809.

Chinard, Gilbert. *L'exotisme américain dans l'oeuvre de Chateaubriand.* Translations in this text by John Haller. Paris: Hachette et Cᶦᵉ., 1918.

Cubberley, E. P. *Public Education in the United States.* Boston: Houghton Mifflin Co., 1919.

Donaldson, Thomas Corwin. *The Public Domain.* H. Misc. Doc. 45, pt. IV, 47th Cong., 2d Sess. 1884.

Eby, Frederick. *Development of Education in Texas.* New York: The Macmillan Co., 1925.

Eby, Frederick. *Education in Texas: Source Materials.* Austin: University of Texas Press, 1921.

General Laws of the State of Texas, 21st Legislature, Reg. Sess., 1889. Austin: State Printing Co., 1889.

Giles, Bascom. *History and Disposition of Texas Public Domain.* Austin: 1940.

Gillespie, James E. *The Influence of Oversea Expansion on England to 1700.* New York: Columbia University Press, 1920.

Graham, R. B. Cunninghame. *The Conquest of New Granada.* London: W. Heinemann, 1922.

Hill, Lister. "A Bonanza for Education," *Harper's Magazine*, March, 1952, pp. 29–31.

Jefferson, Thomas. *Notes on the State of Virginia.* Richmond: 1853.

Journal of the House of the Republic of Texas, 3d Cong., Reg. Sess., December 20, 1838.

Keynes, John Maynard. *A Treatise on Money,* vol. II. New York: Harcourt, Brace & Co., 1930.

Kouwenhoven, John A. *Made in America: The Arts in Modern Civilization.* Garden City: Doubleday and Co., 1948.

Lowes, John Livingston. *The Road to Xanadu.* Boston: Houghton Mifflin Co., 1927.

Mencken, H. L. *The American Language.* 4th ed.; New York: Alfred A. Knopf, Inc., 1941.

Parker, Edith. "History of Land Grants for Education in Texas," unpublished Doctor's dissertation, University of Texas, Austin, Texas, 1951.

Reisner, Edward H. *The Evolution of the Common School.* New York: The Macmillan Co., 1930.

Steinbeck, John. *The Red Pony.* New York: The Viking Press, 1945.

Swift, Fletcher Harper. *History of Public Permanent Common School*

Funds in the United States, 1795–1905. New York: Henry Holt & Co., 1911.

Thorpe, Francis Newton. *Federal and State Constitutions*, vol. II. Washington: Government Printing Office, 1909.

Bibliography of Special Studies on the Great Frontier

THE FOLLOWING BIBLIOGRAPHY is comprised of special studies made by graduate students at the University of Texas. These unpublished studies consist of Master's theses and Doctoral dissertations and should be of value to those who may be interested in further study of special phases of the Great Frontier. These theses and dissertations are on deposit in the Library of the University of Texas at Austin.

MASTER'S THESES

Craddock, Emmie. "The Influence of the Frontier on the Idea of Progress in the United States" (1949).

Eakle, Betty Brooke. "The Frontier and Population: A Study of the Influence of the New World on Population Growth" (1948).

Laing, Richard Davis. "The Effect of the Frontier on Military Science and Tactics" (1950).

Lancaster, Michael O. "Some American Plant Migrants: Their Influence on Western Civilization" (1948).

Moore, Martha. "The Philosophy of Work as Developed on the American Frontier" (1952).

Parker, Edith Helene. "William Graham Sumner and the Frontier" (1947).

Trahan, Mrs. Mauree P. "American Methodism and the Frontier" (1950).

DOCTORAL DISSERTATIONS

Klose, Nelson. "Foreign Plant Introduction by the Federal Government" (1947).

Mondy, Robert William. "Jesse Mercer: A Study in Frontier Religion" (1950).

Parker, Edith Helene. "History of Land Grants for Education in Texas" (1952).

Renfer, Rudolph A. "Protestant Integration as Reflecting Corporate Trends in America." In progress.

Weinberger, Abe L. "Judaism in America: The Influence of a New World Frontier upon Judaism of Tradition." In progress.

Wiederaenders, Arthur G. "The American Frontier as a Factor in Protestant Denominationalism in the United States" (1942).

Wolfskill, George. "The New World Frontier and International Law" (1952).

INDEX